Wisdom Learning

In traditional business circles, wisdom is viewed with a certain scepticism, which is in part due to its historical associations with wisdom traditions and spiritual cultures. However, in business today, wisdom is emerging not only as a viable but also a necessary organizational and management practice. In particular, practical wisdom is being updated and retranslated for today's issues and concerns in organizations. In recent years, leadership and organizational studies have initiated important changes in the way in which business-as-usual is conducted.

In response to the increasingly complex and uncertain conditions of our international business environment, a growing community of 'scholar-practitioners' are pushing the boundaries of traditional organizational and leadership thinking and acting, making inroads into processes and applications of practical wisdom and ways of wise leading and managing. Given the unprecedented levels of challenges, dynamics and uncertainties that today's organizations are exposed to, there is a need for a more integrative and sustainable approach to managing.

Following the need for a reconsideration and revival of the meaning of wisdom, the editors explore vitalizing possibilities for the learning of wise practices in organizing and leading. This expansive range of domains where wisdom is currently being explored suggests a promising number of perspectives and possibilities for future inquiries and explorations into the nexus of wisdom and organization, leadership/management education and learning that benefits from cross-disciplinary synergies.

This book will be of interest to those seeking to understand the growing significance of wisdom in relation to learning and teaching, especially in business and management education.

Wendelin Küpers is Professor of Leadership and Organization Studies at Karlshochschule International University in Karlsruhe, Germany. Combining a phenomenological and cross-disciplinary orientation, his research focuses on embodied, emplaced, emotional, creative and aesthetic dimensions of organizing and managing. In his current research and teaching he is focusing on more responsive, responsible and wiser forms of organizations and management/leadership that are contributing towards more integral and sustainable practices.

Olen Gunnlaugson is an Associate Professor in Leadership and Organizational Development within the Department of Management in the Business School at Université Laval, in Quebec City, Canada. He brings a cross-disciplinary approach to his current research in collective leadership training (i.e. conversational leadership, dynamic presencing, we-space practice and facilitation), wisdom-based learning methods, inner management skills and leadership coaching which have been published in several books as well as numerous international academic journals and presentations at leading conferences. He is currently collaborating with colleagues on a number of books, articles and consulting offerings. More recently, he was the chief co-editor of the management book, *Perspectives on Theory U: Insights from the Field*, an anthology featuring applied research on Theory U by 30 faculty members and associates from North America and Europe.

The Practical Wisdom in Leadership and Organization Series

The Practical Wisdom in Leadership and Organization Series provides a platform for authors to articulate wiser ways of managing and leading and of reassessing both practice within organizational settings and organizational research. Books in this series focus on the art and practice of inquiry and reflexivity and explicitly connect with challenges and issues of 'praxis' in the field of organization and management, be that academic research or in situ management practice. Rather than offering closure and final answers, contributions to this series invite further critical inquiry, cross-disciplinary conversations and explorations. The aim is to engage authors and readers – students, academics and practitioners alike – in inspiring, reflexive and critical dialogue. By thus engaging readers, we hope that these books play an important role in informing, teaching and learning in educational contexts and public forums as well as among practitioners and in management boardrooms.

The Series Editors

Dr Wendelin Küpers *is Professor of Leadership and Organization Studies at Karlshochschule International University, Germany and* Dr David Pauleen *is an Associate Professor of Business Information Systems at Massey University, New Zealand.*

A Handbook of Practical Wisdom
Leadership, Organization and Integral Business Practice
Wendelin Küpers

Practical Wisdom in the Age of Technology
Insights, Issues and Questions for a New Millennium
Edited by Nikunj Dalal, Ali Intezari, Marty Heitz

Wisdom Learning
Perspectives on Wising-Up Business and Management Education
Edited by Wendelin Küpers and Olen Gunnlaugson

Wisdom Learning

Perspectives on Wising-Up Business and Management Education

Edited by
Wendelin Küpers
and Olen Gunnlaugson

Routledge
Taylor & Francis Group
LONDON AND NEW YORK

First published 2017 by Routledge

2 Park Square, Milton Park, Abingdon, Oxfordshire OX14 4RN
52 Vanderbilt Avenue, New York, NY 10017

Routledge is an imprint of the Taylor & Francis Group, an informa business

First issued in paperback 2019

British Library Cataloguing in Publication Data
A catalogue record for this book is available from the British Library

Library of Congress Cataloging in Publication Data
A catalog record has been requested for this book

ISBN: 978-1-4724-6393-7 (hbk)
ISBN: 978-0-367-88130-6 (pbk)

Typeset in Sabon
by Book Now Ltd, London

To present and future teachers and students in management and business education who try to incorporate wisdom into their teaching and learning

Contents

Figures

Tables

Contributors

Monika Ardelt is Associate Professor of Sociology in the Department of Sociology and Criminology & Law at the University of Florida, USA.

Stewart Clegg is Research Professor at the University of Technology Sydney, Director of the Centre for Management and Organization Studies Research, and a Visiting Professor at Nova School of Business and Economics, and at Newcastle University Business School, UK.

Cynthia V. Fukami is Associate Chair and Professor of Management at the Daniels College of Business, University of Denver, USA.

Vincenzo Mario Bruno Giorgino is Professor of Economic Sociology the Department of Economic and Social Sciences, Mathematics and Statistics, University of Torino, Italy.

Olen Gunnlaugson is an Associate Professor in Leadership & Organizational Development within the Department of Management in the Business School at Université Laval, in Quebec City, Canada.

Jay Martin Hays is the Program Leader, Master of Education, in the Department of Education at Unitec Institute of Technology, Auckland, New Zealand.

Nina Kongsbakk is an HSE advisor for an occupational health and safety training and educational services organization in Norway.

Wendelin Küpers is Professor of Leadership and Organization Studies at Karlshochschule International University in Karlsruhe, Germany.

Bernard McKenna is Associate Professor in the University of Queensland Business School, Australia, where he teaches mostly at graduate level.

Ksenija Napan is Associate Professor at Massey University, Auckland, New Zealand, College of Health, School of Social Work and a Programme Coordinator for Master of Applied Social Work programme.

Charles Oden is a retired US Naval Officer and an Assistant Professor of Business at Saint Leo University, Florida, USA.

Miguel Pina e Cunha is a professor at Nova School of Business and Economics, Universidade Nova de Lisboa, Lisbon, Portugal.

Arménio Rego is an associate professor at the Universidade de Aveiro, Portugal.

Xabier Renteria-Uriarte is Professor of World Economy and Management at the University of the Basque Country, Spain.

Filipa Rocha Rodrigues is a PhD student in Management at Nova School of Business and Economics, Universidade Nova de Lisboa, Lisbon, Portugal.

David Rooney is Professor of Management and Organization Studies in the Faculty of Business and Economics, Macquarie University, Australia.

Matt Statler is the Richman Family Director of Business Ethics and Social Impact Programming and a Clinical Associate Professor of Business and Society at NYU Stern School of Business, USA.

Marilyn M. Taylor is a professor in the School of Leadership Studies at Royal Roads University, Canada.

Steven S. Taylor is a professor of leadership and creativity at the WPI Foisie School of Business, USA.

Mike J. Thompson is a professor of Management Practice and director of the Euro-China Centre for Leadership and Responsibility at the China Europe International Business School, Shanghai.

Dennis W. Wittmer is Chair of the Daniels College of Business Department of Management and Professor of Management at the University of Denver, USA.

Foreword

This book addresses a critical need in business and management education: the incorporation of wisdom in its various facets into management pedagogy and from there into management practice.

At a moment in history when business people have come to believe that they are eminently qualified to enter politics and run governments, it begs the question, did they learn enough of lasting value in university to allow them to manage wisely, let alone govern wisely?

Are Wharton, Harvard and the other global graduate and MBA (Master of Business Administration) mills, which are churning out self-important and overconfident graduate and MBAs, properly preparing these students to manage organisations in times of great environmental stress and challenge? Courses in sustainability, corporate social responsibility and ethics are fine, but what the world needs are managers and leaders steeped in wisdom – with wisdom as philosophy and practice that guides management decisions and actions.

There is an urgent necessity and there is only good in educating and inculcating MBAs and other management school graduates in the finer points of practical wisdom. People, organisations and society will only be the better for it. May the talent, intelligence and yes, wisdom, of the authors gathered together in this book lead the way in espousing, explaining and demonstrating how practical wisdom can become a part of our education of leaders.

David Pauleen (Series Editor)

Introduction

Context and complexities: Wisdom learning today for a sustainable tomorrow

Wendelin Küpers and Olen Gunnlaugson

> We are drowning in information, while starving for wisdom. The world henceforth will be run by synthesizers, people able to put together the right information at the right time, think critically about it, and make important choices wisely.
>
> (Wilson, 1998: 294)

As part of the series on Practical Wisdom Leadership, Organization and Integral Business Practice, this book gathers contributions that address the growing significance of wisdom in relation to learning and teaching, especially in business and management education. The following outlines some reasons and motivations for exploring this conection and contextualising wisdom in relation to education.

In recent years, organizational management practices and studies are processing new ways concerning how organizations, leadership and business are conducted and approached, especially in more responsible ways. In response to the increasingly complex and uncertain conditions of environments and limitations of conventional forms, a growing community of practitioners and scholars are pushing the boundaries of traditional ways of thinking, learning and acting, connecting and qualifying them in relation to practical wisdom. Accordingly, wiser forms organizing and leading as well as possibilities of preparing or learning them are increasingly processed and studied (Küpers & Pauleen, 2015).

While traditionally viewed skeptically, today wisdom and its learning have been rediscovered as viable and worthwhile orientation and practices, as are possibilities for developing wisdom through education (Ferrari et al., 2017).

This re-evaluation is bourgeoning also because of the need to deal with acute and expectable issues and concerns of unsustainable operations with its unprecedented challenges, dynamics and implications in contemporary society, economies and organizations, as well as its management. Especially in organizational and management-related contexts as well as the task of higher education, wisdom needs to be updated and re-translated as well as in re-integrated conceptually and practically.

In fact, this book series on Practical Wisdom Leadership, Organization and Integral Business Practice is a manifestation of this revisiting and exploring renewed meanings as well as practices of wisdom in relation to various organizational and leadership issues and areas.

This book focuses on one essential dimension of developing practical wisdom: business and management education as well as learning. This is important for bringing wisdom into our world, theoretically and pragmatically, as we need to investigate and identify potential relevancies, promising prospects and actual or potential educational practices of teaching and learning wisdom. In particular, conceptual and practical possibilities for wisdom learning in relation to business and management or leadership education serve as integrative catalyst towards more sustainable development (Leal Filho et al. 2015; Leal Filho & Zint, 2016).

Since wisdom and its learning are multi-dimensional and emerge from a synergistic interplay of different forms of knowledge, understandings, reflections and creative thinking, there are many issues, quests, questions and quandaries that are challenging and of interest. Therefore, we invited contributions from diverse viewpoints and disciplinary backgrounds or cross-disciplinary work related to forms of learning, teaching or education of wisdom. In deference to the plurality already existing in organizational, management and education research on wisdom, we called a variety of conceptual and practical investigations as well as empirical studies. Accordingly, the individual chapters of this book are dedicated to specific themes, selected to present conceptualising and/or pragmatic contributions.

Before introducing these particular chapters, the following contextualizes wisdom and its learning. First, the absence of wisdom in forms of hubris, hyper-orientations and hydra-monsters and moves towards rethinking wisdom are discussed. For interpreting the multi-layered contexts then, on a mundo- or macro-level, the so-called Anthropocene, on a meso-level, some realities and deficits of exiting business- and management education and on a micro-level, dispositions and capabilities are addressed.

The first section of this introduction finishes with elaborating the role of "in-between," for learning and education of wisdom.

In the second section we then provide an overview and of the individual chapters and in conclusion we offer some perspectives on and open questions about research and practices of wisdom learning.

Contextualizing wisdom and its learning – hubris, hyper, and hydra

Imagine if we were to ask a group of acclaimed wise people from history about what they think is generally over- and undervalued by people, economies and societies today; what would they answer? How would they see the role and importance of truth, beauty and goodness in current economy and society, including its reframing (Gardner, 2011)?

How and what would they respond to the question about what the main obstacles are that prevent young adults and supposed mature people from finding true happiness as well as learning and living practically wise? What would they say about why it makes sense and how to cultivate and learn wisdom?

With this imaginative inquiry, many more open questions emerge: Why is the capability to ask about and to do the right thing, at the right time, for the right reason, imperative in relation to today's particularities? How and when can we choose the right means for attaining the right ends today and for a tomorrow to come? Why is living well and sustainably significant and learning to become wise life-worthy? How can these aspirations be again purposeful and part of contemporary education?

Reading the news about the current turmoil, looking at images and hearing voices about what is going on (or just not) in our world, confirms a mounting realization of prevalence of nonsense and folly. It seems that the dynamics and powers of technological, economical, and societal, but also individual proficiencies and life-worldly practices are fundamentally out of touch or lack wisdom. Demonstrating a tremendous dearth of wisdom, our existing realities are recklessly full of inattentive, mindless, inconsiderate attitudes, orientations, and structures as well as imprudent, careless, and irresponsible actions.

In a way, these realities reflect some of the experiences of horror, anxiety, and a loss of reverence, while wandering through ruins that Gabriel Marcel described in his book on "The Decline of Wisdom" (see Steel, 2014). There seems to be a correspondence to a mass-scale civilizational rejection or non-realization of wisdom in our times, which evokes a feeling of growing impatience and despair. In the words of Marcel, this refers to a growing exasperation with what tends increasingly to be regarded as obstacles to the advent of a new world, even of a renewed humanity and of planetary life at all.

Historically wisdom has always acted as a counterweight to hyper-uplifting hubris, thus an exaggerated and blinding pride of feeling superior and insolent that leads to excessive violent and wrongful behavior. But what happens when cautionary counteracting and balancing orientations or rectificational forces are lacking, while fallacies of invincibility or delusions of omnipotence or narcissism dominate? Does arrogant pride and lack of correcting wisdom not only prevail, but lead to a downfall?

Indicating not only a lack of humility and well-balanced quality (sophrosyne), but also a loss of contact with reality and overestimation of one's own competencies, hubris without wisdom makes going astray inevitable. Disposed of presumptions hubristic humans fail to realize or recognize their limitations and precariousness of the entire condition. We are dangerously tearing apart the materio-biological and socio-cultural fabric of life and existence of which we are all a part of. Interestingly, Bateson already reinterpreted hubris as the lack of systemic wisdom, the tragic blindness that occurs when any part of an ecological system ignores the fact that it is participating in a system larger than itself, one upon which its very existence is predicated (Bateson, 1972: 433).

The lack or regression of sensitivities, integral sense-making, and prudent reason and wisdom in our time has caused individuals, organizations, and leadership, as well as economies, societies, and the planet to be dominated by poor reasoning, stupidity and madness, and amoral or unethical practices (Küpers & Pauleen, 2013).

Functional stupidity as inability and/or unwillingness to use reflective capacities, justification and substantive reasoning (Alvesson & Spicer, 2012) reigns not only in organizational and management contexts, but seems to have become systemic. We are under the reign of forces that show a lack of wisdom, while facing an ecological, social, and economic crisis of various local impacts and global proportions or, better to say, that is out-of-proportion on all levels.

The unbalanced and shocking "States of Shock" and "Lost Spirit of Capitalism" (Stiegler, 2014a,b) in our contemporary world manifest a prevailing disbelief, discredit, and destruction of the *savoir-vivre*. Reinforced by advanced technology and technics of hyper-industrial society with its hyper-busy schedules and its mechanism of monetized sensibility of the "other," what we can observe is an actual and symbolic misery. This orientation is characterized by a loss of genuine singularity and engaged participation, estranging experiences and detrimental practices of a hype(r)-modern epoch.

Connected to the mentioned hubris, hyperbolic phenomena and experiences are forms of excess, in which that what appears, exaggeratedly transcend what they are. Hyper-phenomena cross thresholds of the alien, without overcoming them, while they slip from normative regulation and can turn violent. In order to understand the hyperbolic(al) we need indirect descriptions, moving at the margins (Waldenfels, 2012).

Ever more our late-modern days are characterized by hyper-accelerated lives, hyper-corporatized pursuit of short-term growth at any cost, and corresponding hyper-economies and hyper-societies that become increasingly uncontrollable, profoundly irrational, and incapable of inspiring hope, while generating dead-end futures. This monstrous hyper-capitalism ranges from zombie-cultures of unsustainable mass-production and mass-consumerism of carbon- and calorie-hungry systems to devastations of the bio- and socio-spheres on all levels, exceeding situated and planetary boundaries.

How can we relate critically to a capitalism that functions as a monstrous system, a "capitalist monsterology" (McNally, 2011: 2) that systematically threatens the integrity, through invisible processes of exploitation, and unmeasurable experiences of psychic and corporeal disintegration? Following its etymological origin (*monere* = "to warn"), what do contemporary phenomena and fables of monsters of disembodied, occult (financial other) economies, markets, and organizations warn us about; not only of what may happen but also of what is already happening?

The sprawling monster of a hydra-headed menace of today's calamities is fed by neoliberal over-leveraged "Disaster Capitalism" (Klein, 2007), that – with its hubristic mind-set – is imploding. With its techno-scientific devising paws, this system monster colonizes and devours the natural, socio-cultural, and political life-worlds. It exploits these worlds of life by a strategic and instrumental rationality through an encroachment and pervasive hegemonic and homogenizing reduction of all spheres to the over-consuming economic logic and purpose-driven dominance.

Enacting foundational value-claims, the ideology of a growth or development at any cost, the glorification of competition in a battlefield, and, above all, the supposed pre-eminence of economic "value" over all other values turn out to devalue and ultimately destroy life. Are we now punished and cursed by the inevitable and inexorable nemesis, the goddess of fate and retribution; and the vengeance of infernal furies as cataclysmic "Revenge of Gaia" (Lovelock, 2006)? Is it this retaliation that causes ecological and social catastrophes and destruction of the planet, thus turning it into a hellish place, as major ecosystems on the Earth are subsiding into environmental degradation, all falling into decline in an escalating spiral of nihilistically productive Thanatos?

Not only the bio-material resources and spiritual sources, but also the social imaginary of the capitalist project of unlimited expansion and mastery (Castoriadis, 2003: 379, 2013) comes to an end. Does this open up a transition to a new imaginary vision and practice, as the old images and narratives with their subsequent practices and effects, and unintended consequences, are disassociating and disintegrating?

Disintegration and disorganization, and rethinking

We are living in times characterized not only by a lack of integration, but pervasive disintegration and disorganization. As Rudolphe Durand (HEC Paris) in a recent book stated:

> Our society, our economy and our politics project the impression of a continuous process of disorganization and reorganization that is pointless and absurd – a permanent state of dismembering, repeated instability, recurrent uncertainty.... Everything collapses, but does anything change? Unstable stability, change without change. The world resumes its rotation, but at every turn, my world loses its reality. My world becomes unreal, unbalanced and unquestionably incoherent.
>
> (Durand, 2014: 2)

What is our response to this loss? While sensing more and more the finitude of our being entwined with the finitude of the Earth, rendering us in the throes of despair, "we exhaust ourselves to avoid exhaustion. The social and economic world has no meaning or direction, the dominating values manifest as selfishness, deceit and profiteering" (Durand, 2014: 3). More and more people experience the dismay of a disorganized world caused by internal disturbances, loss of legitimacy, and meaning depreciations in relation to individuals and organizations. According to Durand, this situation is calling for us to engage in a reprise of our known worlds and a new order for reality via a "re-sensing" of the world, that is, to correctively re-evaluate the position within the myriad of organizational associations that individuals and groups maintain and to establish a revived sense of (motivating and framing) meaning (ibid.: 131). For Durand, re-sensing starts with a reprise that is both *reprendre* (to take again or to repeat), and a *reprise* (to repair), entailing a new posture, a fresh way to engage differently with the organizations to which we are linked, but also to resist organizational orders and injunctions, as well as to rearrange scattered fragments of meanings into a more sensible universe (ibid.: 131).

We are living in a time to reorganize, for which we require a wise rethinking. Such reconsideration of existing business, management, and further life-practices, implies that we both remember and reclaim the value or practical wisdom. Remembering can be taken as literally reconnecting "members" and integrating senses, affects, bodies, feelings, and further dimensions that are only reductively and narrowly seen in instrumentalized "practicalist" modes. Thus, returning to wisdom goes along with refusing or ever more resisting managerialist and unsustainable positions or one-sided reification and unreflected practicalism while also redesigning and redoing management in more responsible ways (Küpers et al., 2016).

Cultivating and enacting practical wisdom – as part of living well, i.e. individual, societal, and ecological flourishing – has never been more important than it is today and for a sustainable world to come, as actual and possible lives are at stake, and even more, the stakes are burning already. Facing these dynamics, we need to see the limit-character of the current situation of auto-destructive hyper-systems and be mindful of its undermining manifestations, calling for a mutation and transition, beyond "overcoming,"[1] while raising crucial questions:

- How can we situate wisdom and its learning in our current age of the Anthropocene that is calling for a reconfiguration of relationships between humans, nature, and society related to local and planetary perspectives?
- What are the possibilities but also the tensions between wisdom learning and existing or future realities of business- and management education?
- What roles do individual and collective dispositions and capabilities play for learning processes of wisdom?
- What significance has an "in-between" for learning and education of wisdom as an relational event and practice?

Corresponding to these questions, the following reflections sketch some contours of our contemporary being-in-the-world, related to wisdom learning. On a more overarching mundo- or macro-level, first the Anthropocene age with its problematic realities and dangerous developments is addressed, as it calls for a revived reconsideration and engaged practice of wisdom and its learning. Positioned more on a meso-level, the need and shapes of wisdom learning in actual and possible business- and management education are then outlined and alternative perspectives offered. Building on a critique of existing business education, subsequently, on a micro-level, the role of dispositions and capabilities are discussed. As an inter-relational sphere and processual inter-practice we emphasize the significance of an "in-between" in the sense of a "*metaxis*" for learning and educational practices of wisdom.

In the second section of this introduction we provide an overview and a brief introduction into the chapters. In concluding, we offer some perspectives on and open questions about research and practices of wisdom learning.

Wisdom learning in the Anthropocene age

As hinted before, what we are facing currently is a kind of "ecocidal" ongoing nihilism that is characterized by the destruction and loss of diversity, meanings, and thereby viability of local, regional, and global-planetary life.[2] The revival and cultivation of wisdom learning may therefore become a question of urgency, if not survival in a time of a crisis that manifests as a so-called Anthropocene age (from Greek *anthropo-* meaning "human" and *-cene* meaning "new" or "age").

Historically, this epoch has been emerging over a longer period of time, starting with various forms of taming nature by one of its creatures, intensified ever since the Industrial Revolution up to our contemporary late capitalist society and economy. Human activities and impacts are seen now as permanent, even on a geological time-scale (Steffen et al., 2011a, b).

Today, under the "techno-human condition" (Allenby & Sarewitz, 2011), human-induced environmental change and domination of the Earth's ecosystems have reached a global scale and have accelerated in terms of resource use, agricultural intensity, economic output, overload of sink functions, and endangered ecologies.

Each of these and further anthro-bound phenomena are part of a dramatic increase in economic growth, spread of global markets, commodity production and consumption, and thus globalization, since World War Two. Increasingly, these developments and impacts are all-pervading in pungent ways of hyper-modernistic, neo-liberal market-oriented globalism, reaching and surpassing boundaries of what planet Earth can bear.

In addition to globally aggregated planetary boundaries and processes that manifest its reach, like climate change, also regional-level boundaries can be recognized with regard to atmosphere and biosphere integrity, geo-bio-chemical flows, land-system change, freshwater use, etc., that all have been crossed as a result of human activity.

Concretely, too much greenhouse gas going into the atmosphere, too much fertilizer running off into waterways, and an increased soil and ocean acidification, as well as overharvesting and overfishing are changing the organic makeup of life. Furthermore, too little forest and the implications of increased urbanization, contaminations, losses of forests, wild-life, thus biodiversity or species extinction and, further forms of human-caused destruction, has put Earth's ecological environment and ecology into a state that can no longer provide healthy and sustainable habitats. Even more, the complexities of today's interwoven, multifaceted problems that arise from our domination of the planet call for evolution, and change with those circumstances.

Transgressing natural and planetary boundaries increases the substantial risk of destabilizing the "Holocene state." As a consequence, human activities could inadvertently drive the "Earth system" into a much less hospitable state, damaging efforts to reduce poverty and leading to a deterioration of human well-being in many parts of the world (Steffen et al., 2015).

Importantly, the Anthropocene is a malleable concept that accommodates several co-existing and, at times, contesting narratives. While the significance and meaning of the Anthropocene remains disputed and unsettled, there is a distinct story emerging that is affecting how the conversation on, and more sustainable practices with regard to, the future of Earth currently is unfolding. Ontologically, epistemologically, and practically the Anthropocene challenges familiar distinctions and separations between nature and culture etc. that structure the order of approaches toward and knowledge about the world.

As Anthropocene-related analyses showed, humankind has become a global-scale force with the ability to fundamentally reshape the planet as in this era "when natural forces and human forces are so intertwined that the fate of one determines the fate of the other" (Zalasiewic et al., 2010: 2231). This fusing together of human and non-human histories leads to what has been called a post-natural ontology of the Anthropocene (Barry et al., 2013). Such ontology is characterized by crossing the human–nature divide inherited, especially in the Western world, from Platonian–Cartesian–Newtonian paradigms and the Enlightenment and Modern eras. This has led to the functioning of an "anthropological machine" (Agamben, 2009) by which animals are humanized or men animalized. The operation of anthro-machines has gradually led to immoral dehumanizing acts and a mechanization of embodied life that implied the loss of meaning and the valorization not of bare life but of the efficiency, along with exchangeability and disposability of all that can assembled or disassembled.

Nature has been and is domesticated, technologized and capitalized to the extent that it can no longer be considered "natural." While nature is "humanized" in the sense of anthropo- and sociogenic practices, the same are "natural," that is, part of natural occurrences.

Realizing humanity's material dependence, embodiment, and fragility invites us to rethink long-held assumptions about the autonomous, self-sufficient rational human subject that begins and ends with itself (Wakefield, 2014), decentering an anthropocentric positioning, while critically problematizing tendencies towards re-elevated humans as reborn Prometheus (Baskin, 2015) or Earth-masters that are now "playing God with the climate" (Hamilton, 2013) by pursuing an updated eco-modernist agenda.

As the capacity to discern a relearned wisdom can help to differentiate the multiple and unequal social values, relations, and practices of power that accompany the "essentialized" humans and their individual and collective behaviors, it is wise to avoid the glossing of universalizing tendencies. This is especially so when materio-natural phenomena and environmental changes are related to social cultural categories and realities, such as class, race, gender, power, and capital. With a wisdom-lens, anthrogenic and androgenic practices and eco-authoritative claims (Howe, 2013) can be seen as emerging from different socio-political narratives and bio-power(ful) settings that produce vulnerabilities, rendering various responses. Wisdom might facilitate processing multiple futures of Anthropocenes beyond an age of humans (Berkhout, 2014). This even more as the "anthropos" has never been only human (Pyyhtinen & Tamminen, 2011).

In these ways, a revived wisdom learning may serve as a medium for developing an anthro-decentric orientation that is questioning the "anthropos" of the Anthropocene while it allows us to envision a new understanding of "Gaia." Gaia is then more an inter-relational, anthro-decentered "humanimality" or "hum-animism" (Küpers et al., 2016) as part of an entwined "natureculture" in the geo-storied sense of a secular multiplicity or assemblage and distributed agency (Latour, 2013).[3] Engaging with Gaian emergence of the planetary system and dynamic living patterns may catalyze breakthrough-learning for wisdom as part of a sustainability and regenerative education that is contributing to enhanced ethical actions (Hauk, 2014).

A critical usage of Anthropocenian concepts provides a chance for developing different understandings and practices. These concern not only multi-speci(es)fied arrangements, but also normatively guided, prudent sense-makings, practical wise stories, policies, actions or non-actions, and forms of leadership and governance. Furthermore, it can help challenging imperatives of progress and growth as well as further belief systems that underpin economic, organizational, and managerial thinking, constructing, and acting.

The revived learning of wisdom may contribute to a transformative transition from a human-centered and deadening Anthropocene toward an enlivening eco- or *zoë*-cene. The Greek word *zoë* refers to meanings of life in its felt sense, and including the whole animated/animating Earth (Weber, 2013). Oriented towards such *zoë* via a Gaian Prax*eco*logy integrates and learns from the "proto-wisdom" of plants and animals in the sense of an integral eco-sophy.

In this way, the Anthropocene concept represents a tremendous opportunity to engage more wisely and transformatively with questions of ecology and its inhabitants. These concern reconsidering and reintegrating meanings, values, and responsibilities, as well as resonances (Rosa, 2016) and practices in alienating times of rapid and escalating change (Rose et al., 2012: 1) and technical and social acceleration (Rosa, 2013). The Anthropocene marks the transformation of the Earth twisted by practices of the anthropos that in order to radically alter business and organization on a meso-level calls for a different education.

Wisdom learning in business and management education

In a speech made at Cambridge University in 1912, Whitehead said that:

> Above all things, we must be aware of inert ideas, that is to say ideas that are merely received into the mind without being utilized, or tested, or thrown into fresh combinations. Education with inert ideas is not only useless; it is above all things, harmful.
>
> (Whitehead, 1929)

Stating this, he was criticizing the paralysis of thought induced in students by the aimless accumulation of precise knowledge, inert and unutilized.

Interestingly, he made similar assertions at a later address, given to Harvard University Business School in 1929. Here again he specified that education for him is a discipline for the adventure of life. Importantly, it is the function of the teacher to evoke into life wisdom and beauty (ibid.: 98). All efforts should be directed towards practical realization of values and enacting "wisdom as an artistic sense" (ibid.: 39). For him, this orientation needs to be dialectically processed through being romantically informed, followed by precision-exercising modes of learning then leading to synthesizing generalization. Interestingly, the habit-forming body is integrated in Whitehead inductive–deductive rhythmic interweaving of modes of learning and a mental cultivation that are connected to the enhancement of ordinary everyday life by heightened value quality. For him the wisdom-oriented process of knowing and learning is transformative and emergent in the sense that a dynamic movement between qualitatively different stages affords new abilities and knowledge, and, at the same time, provides a ground for further exploration and development. Overall, he essentially reminds us that "an education which does not begin by evoking initiative and end by encouraging it must be wrong. For its whole aim is the production of active wisdom" (Whitehead, 1957: 37) and "moral education is impossible apart from the habitual vision of greatness" (ibid.: 69).

The active part of wisdom lies for him and for us in the molding of our future actions in accordance with insights into general principles that help to understand the particular events in our experiences. The emergence of a responsible, ethically oriented and wise student is Whitehead's vision of the "outcome" of multiple rhythms of education.

> For Whitehead, this symphony of rhythms – this rich pedagogy of repeating and alternating differences – is united in a drive towards a value-oriented growth and novelty, with art as an important mediator, and the art of life as its goal. Teachers contemplating these ideas might get in touch with the greater perspectives of education and thus see the links between everyday classroom activities and the ethical challenges of humanity as a whole.
>
> (Mathisen, 2015: 48)

In stark contrast to these programmatic and educational aspirations are existing realities of business and management education practices. The dire status, problems, and failures of this contemporary education with its underlying, unwise principles have been criticized extensively, as outlined exemplarily in the following.

Management education is in a parlous state (Grey, 2004) as its research and teaching missions are compromised – perhaps fatally (Starkey & Tempest, 2005), its degrees not correlated with career success influential on management practice, calling into question the professional relevance of management scholarship (Pfeffer & Fong, 2002). Following a *tékhnê*- and *episteme*-oriented approach, traditional business and management teaching in business schools is too focused on "scientific" research at the expense of other approaches, including ethical ones (Bennis & O'Toole, 2005). This education is too reductive with a functional "silo type" disciplinary mentality (Chia, 2005) that compartmentalizes instead of helping to cross and to integrate. The dominant curriculum puts too much emphasis on teaching students sets of analytical tools, leaving them with the false perception that management problems can be defined as neat technical packages (Raelin, 1995) dissolved in simplistic ways.

Conveying forms of "Unenlightened Economism" (Huehn, 2008), management students are trained to become executors of the economic principle, causing bad corporate governance and ethical decline (ibid.: 2008: 831; 2014). Such unwise forms of teaching produce management graduates, who display analytic detachment to the detriment of insight. Even more bad management theories and teachings are destroying good management practice (Goshal, 2005). Students seem to learn the wrong things in the wrong ways because they are being taught the wrong things in the wrong ways. Considering the past, present, and future perspectives of management learning, education, and development (Armstrong & Fukami, 2009), the call for teaching leadership critically intensifies with a new pedagogy that considers the dynamics of power and the influence of contexts and agencies and a more questioning approach (Collinson & Tourish, 2015).

Recognizing the impasses and limitations of conventional business education, suggestions for its reassessment and redesign have developed (Colby et al., 2011). Accordingly, management education and business schools seem to have increasingly recognized the importance of teaching responsible management/leadership as a subject, and drawing attention to [ir]responsible practices and behaviors. However, despite calls for management and business educators to develop a more holistic, emotion-integrating, non-cognitive, and responsible approach, very little has been done to directly include subjects in the management curricula that add clarity to responsible leadership (Peach Martins et al., 2016), also bound to management curricula biases. The existing forms and contents are insufficient, manifested in the reduction of leadership to a set of skills functioning as defense against, but a poor preparation for, the ambiguity and precariousness of leadership in contemporary workplaces (Petriglieri & Petriglieri, 2015).

Failing to educate with appropriate, ethical, responsible, and aesthetic orientations and practices in teaching and learning manifests not only a lack of wisdom. Rather, with its obsolete designs, learning objectives, and "subjects," traditional mainstreaming (business) education contributes to reproducing an unsound, non-sustainable thus non-viable status-quo education, implicitly and complicitly.[4] In this way, conventional education puts all stakeholders into danger and imperils the acute situation, missing chances for radical transformation.

While facing multifaceted socio-ecological, social, and cultural issues and problems, due to their fatally flawed structures and nihilistically "productive" progress-driven mechanisms, existing outmoded forms of education appear as uncanny and ghostly in its morbid decadence. From this perspective, practices and protagonists of current business and management education are a kind of "zombie jamboree," i.e. minds being possessed by the dead. As such they are engaged in a dance macabre that is laying waste to the planet, rather than in preparing future generations for more integral and wiser forms of living in mutual responsive resonance with the planet that would require a "de-schooled" learning with "Earth-in-mind" (Mitchell, 2014).

Many of the mainstream approaches are institutionalized in homogenizing forms, while education is increasingly standardized with national qualification frameworks emphasizing student learning outcomes and quantifiable measures (Bologna Working Group, 2005; OECD, 2009) and metrics, including leveraging measures of quality (Pettersen, 2015).

Likewise, challenging the perceived (lack of) wisdom of management theories and practice, Baden and Higgs (2015) demonstrated that management models that measure success in purely financial terms are foolish as they are conflating the means with the end. According to these approaches, if business and its schools are to retain their legitimacy and benefit to society, profit needs to be seen as a means to sustainable business as an end, not as an end in itself, which requires changes beyond superficial inclusion of ethical issues. Rather, it requires updating the business curriculum with more pro-social management theories and a reprioritization of the goal of social welfare over individual business profit maximization.

An Apollonian order of logic and its pressuring regimes that define uniform learning objectives, measurable certainties and skill- and outcome-based imperatives are limited. Therefore the call for alternative education practices that allow a multidimensional and qualitative learning grows, while the need for more wisdom- and sustainability-oriented learning is pressing. With John Dewey we can say, "If we teach today's students as we taught yesterday's, we rob them and future generations of tomorrow."

The cultivation of practical wisdom and embodied wisdom learning (Küpers & Pauleen, 2015) is part of the urgent need, even necessity for developing and enacting more integral and transformational approaches to business and management education. Such integration re- and interconnects business, organization, and management to life-worldly and societal *prâxis* as emerging in situated sayings, doings, and relating (Kemmis, 2012: 150).

In *prâxis*, the disposition of practical reasoning and wisdom is realized, as it is the action of doing what is right and proper in a given situation in accordance with a greater community and with principles that go beyond self-interest. Accordingly, *prâxis* might be understood as formational history-making, "action that is morally committed, and oriented and informed by traditions in a field" (Kemmis & Smith, 2008: 4).

Bound up with lived experiences and embodied reason, rather than abstract context-free rationality (*episteme*) and not a set of techniques to be deployed (*tékhnê*), practical wisdom (*phrónêsis*) is entwined with *prâxis*. Accordingly, *phrónêsis* can and is used in and for *prâxis* as acting for the common good. Thus, be(com)ing wise manifests a situated practical reasoning, knowledge, and habit, which directs action for acting well (*eu prâxía*) and living well (*éu zén*). This understanding of *prâxis* is closely connected to that of an integral understanding of education in the sense of "*Bildung*." As educational *prâxis*, "*Bildung*" can be interpreted as a process by which learners

> are initiated into forms of understanding, modes of action, and ways of relating to one another and the world, that foster (respectively) individual and collective self-expression, individual and collective self-development (to secure a productive sustainable economy) and individual and collective self-determination (to secure a just and democratic society), and that are, in these senses, oriented towards the good for each person and the good for humankind.
>
> (Kemmis et al., 2014: 26)

This proposition implies a double purpose of education that is to prepare people to live well in a world worth living in. What counts as the good life individually and collectively, must of course always be determined anew for changing times and circumstances.

With such orientation, practical wisdom in relation to educational *prâxis* refers not only to a poietic competent "making" of goods, following instrumental reasoning, but doing something habitually "right" and living excellently, while contributing to the well-be(com)ing of the organization, its members, and beyond. Being practically wise does not mean to know or to generate "the right answers," but to perform a (re-)habituated pattern of human and organizational actions or a "wise practice" situated as *prâxis*. As this *prâxis* integrates embodied experiences, reflection, and actions, it is a condition of the possibility of *phrónêsis* and its development (Kemmis, 2012) also in organizations as structured and functional settings. *Prâxis* implies not only acts of engaging, applying, exercising, realizing, or practising ideas and knowledge with prudent decisions in relation to reflective, critical, and political interaction, but is directed also towards sedimented structures and practices to be transformed.

However, the dominant logos and "makings" of *tékhnê* in our contemporary times with its increasingly instrumentalized and institutionalized contexts of neo-liberal, neo-conservative regimes, and auditing constraints of professional practice, encumber practitioners' prâxical and phrónêtic capacities.

Metaphorically speaking, the "desert grows … woe to him who conceals the desert within him" as Nietzsche expressed in the Dithyrambs of Dionysus (2006). This desert is a "hostile ground for growing phrónêsis" (Pitman, 2012). It is characterized by an increasing managerialism, systems of surveillance and accountability in the professions, in which professionals have numerous and frequently conflicting ruling bodies to which they are held accountable.

How can business education go beyond mere *tékhnê*-based trainings of cognitive, disciplinary knowledge and competencies, functioning as a career preparation for efficient (business-as-usual) work and reproduced unhealthy hyper-modern (post-) industrial economies and societies? Teaching business as a factory-style training reduces itself to a cramming that produces consumable, short-term-oriented, and shallow knowledge.

> Education that focuses exclusively on the knowledge and skills necessary for socio-economic success not only precludes education for wisdom, but is detrimental to it, by reinforcing cultural, political and especially economic forces that tend to shape students into alienated individuals aggressively competing with others in the pursuit of unexamined, market-manipulated desires.
>
> (Maughn, 2009: 118)

Such an instrumental approach is problematic as it is a moralizing normative imposition that focuses on advising what ought to be done in different situations. While the instrumental orientation seems to under-specify the link between wisdom and ethical principles and (intra- und inter-)action, the normative thrust often appears to be disconnected from many pragmatic and wisdom- or ethics-related issues of messy business and management realities in which various Others are encountered. It is an openness and orientation towards Others (Durand & Calori, 2006) and "Othering" that characterizes a practically wise agent that in turn also influences the organizational accountability (Durand & Huy, 2008). Practical wisdom manifests in organizational and social contexts through the relational and respectful practice of reciprocity – including mutual abandonment of self-certitudes and creation of balanced non-dominating interpersonal relationships – as well as moral exemplarity (Durand & Calori, 2006).

What does it mean to pose the ancient question about whether wisdom can be taught and learned again, especially in relation to management and business education? What does it imply that practical wisdom cannot be directly learned as there are no formal procedures for getting to it or formulaic element to be able to discern (morally) and becoming prudent?

Being neither a method, nor a reducible set of universal or heuristic rule, learning wisdom is more about a situational and even improvisational way of dealing with and living through practices and in *prâxis*.

If learning practical wisdom is more than knowing why things happen (*episteme*), or knowing how to make things happen (*tékhnê*), how can a learner get to know what to do in a particular situation but in relation to the common good, that is, to know how to act to achieve good ends, in a good way? Moreover, if wisdom is not just a transferring of knowledge, but its learning and realization better understood as an embodied practice, how then can it be learned? Correspondingly, what role do experiential processes and affective and tacit dimensions of wisdom (Fukami, 2007)[5] as well as de- and re-habitualization and improvisation play in such embodied wisdom learning and educational practices? Furthermore, knowing what to do and doing it in a *tékhnê*-based way is not enough. Rather, there is the need to facilitate wisdom-oriented dimensions as well as the conversion of knowledge into action (Pfeffer & Sutton, 1999).

More innovative approaches to embody teaching, learning, and assessment are required that shift from *tékhnê*- and tool-oriented, lecturer-centered, or tutor-driven formal teaching to that which integrates participation and engagement of learners and co-inquiry and peer-oriented learning. In such a form, students take significantly more responsibility for their own learning with higher levels of involvement and Gestalt-switching in social transformative social practices while living with uncertainty (Wals, 2010).

Such learning requires educational arrangements that allow experimentation and invite "rhizo-activity" (Kang, 2007) of mutual, co-evolving modalities and transformative processes, while integrating aesthetical qualities and art-based initiatives for developing and enacting ethical practices and wisdom (see Chapter 12 by Küpers in this volume).

The various dimensions addressed situate business and management education as being part of a move toward a more integral education, pedagogy, and learning practice (Esbörn-Hargens et al., 2010). Many elements of such an integral approach are highly relevant for wisdom learning. These include among others exploring multiple perspectives, comprising first-, second-, and third-person methodologies and various styles of learning and teaching, as well as multiple ways of knowing. Further elements encompass weaving together the domains of nature, culture, and self, combining experiential feeling with critical thinking, recognizing various types of learners and teachers as well as honoring other approaches to education and many more (Esbörn-Hargens et al., 2010: 5–6).

Interesting for a wisdom-learning approach are interpretations of (non-authoritarian) integral education arising from a historical perspective, including the following (Molz & Hampson, 2010):

- a lifelong and life-wide practice across formal and informal learning opportunities;
- engagement with dimensions and aspirations of the whole human being in a dynamically harmonious way;
- cultivation and facilitation of inner qualities (for all ages and in all domains of life);
- connectivity, such as that between disciplines; occupations; cultures; theory and practice; private and public; beauty, truth, and goodness;
- engagement with the challenges and opportunities of the given era (regarding, for example, governance, technology, social justice, ecology);
- respect for the evolving freedom and uniqueness of the learner – education as self-determined, unfolding in an emancipatory way along individual trajectories;
- facilitation of a non-dogmatic, critical, experimental, and experiential enjoyment of being, becoming, doing, relating, and caring.

How can we provide opportunities to exercise wisdom, that is, to actually and critically practice virtuously in dealing with organizational challenges in concrete situations that call for collaborative work, dividing labor, reaching consensus, resolving conflicts, and creative problem solving (Lickona et al., 2007: 2)?

What are needed are open-ended forms of co-learning that are recognizing an integral pluralism (Molz, 2009) and give space for processing complexities and ambiguities as well as ethical and wisdom-related experiences, decisions, and practices. Accordingly, inquiry-based learning approaches for management education have been suggested (Bachmann, 2014; see chapter by Napan in this volume) and possibilities for developing wisdom through education offered (Ferrari et al., 2017). These innovative forms of inquiry-oriented learning are also complementary with forms of civic and service learning (Butin, 2005).

Furthermore, for cultivating more responsible ways of thinking and acting by business students, suggestions have been made to complement the moral case and the economic case with a governance case based on practical wisdom as "middle ground" of thoughtful action (Roos, 2015). Case-based learning offers possibilities to configure opportunities to learn wisdom by being exposed to real-life situations that require decisions, where uncertainty, anxiety, and risks generate demanding challenges, including the opportunity to fail (Grint, 2007: 243).

Wisdom itself

> facilitates learning in order to enable us to face the complexities of life and to do things as they should be done: phronesis invites us to adopt the best decision on each occasion and to conduct life.... It is a means of foresight in the light of what may occur, a form of knowledge that can use the experiences of the past as a means of anticipating future events.
>
> (Couceiro-Bueno, 2011: 181)

Overall, wisdom learning is called to cultivate, activate, and use dispositions and capabilities for be(com)ing ethical and wise, as these are prerequisites to societal and cultural transformation.

Disposition – wisdom as capability

Practical wisdom is itself a disposition and in particular a capacity or capability. Generally, disposition refers to being prepared, a learnable state of readiness, or a tendency to act in a specific way. Wisdom, learning, and disposition are closely connected (see chapter by McKenna in this volume). According to Aristotle "Virtue is a purposive disposition" inherent in the "prudent [hu]man" (Aristotle, 1998: II: 1107a1), and *phrónêsis* as practical or prudential wisdom is a reasoned and true state of capacity to act with regard to human goods (ibid.: 1140), essentially rooted in action. Specifically, Aristotle describes ethical virtue as a *hexis* that is a state or condition, thus a tendency or disposition that is induced by our habits and to have appropriate feelings (ibid.: 1105b25–6).

Habitual dispositions suggest that we have a "natural" capacity to develop being disposed through learning by doing. Moral excellence is based on or mediated through habit and not teaching. The difference between a virtue, like wisdom, and a craft is that although both require inquiry and deliberation, the latter is more concerned with an end product, while practical wisdom only includes the correct use of capacities towards ethical action. The right thing done for the wrong reason does not count as a virtuous or wise action.

Accordingly, with regard to being a capability, practical wisdom refers to more inclusive, deeper, and higher levels of operation and practice than that typically captured in most notions of competence or logic and analytic skills. Having the potential to become competent, as such it is a feature, faculty, or process of how then applied and "sagacious" competencies (Bernstein, 1996) can be developed, deployed, or improved.

Furthermore, someone capable is able to know what level of competence is needed and to exercise it wisely. Moreover, capability includes being aware of the limits of competencies as well as how to overcome them in any given situation.

Capable persons take an inquiring approach and work their way around problems, rather than accept practices and assumptions as given. Rather than waiting to be prompted and trained, they develop new skills and abilities in response to new demands or to improve practice. Importantly, they make sound judgments in the face of incomplete information and divergent problems (Schumacher, 1977) or even process negative capabilities *in sensu* Keats.[6]

Implying being able to become more or better able, a responsive capability implies not only a capacity to develop additional competencies, but to move beyond competence-based approach to work effectively in unpredictable situations and changing contexts. Such orientation requires the integration of skills, knowledge, and judgment, including dealing with unfamiliar problems in unaccustomed contexts (Stephenson, 1998). Also the connections between practical wisdom and emotional capability (Huy, 1999) have also been studied as antecedents of organizational accountability in revolutionary change processes (Durand & Huy, 2008).

If critical and applied, philosophy (Painter-Morland, 2015) and education are activities by means of which learners prepare for and cultivate wisdom. But developing and exercising these proto-wisdom activities need

> necessarily consist not merely in speaking and discoursing in a certain way, but also in being, acting, and seeing the world in a specific way. If then, philosophy [and education] is not merely discourse, but a choice of life and its course that is an existential option and a lived exercise; this is because it is the desire for wisdom.
> (Hadot, 2002: 230)

A capabilities approach has also been developed as a flexible and multi-purpose framework, and a paradigm for policy debate in human development and well-being on a macro-level for overcoming poverty as capability-deprivation (Sen, 1985; Comim et al. 2008, Nussbaum, 1988, 2003, 2005; Ballet et al., 2014). It is a normative orientation as it demands that social arrangements should be primarily evaluated according to the extent of freedom and dignity people have to promote or achieve functioning (being and doing) they also intrinsically value. Specifically, it can be used for a range of normative exercises, including the evaluation of individual and social well-being, and the design of policies or proposals about social change in economy and society.

The capacity for wisdom involves openness and vulnerability, and in learning/teaching needs to be linked to encounters based on the principle of a genuine under-standing, as to "stand among" as opposed to apart from (Hart, 2001) extended towards a rhizomic "inter-standing" (Taylor, 1995). The next section explores in more depth the role of the mediatrix of this "inter-" and "in-between" for wisdom learning.

Wisdom learning as inter-practising movement "in-between": metaxis

Wisdom and sustainability learning takes place in in-between spaces that "emerge from the differences of various knowledge fields and fields of action [and] provide opportunities to link knowledge production and societal transformation" (Vilsmaier & Lang, 2015: 51).

What does it mean to understand wisdom learning as an event that moves in-between, and to interpret it as an inquiring journey in *metaxis* (Linds, 2009; Linds & Trull, 2012)? *Metaxis*, *metaxu*, or *methexis* – in Greek meaning "between" and "in" – refers to the state of being in the middle, betwixt, between, between-whiles, in the interval, neither good nor bad (Allern, 2002).

Plato used the term *metaxis* to refer to the state of existing and oscillating between two opposite poles. "All spirits occupy the middle ground between humans and gods. As mediators between the two, they fill the remaining space, and so make the universe an interconnected whole" (Plato, 1994: 43–44). Further examples include moving at the border between the real and the fictional, or simultaneously being an individual and a member of a group, or being an observer and also a performer, oscillations of and between chaos and harmony, irony and sincerity, naivety and knowingness, ignorance and wisdom, relativism and truth, optimism and doubt, etc.

For Plato, *metaxu* is a dynamic space or sphere between two "separate" and distinct things or phenomena while mediation keeps them and the universe together. Eric Voegelin calls this the tension "in-between the poles of man and of the reality he experiences" (1989: 72). Rather than seeking to move to one pole or the other, we are invited to explore this in-betweenness. Being situated in this intermediate *(metaxu)* position – between need and resource, ignorance and knowledge, etc., the very lack of what one desires can become a guiding form of contact with the objects of human desire. Focusing on intermediacy, philosophizing and searching for wisdom is a kind of "being in-between," an aspiring love for wisdom – *philo-sophia* – rather than the possession of it (Scott & Welton, 2009).[7]

Importantly,

> [a] different kind of knowing emerges from this process between the observing, the in-situ, and our interactions. We begin to see everything in new ways. We hold up a mirror to the world and, instead of trying to represent it, find it accessible. We can see that this co-emergent self/other/world is flexible, dynamic, and changeable. Observation through metaxis allows us to experience knowing as it is enacted, and, as it occurs in/through the artist's body, embodied in each moment of the present.
>
> (Linds, 2009)

This experienced process mediates an aesthetic transformation.[8]

In ancient traditions the embodied and aesthetic in-between of wisdom learning referred to body-sensitive habits of diet and exercise, the joy, but also discipline of desire, the cultivation of worthy passions, meaningful relationships, especially friendships. Furthermore, it comprised helpful attitudes toward death, and other aspects of caring for the self, the community, the stranger, and the natural world. All of them are part of an open-minded and self-corrective existential and moral as well as collaborative inquiry in a community of joint research, mutual assistance, and spiritual support (Hadot, 1995: 274).

Somantic active and semantic contemplative exercises are practical methods – technologies or "therapies" – for realizing ethical and wise ideals like quieting the ego, facing suffering with equanimity, and taking compassionate action. Such a relational approach cultivates a more "plastic" wisdom learning. The plasticity of practical wisdom would offer a dynamic "difference-unity" of acting (giving form = activity) and being acted upon (receiving form = passivity), that is, something modifiable, formable, and formative at the same time. Such wisdom practice allows spontaneity and receptivity, serving as a medium for differentiation and integration of opposites, contradictions, paradoxes, dilemmas, and "trans-subjectivation," offering a meta(-morphising) dynamic stability through structural and processual integrity.

Wisdom and its learning is both a flourishing journey and provisional destination, constantly developing and be(com)ing a state of readiness to engage at any time with a higher purpose of flourishing self and others. Part of evoking the transformation toward wisdom and its inter-relational learning is to re-orientate with new images and apt metaphors.

Wilma Fraser and Tara Hyland-Russell in their article on creating wisdom-spaces in adult education, suggested convincingly the spiral as generative metaphor of wise development und unfoldment.

For example, the spiral nautilus can serve as a profound and dynamic metaphor for the deepening awareness and integration of personal, relational, and cultural stories and practices of wisdom. This shell is constructed as a series of chambers that lead deeper into further chambers, spiraling around the "inner self" (Figure I.1). Importantly, these chambers also open outward, connecting the inner creature with the surrounding sea.

> Using a spiral metaphor for wisdom learning processes provides a model through which to evaluate and mediate among conflicting discourses and social pressures,

not least of which are the current economic paradigms, and values the wisdom that emerges from one's personal and communal journey.

(Fraser & Hyland-Russell, 2011: 29)

What would a pedagogy of possibility or a metaxic education of wisdom learning as one of the "in-between" (Steel, 2014) involve? How can we develop a metaxic business and management education, educating as and in an in-between that is part of pursuing and enacting wisdom? In metaxic wisdom learning, embodied selves sense spaces of possibilities as processes of constantly co-enacting and re-enacting their encounters, moving in-between, which they long for and belong to, of which they are always already a part, and in which they participate. The task as "enactors then becomes awaiting, performing, testing, noticing, listening to choices and options that keep the space of possibility alive" (Linds, 2006: 117). S/he knows that metaxic in-between (Linds, 2001) is not empty but alive with intentions, responses, and actions arising from the prior history, experiences, memories, sediments, habits, prejudices, and foreknowing. Such *metaxis* as transition between (real and virtual) worlds has various implications for education (Falconer, 2011). Through metaxic wisdom learning, task and relationship in followership and leadership would not be seen as an upward orientation of followers that try to satisfy the demands of their

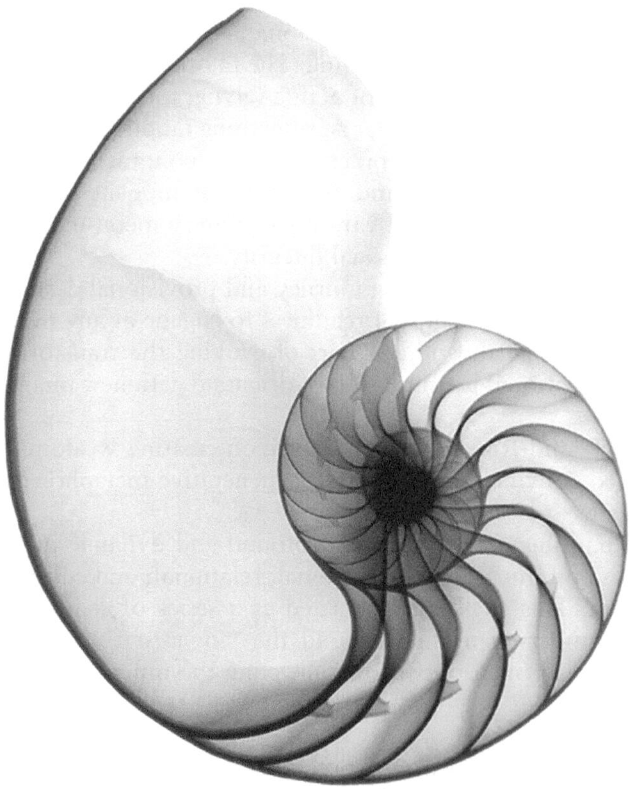

Figure I.1 Nautilus shell spiral.

superordinates (Orpheans), or a downward-focused one to the demands of subordinates (Prometheans) but would be a capacity that tries to look both ways (Janusians) (Cowill & Grint, 2008).

Possibilities for *metaxis* occur in moments in which questions arise, when (wisdom) learners ask: Will this work over time, and long-term? What are the direct and indirect consequences? Does this fit with our goals and goals of stakeholders? Is this part of the problem or part of the solution? Does this represent excellence? Is this fair? Is it right? Is action needed or not needed? Does it make sense in terms of the general welfare? What if things and realities could be different? When unseen, unknown, and unrecognized spaces and possibilities are discovered within themselves, other communities and life-worlds are experienced as vibrant and creative milieus, offering opportunities for explorative movements and interrogations.

Metaxis education facilitates a deep learning, by which students make connections between ideas and issues, examine underlying reasons and arguments, explore root causes of problems, and engage in active learning (Warburton, 2003) that also helps to translate the learned into ways of acting in everyday situations.

The wisdom learner can become a transformative mediator between worlds; a trickster-kind of actor who, being in-form and in-formed, is playing the wild card and various roles, including the "Joker," zooming in and out, enabling more "metaxis to occur by constantly stretching the space to engage in a discourse of embodied critique and possibility" (Linds, 2006: 123), thus a maieutics of body and spirit:

> Like the midwife, the Joker enacts and enables the conditions of metaxis so that (wisdom) stories can emerge into and from the world processed in classrooms, in professional workshops, in clinical practice and by doing so assisting people to discover and co-create their own wisdom (Randall and Kenyon, 2004: 342; Randall, 2014). This task enables different voices, worldviews, value systems, and beliefs to converse with one another. Through this process, knowing is an unfolding, dancing metaxis into being.
>
> (ibid.)

Also the forms of "inter-being" as described by Thich Nhat Hanh have been discussed that resonate with a *metaxis* approach to learning. From the perspective of inter-being, selves are active co-participants in a holistic shifting matrix of mutual causality and interrelationship.

> When viewed within a contemplative educational context, interbeing brings attention to how the students, the classroom subject of inquiry, the process of inquiry and educator shape and co-constitute one another .... By valuing and amplifying our shared experience of consciousness, the lens of interbeing brings into focus the more subtle unseen aspects and sinews of interrelatedness with our students, the subject and process of inquiry. This helps us relax the habituated compulsion to know and deliver an authoritative view to our students. In the context of classroom inquiry, interbeing can help students and educator regard the classroom as a place for occasions of interconnectedness and the co-constitution of shared meaning .... Nhat Hanh's depiction of inter-being offers a means for working with the resistances in ourselves to what is 'other' in our classrooms, as well as

> to the elements in our students and ourselves that we may resist and for whatever reasons, cannot or refuse to openly engage with. By identifying and finding a basis to transform the elements in ourselves that prevent us from recognizing our interrelatedness with our difficult students, we become more prone to experiencing our students and our selfhood as interdependent and thus our processes of inner transformation and our students' transformation as likewise interdependent.
>
> (Gunnlaugson, 2009; 32–33)

As wisdom occupies the "fertile hinterland between spirit and matter, mind and body, and heaven and Earth" and "slips easily between them, retaining that 'strange poise – an echo, a reminder of a basic wonder/wander that drives human endeavors" (Chia & Holt, 2007: 524), what is needed is to move likewise, in dialogue with this in-between.

In a certain way, the entire book invites to enter a dialogical in-between here with the authors, who offer their insights, discourses, and findings about requirements and possibilities as well as limitations and challenges of learning, teaching, and educating wisdom, especially related to management and business.

Introduction to specific chapters

We divided the book into two parts. While the first part covers more conceptual contributions and alternative perspectives on Wisdom Learning, Teaching and Education, the second presents more empirical and practical contributions.

The first chapter by Bernard McKenna, "Business Schools' Role in Embodying a Wise Graduate Disposition," explores how wisdom can be developed by cultivating a disposition in business courses that includes reflection of context, embodiment, and agencies, as well as enacting character. Adopting a stoic approach that takes this philosophy as a holistic "eudaimonian" approach and practice, wisdom is proposed as an appropriate expertise to which emerging leaders should aspire. Responding to the guiding question on how business education can shape a disposition that is founded on wisdom virtues in relation to values and behavior, he develops a framework for research and teaching. This framework provides a conceptual base for moving toward developing and inculcating "the right stuff" and appropriate expertise in business graduates as aspiring emerging leaders who are enacting their life narrative. Proto-integrally, wisdom for him involves a world-orientation that brings together the physical, the ethical, and the cognitive/logical, that are all embodied in a disposition leading to habitual and resilient forms of wise action.

Matt Statler and Steven Taylor contribute with a chapter on a powerful pedagogical tool, "Catharsis," and explore its role "in the classroom." For them, catharsis serves as an approach and means for fostering the development and learning of wisdom, experientially and practically. Building on a critique of conventional teaching at business schools, and facing the current crisis, they raise the question of what and how these institutions could be teaching and learning differently. Following the idea of a "knowledge-by-exemplification" as an essentially theatrical or dramatic phenomenon, they demonstrate how the role of affective moods, normative values, and aesthetic perceptions and judgments could be evaluated in view of presence, distribution, and relative intensity of catharsis experienced by students.

Specifically they present a matrix of four different case illustrations of catharsis in the classroom varying according to how pedagogical processes integrate dramatic contents and/or theatrical process techniques. Related to these possibilities, they offer reflections on the existing research that deals with catharsis and the role of theater and drama in organizational contexts and then on the broader concept of social materiality as it pertains to the business school classroom, followed by complex issues associated with the design and facilitation of pedagogical processes that make catharsis more rather than less likely to occur. Finally, they conclude by raising some questions for future research, particularly with regard to the teaching and learning of wisdom.

The third chapter explores the possibilities for "Cultivating Practical Wisdom Through Emergent Learning." As leadership wisdom is recognized as increasingly critical for organizations to navigate the turbulence and unpredictability of our complex world, the question of how practical wisdom can be catalyzed has become pivotal. In her chapter, Marilyn Taylor points out our collective preoccupation with acquiring knowledge that has eclipsed the importance of a deeper guiding wisdom. After making a case for a radically different approach to wisdom learning, this chapter presents a process model of emergent learning that can be considered a path toward the development and enhancement of wisdom. Constructed phenomenologically from common patterns of experience of people confronting the unexpected, elements of the process align with six dimensions of wisdom as reflected in the literature. It begins with what represents a common challenge in our complex world – a distressing experience of confusion that arises from a surprising discovery that we do not know something vital to what we are trying to accomplish. The subsequent process is configured as four distinctive phases or "seasons" of experience and four phase transitions that engage our senses, emotions, and relationships with others, as well as our minds. While the process patterns are affected by unique individual qualities and contextual differences, the configuration provides a "map" of challenges in engaging the unknown in ways that enhance specific dimensions of wisdom.

Filipa Rocha Rodrigues, Miguel Pina e Cunha, Arménio Rego, and Stewart Clegg set up "The Seven Pillars of Paradoxical Organizational Wisdom: On the Use of Paradox as a Vehicle to synthesize Knowledge and Ignorance." Showing that complex times require complex management, in which wisdom prevails, they introduce the concept of paradoxical wisdom as a way of articulating organizational polarities that align with an Aristotelian virtuous golden mean in a duality. Various approaches to paradoxes and their implications are outlined and the role of wisdom in the management of paradox revealed, as well as in turn how paradox sustains wisdom. They argue that paradox requires an attitude of flux rather than rigidity between forces that may be contradictory themselves and suggest that paradoxical wisdom may be diffused within organizations via a specific cultivation (of seven pillars). Deliberately engaging with paradox is an exercise in learning and unlearning, acting and reflecting, doubting and being confident, gaining comfort with contradiction, understanding and influencing, as well as (its) dialectics.

For them, managers and organizations can cultivate wisdom by exposing themselves to paradox, by synthesizing knowledge and ignorance. Engagement with paradox in search for solutions that transcend habitual dichotomies offers a fertile ground to acquire knowledge and to gain awareness about the limits of the knowledge acquired.

In their chapter "Too busy to learn: Wisdom, mindfulness, and grounding learning" Nina Kongsbakk and David Rooney bring together time, values, and identity-related barriers that prevent organizational learning by using a mindfulness and wisdom framework. Their empirical data and analysis demonstrate how issues linked to identity, like values conflicts, as well as time pressure, negatively affect learning and knowledge sharing by not grounding learning. By contrast, mindfulness helps identity and enacts values to interact in positive ways to ground learning and the sharing of knowledge in a time poor organization. Specifically, they present an eight-step framework to manage mindful organizational learning and knowledge sharing.

The subsequent chapter asks an important question: "Is Practical Wisdom and Learning Literature Actually Wise on Its Right to Speak?" Following the reflection on mindfulness of the previous chapter, the synergistic interplay of different business practices and creative ways of thinking that emerge from wisdom and its learning is explored by Vincenzo Mario Bruno Giorgino and Xabier Renteria-Uriarte. They look more in depth at some of the inner dimensions of unity and integrity that subsume these multiple and only apparently separated dimensions. The authors remark that traditionally this issue is addressed by a specific side of ancient wisdom traditions, some western scientific currents and, also as instrumental and practical tools, by meditation and contemplative practices. The chapter makes a contribution by reconsidering traditional occidental and oriental arguments. On this basis of an integrative understanding, the authors argue that, among innovative social science perspectives, modern contemplative sciences seem the most suited to inquiry into vitalizing possibilities of learning of wise practices in organizing and leading. Nevertheless, how to implement practical wisdom learning in social sciences and education remains a fundamental challenge. As a whole, the authors devote their main attention to what this vision means in terms of practice for academic teaching and training.

In the second part of the book, the chapters provide more empirical and practical contributions. They concretize how to put wisdom learning, teaching, and education into practice and what challenges and implications are involved in doing so.

The chapter by Charles Oden and Monkia Ardelt on "Practical Wisdom and Professional Development: Engagement for the Next Generation of Business" situates wisdom in relation to recent context: it points out that a number of transformations are underway in our world presently that will significantly influence the next decade as one of rapid change in business led by innovations in 3D printing, use of drones, driverless vehicles, and development of the internet of things. Retiring Baby Boomers will be leaving the workforce in droves creating a global workforce crisis, being replaced by Millennials. The authors point out that the new business environment will be more connected, flexible, and expressive, requiring greater team cohesiveness and interpersonal trust than ever before in history. Correspondingly, they make the case for developing personal and organizational wisdom as a basis for stewarding and implementing such dramatic changes successfully. The study in this chapter on the whole proposes that organizations will benefit if the development of wisdom becomes the goal of professional training within organizations. Based on a comprehensive empirical research, including full-time non-instructional staff from both a traditional university setting and numerous branch offices, interesting findings were gained. The results indicated that the personal wisdom of individuals in a business setting, measured as a composite of cognitive, reflective, and compassionate dimensions of wisdom, was positively related to team cohesiveness and both cognitive-based and affective-based interpersonal trust. On the whole, this chapter forwards the view that personal wisdom will play an increasingly pivotal role in professional development and organizational success in the future.

Jay Martin Hays' chapter on "A Wise Course: Educating for Wisdom in the Twenty-First Century" sets forth the key features of "a wise course" or curriculum, including suggestions on course design and delivery, and how elements of wise thought and action can be developed, elicited, and assessed. To explicate this approach he uses his definition of wisdom as "doing the right thing for the greater good, all things considered." As the heart of this "wise course" he has conceptualized a model that unites "Reasoning, Judgement, and Reflective Action" (RJRA) that encompass highly demanded capabilities and dispositions for our world. It involves skills, tools, processes, and disciplines related to RJRA as well as critical thinking, complex problem-solving, creativity, decision-making, and planning. All of them are viewed through an ethics lens, and continually referenced to the local and global context. Furthermore, his conceptualization and suggestions for "wising up" management education embodies sustainability and engender sustainable teaching and learning practices.

The next chapter by Mike Thompson provides insights into a phronetic research study that explored the question of "how managers understand wisdom in decision-making." The study is based on a Wisdom Project conducted at the China Europe International Business School as a research enquiry into the way in which senior managers understood the role of wisdom in processes of making decisions and how someone might acquire wisdom. As over half of the survey participants were senior Chinese managers, the study pursues also a comparative analysis between Chinese and Western understandings of wisdom in management. Similar concepts were grouped and five constructs of management wisdom identified, comprising: (i) Rational Capability; (ii) Intuitive Insight; (iii) Humane Character; (iv) Self-awareness; and (v) Emotional Regulation. A subsidiary objective was to test the extent to which the descriptions collected through the research survey aligned with the five principles of Social Practice Wisdom (SPW), namely: (1) wise leaders use reason and careful observation; (ii) wise leaders allow for non-rational and subjective elements when making decisions; (iii) wise leaders value humane and virtuous outcomes; (iv) wise leaders and their actions are practical and oriented towards everyday life, including work; and (v) wise leaders are articulate, understand the aesthetic dimension of their work, and seek the intrinsic personal and social rewards of contributing to the good life. Interestingly, the survey confirmed that the identified concepts were associated with all five principles of SPW. This study invites important questions and implications for management education.

The next contribution by Dennis Wittmer and Cynthia Fukami is connected to the previous one on decision-making and continues the prior discussion on curriculum design. In this chapter entitled "Educating Future Business Leaders to Be Practically Wise: Designing an MBA Curriculum to Strengthen Good Decision-Making" the authors develop a case for enhancing and strengthening practical wisdom as a primary goal for an MBA education. After exploring a conception of practical wisdom, the chapter develops and unpacks what educating for practical wisdom looks like in an MBA and leadership context. Finally, the chapter summarizes and outlines various curricular innovations that have been adopted at a number of business schools, in turn exploring possible strategies and metrics for assessing success of the program and curricular changes.

The eleventh chapter "Exploring Practical Wisdom: Teaching Management in a Spirit of Co-creation" also provides innovative forms of teaching and learning practical wisdom. In her revealing elaboration, Ksenija Napan focuses on the process of development of practical wisdom with a group of reluctant learners enrolled in the "Management in the Social Services" course within a Master of Applied Social Work. For this she presents and discusses the context, processes, and evaluation of the specific and meaningful way of teaching called "Academic Co-creative Inquiry." This teaching approach intends to build on students" strengths and abilities, and to enhance their understanding of the context of their future practice. It utilizes their prior knowledge and encourages them to transform from passive recipients of knowledge into wisdom seekers. Importantly, a special focus is placed on students' ways of managing themselves, their collaboration with peers, discovery of their leadership potential and passion for "bringing forth" the world. As the author demonstrates, these features enable practical wisdom to emerge, evidenced in students' choice in composing creative, relevant, and practical assignments. Specific qualities that emerged as being essential for effectiveness of the academic co-creative inquiry are presented, critically analysed, and illustrated with examples of student work in relation to different ways of how they engender practical wisdom in management education. This enlightening presentation can indeed inspire educators and other practitioners to experiment and play with various ways of applying inquiry learning in order to engender practical wisdom in future leaders and managers. Moreover, it also offers theoretical, methodological, and practical implications for educating future managers and leaders in social work services.

As an example of an experiential and experimental approach, the final chapter by Wendelin Küpers, "Embodied "Aesth-Ethics" for Developing Practical Wisdom in Management Education/Learning" discusses the role of embodied ethics and aesthetics for a different kind of management learning and education. Based on a phenomenology of embodied learning, the author presents and discussed the experienced teaching and learnings practices of a module on "Ethics and Aesthetics" that is an integrated part of a Master-study at a German Business School. Furthermore, the significance of wonder and wondering in management learning and education is discussed and concluding implications and perspectives outlined.

Research agenda and open questions – overall conclusions and perspective

It is our hope that this book gives voice to some current and future-oriented perspectives and research on wisdom learning. In this way, it might contribute to the movement into the field of theory development and further exploring critical avenues of practices of wisdom learning in business and management education, as well as beyond. This may then help to grow a radically different kind of organization and management engagement in our world that will not survive if it continues its existing unwise forms of organizing, leading, and governing.

The following lists of open questions offer some indicating directions and programmatic suggestions for research, practice, and experimentation. They aim to open up an agenda with various challenges, issues, and areas of wisdom learning, some more specifically addressing organization and leadership and/or business and management education.

(Research) approaches and methodologies for wisdom learning

- What are the ontological, epistemological, and methodological assumptions or underpinnings that are needed to ground and apply a (meta-) theory of wisdom learning in organizations?
- To what extent can wisdom learning be theorized as an individual, collective, and/or (inter-) relational phenomenon in organizations and management?
- How can a more integrative understanding of wisdom learning be developed and enacted within and by employees, leaders, teams, and entire organizations and stakeholders in their interrelationships?
- Of the existing philosophical and psychological conceptualizations of wisdom (i.e., traits, dispositions, capabilities, competences, processes of creative enactment), how might these concepts support or extend current organizational research on wisdom learning and education?
- What innovative social science or cross-disciplinary perspectives and approaches seem most suited to inquiries into wisdom learning? Are there particular art-based approaches, or integral or process philosophies that could help in further exploring these issues methodologically?
    - How can, in a cross-disciplinary practice, humanities and liberal arts be integrated in management education and with what implications and outcomes?
    - What non-mainstream "management as unusual" contents can be incorporated or explored?

Methodological study

- How can we develop a "thick" description and understanding[9] of practical wisdom in relation to the Anthropocene and the processes of both survival and revival?
    - Specifically, how can we situate and methodologically study wisdom learning and seeing the current transition as part of a broader process of the problematization and searching for ways of global, regional, and local survival?
        - What does it imply and how can we interpret that this is a process which induces and includes also a revival of meaningful life through reconfiguration of relationships between humans, nature, and society within a local and planetary perspective?

Values and wisdom learning

- How are or can values and ethical orientations that are underlying wisdom learning be taken into account by individual and collective actors?
- To what extent can wisdom learning be associated with "positively valued" phenomena such as appreciation, happiness, eudaimonia, and/or well-being in organizations? What links exist between wisdom learning and positive psychology?
    - How do forms of wise/wisdom learning practices provide media for fulfilling pragmatics of everyday life, especially for developing an art of living well, individually and collectively?

- How does wisdom learning lead towards a more prudent and proactive orientation and contribute to a more responsible and sustainable way of organizing and managing?
- Can the exercise of wisdom learning practices make organizations more prepared to deal with unexpected events and uncertainty?
- What is the significance of mindfulness (Sauer & Kohls, 2011) and spirituality for an inspiring responsible leadership education (Blakeley, 2015) and wisdom learning?
    - What insights can be learned about wisdom practice from non-Western and spiritual traditions and philosophies?

Knowledge and wisdom learning

- Can wisdom learning be theorized in more process-oriented ways that stress ongoing performance and be(com)ing, rather than static knowledge as a "state of having"?
- How can wisdom learning contribute to the development of different ways of knowing about knowledge creation, sharing, and implementation processes and outcomes in organizations?
- How might implicit and tacit knowing, and intuition or storytelling be related to or inform or part of wisdom learning?
- What would it mean to appreciate the fallible nature of that knowledge and seeing knowing what we do not know as part of wisdom and its learning?
- Is it wiser to pursue incomplete, messy, contextualized, uncertain knowledge that enriches our understanding of how to promote human welfare than to amass lots of clean data that is easy to manipulate and present, but yet is based on false assumptions (Baden & Higgs, 2015)?

Design(ing) wisdom learning/pedagogies

- How can we get "beyond" to become "Future Wise" (Perkins, 2014):
    - beyond basic skills – to twenty-first century skills and dispositions such as collaboration, critical thinking, and entrepreneurship;
    - beyond traditional disciplines – to hybrid themes such as bioethics, ecology, and challenges of our time;
    - beyond discrete disciplines – to interdisciplinary topics and problems;
    - beyond regional matters – to global perspectives, problems, and citizenship;
    - beyond mastering content – to connecting content to life situations and productive action;
    - beyond prescribed content – to learner choices in what to study?
- Whose responsibility is it to develop wisdom-based pedagogies and designs?
- What materials, subjects, and contents could or should be included in wisdom pedagogies and life-worthy curricula and how can they be didactically conveyed?
    - Where in the curriculum could wisdom-related contents and learning practices be positioned and how can they be linked to other courses and contents?

- How can we apply a wisdom learning perspective to the functional areas of Business School education, like finance- or HR management or marketing, that defines business success in terms of the terminal value of societal welfare (Baden & Higgs, 2015)?
- What would be the learning outcomes of a wisdom program in educational or organizations and management pedagogies? How will the "achievements" of certain key outcomes be assessed?
- Who is teaching and how? How can we teach teachers wisely?
    - What is the role of disposition, capabilities, virtues, and character of teachers or educationalists?
    - Concerning being–doing–teaching wisdom learning, can educators help make their students a more integrally oriented whole if they are not committed to becoming proto-integral themselves and in all that they do or do not do?
    - How can those engaged in teaching students embody the key components of wisdom in their own practice, and thereby effect changes in a business and management education that contribute to the unfolding of practical wisdom?
    - What is the significance of role modeling, specifically the ways in which role models serve to shape individual wise decisions and choices related to their actions?
- What does it imply for learning/teaching that rules and incentives can never provide an adequate substitute for people who have the character to want to do right by, for and with others, and the judgment to figure out what doing right requires?
- How can we prepare the cultivation of wisdom learning as requiring devoting interest, effort and passion as well as love or *eros* to that cultivation?
- How can education itself be informed by a wisdom-based and future-oriented strategic framework and enact wisdom-augmented practices that keep an unfolding and flourishing of self and others as the ongoing emerging outcome?

Context and conditions, practices and problems with wisdom learning

- In what sense does wisdom learning have temporal and spatial qualities? How does wisdom learning build over time and is it placed in relation to events in particular life-worldly and organizational contexts?
    - How can we deal with the challenge that wisdom as mastery of the habit of practical wisdom requires more time, perhaps a life-time, to develop than is available in brief classroom meetings? How can we encourage and evaluate an incremental development?
    - In what ways is wisdom learning practice manifest in specific situations and not in others? How should the dynamics of wisdom learning be assessed and described to optimally serve the processes involved?
    - Can wisdom learning become part of a "slow education" to counter the "edu-anxiety" and enhance our ability to respond to the crises and stresses of late modernity (Bussey, 2012)?

        - While this slowness challenges the speed, disorientation, crisis addiction, and homogenization of current educational practice, how can it – like slow food – be interested in the relationships of production of local relevance; social health; the 'taste' of a subject of study; the time students and their teachers have to develop scholarship, meaning, relevance, relationship, and rigor; the sense that learning needs to be more than just functional in nature and that scholarship has intrinsic merit (Bussey, 2008)?

    - How can we reincorporate *skhole*, that is, a contemplative and receptive attitude and practice of leisure associated with connectedness, with growth in insight and knowledge as well as understanding of truth?

- What are the relationships between wisdom learning and material, bodily, emotional, socio-cultural, and historical conditions and interlinking factors or multiple dimensions that co-constitute its occurrence and development?
- How can digital and other learning technologies facilitate the development of wisdom?
- What about resources in relation to practical wisdom learning, including material, infra-structural intellectual resources, and the status of institutional settings?
- Learners who cultivate or take special care to develop virtues, including practical wisdom, are inevitably influenced by what the dominant institutions of their societies prize and value. How then can we deal with the fact that our currently dominant set of political, economic, and educational institutions do not prioritize the cultivation of theoretical and practical wisdom?
- What does it mean concretely that transformations of educational practice depend on complementary transformations in classroom- and system-level organizational cultures, resourcing, and politics (Kemmis et al., 2014)?
- How might the status of wisdom and its learning in organizations be transformed, e.g., by the trends toward increased globalization, uncertainty, complexity, technological advances, and the steep growth level and demand for interpreted data, information, and knowledge?
- What role does transformative learning and its extensions play in relation to wisdom?

Integrations in wisdom learning

- How can we balance and integrate the empathy of care and concern with a detachment that permits clear thinking and suitable action?
- Can we allow for perceiving and treating the "others" in teaching and learning, not just as "students" but as "fellow travelers"?
- What would our teaching and learning look like that bring together the ability to perceive, to have suitable feelings or desires, and to deliberate on what is appropriate in specific circumstances, to value, to respond, and to act adequately?

    - How can we teach and learn through the integration of modes in relation to our self, others, and the world (including embodied, sensual and tacit knowing, intuition and emotions and reasoning practically) that gradually acquires experiences (*empeiría*) by practising and deliberating with and for virtuous others?

- What classroom activities or experiential formats outside integrate senses and make sense for fostering wisdom?
- What does it imply that understanding that the aspiration of becoming practically wise is more as a steady state than a final endpoint or final product? What follows to interpret it as an open process that is always moving towards the good and ideal, thus a never-quite-achieved telos and that is calling for a continuous reappraisal and adaptation of strategies for approaching virtuosity and goodness, respectively the potential for good in particular?

Wisdom learning practice in organization and leadership

- To what extent does the cultivation of an ethos and learning of wisdom in the practices of organization and their members require an understanding that is embodied and performed as a presencing event?
- What management education and organizational learning processes facilitate the development and thriving of wisdom? What organizational interventions support the practice of wisdom learning and how can they be assessed and evaluated? On what grounds would someone be responsible for initiating the wisdom learning processes?
- What specific educational processes as well as institutional and HR-related requirements are needed for organizations, management, and leaders to learn how to become wise?
- Are there specific forms of practices that enable or preclude wisdom learning?
- In what domains can wisdom be "misused" or why is it sometimes seen as negative, counter-productive, or irrelevant? What is the shadow side of wisdom learning?
- What are the implications of wisdom learning in institutionalized power relations? What are the conflicts, political issues, and ramifications of the learning of wisdom?
    - How can learning individuals be equipped to act at institutional and structural levels (i.e. advocating for changes in policy and practices)?
- How can the emerging practice turn in organization and leadership/management studies (with its focus on the everyday processes including its moral, emotional, and relational aspects) be connected to wisdom learning?
- What would a "leadership-as-(wise)-practice" approach imply (Raelin, 2016)?
- How can we link a practice of leadership with wisdom learning as part of the co-creation of social organization (Raelin, 2011) following the democratic post-heroic tenets of collectiveness, concurrency, collaboration, and compassion (Raelin, 2003)?
- How can wisdom learning be connected to a leaderful development process?
- What role do milieus of in-between, intermediary entities we call organizations – as mediators between individual and macro-level phenomena – play in this, related to wiser forms and transformations?
- What is the role of initiatives such as the United Nations "Principles for Responsible Management Education" and how do they affect wisdom learning practices and curricula?

Notes

1 A proper response is not trying to overcome (*Überwindung*), but more of a wise "*Verwindung*." Meaning neither going beyond, nor leaving behind, the term "*Verwindung*" (used by Heidegger and Vatimo) is a complex term that is difficult to translate. It can mean convalescence (or recovery), to be cured of an illness while still bearing the traces of it, and also distortion (from "*winden*" which means to twist). So we need twisting-free from metaphysics that guides the monster through a kind of active re-signation to it in the sense of a new "signing." This implies a critical acceptance of the necessity to think in the metaphysical categories that have been handed down to us (traditionally), but bereft or freed of their secure foundation(alism) to a reference (of a supposed known Being). Can we work within what we are in in a *verwindend* relation to it? Such *Verwindung* (of capitalism and other "-isms") would be by no means an uncritical surrender to or affirmative celebration of real-existing "-isms," but an injunction to undermine or unearth its violent, meta-physical actual ideological tendencies (even by helping it fully realize its nihilistic vocation?) in order for contributing to a dissolution of inherent metaphysical absolutes. Perhaps such under-minding move through a positive nihilism lead to opening up a new field of possibility and expressions of multiple voice and choices, where non-alienated feelings, thought, actions, and life will relinquish the nostalgic desire to hold fast to foundations, while navigating the difficult passage between Scyllaian rocks of dogmatic modernism and Charybdisian whirls of postmodern relativism.

2 Overpopulation, destruction of the ozone layer, global warming, extinction of species, loss of genetic diversity, acid rain, nuclear contamination, tropical deforestation, the elimination of climax forests, wetland destruction, soil erosion, desertification, floods, famine, the despoliation of lakes, streams, and rivers, the drawing down and contamination of ground water, the pollution of coastal waters and estuaries, the destruction of coral reefs, oil spills, overfishing, expanding landfills, toxic wastes, the poisonous effects of insecticides and herbicides, exposure to hazards on the job, urban congestion, and the depletion of nonrenewable resources. The rise and expansion of the Western industrial regime made humanity an equipotent force with nature. The relationship between humans and Earth became increasingly out of balance; geologists and climate scientists base the Anthropocene hypothesis (itself an outgrowth of the recent interdisciplinary understanding of the Earth as an evolving planet) on a number of human-driven processes that are likely to leave a lasting mark on the planet; lasting meaning likely to leave traces that will last tens of millions of years. These include rising oceans due to the emission of greenhouse gases; ocean acidification, which is changing the chemical makeup of the seas; urbanization, which is vastly increasing rates of sedimentation and erosion; and habitat destruction and the introduction of invasive species which are causing widespread extinctions. Interestingly, Wilson (1998) stated as the worst thing not energy depletion, economic collapse, limited nuclear war, or conquest by a totalitarian government, but loss of genetic and species diversity by the destruction of natural habitats as an ongoing process that will take millions of years to correct. For him this is the folly that our descendants are least likely to forgive us.

3 If the Anthropocene represents a new epoch of thought, it also represents a new form of materiality and historicity for the human as strata and stratigrapher of the geologic record. This collision of human and inhuman histories in the strata is a new formation of subjectivity within a geologic horizon that redefines temporal, material, and spatial orders of the human(imality) and thus nature. Anthropocene contains within it a form of *Anthropogenesis* understood as a new origin story and ontics for man and the in-human. As such it radically rewrites material modes of differentiation and concepts of life, from predominantly bio-political notions of life towards an understanding of life's geophysical origination or "geontics" (Yusoff, 2016). According to Yusoff, this comprises the production of a mythic Anthropos as geologic world-maker/destroyer of worlds, and a material, evolutionary narrative that reimagines human origins and endings within a geologic, social body and communization, rather than an exclusively biological context.

4 With regard to commercialization of higher education (Bok, 2009) investigation on the impact of auditing and monitoring interventions found a specific complicity in tension with a labor of love. While being complicit with new public management demands for audit, accountability,

and performance, there is disquiet and dissatisfaction in relation to working in a business school and the aspiration of a "labor of love" where work is an end in itself is being stretched to its limits as academics are increasingly subjected to loveless or instrumental demands (Clarke et al., 2012).

5 Interestingly, tacit knowing can be traced back to the ancient Greeks in wisdom (Baumard, 1999), being a knowledge that is embodied, "personal," profound, non-scientific, and "generated in the intimacy of lived experience" (ibid. 53). Fukami (2007) also links tacit knowing to phronesis as the integration and transformation of knowledge such that it may be interpreted and applied within a given context. While considering whether wisdom can be taught in business schools, Fukami claims that business schools focus too much on disseminating codified knowledge and explicit information and neglect the development of tacit knowledge.

6 Keats describes this negative form of capability as "capable of being in uncertainties, Mysteries, doubts without any irritable reaching after fact & reason" (Keats in Gittings, 1970: 43). This "being in uncertaint[y]" and state of intentional open-mindedness is a place between the mundane, ready reality, and the multiple potentials of a more fully understood existence. Not trying to reconcile contradictory aspects or fit it into closed and rational systems, this ability implies the capacity to sustain reflective inaction also in relation to leadership (Simpson et al., 2002) and to resist the tendency to disperse into actions that are defensive rather than relevant for transitional states and tasks. Negative capability indicates the capacity to live with ambiguity and paradox in a way that holds or contains them in order to be a medium. This is a mediality that serves as a sounding board, like an Aeolian harp that is "serenely brilliant such should Wisdom be" (Coleridge, *The Eolian Harp,* 1795) to a music that is there but unheard. In unheard sound it is like an unthought, known or resonance field for voices or visions "to pass on a message, translating it, flawlessly, into another more easily apprehended tongue" (Symons, 1901: 1627). In a certain sense, through the exercise of negative capability, members of organizations become *membranous* media. Metaphorically expressed, they mediate like the strings of a lyre, an instrument here not for performing music or poetry but serving organizational inquiries, learnings, creativities and actions (Simpson et al., 2002). Whereas positive capabilities enable things happen fast and effectively, conversely negative capability is the capacity to wait without expectations. It is a capability to hold back the tensions and pressures for solutions or quick fixes in response to problems, ambiguities and uncertainties of the paradoxical movements. Negating of habitual patterns of pressured action and straight or simple solutions allows creative processes appropriate time to prevent premature closures and to unfold its own rhythms. Interestingly, the root meaning of "capable', like "capacity" and "capacious" are derived from the Latin word "capax" and "capabilis" – "able to hold much'. Thus, it refers to "containing" or "spacious', whereas the volume of a container is a measure of its internal "negative" space. Accordingly, negative capability implies "containment" and the capacity to endure, rather than the capacity for active intervention. It invites "the cultivated resilience to resist premature closure in the face of vagueness, uncertainty and equivocality ... resisting the tendency to gravitate all too quickly towards recognizable forms of comprehension associated with positive capability, whether this is a capability of the intellect or of intuitive belonging" (Chia and Holt, 2009: 211). Correspondingly, the "negativeness" of this capability does not indicate negativity, deficiency or insignificance; it indicates refraining from hasty action or practically-driven "actionism'. The focus is "negative" in the sense of negating what is known and leaving a space open for the emergent. The deeper aspect of the creative process then gets a chance to operate when such a space of the possible is kept open. Negative capability is both the ability to resist the inappropriate pressure for all too easy solutions and the capacity to hold the creative tensions involved. This capacity requires a specific attitude that includes tolerance for ambiguity and considerable sensitivity, especially for timing, in order to remain detached enough to know not only how, but also when to act that is to catch the ripe moment of kairos. Overall, negative capabilities can create intermediate spheres and a corresponding receptive state of intense and lived waiting, attending to the deeper patterns of meanings that may unfold.

7 Such interpretation of the in-between nature of erotic wisdom sees wisdom and its learning as a kind of love affair. Complementing different interpretations of love, like philia (friendship) or agape (benevolence), *erôs* (ἔρως) as passion and desire – personified as a *daimon*

(202e–204c) – is part of wisdom. Even more, *erôs* refers to the desire for good things and happiness (e.g., *Symp.* 205df.), whose highest expression is the desire for wisdom (210df.). What does it mean to love wisdom? The philosopher as lover of wisdom (*philosophein*) is not sterilizing but inseminates, fertilizes, and gives birth in a figurative sense. According to Plato's Diotimas, teaching the art of love (*ta erôtika*) refers to *erôtan* as the art of "asking questions." The process of learning requires an active and autonomous learner: the soul gives birth itself to its own wisdom when it comes across a beautiful person, a beautiful branch of knowledge or beauty itself, and not by learning a lesson from an outside authority. In order to become wise, one must be previously pregnant with wisdom and crave to give birth to it. In other words, one cannot acquire knowledge of anything without being primarily in love with this knowledge (empirically), following (1) the nature of Socrates' wisdom about love (it is an empirical, rather than a theoretical knowledge); (2) the nature of love itself (it is an active force striving for knowledge rather than a passive object of knowledge); and (3) the nature of any good teaching on love (one must communicate the *eros* of knowledge rather than the knowledge of *eros*). As Belfiore stated: "when we love something and recognize that we do not possess it, we ask questions about this object and attempt to find out how to acquire it. That is, loving leads people to like wisdom: philo-sophein" (Belfiore, 2012: 154, 83). This need to be connected to beauty (*kalon*), as all *eros* is concerned with the beautiful (Platon, 206e). If something is perceived to be beautiful, then Eros desires it; wisdom is perceived to be beautiful; therefore Eros desires wisdom. Further, wisdom is desired because it is one of the most beautiful things (204b2–3). So, Eros is concerned with the beautiful; the more beautiful an object the more Eros desires that object; wisdom is one of the most beautiful objects; therefore Eros is most especially a lover of wisdom. Socrates thinks it follows from the fact that *eros* is that part of desire specifically related to beauty, and wisdom is amongst the most beautiful things, that philosophy is an important activity of *eros*. Seeing wisdom as one of the most beautiful things means that one will set after it in a very particular kind of way: one will see it as something intimately connected to *eudaimonia* (*Symp.* 205d), and this will manifest itself in creative pursuits designed to secure that end (206b). *Eros* and erosion = The mania of *eros* undermines the notion of the self as a transparent, autonomous and continuous unity. Why is there Philo-Sophia but not Philo-Phronesis?

8 For Boal (1995), *metaxis* as the state of belonging completely and simultaneously to two different, autonomous worlds: the image of reality and the reality of the image. The participant shares and belongs to these two autonomous worlds; their reality and the image of their reality, which she herself has created (Boal, 1995: 43). Then we play with the reality of the images before us. The storyteller must forget the world outside the workshop which was the origin of the image, and play with the image itself in its artistic embodiment. S/he must practice in this second world (the aesthetic), in order to modify the first (the perception). Boal calls this aesthetic transubstantiation (ibid.: 43): "knowledge acquired aesthetically is already, in itself, the beginning of a transformation" *(Boal*, 1995: 109). Through the process of *metaxis*, drama becomes the interplay between the imagined and the image, the tangible and the ephemeral. Knowing begins to unfold, to emerge, and to become more explicitly known. Because it happens *through* the body, learning becomes more tangible and is made available for future deepened exploration (Linds, 2001).

9 Such a "thick" understanding of practical wisdom today would refer to a concept or description that includes particular features and circumstances, in contrast to a "thin" one (like "good") that remains couched in general and abstract terms. As deployed in a pheno-practical, real-political theory and understanding, such thick orientation and interpretation of wisdom (and its virtues like courage or lack of it, e.g. cruelty), are applied to concrete features of the world and specific situations of our contemporary and imagined realities. A thick understanding requires to bear also a kind of breakdown of speech, an apophasis (literally "un-saying" or "speaking-away" (Sells, 1994: 2). Valuable knowledge and wise action arises when ignorance is embraced and when we allow being immersed "in a thick cloud in which we lose all our familiar bearings and *do not know* either where we are or where we are going" (Case et al., 2012: 10). Not knowing as a medium for and of uplifting, deep knowing, and action can then move to expressions in the spirit of cataphaticism; *kataphasis* meaning "affirmation, saying, speaking-with" (Sells, 1994: 31).

References

Agamben, G. (2009). *The Open Man and Animal*. Stanford, CA: Stanford University Press.

Allenby, B.R. & Sarewitz, D. (2011). *The Techno-human Condition*. Cambridge, MA: MIT Press.

Allern, T.-H. (2002). Myth and metaxy, and the myth of "metaxis." In B. Rasmussen & A.L. Østern (Eds.), *Playing Betwixt and Between: The IDEA Dialogues 2001* (pp. 77–85). Bergen: Idea Publications.

Alvesson, M. & Spicer, A. (2012). A stupidity base theory of organization. *Journal of Management Studies*, 49(7), 1194–1220.

Aristotle (1998). *Nicomachean Ethics*. London: Dover.

Armstrong, S. & Fukami, C. (2009). Past, present and future perspectives of management learning, education and development. In S. Armstrong & C. Fukami (Eds.), *Handbook of Management Learning, Education & Development* (pp. 1–22). London: Sage Publications.

Bachmann, C. (2014). Can practical wisdom be taught in business schools? An inquiry-based learning approach for management education. In P. Blessinger & J.M. Carfora (Eds.), *Innovations in Higher Education Teaching and Learning, Volume 2* (pp. 277–302). Bingley: Emerald Group Publishing.

Baden, D. & Higgs, M. (2015). Challenging the perceived wisdom of management theories and practice. *Academy of Management Learning & Education*, 14(4), 539–555.

Ballet, J., Bazin, D., Dubois, J.-L. & Mahieu, F-R. (2014). *Freedom, Responsibility and Economics of the Person*. New York: Routledge.

Barry, J., Mol, A. & Zito, A. (2013). Climate change ethics, rights, and policies: an introduction. *Environmental Politics* 22(3), 361–376.

Baskin, J. (2015). Paradigm dressed as epoch: the ideology of the Anthropocene. *Environmental Values*, 24, 9–29.

Bateson, G. (1972). *Steps to an Ecology of Mind*. New York: Ballantine.

Baumard, P. (1999). *Tacit Knowledge in Organizations*. London: Sage Publications.

Belfiore, E. (2012). *Socrates' Daimonic Art: Love for Wisdom in Four Platonic Dialogues*. Cambridge: Cambridge University Press.

Bennis, W.G. & O'Toole, J. (2005). How business schools lost their way. *Harvard Business Review*, May, 96–104.

Berkhout, F. (2014). Anthropocene futures. *The Anthropocene Review*, 1(2), 154–159.

Bernstein, B. (1996). *Pedagogy, Symbolic Control, and Identity: Theory, Research, Critique* (2nd edition 2000). London: Taylor & Francis.

Blakeley, K. (2015). Inspiring responsible leadership in business schools: can a spiritual approach help? In C. Mabey & W. Mayrhofer (Eds.), *Leadership Development: Questions Business Schools Don't Ask*. London: Sage.

Boal, A. (1995). *The Rainbow of Desire: The Boal Method of Theatre and Therapy* (A. Jackson, Trans.). New York: Routledge.

Bok, D. (2009). *Universities in the Marketplace: The Commercialization of Higher Education*. Princeton, NJ: Princeton University Press.

Bologna Working Group on Qualifications Frameworks (2005). *A Framework for the Qualifications of the European Higher Education Area*. Copenhagen.

Bussey, M. (2008). Embodied education: reflections on sustainable education. *International Journal of Environmental, Cultural, Economic and Social Sustainability*, 43(3), 139–147.

Bussey, M. (2012). When no crisis is the real crisis! The endless vertigo of capitalist education. In D.R. Cole (Ed.), *Surviving Economic Crises through Education* (pp. 247–255). New York: Peter Lang.

Butin, D.W. (2005). *Service-learning in Higher Education: Critical Issues and Directions*. Basingstoke: Palgrave Macmillan.

Case, P., French, R. & Simpson, P. (2012). From theoria to theory: leadership without contemplation. *Organization*, 19(3), 345–362.

Castoriadis, C. (2003). *The Rising Tide of Insignificancy* (Trans. from the French and edited anonymously as a public service). Retrieved from www.costis.org/x/castoriadis/castoriadis-rising_tide.pdf.

Castoriadis, C. (2013). La rationalite du capitalisme. In C. Castoriadis (Ed.), *Démocratie? Tome 2 – Ecrits politiques 1945–1997* (pp. 627–656). Paris: Editions du Sandre.

Chia, R. (2005). The aim of management education: reflections on Mintzberg's managers not MBAs. *Organization Studies*, 26(7), 1090–1092.

Chia, R. & Holt, R. (2007). Wisdom as learned ignorance: integrating east–west perspectives. In E.H. Kessler & J.R. Bailry (Eds.), *Handbook of Organizational and Managerial Wisdom* (pp. 505–526). Thousand Oaks, CA: Sage.

Chia, R. & Holt, R. (2009). *Strategy Without Design: The Silent Efficacy of Indirect Action.* Cambridge: Cambridge University Press.

Clarke, C., Knights, D. & Jarvis, C. (2012). A labour of love? Academics in business schools. *Scandinavian Journal of Management*, 28(1), 5–15.

Colby, A., Ehrlich, T., Sullivan, W.M. & Dolle, J.R. (2011). *Rethinking Undergraduate Business Education: Liberal Learning for the Profession.* New York: Jossey-Bass.

Collinson, D. & Tourish, D. (2015). Teaching leadership critically: new directions for leadership pedagogy. *Academy of Management Learning & Education*, 14, 576–594.

Comim, F., Qizilbash, M. & Alkire, S. (Eds.) (2008). *The Capability Approach. Concepts, Measures and Applications.* Cambridge: Cambridge University Press.

Couceiro-Bueno, J.C. (2011). How to conduct life (arete and phronesis). In A-T. Tymieniecka (Ed.), *Phenomenology/Ontopoiesis Retrieving Geo-cosmic Horizons of Antiquity* (pp. 181–187). Berlin, New York: Springer.

Cowill, R. & Grint, K. (2008). Leadership, task and relationship: Orpheus, Prometheus and Janus. *Human Resource Management Journal*, 18(2), 188–195.

Durand, R. (2014). *Organizations, Strategy, and Society: The Orgology of Disorganized Worlds.* London: Routledge.

Durand, R. & Calori, R. (2006). Sameness, otherness? Enriching organizational change theories with philosophical considerations on the same and the other. *Academy of Management Review*, 30, 93–114.

Durand, R. & Huy, Q. (2008). Practical wisdom and emotional capability as antecedents of organizational accountability in revolutionary change processes. In W.J. Zerbe, C.E.J. Härtel & N.M. Ashkanasy (Eds.), *Emotions, Ethics and Decision-making Research on Emotion in Organizations*, Volume 4 (pp. 311–332). Bingley: Emerald Group Publishing.

Esbörn-Hargens, S., Reams, J. & Gunnlaugson, O. (2010). The emergence and characteristics of integral education: An introduction. In S. Esbörn-Hargens, J. Reams & O. Gunnlaugson (Eds.), *Integral Education: New Directions for Higher Learning* (pp. 1–16). New York: SUNY Press.

Falconer, L. (2011). Metaxis: the transition between worlds and the consequences for education. *Innovative Research in Virtual Worlds*, University of Coventry, 3–4 November. Retrieved from http://eprints.uwe.ac.uk/1661.

Ferrari, M., Westrad, N. & Miller, J. (2017). *Developing Wisdom through Education: The Science and Practice of Wisdom-based Teaching.* Berlin: Springer.

Fraser, W. & Hyland-Russell, T. (2011). Searching for Sophia: adult educators and adult learners as wisdom seekers. *New Directions for Adult and Continuing Education*, 131, 25–34.

Fukami, C. (2007). Strategic metaphysics: Can wisdom be taught. In E. Kessler & J. Bailey (Eds.), *Handbook of Organizational and Managerial Wisdom* (pp. 459–476). London: Sage.

Gardner, H. (2011). *Truth, Beauty, and Goodness Reframed: Educating for the Virtues in the 21st century.* New York: Basic Books.

Ghoshal, S. (2005). Bad management theories are destroying good management practices. *Academy of Management Learning & Education*, 4, 75–91.

Gittings, R. (Ed.) (1970). *Letters of John Keats*. Oxford: Oxford University Press.

Grey, C. (2004) Reinventing business schools: the contribution of critical management education. *Academy of Management Learning and Education*, 3(2), 178–186.

Grint, K. (2007). Learning to lead: can Aristotle help us find the road to wisdom? *Leadership*, 3(2), 231–246.

Gunnlaugson, O. (2009). Establishing second person forms of contemplative education. *Integral Review*, 5(1), 25–50.

Hadot, P. (1995). *Philosophy as a Way of Life: Spiritual Exercises from Socrates to Foucault*. (M. Chase, Trans.). Malden, MA: Blackwell Publishing.

Hadot, P. (2002). *What is Ancient Philosophy?* Cambridge, MA: Harvard University Press.

Hamilton, C. (2013). *Earthmasters: Playing God with the Climate*. Crows Nest, NSW: Allen & Unwin.

Hart, T. (2001). Teaching for wisdom. *Encounter: Education for Meaning and Social Justice*, 14(2), 3–16.

Hauk, M. (2014). Gaia e/mergent: earth regenerative education for empathy, creativity, and wisdom (Doctoral Dissertation, Prescott College). ProQuest Digital Dissertations, UMI 3630295.

Howe, C. (2013). Anthropocenic ecoauthority: the winds of Oaxaca. Energopower and biopower in transition. *Anthropological Quarterly*, 87(2), 381–404.

Huehn, M.P. (2008). Unenlightened economism: the antecedents of bad corporate governance and ethical decline. *Journal of Business Ethics*, 81, 823–835.

Huy, Q. (1999). Emotional capability, emotional intelligence, and radical change. *Academy of Management Review*, 24, 325–345.

Kang, D.J. (2007). Rhizoactivity: toward a postmodern theory of lifelong learning. *Adult Eduaction Quarterly*, 57(3), 205–220.

Kemmis, S. (2012). Phronēsis, experience, and the primacy of praxis. In E.A. Kinsella & A. Pitman (Eds.), *Phronesis as Professional Knowledge: Practical Wisdom in the Professions* (pp. 147–162). Rotterdam: Sense.

Kemmis, S. & Smith, T.J. (2008). Praxis and praxis development. In S. Kemmis & T.J. Smith (Eds.), *Enabling Praxis: Challenges for Education* (pp. 3–13). Rotterdam: Sense.

Kemmis, S., Wilkinson, J., Edwards-Groves, C., Hardy, I., Grootenboer, P. & Bristol, L. (2014). *Changing Practices, Changing Education*. Singapore: Springer.

Klein, N. (2007). *The Shock Doctrine: The Rise of Disaster Capitalism*. New York: Metropolitan Books/Henry Holt.

Küpers, W. & Pauleen, D. (2013). Introducing a handbook of practical wisdom for our times. In W. Küpers & D. Pauleen (Eds.), *A Handbook of Practical Wisdom: Leadership, Organization and Integral Business Practice* (pp. 1–18). London: Ashgate Gower.

Küpers, W. & Pauleen, D. (2015). Learning wisdom: embodied and artful approaches to management education. *Scandinavian Journal of Management*, 31, 493–500.

Küpers, W., Sonnenburg, S. & Zierold, M. (2016). *Rethinking Management*. Berlin: Springer (forthcoming).

Latour, B. (2013). Facing *Gaia*: a new enquiry into natural religion. The Gifford Lectures. University of Edinburgh, www.bruno-latour.fr/node/486.

Leal Filho, W., Brandli, L., Kuznetsova, O. & Paço, A.M. (2015). *Integrative Approaches to Sustainable Development at University Level. Making the Links*. Berlin: Springer.

Leal Filho, W. & Zint, M. (2016). Social sciences and campus sustainable development: the way forward. In W. Leal Filho & M. Zint (Eds.), *The Contribution of Social Sciences to Sustainable Development at Universities*. Berlin: Springer (forthcoming).

Lickona, T., Schaps, E. & Lewis, C. (2007). *CEP's Eleven Principles of Character Education*. Washington, DC: Character Education Partnership.

Linds, W. (2001). A journey in metaxis: been, being, becoming, imag(in)ing drama facilitation (unpublished Doctoral Dissertation, University of British Columbia).
Linds, W. (2006). Metaxis: dancing (in) the in-between. In J. Cohen-Cruz & M. Schutzman (Eds.), *A Boal Companion: Dialogues on Theatre and Cultural Politics* (pp. 114–124). London: Routledge.
Linds, W. (2009). A journey in metaxis: been, being, becoming, imag(in)ing drama facilitation (T). Retrieved from https://open.library.ubc.ca/cIRcle/collections/831/items/1.009055.
Linds, W. & Trull, A. (2012). Developing ethical practice through inquiry: it's not know-what, it's know-how. In C. Wankel & A. Stachowicz-Stanusch (Eds.), *Handbook of Research on Teaching Ethics in Business and Management Education*. Hershey, PA: IGI-Global.
Lovelock, J. (2006). *The Revenge of Gaia: Earth's Climate Crisis and the Fate of Humanity*. New York: Basic Books.
Mathisen, A. (2015). Rhythms in education and the art of life. *RoSE*, 6(2), 36–51.
Maughn, G. (2009). Ethics education and the practice of wisdom. *Teaching Ethics*, 9(2), 105–130.
McNally, D. (2011). *Monsters of the Market: Zombies, Vampires, and Global Capitalism*. Boston: Brill.
Mitchell, L. (2014). Nomadic dimensions of education with the earth-in-mind. In D.A. Vakoch & F. Castrillón (Eds.), *Eco-psychology, Phenomenology, and the Environment, The Experience of Nature* (pp. 109–126). New York: Springer.
Molz, M. (2009). Toward integral higher education study programs in the European higher education area: a programmatic and strategic view. *Integral Review*, 5(2), 152–226.
Molz, M. & Hampson, G.P. (2010). Elements of an underacknowledged history of integral education. In S. Esbjörn-Hargens, O. Gunnlaugson & J. Reams (Eds.), *Integral Education: New Directions for Higher Learning*. Albany: SUNY Press.
Nietzsche, F. (2006). *Thus Spoke Zarathustra* (Pippin, R., Ed., A. del Caro, Trans). Cambridge: Cambridge University Press.
Nussbaum, M. (1988). Nature, functioning and capability: Aristotle on political distribution. *Oxford Studies in Ancient Philosophy*, 6, 145–184.
Nussbaum, M. (2003). Capabilities as fundamental entitlements: Sen and social justice. *Feminist Economics*, 9(2/3): 33–59.
Nussbaum, M. (2005). Well-being, contracts and capabilities. In L. Manderson (Ed.), *Rethinking Well-Being* (pp. 27–44). Perth: API Network.
OECD (2009). *Roadmap for the OECD Assessment of Higher Education Learning Outcomes Feasibility Study* (2nd version). Paris: OECD.
Painter-Morland, M., (2015). Philosophical assumptions undermining responsible management education. *Journal of Management Development*, 34(1), 61–75.
Peach Martins, L., de Four-Babb, J., de Lourdes Lazzarin, M. & Pawlik, J. (2016). [Ir]responsible leadership: Addressing management and leadership curricula biases. In BAM Conference PDW 2015. Retrieved from Middlesex University Research Repository: http://eprints.mdx.ac.uk/19063/.
Perkins, D. (2014). *Future Wise: Educating Our Children for a Changing World*. San Francisco, CA: Jossey-Bass.
Petriglieri, G. & Petriglieri, J.L. (2015). Can business schools humanize leadership? *Academy of Management Learning and Education*, 14, 625–647.
Pettersen, I.J. (2015). From metrics to knowledge? Quality assessment in higher education. *Financial Accountability & Management*, 31(1), 23–40.
Pfeffer, J. & Fong, C. (2002). The end of business schools? Less success than meets the eye. *Academy of Management Learning and Education*, 1(1), 78–95.
Pfeffer, J. & Sutton, R.I. (1999). Knowing what to do is not enough: turning knowledge into action. *California Management Review*, 42, 83–108.

Pitman, A. (2012). Professionalism and professionalisation: hostile ground for growing phronesis? In E.A. Kinsella & A. Pitman (Eds.), *Phronesis as Professional Knowledge: Practical Wisdom in the Professions* (pp. 131–146). Rotterdam: Sense Publishing.

Plato (1994). *Symposium*. Oxford: Oxford University Press.

Pyyhtinen, O. & Tamminen, S. (2011). We have never been only human: Foucault and Latour on the question of the Anthropos. *Anthropological Theory*, 11(2), 135–152.

Raelin, J. (1995). Reformulating management education: professional education, action learning, and beyond. *Selections, Graduate Management Admissions Council*, Autumn, 20–31.

Raelin, J. (2003). *Creating Leaderful Organizations: How to Bring Out Leadership in Everyone*. San Francisco: Berrett-Koehler.

Raelin, J. (2011). From leadership-as-practice to leaderful practice. *Leadership*, 7(2), 195–211.

Raelin, J. (Ed.) (2016). *Leadership-as-Practice: Theory and Application*. York: Routledge Studies in Leadership Research.

Randall, W. (2014). *The Stories We Are: An Essay on Self-Creation*, 2nd ed. Toronto: University of Toronto Press.

Randall, W. & Kenyon, G. (2004). Time, story, and wisdom: emerging themes in narrative gerontology. *Canadian Journal on Aging*, 23(4), 333–346.

Roos, J. (2015). Practical wisdom: making and teaching the governance case for sustainability. *Journal of Cleaner Production*. DOI: 10.1016/j.jclepro.2015.10.135.

Rosa, H. (2013). *Social Acceleration: A New Theory of Modernity* (J. TrejoMathys, Trans.). New York: Columbia.

Rosa, H. (2016). *Resonanz*. Berlin: Suhrkamp-Verlag.

Rose, D.B., van Dooren, T., Churlew, M., Cooke, S., Kearnes, M. & O'Gorman, E. (2012). Thinking through the environment, unsettling the humanities. *Environmental Humanities*, 1, 1–5.

Sauer, S. & Kohls, N. (2011). Mindfulness in leadership: does being mindful enhance leaders' business success? In S. Han & E. Pöppel (Eds.), *Culture and Neural Frames of Cognition and Communication* (pp. 287–307). Berlin: Springer.

Schumacher, E.F. (1977). *A Guide for the Perplexed*. London: Jonathan Cape.

Scott, G.A. & Welton, W.A. (2009). *Erotic Wisdom – Philosophy and Intermediacy in Plato's Symposium*. Albany: SUNY Press.

Sells, M. (1994). *Mystical Languages of Unsaying*. Chicago: The University of Chicago Press.

Sen, A. (1985). *Commodities and Capabilities*. Amsterdam: North-Holland.

Simpson, P., French, R. & Harvey, C. (2002). Leadership and negative capability. *Human Relations*, 55(10), 1209–1226.

Starkey, K. & Tempest, S. (2005). The future of the business school: knowledge, challenges and opportunities. *Human Relations*, 58(1), 61–82.

Steel, S. (2014). *The Pursuit of Wisdom and Happiness in Education: Historical Sources and Contemplative Practices*. Albany: SUNY Press.

Steffen, W., Broadgate, W., Deutsch, L., Gaffney, O., & Ludwig, C. (2015). The trajectory of the Anthropocene: the great acceleration. *The Anthropocene Review*, 2(1), 81–98.

Steffen, W., Grinevald, J., Crutzen, P. & McNeill, J. (2011a). The Anthropocene: conceptual and historical perspectives. *Philosophical Transactions of the Royal Society* A, 369, 842–867.

Steffen, W., Persson, Å., Deutsch, L., Zalasiewicz, J., Williams, M., Richardson, K., et al. (2011b). The Anthropocene: from global change to planetary stewardship. *AMBIO*, 40(7), 739–761.

Stephenson, J. (1998). The concept of capability and its importance in higher education. In J. Stephenson & M. Yorke (Eds.), *Capability and Quality in Higher Education*. London: Kogan.

Stiegler, B. (2014a). *Lost Spirit of Capitalism: Disbelief and Discredit, Volume 3*. Cambridge: Polity.

Stiegler, B. (2014b). *States of Shock: Stupidity and Knowledge in the 21st Century* (D. Ross, Trans.). Cambridge: Polity.

Symons, A. (1901). John Keats. *Monthly Review, 5*. Reprinted in C. Franklin (Ed.), *British Romantic Poets* (1621–1631). London: Routledge.

Taylor, M. (1995). Rhizomic folds of interstanding, *Tekhnema*, 2, 24–36.

Vilsmaier, U. & Lang, D.J. (2015). Making a difference by marking the difference: constituting in-between spaces for sustainability learning. *Current Opinion in Environmental Sustainability*, 16, 51–55.

Voegelin, E. (1989). *Autobiographical Reflections*. Baton Rouge, LA: LSU Press.

Wakefield, S. (2014). The crisis is the age. *Progress in Human Geography*, Special Forum on the Anthropocene, 12–14.

Waldenfels, B. (2012). *Hyperphänomene: Modi Hyperbolischer Erfahrung*. Berlin: Suhrkamp.

Wals, A.E.J. (2010). Mirroring, Gestalt-switching and transformative social learning: stepping stones for developing. *International Journal of Sustainability in Higher Education*, 11(4), 380–390.

Warburton, K. (2003). Deep learning and education for sustainability. *International Journal of Sustainability in Higher Education*, 4(1), 44–56.

Weber, A. (2013). *Enlivenment: Towards a Fundamental Shift in the Concepts of Nature, Culture and Politics*. Retrieved 15 October 2013, from: www.autor-andreas-weber.de/downloads/Enlivenment_web.pdf.

Whitehead, A.N. (1929/1957). *The Aims of Education and Other Essays*. New York: MacMillan.

Wilson, O. (1998). *Consilience: The Unity of Knowledge*. New York: Knopf / Random House.

Yusoff, K. (2016). Anthropogenesis: origins and endings in the Anthropocene. *Theory, Culture & Society*, 33(2), 3–28.

Zalasiewic, A, Williams, M., Steffen, W. & Crutzen, P. (2010). The new world of the Anthropocene. *Environmental Science and Technology*, 44, 2228–2231.

Part I

Conceptual contributions and alternative perspectives on wisdom learning, teaching and education

Chapter 1

Embodying a wise graduate disposition in business school education

Bernard McKenna

Introduction

We know that business schools have a poor record in producing people who are sufficiently emotionally, cognitively and morally fit to make decisions that benefit not only their organisation but also the society in which those organisations operate. We could assume, therefore, that we simply need to change the curriculum in order to produce more cognitively and morally capable people to take up positions of power in industry, commerce, government and non-government organisations. But is it as simple as that?

Let us begin with what *should* be before dealing with what *is*. This unapologetically normative orientation is taken because norms and values, often unarticulated, underlie any set of practices that are often presented as 'free of ideology'. However, every practice is infused with social or individual norms, most usually both, based on particular values and beliefs. To be clear, I propose that the 'what should be' deontic of human existence is unashamedly any set of practices that contributes to human flourishing and sustainability. This is Aristotle's notion of *eudaimonia*, the perfect end chosen for its own perfect good, and not for a more limited or strategic end (Fiasse, 2001, p. 331). While it is appropriate to adopt a humane orientation to give meaning to our existence, the difficult part is being true to our word in our deeds. The Stoics, whose works initially preceded Aristotle and even Socrates, provide a holistic orientation to good practice through their notion of *pneuma*, a force underlying our physical existence. They link the ethical with the physical within a broader context of humans in nature. The foundations of Stoicism were neatly summarised by Plutarch nearly 500 years after the death of Zeno, the founder of Stoicism:

- Wisdom requires knowledge of human and divine matters.
- Wisdom requires fitting expertise, the pinnacle of which is excellence (*aretē*).
- These excellences are seen in nature, behaviour and reasoning.
- Consequently, a philosophical orientation to the world involves the physical, the ethical and the logical (drawn from Brouwer, 2014, p. 8).

The notion of the divine in a secular discussion of business may seem ill-fitting. However, the divine is understood as the pinnacle of excellence and not as an endorsement of a theological orientation. Excellence is the ideal of both practical matters and moral matters as is evident in, say, Plato's *Republic*, where the noblest human, the philosopher king, seeks human and divine excellence to attain wisdom.

Stoic philosophy, which is consistent with (but goes beyond) Aristotle's later work, *Nicomachean Ethics*, is a useful orientation to wisdom in business schools because of its distinction between philosophical discourse and philosophy as a way of life. That is, the Stoic approach to wisdom is not just philosophical, but practical. Aristotle drew a similar distinction between *technē* and *sophia* which is combined in *phronesis*. The latter is defined as the capacity to deliberate well on significant matters by reason, sceptical apprehension of the relevant facts, intuition and human understanding in order to make a decision. This in turn is based on sound values to resolve a particular issue, while taking into account the social good at a particular time and context as well as in the future.

A simple rendition of Stoic philosophy is, according to Cleanthes, 'to live in consistency with nature'. This was elaborated by Diogenes to mean 'to live according to the nature of oneself and according to the nature of the universe' (Brouwer, 2014, pp. 26, 28). In other words, the actions of our body inescapably relate us to nature. By aligning with nature, a wise person ingests a *pneuma*, a force or 'breath' in Greek, that underlies substance and is not reducible (Hahm, 1985). Essential to an individual's disposition, for the Stoics, is to be intellectually and morally humble; no Stoic, for example, called themself a sage, and ascribed true knowledge only to the gods. On induction, the wise person 'often does not even perceive that he has acquired [virtue and happiness], and fails to notice that he has now become prudent and blessed' (Plutarch in Brouwer, 2014, p. 80). Seneca, the Roman Stoic, believed that it was impossible to find a human sage, and that the optimum was 'the least bad' person (p. 105). Consistent with this humility is the reduction to three parts of a philosophical direction to guide our lives: physics, ethics and logic. While physics considers 'the world and the things in it' as part of a larger cosmos, ethics considers the *telos* of human life. Logic is reason-based knowledge of what is true and false (Brouwer, 2014, pp. 20–22). Thus it is in practice that we attain wisdom. The Stoics understood philosophy as 'living being' (p. 23) in which the mentioned three parts are connected, and not discrete. That is, knowledge cannot be dissected from virtue. Crucially, our physical sense perceptions help us to shape our mental representations, that is, the 'real' is conditioned by physics or Fate: 'without an explanation of the natural world justice towards other human beings and piety towards the gods is impossible' (Brouwer, 2014, p. 40).

Clearly then the Stoics provide us with a holistic philosophy in which practice is a fulcrum for mind and body within nature. While not understating the complexity of their task, the Stoics valued simplicity in lifestyle. It is true that some Stoics, such as Seneca and Marcus Aurelius, were wealthy and powerful. However, history seems to show that they adhered to their principles by living lives relatively indifferent to their wealth, administering wisely, and, in the case of Seneca, dealing with appalling vicissitudes. The Stoic disposition is 'the single-minded pursuit of virtue – conceived as life lived in accordance with reason and with a minimum of disingenuous affectation' (Ferraiolo, 2011, p. 40). Virtue, for the Stoic, defined as an absence of vice, emerges from 'a disposition in favour of the rational governance of desire and aversion and, in particular, the renunciation of pretense' (Ferraiolo, 2011, p. 48). To live the Stoic philosophy 'meant practising how to 'live': that is how to live freely … in that we give up desiring that which does not depend on us and is beyond our control' (Hadot, 1995, p. 86). Thus a Stoic lives a virtuous life by acquiring holistic knowledge, practising contemplation and maintaining ethical discipline. The Stoic aspires to the perfection of the gods, knowing that this is not possible, but is worthy of the pursuit nonetheless. And it is from this orientation the stoic acquires humility and lacks pretension. The Stoic does not check opinion polls or the prevailing fashion before venturing an opinion or judgement. Although Stoic has now come to mean a capacity to deal with misfortune, in philosophical tradition it means rather a sense of equanimity. However, Epictetus, a Roman Stoic rendered lame by mistreatment as a slave and later banished from his homeland, does provide a living embodiment of this sense of Stoic:

> I must die. But must I die groaning? I must be imprisoned. But must I whine as well? I must suffer exile. Can any one of them hinder me from going with a smile, and a good courage, and at peace?
>
> (Quoted in Russell, 1961, p. 270)

A philosophy that implies simplicity, humility and reflectiveness in pursuit of the common good does seem rather at odds with the spirit of an age in which self-interest and acquisitive materialism are valorised and materialised in the everyday practices of mindless tweets, the selfie and consumer brand displays. The question is whether there is a way to identify and develop attributes in business school students that predispose them to making wise decisions, when they serve in managerial and leadership positions. Let us assume that business schools can certify that students are skill-competent, particularly in professional (e.g., accountancy) and quasi-professional areas (e.g., human resources, finance, marketing) to perform the tasks of their (quasi-)profession in the workplace (Lester, 2014, p. 32). However, effective performance requires far more than this: it requires a proper disposition. For example, airline pilots, emergency personnel and military leaders must have low anxiety and high stress-resistance. In some potential high-stress situations, certain otherwise undesirable traits such as being controlling, and high-practical, low-abstract problem-solving capability may provide the appropriate disposition (Flin & Slaven, 1996). That aside, all professional and managerial roles require good judgement, for which skill-competence is a necessary, but insufficient condition. Good judgement – wise judgement – involves ethical commitment, emotional sensibility, intuition, advanced reasoning skills, reflexivity and contextual awareness (McKenna, Rooney & Boal, 2009). Thus, good judgement rests on a disposition identified by the presence of certain attributes.

The idea of a wisdom disposition is not new. In his *Nicomachean Ethics*, Aristotle (1984) stated that 'Virtue is a purposive disposition' inherent in the 'prudent [hu]man' (II: 1107a1), where virtue was understood as a set of intellectual and moral qualities. Such a surmise comes with considerable qualification. The thought of an instrumentalist programme of instruction that ultimately tests for virtue is clearly oxymoronic. Similarly, Tom Wolfe's (1980) *The Right Stuff* alerts us to the deep ideological assumptions and the historical and proximal contextuality of appropriate 'virtues'. That is, the political assumptions of military, scientific and technological supremacy, the project of 'conquering' space and the valorising of 'manly' virtues and exceptional bravery (one in four test pilots died) necessary to maintain the space programme now seem like an anachronism. Are there, however, timeless virtues that humankind needs in order to produce socially desirable outcomes?

This chapter proposes that the philosophical attributes of wisdom are certainly desirable. But it asks whether business schools are able to do more than developing and certifying competence. In particular, is it possible for a university course to shape a *disposition* founded on wisdom virtues that graduates can draw on as business leaders? Dispositional traits (in the broadest sense, not just a psychological sense) strongly 'influence behavior across time, situations, activities, and environmental circumstances' (Bandura, 2015, p. 1040).[1] Immediately we run into terminological problems given that traits are widely understood from a psychological perspective as the 'big five': conscientiousness, agreeableness, openness, extraversion and neuroticism (Judge, Higgins & Thoresen, 1999). Traits are phenotypical habits, attitudes, skills, roles and relationship orientations that are developed internally along with other dynamic processes such as cognition and morality. Thus, traits here are understood in a wider sense to include conation (Biloslavo & McKenna, 2011), for example. However, a moral and *eudaimonic* disposition is a foundational underpinning that is oriented to the social and long-term good of humankind. A more useful way to understand the relationship between virtues, values and disposition is provided by Peterson and Seligman (2004, p. 74): 'Virtues embody values when the behavior they organise and direct becomes habitual'. Thus, we can say that habitual behaviours, which characterise a person (in this case a business manager or leader), emerge from a disposition, which incorporates values. However, we must also account for largely genetic, but adaptable traits, and other internal factors such as forms of cognising, emotions, motivations and even more deeply unconscious drives. Given this complexity, and the further complexities from a sociological and cultural perspective, of the spatio-temporal context (the time and place in which a person's narrative unfolds), it is obvious that shaping a person's disposition in a business school curriculum is no easy task.

I will now consider the potential and worth of devising a business school course that attempts to shape a wise disposition by considering whether timeless virtues is a meaningful concept; whether a wise disposition produces a better life; and whether human traits are hard wired or are in some sense adaptable. To focus only on individual disposition in teaching for performing well in an organisation would be like building up athletes at a gym, but failing to explain the rules of the game or not playing against other teams prior to the competition. In other words, a comprehensive business course is one that provides their students with a reflexive understanding of their inner mechanisms as part of an embedding context. The concepts of agency and embodiment are central to this educative process.

Is 'timeless virtues' a meaningful concept?

The notion of being timeless incorporates both time and space: that is, timeless implies a constant state over time and universality at any given time. In a world where the news includes Islamic State and 'Medecins Sans Frontieres', Donald Trump and Aung San Suu Kyi, is it sensible to talk of values being timeless and universal? Well, yes. That is, reassuringly, despite historical blips such as Stalinist Soviet Union, Pinochet's Chile, or Pol Pot's Kampuchea, invariably, but not always, sufficient good people eventually gather from their disparate, contented lives to oppose and overthrow evil because of its inhumanity. Over time, sufficient people feel the pulse of humanity in their veins giving strength and courage to their bodies to risk their lives for a principle, for the good of others. There is evidence that timeless and universal values and virtues do exist, although they find a timely expression in different contexts. For example, a study of philosophical and religious traditions in China (Confucianism and Taoism), South Asia (Buddhism and Hinduism) and the West (Athenian philosophy, Judaism, Christianity and Islam), Dahlsgrad, Peterson & Seligman (2005) found six core virtues that recurred: courage, justice, humanity, temperance, wisdom, and transcendence. Another study by Ronald Inglehart, the Director of the World Values Survey, covering 80 societies containing 90 per cent of the world's population, provided a two-dimensional description of cultural values, understood as shared ontological and teleological assumptions: Survival vs Self-expression; and Traditional vs Secular-rational. The dividing line that he proposes is modernisation represented by the Industrial Revolution when industrialised societies shifted from traditional to secular-rational values. In the post-industrial phase of modernisation, the shift from survival values to post-material and self-expression values brings increasing emancipation from both religious and secular-rational authority (Inglehart, 2006). Thus, he sees the changes in values as emanating largely from economic and technological changes. This would seem to suggest that perhaps universal values are not necessarily timeless. However, given the ancient roots of Confucianism, Buddhism, Hinduism, Judaism, Christianity and Islam considered in Dahlsgrad et al.'s research, it may be that pre-industrial societies were far less democratic and far more regulated and that, consequently, the societal expression and enactment of those virtues and values was far more difficult.

From a philosophical perspective, a universal approach might be attacked as 'foundationalist', a criticism that I believe almost always leads to an undesirable state of extreme ethical relativism, if not nihilism. However, Bok (1993) provides an elegantly simple response to this challenge. Acknowledging the quite reasonable concerns about the outcomes of religious foundationalism, which are, to my mind, dangerously based on doctrinal revelation, Bok adopts a 'minimalist' approach to identify those values that empirically meet two characteristics: that they are held in common by most human beings, and that they have had to be resolved in all human societies. The claim to universalism is not based on divinely ordained moral values; nor is it based on claims to be part of the supposed 'natural order'; that they are eternally valid or valid without exception; that they are directly known by any rational human being; that they can be perceived by a 'moral sense'; or that they exist independently of human beings (p. 351). In other words, it can be claimed that certain values are 'universal' in the minimal sense of simply occurring as dominant values in most human societies in order to work out a way for humans to get on well and achieve socially desirable outcomes. To sum up, it seems to be a defensible surmise that there are universal and timeless values which are qualified as life-affirming and life-sustaining.

Values, behaviour and society

The psychological foundations of values are extremely well elaborated by Shalom Schwartz whose work builds on Milton Rokeach's (1973) book *The Nature of Human Values*. Schwartz's (1992, 1994) earlier work has now been tested and refined across various cultures to confirm that it is valid and reliable. His most recent modifications (Cieciuch & Schwartz, 2012) propose that basic human values can be arrayed on a circular motivational continuum (Schwartz, 1992), comprising ten distinct values and clustered into four higher-order categories. Although these four categories are diametrically opposite (Self-enhancement vs Self-transcendence and Conservation vs

Openness to Change) and adjacent, not all of the individual values necessarily sit in this diametric or adjacent relationship. For example, universalism was found to be adjacent to conformity/tradition (Cieciuch & Schwartz, 2012). Furthermore, Cieciuch and Schwartz (2012) found sub-types in some of the values: e.g., security included the sub-types of personal security (avoiding danger, staying healthy) and national security (such as limiting terrorism). These sub-types may affect future empirical results in predicting behaviour and identity. For example, the value of tradition incorporated the expected sub-type of keeping traditional ways and religious practice but also now includes humility defined as satisfaction with what one has, and being humble and modest. In the value of benevolence, two sub-types were identified: protecting the environment and societal concern (social justice and harmony). Consequently, empirical research on values may be adversely affected by imprecise concepts.

Two aspects of values are particularly relevant to a business school curriculum: their relationship to behaviour, given that this is what we intend to affect, and the link between this internalist feature and society. Dealing with the first issue, values are distally related to behaviour for various reasons. The most important is that situational forces can overwhelm values. Another reason is that, when values are held without strong cognitive support, they are weakly linked to behaviour (Hitlin & Piliavin, 2004, pp. 381–382). Nonetheless, holding a constellation of values that form part of self-identity aligned to particular group identity can influence behaviour. Integral to personal identity are central values, those that are most prominent in an individual's idiosyncratic value system (Hitlin, 2003; Verplanken & Holland, 2002). These central values 'when energized, lead to behavior congruent with those values' (Hitlin & Piliavin, 2004, p. 382). It is best to consider the link between personally held values and society by considering self-concept. Self-concept emerges not just internally but also by being inducted in childhood to socially shared values and then by a constant process of self-monitoring in our relationships with others. Whereas low self-monitors link their attitudes, a determinant of behaviour (Fishbein & Ajzen, 2010), to their values, high self-monitors often shift their attitudes to align with situational pressures (Hitlin & Piliavin, 2004, p. 383). To sum up, it is possible to link internalist value structures with social outcomes by assuming an agentive individual, whose value-driven choices impact on social reproduction (Hitlin & Piliavin, 2004, p. 384). Helping students to identify their values and their relation to social behaviours, business schools fulfil the first step in creating a wise disposition. However, providing the capacity to enact these values is a much more difficult task.

Can a wise disposition produce a better life?

Sceptics may well argue that, while it would be nice to live in a world where people behave in ways that produce socially desirable outcomes, the reality is that life isn't like that. We are essentially selfish, they might argue, and we all desire material goods, wealth and status that can be produced only by adhering to a competitive system with winners and losers where self-interest is crucial for survival and advantage: ergo, we're all on the look-out for 'competitive advantage'. However, even conservative economics, perhaps somewhat motivated by the apparently intractable incapability of Western economies to provide secure employment and desirable social infrastructure, is increasingly acknowledging – and even accepting – that contemporary economics needs a paradigmatic refit. The previously sterile discourse of economics is now incorporating words such as happiness, well-being and life satisfaction. This means that orthodox economics, which has assumed a social environment that is built on satisfying personal preferences through consumption of goods and services, is now admitting new humane concepts. Psychological well-being, human flourishing and positive relatedness are now entering the economic lexicon. This movement to 'happiness economics' (MacKerron, 2012) is hardly mainstream, but it does indicate that consideration of human values is challenging the established assumptions of *homo economicus* that is the cornerstone of business schools.

Turning from economics to psychology, is it true that certain types of person live a 'better life', not only for themselves but also for others? A considerable number of studies have considered whether certain traits produce better life outcomes. Without doubt this is so, according to Roberts et al. (2007, p. 336): 'It is abundantly clear … that specific personality traits predict important life outcomes, such as mortality, divorce, and success in work'. This is supported by impressive evidence. The trait of conscientiousness in children was positively correlated with longer lives, and was a strong protective factor in elderly people. Also associated with longevity was the trait of extraversion, or positive emotionality, while neuroticism and pessimism predicted a higher risk of premature death. Neuroticism also increases the probability of divorce, while more conscientious and agreeable people tended to remain longer in their marriages and avoided divorce. These findings are significant in two ways. First, they provide strong evidence that socially positive traits produce socially desirable outcomes. Second, they suggest a holistic understanding of the individual as a social actor. For example, there is medical evidence that personality differences may be related to pathogenesis, or to health-promoting or health-damaging behaviours such as the evidence that extraverted people may develop more or stronger social relationships, an important protective factor from ill health (Roberts et al., 2007). There is also good evidence of the positive relationship between neuroticism and unsatisfying relationships, conflict and abuse. It seems clear, then, that positive psychological traits produce personally and socially desirable outcomes. The question remains whether other positive features of our disposition such as emotional sensibility, resilience and moral orientation –understood from the Stoic perspective as a set of intellectual and moral qualities, or 'virtues' – also produce socially and personally desirable outcomes.

Are traits adaptable?

It is now well established that personality descriptors are 'almost completely accounted for by five robust factors' (McCrae & Costa, 2008, p. 159). Notwithstanding that the subconscious may also impel a human's observable actions, the 'big five' traits – conscientiousness, agreeableness, openness, extraversion and neuroticism – still provide strong correlations with certain behaviours and life outcomes to such an extent that makes them useful variables to test and potentially manipulate to produce a greater propensity for certain desired behaviours resulting from a particular multi-factor disposition. However, a useful theory of behaviours must incorporate not just traits, but also the social context within which one finds oneself, life experiences and self-concept in a dynamic model, which produces adaptations in life goals, beliefs and attitudes. A useful model, displayed in Figure 1.1, is that provided by McCrae & Costa (2008).

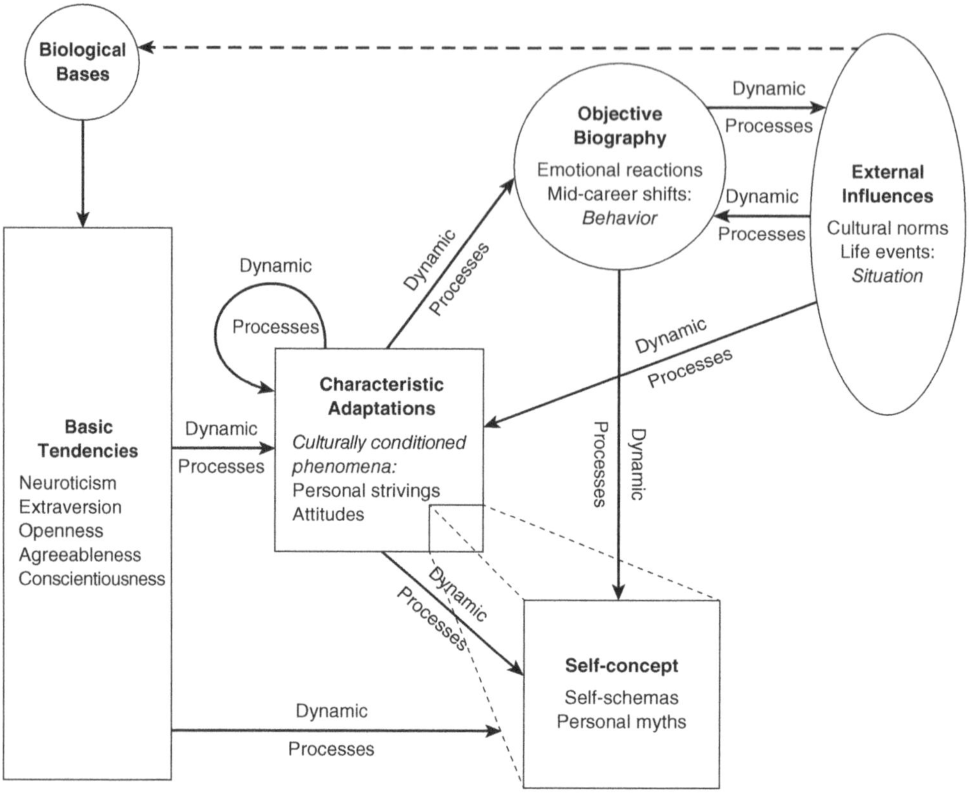

Figure 1.1 Five-factor theory of personality. Core components in rectangles; interfacing components in ellipses.

Source: McCrae & Costa, 2008, p. 163.

Briefly, the model begins with an assumption that by early adulthood, individuals have relatively immutable traits (about 60–80 per cent stable), although I later contest this. However, over our life course, adaptations occur in motivations and socio-cognitive functions wrought by social roles in particular socio-temporal contexts (McAdams & Pals, 2006, p. 208). Dynamic feedback cycles can produce increased efficacy in performing certain tasks, which in turn 'improves' a particular trait. Humans construct a sense of self (or to use the post-structural sociological term, subject position) using their capacity for 'conscious awareness of past and future and our own changes over time' (Pasupathi, Mansour & Brubaker, 2007, p. 106). All of us encounter positive and negative experiences as we live our lives. We account for these experiences to explain who we are in autobiographies and identities that are continuously 'constructing relations between who we are, and what we experience' (p. 106).

Thus, it is evident that we are not the prisoner of the traits which we have largely inherited and have developed into early adulthood. While useful, the model does not include important aspects, particularly external influences, which contains cultural norms but excludes the political-economic considerations of ideology and the individual's role in the processes of production. Objective biography interacts with 'Self Concept', but only in psychological terms. Objective biography must include not only one's education and work, but also one's experiences as a child, an adolescent and an adult, such as the conditions of family life, the level of material welfare, one's home and neighbourhood, significant life events such as deaths, sibling births and illness, as well as social participation, travel and the like. Thus, Characteristic Adaptations emerge as manifestation of an objective biography, Self Concept and Basic Tendencies.

This complex model of personality is very useful because it moves beyond measurable psychological traits as an account of behaviour to include narrative, self-concept, life events, and context. I have already incorporated a political-economic aspect of ideology and the productive process, which is relevant to the formation of the self within a dynamic environment. This self composes an autobiographical narrative that explains the relations between who we are and what we experience in an evolving context. Underlying this account of our ongoing formation is the assumption that we have a capacity to make decisions that influence our life outcomes: that is, we have varying degrees of agency.

Agency

So far, we have moved from the internalist account of behaviour, in terms of traits, to see that this behaviour is acted out in a social context. At the macro-level, the context is structured by global, national, regional and ethnic ideologies and social, political and economic relations. At the meso-level the social constitutes the sites of human activity including home and family, the workplace, social organisations (religion, sport, etc.) and sites of commercial exchange (banks, shopping centres, etc.). The construction of the self is continually created and re-created, within limits, in a process best explained by Giddens's (1984) structuration theory. This theory is usefully applied here because it is a humanist sociological approach, incorporating interpretivist and subjectivist dimensions, to explain a dynamic relationship between 'system', 'institution' and subject. Structuration theory has two further positive features. First, it assumes an agentive subject who is not bound by an 'iron-cage'. Second, it assumes an interactive relationship between institutional structure, organisational structure and the human agent that produces and reproduces both system and subject in a 'duality of structure' (Giddens, 1979).

The significance of this theory is that it establishes that organisational members have varying degrees of agency, while acknowledging that institutions and organisations maintain a structure that is reproduced predominantly by a prevailing ideology, dominant discourse, and formal and informal rules of procedure. That is, while action is constrained by relatively stable discourses and 'rules' (authority structures, approved procedures, accountability and audit processes, etc.), these do not produce absolute rigidity. It is the multiple micro-processes of organisational agents that produce the perpetuating (re-)structure of the organisation. Yet, one further complication needs to be admitted: while agency is understood as 'the capacity to be in or to take action' (West & Zimmerman, 1987, p. 259) that organisationally produces a transformative capacity, it is not understood in the Promethean and liberal sense (i.e., the capacity to completely control our lives). Institutions, ideology, regulatory power and social responsibility limit our agentive capacity in such a way that we become adaptive to varying degrees. A further consideration is that even absolute agency – though it does not exist – would always produce unintended consequences. Taking this into account, then, leads us to a more realistic understanding of the individual and the organisation as being in a state of creative (co-)evolution (MacKay & Chia, 2013, p. 209). Thus a business graduate needs to understand not only their capacity for making decisions that will impact on them and others, but also the complex relationship between those individual decisions and the social structures such as their workplace and their profession in which they operate.

Character

We have thus far posited the person, subject or individual, depending on your theoretical orientation, as agentive, possessing inherited and adaptable traits, and holding certain values that determine their predisposition to certain behaviours, virtuous or otherwise. This ensemble might rightly be classified as a person's character which, within various contexts, reveals itself through action. These actions, or events, are reflexively understood as a coherent self-narrative. However, this character is developmental as a person develops cognitively, physically and socially in identifiable life stages (e.g., infancy, childhood, adolescence and adulthood). A person's character also develops as s/he encounters largely exogenously determined situations. How they deal with these encounters is understood as a test of character, but they also modify the character in some way. The familiar saying that 'what doesn't kill us makes us tougher' acknowledges the sometimes positive transformational effects of successfully negotiating life's vicissitudes whether it be a bereavement, losing a lover or losing a job. On the other hand, a profound life-crisis, or more likely a cluster of crises, can completely break a person's mind, spirit and will.

The best-known theories of developmental stages include Erikson's (1963) eight stages of psycho-social development from infancy to maturity, where various crises lead to the development of certain virtues such as hope, fidelity and wisdom. Kohlberg's six stages of moral development, an elaboration of Piaget's three stages of cognitive development, also provides discernible stages, although it assumes that most people do not reach the sixth stage of development (Rest, Narvaez, Bebeau & Thoma, 1999). Other developmental models related to character have more to do with personal fulfilment. The best known is Maslow's self-actualised individual. Another influential model is Ryff and Keyes's six dimensions of well-being: acceptance of self; positive relations with others; autonomy; environmental mastery; purpose in life; and personal growth (Ryff & Keyes, 1995). Personal well-being approaches to character are consistent with positive psychology, which considers not just the importance of positive subjective experience but also the values of hope, future mindedness, courage, spirituality and responsibility that increase the capacity for individuals and societies to flourish (Seligman & Csikszentmihalyi, 2000).

Although such psychological developmental models can be criticised for possible universalist cultural claims, implied ideological assumptions, and sequential, linear development processes, they do provide useful guides to desirable psychological and social developments. Furthermore, they provide sound evidence that virtuous behaviour, personal well-being and positive social outcomes are correlated. Thus it would seem that developing 'good character' as foundation of wisdom is an appropriate and desirable goal and outcome for any educational system.

Embodiment

It is assumed here that to be wise, whether they be in business or any other walk of life, people must enact wisdom (Rooney, McKenna & Liesch, 2010). The capacity of wise people to integrate the dialectics of self and life (Staudinger & Glück, 2011) into understandings and embodied processes was reinforced by Yang's (2008) process view of wisdom. Based on a study of 66 Taiwanese people nominated by others as wise, Yang found three processual features of wise people: the ability to integrate the dialectics of life; to embody wisdom in their own personal practices; and, as a result of this wise practice, to contribute towards well-being. Other wisdom theorists have agreed on the need for embodiment (Baltes & Staudinger, 1993; Kekes, 1995; Küpers & Pauleen, 2015)

Two useful and related ways to consider embodied wisdom are provided by phenomenology and Bourdieu's theory of habitus. From a phenomenological perspective, the human subject is understood, according to Merleau-Ponty, as having a 'primordial relation to the world [which] consists in their embodied (practical) action within it'; such beings produce meaning 'by an engaged body-subject' (Crossley, 1996, p. 101). The human's interaction with the world is somatic, inter-subjective, communicative, and understood through consciousness (Harries-Jones, 2003). In this sense, humans can be seen as part of a social fabric, or as an agentive organism, with the capacity for embodied conscious reflection in a dynamic ecosystem. This relationship between the somatic experience and consciousness is a phenomenological one: 'being embodied implies that practitioners are dynamically incarnated in and mediated through situated experiences, living and interrogating perceptions, receptive affectedness, emotions and being-at-tuned in moods as well as cognitions and actions' (Küpers, 2013, p. 337). Thus the human continuously makes meaning of their 'life-world' through multiple inter-subjective engagements based on their pre-reflective perceptions (Crossley, 1996; Gherardi, 2009; Küpers, 2013) and a pre-subjective involvement, 'enfleshed' with others and the world (Küpers, 2015). Because embodiment 'is irreducibly both corporeal and social' (Dale, 2005, p. 659), experience cannot be reduced just to language, psychological states, cultural practices, or relations of power but is a compilation of all of these as they are *phenomenologically* experienced and processed. Such an understanding can be applied to organizational practices, which can be understood as 'the entwinement of life with world . . . as we engage in our activities and projects' (Sandberg & Dall'Alba, 2009, p. 1351). But these activities and projects are not like the actions of eukaryotes, pushed around by flagella and asexually reproducing in order to fulfil a genetically pre-ordained purpose of reproducing DNA. Human entwinement with a life-world is, although partly exogenously determined by the circumstances of a time and place, enacted by (bounded) agentive subjects forming intentions and purpose that are enacted in practice. Because of our human capacity for reflectiveness, 'we come to understand ourselves as practitioners, practice as consisting of particular activities' (Sandberg & Dall'Alba, 2009, p. 1356). The implication for business education is the need to develop an awareness within students of the role of the body in enacting wisdom as a social practice: the habitus of wisdom.

Bourdieu's theory of habitus shares with phenomenology the socially constructed body engaged in social practices. Central to Bourdieu's theory is the way in which habitus socially reproduces practices. According to Bourdieu, habitus is:

> the durably installed generative principle of regulated improvisation, [that] produces practices which tend to reproduce the regularities immanent in the objective conditions of the production of their generative principle, while adjusting to the demands inscribed as objective potentialities in the situation.
>
> (Bourdieu, 1977, p. 78)

Habitus, thus, is 'a mediating structure; it is medium for, and result of, social actions as well as of social structures' (Fuchs, 2003, p. 403). The habitus that one develops (re-) produces practices, but is itself the consequence social practices, a form of dynamic feedback (in psychological terms). This is because the social structures in practice have been embodied or internalised by social actors. This complex notion was nicely revealed in Bachen and Illouz's (1996) study in which children were interviewed to reveal cultural models of what it means to 'do romance'. Although it was a cognitive-schemata study, the social implications clearly revealed how social roles and types of performance are understood from a young age. For example, asked to choose in which pictures the man and the woman look most like they love each other, a strong consensus chose a couple on the beach or an elegant couple rather than a couple in a domestic situation. Asked what people usually do on a first date, the most frequent scenario involved a boy picking up a girl, taking her by car to a restaurant or movie and returning her home. These taken-for-granted understandings and perceptions of social roles show how external social conditions and practices are internalised, even by early childhood. A theory of habitus is not reductive because the theory admits innumerable and unpredictable human practices (Bourdieu, 1990), although these can be grouped into typologies of habitus characterised by certain groups of people. These micro-practices serve to reproduce social practices that maintain and reproduce a social order that is itself undergoing microbial levels of adaptation. Drawing on structuration and complexity theory in elaborating habitus, Morrison (2005, p. 316) explains that through 'feedback, recursion, perturbance, auto-catalysis, connectedness, interdependence and self-organisation, differentiated, new forms of society, behaviour, systems and organizations arise from lower levels of complexity and existing structures, which are not reducible to these'. The implications of such an understanding for education are outlined in Küpers (2011).

Enacting character

Although psychology provides useful, sometimes measurable, constructs that help us to understand character from a moral perspective, we have seen that internalist accounts of personality, motives, emotions, cognitions and the like are insufficient because they exclude situational factors, including economy and politics, wider social norms and the role of embodiment in social interactions. Pleasingly, certain psychologists are attempting to broaden a social psychology of pro-social behaviour by taking these factors into account. For example, Fleeson et al. (2014) provide an account of six classes of psychological study into moral behaviour (e.g., personality, intentions and behaviour, social conformity and deviance), with each having limitations of scope.

They also point out that characteristics such as ideologies, traits and abiding values cannot be easily or consistently manipulated in short-term experiments. Other psychological researchers, Cohen and Morse (2014), conclude after analysing contemporary research into right and wrong behaviour that this moral evaluation should be based on that which regulates social relationships and facilitates group living; consequently moral behaviour is inextricably involved in social relationships. The self develops and defines its uniqueness within an external context, producing a social interaction between the internal world and external circumstance. This tells us, through reflexive awareness, who we are and how we embody that symbiotic relationship. Thus it is the body that is the nexus between the self and our experienced world (Ladkin & Taylor, 2010). Understanding the embodiment of dispositions therefore presents business educators with a profound pedagogical problem.

Education of and training for character in the business school

Returning now to our philosophical starting point in Stoic philosophy, it is clear that education, or training for, wise management and leadership should be directed towards developing both expertise and disposition. At the cognitive level, expertise 'is a system of cognitions unified by training towards some useful end in life' (Brouwer, 2014, p. 45). At the level of disposition, a wise disposition is 'a turn towards the divine', or *metastrophē* (Brouwer, 2014, p. 52). To seek the divine is to seek the pinnacle of excellence, and thus requires radical change (p. 69). The business school initiates – *teletē* – people into the realm of wisdom by seeking perfection but having the humility to accept that it is unattainable. Building this stable virtuous character with the potential to endure, becoming an authentic leader is obviously enormously difficult. It involves the balancing and resolution of paradoxes and tensions, many of which have their origin in bodily and unconscious processes (Ladkin & Taylor, 2010, p. 72) and developmental history. Notwithstanding this difficulty, it is necessary that a pedagogical framework for building the virtuous character be attempted and tentatively designed.

Character may be defined as 'one's standard pattern of thought and action with respect to one's own and others' well-being and other major concerns and commitments' (Hartman, 2006, p. 69). Because character incorporates vice as well as virtue, good and bad dispositions, and positive and negative emotions, a person may present as a good or bad character. Good character does not mean simply doing the 'right thing' for this is deeply socially normative. One must be motivated by good virtues that are based on sound moral values, the 'turn to the divine'. A person's character is already profoundly shaped and habituated by the time they enter business school as an undergraduate, graduate or MBA student. A character is habituated by the application of 'virtues', whether negative or positive, over the course of one's life in various contexts. Acknowledging this should not be a cause for abandoning the project of good character formation in business schools, simply because the school may be the first time they have had time out, either as fresh undergraduates or mid-career MBA students, to ask the ultimate teleological questions: what are you now and what is it that you ultimately want to engage in becoming? The answers may surprise. For example, in a large Master of Business leadership class that I teach containing students from every continent, their responses to the question 'What would you like others to say about you in the eulogy at your funeral?', descriptors of being good to others (kind, helpful, compassionate, caring, loving, thoughtful), particularly their family, were matched by virtues (honest, trustworthy, humble, brave, responsible, resilient, non-judgemental, etc.); only one response had to do with work ethic (hardworking) and a few had to do with themselves (unique, contented, inspiring). The point is that, when asked the ultimate teleological question about their own death, they chose ancient and enduring virtues. Thus, one can see that when derived inductively, students are likely to seek the good path: they have the potential *pneuma*, the irreducible force or 'breath' that underlies the substance of who they are, as mentioned before.

Having elaborated the first of the previously outlined three parts of the Stoic life, a *telos*-oriented ethics, the business school then needs to deal with the second and third components, physics and logic. Physics considers their present and future location in the world, or more appropriately, the cosmos. Rather than perceiving their location in narrow organisational terms, it is vital that they understand the concept of globalisation beyond the narrow technocratic framework founded on neo-liberal economic assumptions (McKenna & Graham, 2000). This perception demands, first, an awareness of the grave threat to the planet's existence (IPCC, 2013; Stern, 2007) because our current economic trajectory is leading to an undeniable environmental catastrophe. Second, it is important to build an awareness of the inescapable connectedness of our privileged Western life-style and the subsistence and dangerous working conditions of those who produce our clothing, furniture and electronic goods.

Being confronted with the 2013 Rana Plaza garment factory collapse in Bangladesh, can temporarily raise awareness of how they, as consumers, are implicated in this institutionalised inequality simply by their choice of clothing. However, introducing the story of the 1911 Triangle Shirtwaist Factory in New York City can raise awareness about the ongoing exploitation of labour, in this instance female workers, as capital moves to cheap labour sites globally. Such juxtaposition then provides an opportunity for discussing the changing nature of contemporary capitalism in which Western economic crises involve 'bailing out' banks while Eastern ones involve bailing out dying workers from buildings.

Another vital element of the 'physics' of a Stoic-based business course is the students' location within an organisation. Of relevance here are the notions of self-identity and moral agency within a specific context to maintain a continuous life narrative. If we assume that integrity and wholeness arise from congruence between our identity, our beliefs and values and our actions, then business schools need to help students negotiate the reformulation, to varying degrees, of their identity, beliefs and values framed as their unfolding narrative, the next chapter of their life which is to (re-)enter the workforce or their own business in some form of leadership role. They need to know what to anticipate in the next phase of their existence. The evidence is clear: they will be tested by the pressures of a market-based economy, conformist isomorphism, and routinised organisational culture and practice. The power of this 'moral seduction' (Moore, Tetlock, Tanlu & Bazerman, 2006) is considerable. Such lures have definable patterns that schools can identify. For example, Messick and Bazerman (1996) explicate theories used by executives in decision making, which do not make for good reading if one assumes that such decisions are based in logic and fact. Among the recognisable patterns of behaviour are overlooking the consequences of actions, discounting the future and denying uncertainty. Physics then is based on the embodiment of students within the wider contexts in which they are placed.

The final element of a Stoic orientation to business leadership courses, logic, is the capacity for reason-based knowledge. Such knowledge is the foundation of *technē,* pragmatic, context-dependent knowledge consciously oriented towards a good or service (Flyvbjerg, 2004). By itself, reason-based knowledge does not potentially produce wise outcomes unless it is epistemologically and axiomatically tested. By understanding that the motivation to act morally is determined not solely by cognitive competence (although there is evidence of a relationship between cognitive and moral complexity, where cognitive complexity is a necessary but not sufficient condition for moral complexity), then business schools are more likely to produce graduates with some enhanced moral capability and awareness. The knowledge that only 20 per cent of adults in the United States reach Kohlberg's sixth level of a principled conscience with an understanding of a commitment to a social contract (Rest et al., 1999) should be a sobering reminder to students not to overestimate potential organisational support when they take a principled stand on an issue.

The most credible explanation of the moral motivation of behaviour may be that it is only partly determined by cognitive processes, and that actions are the outcome of intuitive 'instinctive' urges. This is not unlike the athletic action of the high-performing sportsperson whose on-field performance is built on training and repetition. For example, accomplished cricket batsmen facing a fast ball travelling at 40 metres per second over 20 metres have to make a judgement about shot selection, which also involves feet placement (going back or forward; in line or 'giving room'). They do so first by focusing on the ball (visual saccades) and then using 'mappings … that they have acquired after years of practice' (Land & McLeod, 2000, p. 1344) to choose their shot 'intuitively'. This instinctive, automatic 'shot selection' in the moral realm is called the 'social-intuitionist model approach to moral judgment' (Haidt, 2001). While at one level such responses might be called non-reasoned, it could be argued that the reasoning has been developed in the processes of 'mapping' built up over time. That is, while moral motivation may seem disconnected from moral reasoning processes (Treviño, Weaver & Reynolds, 2006, p. 960), the reasoning processes are embedded not only in the formation stage of education, but also throughout one's working life by critical reflective processes. Business schools can work towards instilling a reflexive or heuristic propensity in its students that encourages the consideration of context, virtue and social, cultural and emotional consequences for oneself and others. Such a propensity obviously requires considerable cognitive capability, but undoubtedly goes beyond mere cognition to a deep 'whole-of-body-in-context' understanding. Heuristic responses are automatic and almost sub-conscious, and thus tend to be very simple. Directing our students to consider the wider context as a first step is an excellent and achievable heuristic that will prompt further consideration before action.

To build the right moral character is to shape 'an individual's disposition to think, feel, and behave in an ethical versus an unethical manner' (Cohen & Morse, 2014, p. 45). Business schools can induct its students into the 'right' disposition by developing habitual qualities or character strengths and the motivational drivers to call on them, when faced with challenges (Crossan, Mazutis, Seijts & Gandz, 2013). This is the phenomenon of embodiment, or habitus, outlined above. Each student brings with them a set of personality traits, or endogenous dispositions. While acknowledging contrary evidence (e.g., Soldz & Vaillant, 1999), Roberts, Walton and Viechtbauer's (2006) meta-analysis provides reasonable evidence to support the propositions that traits do vary over time, though admittedly very much formed in childhood, and that they are influenced by life events and circumstances. Building moral character in leadership training does not imply homogeneity. Rather, the diversity of people's ethnicity, gender, age, traits and experiences should be acknowledged and valued. In fact, the early stages of development could well include the students writing their narrative 'memoir', rather than autobiography. A memoir focuses less on factual detail and more on their subjective experience, specifically identifying significant people and experiences in their formation. The narrative then provides a point of projection about their imagined life course, and how they might get there. This involves the elaboration of a *telos*: what is it that will allow my life to flourish? As previously stated, most people choose positive and enduring virtues as the desired characteristics of their life.

Having done that, students could undertake a self-diagnosis based on well-established surveys such as traits, wisdom, emotional intelligence, psychological well-being and values. These surveys, confidentially provided to individuals, allow them to make their own judgements about their location in relation to others. Because traits are phenotypical, they are observable habits, attitudes, skills, roles and relationship orientations in practice: they are embodied. People's bodies are also endowed to varying degrees with aptitudes and skills, and physicality that produce a certain presence: short, tall; attractive, unattractive; athletic, unathletic and the like. People also have emotional and cognitive capabilities that are both genetically and environmentally determined. They also have a value set that transcends specific situations, which comprises prioritised beliefs about desirable end states or modes of conduct, and so guide choices of behaviour and relationships (Schwartz, 1994). Thus, people arrive at the doors of business school endowed and embodied in unique ways and with a personal narrative determined partly by circumstance and by choice based on the bounded agency available to them in their life so far. Their behaviour will have become habitual in a way that characterises each person's disposition. To truly transform a person into someone with the potential for developing a wise disposition inevitably then must be based on the embodiment of each person within a social context. Business teachers engage in a deeply phenomenological relationship with their students, truly understanding where their disposition and narrative have led them to this point in time. As far as possible, students need to be placed into difficult situations forcing them to confront who they truly are and whether this is the person they want ultimately to be. While case studies can be very useful, they often become cognitive exercises, rather than exercises that 'can tell me who I am'. Other forms include improvisation (Küpers & Pauleen, 2015), aesthetic experience (Kokkos, 2010), contemplation (Morgan, 2015) and reading literature (Hoggan & Cranton, 2015). Importantly, by providing models of virtues, character strengths and values, students are exposed to learning opportunities that they can personally relate to (Crossan et al., 2013). Students will incidentally learn that certain traits and characteristics not only are more likely to direct us to sound moral judgements, but are also wholesome in the sense that they produce a more satisfying life.

Conclusion

The chapter's contribution to the scholarship of wisdom learning is to provide an obviously contestable framework for research and teaching towards developing and inculcating 'the right stuff' in business graduates. Adopting a Stoic approach, wisdom – the pursuit of human flourishing or eudaimonia – is proposed as an appropriate expertise to which emerging leaders should aspire. Wisdom, it has been argued, is a philosophical orientation to the world that involves the physical, the ethical, and the logical. Wisdom is embodied in our disposition to act in certain ways to produce that which is good. Although based on deep self-awareness, heedfulness of the other, worldly understanding and cognitively complex reasoning, wise action ultimately becomes embodied, habitual and resilient. The remaining chapters of our students' life narrative depend very much on the pages where we as teachers become significant characters.

Reflective questions

1 The notion of the divine was used in this chapter as a secular concept. That is, the divine is understood as the pinnacle of excellence in practical and moral matters. Is it sensible or useful to seek an ideal even though it is not attainable?
2 Plutarch's summary of Stoicism's foundations of Wisdom stated that the wise person who seeks excellence (*aretē*) must display this in nature, behaviour, and reasoning. However, we know that to achieve that in the contemporary world is difficult. For example, our carbon-based energy and consumption-based lifestyle profoundly threatens our natural environment. Furthermore, we know that our personal Big Five traits, which influence behaviour, are relatively fixed by early adulthood. Finally, we know that our cultural values are deeply influenced by our cultural upbringing. Is it possible, then, through self-reflection and critique to try to alter the disposition that we have formed so far in our life in order to embody wise practice?

Embodying a wise graduate disposition: Is it possible?

Is it possible to consider a business education degree that requires not just knowledge and skills, but also forms of bodily involvement? Activities of bodily involvement could include undertaking physical tasks never attempted before, attempting to perform acts that are contrary to one's personal traits, or temporarily adopting a lifestyle different to the one currently lived.

For example, in leadership courses undertaken at the University of Queensland Business School, students were asked to undertake a physical activity that took them out of their normal comfort zone. The responses included students who had never jogged before taking up running; another learned how to use a surfboard to overcome her fear of the surf; others began a daily swimming programme. Their reflections showed that they surprised themselves at developing the will to do the action and the conative act of enacting their decision. Although the request was a simple and limited one, students reported not only increased self-awareness about pushing their boundaries, but identified unexpected satisfaction such as acquiring a skill (e.g., surfing), becoming fitter, or enjoying the endorphin rush that comes with physical exercise. Many decided to build this new activity into their lives.

In another exercise, students were required to enact for two weeks a value that they considered core to their identity. One student who wanted to develop a greater sense of community considered the self-knowledge about his 'Big Five' traits, particularly his relatively low score on openness. However, a sense of community was a strong value for him. Thus, he tried to develop this weak trait that he felt limited his capacity to commit to a community. Although an atheist, he chose to go to a church in order to make friends with people who shared different values and to sing with them. His experience was a positive one reinforcing his commitment to community, and strengthening his capacity for openness. However, he also learned that his attempts could be shunned. Rather than being disillusioned by this experience, he accepted that not all communities will be accepting of certain types of people.

Note

1 I acknowledge that the notion of disposition is conceptually vague, as Bandura (2015) points out.

References

Aristotle. (1984). *Nicomachean Ethics* (H. G. Apostle, Trans.). Grinnell, IO: The Peripatetic Press.

Bachen, C. M., & Illouz, E. (1996). Imagining romance: Young people's cultural models of romance and love. *Critical Studies in Mass Communication, 13*(4), 279–308.

Baltes, P. B., & Staudinger, U. M. (1993). The search for a psychology of wisdom. *Current Directions in Psychological Science, 2*(1), 75–80.

Bandura, A. (2015). On deconstructing commentaries regarding alternative theories of self-regulation. *Journal of Management, 41*(4), 1025–1044.

Biloslavo, R., & McKenna, B. (2011). Human flourishing as a foundation for a new sustainability oriented business school curriculum: Open questions and possible answers. *Journal of Management and Organization, 17*(5), 693–710.

Bok, S. (1993). What basis for morality? A minimalist approach. *Monist: An International Quarterly Journal of General Philosophical Inquiry, 76*(3), 349–359.

Bourdieu, P. (1977). *Outline of a Theory of Practice*. Cambridge; New York: Cambridge University Press.

Bourdieu, P. (1990). *The Logic of Practice* (R. Nice, Trans.). Stanford, CA: Stanford University Press.

Brouwer, R. (2014). *The Stoic Sage: The Early Stoics on Wisdom, Sagehood, and Socrates*. Cambridge: Cambridge University Press.

Cieciuch, J., & Schwartz, S. H. (2012). The number of distinct basic values and their structure assessed by PVQ-40. *Journal of Personality Assessment, 94*(3), 321–328.

Cohen, T., & Morse, L. (2014). Moral character: What it is and what it does. *Research in Organizational Behavior, 34*, 43–61.

Crossan, M., Mazutis, D., Seijts, G., & Gandz, J. (2013). Developing leadership character in business programs. *Academy of Management: Learning & Education, 12*(2), 285–305.

Crossley, N. (1996). Body-subject/body-power: Agency, inscription and control in Foucault and Merleau-Ponty. *Body & Society, 2*(2), 99–116.

Dahlsgrad, K., Peterson, C., & Seligman, M. E. P. (2005). Shared virtue: The convergence of valued human strengths across culture and history. *Review of General Psychology, 9*(3), 203–213.

Dale, K. (2005). Building a social materiality: Spatial and embodied politics in organizational control. *Organization, 12*(5), 649–678.

Erikson, E. H. (1963). *Childhood and Society* (2nd ed.). New York: Norton.

Ferraiolo, W. (2011). Stoic simplicity: The pursuit of virtue. *Ethos: Dialogues in Philosophy and Social Science, 4*(2), 47–57.

Fiasse, G. (2001). Aristotle's *phronesis*; A true grasp of ends as well as means. *The Review of Metaphysics, 55*(2), 323–337.
Fishbein, M., & Ajzen, I. (2010). *Predicting and Changing Behavior: The Reasoned Action Approach*. New York: Psychology Press (Taylor & Francis).
Fleeson, W., Furr, R. M., Jayawickreme, E., Meindl, P., & Helzer, E. G. (2014). Character: The prospects for a personality-based perspective on morality. *Social and Personality Psychology Compass, 8*(4), 178–191.
Flin, R., & Slaven, G. (1996). Personality and emergency command ability. *Disaster Prevention and Management: An International Journal, 5*(1), 40–46.
Flyvbjerg, B. (2004). Phronetic planning research: Theoretical and methodological reflections. *Planning Theory & Practice, 5*(3), 283–306.
Fuchs, C. (2003). Some implications of Pierre Bourdieu's works for a theory of social self-organization. *European Journal of Social Theory, 6*(4), 387–408.
Gherardi, S. (2009). Knowing and learning in practice-based studies: An introduction. *The Learning Organization, 16*(5), 352–359.
Giddens, A. (1979). *Central Problems in Social Theory*. London and Basingstoke: Macmillan Press.
Giddens, A. (1984). *The Constitution of Society: Outline of a Theory of Structuration*. Cambridge: Polity Press.
Hadot, P. (1995). *Philosophy as a Way of Life: Spiritual Exercises from Socrates to Foucault* (M. Chase, Trans.). Oxford: Blackwell.
Hahm, D. E. (1985). The Stoic theory of change. *The Southern Journal of Philosophy, 23(Supplement)*(1), 39–56.
Haidt, J. (2001). The emotional dog and its rational tail: A social intuitionist approach to moral judgment. *Psychological Review, 108*(4), 814–834.
Harries-Jones, P. (2003). Consciousness, embodiment, and critique of phenomenology in the thought of Gregory Bateson. *The American Journal of Semiotics, 19*(1–4), 69–94.
Hartman, E. M. (2006). Can we teach character? An Aristotelian answer. *Academy of Management: Learning & Education, 5*(1), 68–81.
Hitlin, S. (2003). Values as the core of personal identity: Drawing links between two theories of self. *Social Psychology Quarterly, 66*(2), 118–137.
Hitlin, S., & Piliavin, J. A. (2004). Values: Reviving a dormant concept. *Annual Review of Sociology, 30*, 359–393.
Hoggan, C., & Cranton, P. (2015). Promoting transformative learning through reading fiction. *Journal of Transformative Education, 13*(1), 6–25.
Inglehart, R. (2006). Mapping global values. *Comparative Sociology, 5*(2–3), 115–136.
IPCC. (2013). Summary for policymakers. In *Climate Change 2013: The Physical Science Basis. Contribution of Working Group I to the Fifth Assessment Report of the Intergovernmental Panel on Climate Change*. New York: Cambridge University Press.
Judge, T. A., Higgins, C. A., Thoresen, C. J., & Barrick, M. R. (1999). The big five personality traits, general mental ability, and career success across the life span. *Personnel Psychology*, 52, 621–652.
Kekes, J. (1995). *Moral Wisdom and Good Lives*. Ithaca, NY: Cornell University Press.
Kokkos, A. (2010). Transformative learning through aesthetic experience: Towards a comprehensive method. *Journal of Transformative Education, 8*(3), 155–177.
Küpers, W. (2011). Embodied pheno-pragma-practice: Phenomenological and pragmatic perspectives on creative 'inter-practice' in organisations between habits and improvisation. *Phenomenology & Practice, 5*(1), 100–139.
Küpers, W. (2013). Embodied inter-practices of leadership: Phenomenological perspectives on relational and responsive leading and following. *Leadership, 9*(3), 335–357.
Küpers, W. (2015). *Phenomenology of the Embodied Organization: The Contribution of Merleau-Ponty for Organization Studies and Practice*. London: Palgrave Macmillan.

Küpers, W., & Pauleen, D. J. (2015). Learning wisdom: Embodied and artful approaches to management education. *Scandinavian Journal of Management, 31*(4), 493–500.

Ladkin, D., & Taylor, S. S. (2010). Enacting the 'true self': Towards a theory of embodied authentic leadership. *Leadership Quarterly, 21*(1), 64–74.

Land, M. F., & McLeod, P. (2000). From eye movements to actions: How batsmen hit the ball. *Nature Neuroscience, 3*, 1340–1345.

Lester, S. (2014). Professional standards, competence and capability. *Higher Education, Skills and Work-based Learning, 4*(1), 31–43.

MacKay, R. B., & Chia, R. (2013). Choice, chance, and unintended consequences in strategic change: A process understanding of the rise and fall of Northco Automotive. *Academy of Management Journal, 56*(1), 208–230.

MacKerron, G. (2012). Happiness economics from 35000 feet. *Journal of Economic Surveys, 26*(4), 705–735.

McAdams, D. P., & Pals, J. L. (2006). A new Big Five: Fundamental principles for an integrative science of personality. *American Psychologist, 61*(3), 204–217.

McCrae, R. R., & Costa, P. T. J. (2008). The five factor theory of personality. In J. P. Oliver & R. W. Robins (Eds.), *Handbook of Personality* (3rd ed., pp. 159–181). New York: Guilford Press.

McKenna, B., & Graham, P. (2000). Technocratic discourse: A primer. *Journal of Technical Writing and Communication, 30*(3), 219–247.

McKenna, B., Rooney, D., & Boal, K. B. (2009). Wisdom principles as a meta-theoretical basis for evaluating leadership. *Leadership Quarterly, 20*(2), 177–190.

Messick, D. M., & Bazerman, M. H. (1996). Ethical leadership and the psychology of decision making. *Sloan Management Review, 37*(2), 37–45.

Moore, D. A., Tetlock, P. E., Tanlu, L., & Bazerman, M. H. (2006). Conflicts of interest and the case of auditor independence: Moral seduction and strategic issue cycling. *Academy of Management Review, 31*(1), 10–29.

Morgan, P. F. (2015). A brief history of the current reemergence of contemplative education. *Journal of Transformative Education, 13*(3), 197–218.

Morrison, K. (2005). Structuration theory, habitus and complexity theory: Elective affinities or old wine in new bottles? *British Journal of Sociology of Education, 26*(3), 311–326.

Pasupathi, M., Mansour, E., & Brubaker, J. R. (2007). Developing a life story: Constructing relations between self and experience in autobiographical narratives. *Human Development, 50*(2–3), 85–110.

Peterson, C., & Seligman, M. E. P. (Eds.). (2004). *Character strengths and virtues*. New York: Oxford University Press & American Psychological Association.

Rest, J., Narvaez, D., Bebeau, M. J., & Thoma, S. J. (1999). *Postconventional Moral Thinking: A Neo-Kohlbergian Approach*. Mahwah, NJ: Lawrence Erlbaum.

Roberts, B. W., Kuncel, N. R., Shiner, R., Caspi, A., & Goldberg, L. R. (2007). The power of personality: The comparative validity of personality traits, socioeconomic status, and cognitive ability for predicting important life outcomes. *Perspectives on Psychological Science, 2*(4), 313–345.

Roberts, B. W., Walton, K. E., & Viechtbauer, W. (2006). Patterns of mean-level change in personality traits across the life course: A meta-analysis of longitudinal studies. *Psychological Bulletin, 132*(1), 1–25.

Rokeach, M. (1973). *The Nature of Human Values*. New York: Free Press.

Rooney, D., McKenna, B., & Liesch, P. (2010). *Wisdom and Management in the Knowledge Economy*. New York: Routledge.

Russell, B. (1961). *History of Western Philospby and Its Connections with Political and Social Circumstances from the Earliest Times to the Present Day*. London: George Allen & Unwin.

Ryff, C. D., & Keyes, C. L. M. (1995). The structure of psychological wellbeing revisited. *Journal of Personality and Social Psychology, 69*(1), 719–727.

Sandberg, J., & Dall'Alba, G. (2009). Returning to practice anew: A life-world perspective. *Organization Studies, 30*(12), 1349–1368.

Schwartz, S. H. (1992). Universals in the content and structure of values: Theoretical advances and empirical tests in 20 countries. In L. Berkowitz (Ed.), *Advances in Experimental Social Psychology* (pp. 1–65). New York: Academic Press.

Schwartz, S. H. (1994). Are there universal aspects in the structure and contents of human values? *Journal of Social Issues, 50*(4), 19–45.

Seligman, M. E. P., & Csikszentmihalyi, M. (2000). Positive psychology: An introduction. *American Psychologist, 55*(1), 5–14.

Soldz, S., & Vaillant, G. E. (1999). The Big Five personality traits and the life course: A 45-year longitudinal study. *Journal of Research in Personality, 33*, 208–232.

Staudinger, U. M., & Glück, J. (2011). Psychological wisdom research: Commonalities and differences in a growing field. *Annual Review of Psychology, 62*, 215–241.

Stern, N. (2007). *The Economics of Climate Change: The Stern Review.* Retrieved from http://mudancasclimaticas.cptec.inpe.br/~rmclima/pdfs/destaques/sternreview_report_complete.pdf.

Treviño, L. K., Weaver, G. R., & Reynolds, S. J. (2006). Behavioral ethics in organizations: A review. *Journal of Management, 32*(6), 951–990.

Verplanken, B., & Holland, R. (2002). Motivated decision making: Effects of activation and self-centrality of values on choices and behavior. *Journal of Personality and Social Psychology, 82*(3), 434–447.

West, C., & Zimmerman, D. (1987). Doing gender. *Gender & Society, 1*(2), 125–151.

Wolfe, T. (1980). *The Right Stuff.* New York: Bantam.

Yang, S.-Y. (2008). A process view of wisdom. *Journal of Adult Development, 15*(1), 62–75.

Chapter 2

Catharsis in the classroom

Reflections on the performance of business education

Matt Statler and Steven S. Taylor

Introduction

In the traditional business school classroom, students sit passively and listen while professors stand and talk. Why? The basic pedagogical proposition underlying the professional business degree is that the students can gain knowledge that will help them to act in the future. These future actions are presumed to take place in organizational contexts – the students speculate that firms will hire them at a good wage based in part on the credential of a business school degree. In this scenario, if students have learned well the lessons that they were taught in business school, then once on the job they will be more likely to perform well, succeeding as business people and thriving as productive members of society.

This familiar situation – students sitting and listening, professors standing and talking – remains prevalent around the world, even in spite of the well-established tradition of case-based, dialogical teaching, as well as the growing emphasis on action-based or experiential pedagogies. The fundamental epistemology of this familiar situation is commonly framed in terms of information transfer. In the classroom, professors educate students by explaining basic facts (i.e., the "know-that") and providing a more subtle procedural sense of how to engage in practice (i.e., the "know-how") (Nahapiet & Ghoshal, 1998). In turn, students are encouraged to grasp the concepts, facts, and analytical techniques since they will generate useful knowledge once they are out on the job. And yet the basic purpose of the curriculum extends beyond information, facts, methods of analysis, and other such cognitive phenomena. Business school graduates are presumed to know something more than people who have not graduated from business schools about how to deal effectively with the ambiguities and dilemmas that perennially arise in human enterprises (see Colby et al., 2011).

In recent years, the global financial crisis, as well as the ongoing litany of ethical and governance crises within firms, has given organizational theorists, business media pundits, and intellectuals reflecting on the broader political economy ample cause to reflect critically on the basic pedagogical proposition offered by business schools. The institution of business – represented primarily by people with business school degrees composed of coursework taught by professional business academics – has arguably perpetuated a state of crisis in society, enriched some while impoverishing others, and squandered natural resources at a rate that will put many future generations at risk (Shrivastava & Statler, 2012). So what and how exactly are people teaching and learning in business school classrooms? What and how *should* they be teaching and learning differently, if indeed they have any hope of avoiding future crises?

One growing stream of recent organizational research seeks to shift the goal as well as the process of business school education away from information transfer and toward the development of *practical wisdom* (Wall, 2003; Nonaka & Toyama, 2007; Eikeland, 2009; Antonacopoulou, 2010; Statler, 2014). This shift of "onto-epistemological assumptions" (Sandberg and Tsoukas, 2011) involves a rejection of the cognitivist and machine-like metaphor of information transfer and an embrace of a variety of additional dimensions of the learning experience, including embodiment, affect, materiality, and normativity. Within this stream of research, organizational phenomena in general, and business education in particular, can be variously conceptualized in terms of practices (e.g., Whittington, 1996; Brown & Duguid, 2001; Jarzabkowski, 2004), processes (e.g., Helin et al., 2014), and/or performativity (e.g., Spicer et al., 2009).

In response to the broad question about what exactly is happening when business students sit in classrooms listening to professors, Chia and Holt (2008) have drawn a particularly useful distinction between "knowledge-by-representation" and "knowledge-by-exemplification." By their account, professors are communicating information, using language to refer explicitly to substantive "bodies" of knowledge and extant forms of organizational practice, while students in turn are listening to these words, understanding their significance, and learning how to apply them in practice (or not). And yet at the same time, professors are also performatively enacting other lessons and communicating them through gestures, tone of voice, rhetorical pacing and timing, arrangement and use of the physical space, etc. These lessons include affective moods, normative values, and aesthetic judgments about what is proper or appropriate in certain contexts or circumstances.

Business students are thus also learning (or not) from these affective, ethical, and aesthetic dimensions of the classroom experience. These lessons – the perceptions, moods, and values – may or may not be coherent with, or even relevant to, the contents of the information that is simultaneously being transferred. Yet by pointing out the existence and importance of these other forms or modes of knowledge, Chia and Holt (2008) have laid the groundwork for further critical reflections on how certain perceptions, moods, and values, might bear upon the various ethical- and governance- as well as further crises that continue to occur within the institution of business.

In this chapter, we consider what Chia and Holt (2008) call "knowledge-by-exemplification" as an essentially theatrical or dramatic phenomenon. The conceit is fairly simple to begin with – business school classrooms provide a physical, architectural, institutional, and social context in which a certain kind of performance or show can take place. Sometimes, the performance sustains the so-called "fourth wall" that separates actors (i.e., the professor) from spectators (i.e., the students), and other times this division breaks down (in Q&A, dialogue, case-based teaching, etc.). Certain notable exceptions notwithstanding (experiential learning, action learning, service learning, etc.), at business schools typically the professor performs a show, and the students give time and money to be in the audience.

Of course, if we judge the theater of the archetypal business school classroom by the aesthetic standards appropriate for professional theater companies, then it might appear as a rather crude and amateur production. The facilitated process of the case method of teaching surely weaves in elements of drama leading to an eventual revelation, yet even many of the professors who excel in the case method could rightly be analyzed as "outsider artists" or practitioners of a theatrical "art brut" to the extent that they deliberately cultivate modes of speaking, patterns of gesture, etc., without much regard for how professional actors and rhetoricians speak about and seek to refine their craft. We may also reflect critically on the cultural trend in which students, as "consumers" of professors' educational "services," appear to enjoy and willingly purchase "edu-tainment," rating it highly on their course evaluation feedback surveys.

But in any case, if we proceed on the assumption that business school classroom experiences can be analyzed using the terms and concepts associated with the theatrical arts, then the basic conceit quickly becomes more complex and interesting. Following Aristotle, the "moral of the story" or the "lesson learned" from a dramatic production has traditionally been described in terms of *catharsis*. Theater taps emotional intelligence by providing a venue for quick-paced, participatory, visual, and fast-moving interaction (Berk & Trieber, 2009). Audiences are invited to experience the multi-dimensional complexity of a scene, and then through interpretation and reflection on this experience they are given the opportunity to develop judgments about character (ibid.).

To take a classical example, and to follow the classical logic, when people experience a theatrical production of *Oedipus Rex*, certain emotions are elicited and released. By watching Oedipus have sex with his mother and kill his father, we are mimetically purged of these desires and thereby inoculated against that tragic eventuality. This inoculation has considerable utility within social, political, cultural, and organizational contexts where incest and patricide are prohibited. Yet beyond this relatively narrow, albeit vitally instrumental utility of the dramatic arts, catharsis may additionally help us to develop the creativity necessary to find new solutions, and it may motivate us to overcome such tragic problems if and when they should arise in the course of our own lives (Meisiek, 2004). The experience of catharsis, following this logic, might help make us wiser, more capable people. Might catharsis in the business school classroom, if such an experience were possible, then contribute to the development of wise managers and business leaders?

Following this line of speculative argument, we propose that the concept of catharsis could help us in practice to judge the effective quality of "knowledge-by-exemplification" in the business school classroom. The effective success of a pedagogy that exemplifies certain affective moods, normative values, and aesthetic perceptions and judgments could be evaluated in view of presence, distribution, and relative intensity of catharsis experienced by students.

As business educators, we are familiar and generally comfortable with how the effective quality of the "knowledge-by-representation" process is assessed. Often learning is assessed through quizzes, tests, and other evaluation techniques, designed to demonstrate whether individual students have retained the information that the professor transferred. But in a typical business school classroom, what emotions are elicited and released, if any? How might the release of certain emotions bear upon the students' future actions as business professionals? Could the experience of catharsis help business students to develop the creativity necessary to find new solutions? Could it make them more wise?

This chapter takes a tentative step toward answering these questions. Ladkin and Taylor (2014) have acknowledged the difficulty of writing about embodiment, physicality, and materiality while maintaining the rhetorical conventions traditionally associated with organizational studies. Thus our approach in this chapter will follow a rather non-traditional tact. We begin by presenting four case illustrations of catharsis in the classroom. Catharsis occurs in each of the four cases, but they differ in terms of how the pedagogical process integrates dramatic contents and/or theatrical process techniques. These differences can be represented in a matrix that describes how dramatic content and theatrical techniques can be integrated into business school classrooms. In view of these possibilities, we present a series of reflections: first, on the existing research that deals with catharsis and the role of theater and drama in organizational contexts; second, on the broader concept of social materiality as it pertains to the business school classroom; and third, on the complex issues associated with the design and facilitation of pedagogical processes that make catharsis more rather than less likely to occur. We close the chapter by articulating a series of questions that may animate future research, particularly with regard to the teaching and learning of wisdom in business schools.

Four illustrations and a discussion

In the following four case illustrations, catharsis occurs, but the experiences differ significantly in terms of how they integrate dramatic contents and/or process techniques. These differences constitute a matrix that can be used to analyze how dramatic content and theatrical techniques may be integrated into business school teaching and learning.

1 *Classroom as theater: The calculus lecture.* In an introductory calculus course offered in a large auditorium to hundreds of students at an elite scientific university, the professor lectures without interruption for one hour, and as he finishes and exits the stage the audience leaps to its feet with spontaneous cheering and applause.
2 *Business tragedy and comedy: An ethical object lesson.* In a senior capstone course required of undergraduate business students at a large, private university, a professor and her two dozen students discuss the tragic case of a jailed low-level investment banker who wrongly assumed that his own legal interests were aligned with his employer's, and one student shudders to realize the implications for his own future career in finance.
3 *Dramatic pedagogical techniques: Improv improves teams.* In an elective service learning course in which teams of students perform volunteer service with children and the elderly in the developing world, an "improv" comedian and coach asks students to get on their feet and engage in a series of funny, interactive exercises. This activity breaks down the physical and emotional barriers that can inhibit trust and collaboration among students.
4 *Collectively embodying leadership: Performing life stories.* In a required MBA leadership course, students write and stage solo performances that deal with who they are as a leader, how they have become that person, and what they struggle with on a regular basis. On the day of the presentations, the collective process of performing and audiencing of several dozen different stories has the effect of bringing many participants to tears.

Discussion

The occurrence intensity, and distribution of the experience of catharsis in any group of students remain difficult if not impossible to verify empirically. Meisiek (2004) laments that "there is no uncontroversial empirical study concerning the cathartic process ... no measures that define the strength or weakness of catharsis ... [and no] benchmark for deciding whether a cathartic reaction has taken place at all" (813). Still, and in order to provoke scholarly debate, we assert that catharsis occurred in each of the four cases, which are drawn from our own experiences as students and educators. The cases differ, however, in several significant respects.

The first case serves to illustrate the notion that the business school classroom inevitably has dramatic or theatrical aspects, even when those aspects may be so ubiquitous or banal that they appear to be completely undramatic. The cavernous lecture hall, the droning figure at the podium, the rows and rows of dazed students: these elements of the business school experience *are* theatrical even though we might hesitate to recognize them as such. A time-traveling hunter-gatherer from a distant human past would stumble into such a room and likely find it completely curious and fascinating, even without the ability to understand the contents of the lecture. The relatively rare, thrilling instance – when a professor's lecture attains such a high degree of excellence, and when the audience recognizes it and immediately expresses profound appreciation – merely brings what is often obscured into the foreground for critical consideration. Organizational theorists have long recognized that even the driest facts are also at the same time stories (Gabriel, 1991). Similarly, any lecture is always a kind of show, and when a lecturer puts a really good show then sometimes people in the audience feel a deep gratitude. As they collectively express this feeling through applause, they experience and possibly learn from a series of perceptions, emotions, and values occasioned by, but otherwise wholly distinct from the contents of the lecture, namely calculus.

The second case illustrates how the affective or thematic contents associated with drama – traditionally characterized most simply in terms of tragedy and comedy – often appear in business school classrooms, and can trigger cathartic experiences even when they are not presented using particularly dramatic pedagogical techniques. The posting of a link on the course website, the downloading and reading of an article, the discussion of the article in a seminar: beyond the banal drama that can accompany such processes, in the second case we see a student learning from the inevitably tragic mood that accompanies a cautionary tale. We believe that this case – where a dramatic subject triggers catharsis in the classroom – may be illustrative of a range of business ethics, strategy, management, marketing, and other courses that purport to teach students how to make decisions and act in practice. Case studies of failure provide a way to clarify by contrast what successful practice looks like (Laditka & Houck, 2006). And while much of this coursework is designed to emphasize the cognitive, rational aspects of the decision-making process, still the affective and normative message rings clearly. Students *should* be afraid of being hung out to dry by their future employer's compliance and enforcement division. The shudder of fear that the student feels when s/he realizes that s/he too had wrongly assumed that his employer would help defend him or her in a criminal prosecution is followed by a sense of relief or release when s/he considers him- or herself therefore less likely to engage in borderline activities in the future.

The third case by contrast illustrates how catharsis is possible even when there is nothing particularly dramatic about the topic, yet a dramatic technique is used. The topics dealt with in the improv exercises were deliberately frivolous and forgettable. But the process techniques made any topic seem ridiculously funny. There is a well-established and long-running tradition of conducting "organizational theater" exercises in the context of management training, leadership development, organizational change, and other learning processes (Meisiek, 2004; Meisiek & Barry, 2007). Dramatic techniques can be effective "to create an awareness of problems, to create togetherness, to stimulate discussion, and to foster a reading for change that can then be drawn upon in various subsequent initiatives" (Meisiek, 2004: 798). Improv techniques have been identified in particular as effective in business school classrooms (Huffaker & West, 2005; Moshavi, 2001). Though the promise of such techniques has led them to be utilized by management as instrumental means of controlling workers, still there is something irreducibly subversive about humor (Westwood, 2004). And yet, even experienced subversives fear the "Monday morning syndrome," where the good feelings and shared experiences generated using a dramatic process technique are quickly forgotten once the students revert to more traditional methods of learning or work. In any case, both the hope for transformation and the fear of its lack suggest that cathartic experiences can be produced when educators utilize dramatic process techniques.

The fourth case illustrates how dramatic process techniques can also be brought to bear on dramatic course contents and trigger relatively intense cathartic experiences. Students who enroll in a leadership development course can reasonably assume that introspective reflection will be a part of the deal (Taylor, 2012). They seek to improve themselves as leaders, and so in addition to the study of other people's leadership successes and failures, they analyze themselves, reflecting on their own past experiences as well as their hopes and fears for the future. Even in today's narcissistic age of the "selfie," people do find occasions to engage in genuine, sustained personal reflection, typically within the relatively private contexts associated with therapy, self-help, religious practice, etc. Yet, while there are traditions of arts-based therapy, and religious practice is often ritualized in a highly dramatic way, it remains relatively uncommon for people to utilize dramatic process techniques to make sense of the drama of their own personal and professional lives. Thus when the students in the fourth illustration engage in the process of articulating and enacting their own leadership stories, and when they listen to multiple stories from fellow students in the same long class session, they have a truly rare and relatively intense experience of the shared, communal or collective aspects of human life (Laditka & Houck, 2006). As the series of performances unfolds, and as the people in the room bear witness to a series of stories, they are overwhelmed with a variety of intense emotions. This peak experience often stays with them in the following weeks and months, shaping their trajectories in often unexpected ways.

Taken together, these four cases can be seen as a 2 × 2 matrix (see Figure 2.1) of different possibilities for the integration of dramatic contents and techniques in a business school classroom. The possibilities include: (1) no dramatic process, no dramatic content; (2) no dramatic process, dramatic content; (3) dramatic process, no dramatic content; and (4) dramatic process, dramatic content.

Quadrant 2 Dramatic Process / No Dramatic Contents	Quadrant 4 Dramatic Process / Dramatic Contents
Quadrant 1 No Dramatic Process / No Dramatic Contents	Quadrant 3 No Dramatic Process / Dramatic Contents

Figure 2.1 Catharsis matrix.

We believe that catharsis did occur in each of these cases, and that they illustrate how catharsis might occur also in other pedagogical contexts. In the following section of this chapter, we reflect on the significance of these cases with respect to: the existing research literature on catharsis and drama in organizational contexts; the more general concept of socio-materiality as it pertains to business school classrooms; and the practical matter of designing and facilitating pedagogical processes that integrate dramatic contents and techniques.

Theoretical and practical reflections

Drama, catharsis, and learning

Meisiek (2004) provides a comprehensive and detailed account of the ancient roots and historical evolution of the concept of catharsis, and considers its relevance to the set of practices known as "organizational theater." The Aristotelian origin of the concept as we have considered it thus far in this essay developed out of a series of ritualized Dionysian ritual practices, including feasts and dances through which sicknesses were released from the body (Barrucand, 1970, cited in Meisiek, 2004). By analogy, drama has a similar purgative effect, releasing negative and unhealthy emotions from the audience. Renaissance thinkers picked up the thread and emphasized the epistemological and ethical dimensions of this process. They thought that catharsis could "enlighten an audience by cleansing them of false beliefs and opening their minds to knowledge" and provide "a route to the moral education of the masses" (Meisiek, 2004: 800).

Twentieth-century psychology pioneers Josef Breuer and Sigmund Freud explored the therapeutic efficacy of a "cathartic method," while sociological theorists emphasized the somatic or physical aspects of the reaction to negative emotions experienced in the theater (Scheff, 1979). Victor Moreno and Augusto Boal independently developed theater traditions that were designed to engage audiences in the active production of catharsis, rather than allowing them to sit passively and observe others performing. For Moreno, because the verbal dimension of dramatic narrative is inadequate, there is a need to get people up out of their seats and actively engaged in the theatrical production (Moreno, 1946). Moreno claims that successful cathartic theater could foster creativity among the participants, enabling them to solve real-life problems when the show is over. For Boal, when the passive audience members become actors and stage the situation of political and social oppression, they experience empathy with the oppressed characters in the play. Boal believes this empathy can increase the participants' motivation to ameliorate the suffering of oppressed people in real life (Boal, 2006).

At the end of his excellent article, Meisiek (2004) reflects on the diversity of these accounts of catharsis and suggests that "the main problem [...] is that as a concept it verges on the all-encompassing" (813). We agree that there is a big difference between purging negative emotions about incest and the political mobilization of people to combat oppression. And yet, we believe that the various conceptualizations of catharsis do share a common, if also complex and mutable, set of defining characteristics. We conceptualize *catharsis as an emotion experienced in response to art that has ethical effects*. We assume that the emotion is always embodied, and that the response is always affective. We acknowledge that some of the effects of a cathartic experience may be judged unethical – Brecht famously avoided catharsis in a rejection of the bourgeois values that he believed it perpetuated. Here we use the term "ethical" pragmatically, as a gesture toward a future conversation in which interested people would reflect on what the experience means in their own context for action. More specifically with regard to the dramatic arts, we believe the response is conditioned by the structure and process of the theatrical production, and by the tension that the structure creates prior to a release or resolution. We think the lack of coherence between and among theoretical accounts of catharsis is due largely to different assumptions about the nature of emotions, art, ethics, and experience. These assumptions and the scholarly debates about them can be pursued without threatening the core meaning of catharsis – namely, *when an artwork gives way to emotions that make life better*. One more iteration, slightly compressed: *catharsis occurs whenever art makes us wiser*.

Yet even if the various conceptualizations of catharsis reviewed by Meisiek (2004) can be collectively understood through this lens, we do think they have another significant ontological and methodological limitation. Most of the recent research and practice remains focused rather exclusively on individual-level psychological phenomena. Even though Moreno and Boal emphasize the importance of activity on behalf of the spectator, they remain anchored to psychological categories of analysis. Indeed, even though Boal's forum theater method is ultimately focused on large-scale political and cultural change, still the point of focus is on group psychology, where a number of independent minds are engaged to realize a collective benefit. The specifically collective or social aspects of the experience of catharsis itself remain to be theorized, as do the dynamically interwoven connections between individual, group, and collective level phenomena.

By the same token, the existing research on catharsis in organizations gestures towards, but does not fully pursue, the embodied, physical, and material dimensions of the phenomenon. Petzold's (1972) notion of intensified role-play involves multiple actors, and seeks to realize benefits at the level of the overall productivity of the enterprise. But it does not take sufficient account of the intersubjective aspects of embodiment, much less the physical setting or the material dimensions of the flour-mill. da Cunha and Orlikowski (2008) contribute an excellent study of catharsis in an organizational change process from a practice perspective, carefully following a series of postings in an online discussion forum and focusing on feelings of anger and shame. Yet they note that "attempts to use online forums to shape others' interpretation of the change can have the paradoxical effect of resisting and facilitating its implementation at the same time" (2008: 152). The notion that a cathartic experience can be beneficial in one respect, but detrimental in another does not, we suggest, involve a paradox – rather it signals a need for more in-depth understanding of the way that material/virtual technologies enable the exercise of learning and power within organizations. In sum, we believe these research contributions point toward a need to consider the socio-materiality of catharsis in the classroom.

The socio-materiality of catharsis in the classroom

Not only do organizations – including educational organizations – involve human relations, they also involve processual relations between human and non-human actors. A variety of theoretical approaches to practice, process, enactment, performativity, etc., can be viewed together as part of a broader research interest in socio-materiality (Carlile et al., 2013; Humphries & Smith, 2014; Orlikowski, 2007; Ropo, Sauer, & Salovaara, 2013; Salovaara, 2014). Leadership and other organizational phenomena can be seen as socio-material practices (Dale, 2005; Jones, 2013; Oborn, Barrett, & Dawson, 2013). Broadly speaking, the two domains – the social and material – "are intertwined in a mutually constitutive way and need to be engaged jointly" (van Marrewijk & Yanow, 2010: 3).

This theoretical orientation allows us to move beyond the individual-level psychological unit of analysis or theoretical point of focus and consider briefly other aspects of the case illustrations presented above. For example, considering the calculus lecture, the experience of one person applauding differs significantly from the experience of hundreds of people applauding. The acoustic resonance of the sound, the percussive movement of the hands and arms, the perceived agreement of multiple individuals: each of these socio-material dimensions bears upon the experience of catharsis, and each merits further study on its own. Similarly, the overall quality of the dialogue in an ethics seminar is conditioned by the physical layout of the room. Indeed the traditional seminar table or hollow square is designed to enable all participants to see each other's faces rather than their backs as in an auditorium. In the case of the improv exercises, consider the simple but important fact that the desks in the room could be moved aside, clearing a space for different forms of physical activity that integrate the body and encourage bodily interactions rather than just dialogue among students. Finally, the autobiographical leadership stories are or can be deliberately staged as theatrical productions, and they are recorded on video so that students can watch themselves later as well as share the clip with other people.

In each of the cases, the values, moods, and aesthetic perceptions that are exemplified by professors are intertwined with physical, material, embodied, and collective dimensions of experience. Thus, if we want to research catharsis in the classroom, we must accept that it is ontologically more than something merely individually experienced, subjectively perceived, or having to do with internal states of mind, etc. Yes, catharsis may be triggered, conditioned, afforded, or sustained by external, objective, intersubjective, and material conditions. But we must recognize that these socio-material dimensions are an integral part of the entire catharsis phenomenon, as they are part of the conditions, part of the people, and part of the effects of the experience. It may be true that these dimensions are complex and thus resistant to reductive theory development, but we believe that they are nevertheless part of organizational life, and part of business education.

So then, what are the socio-material aspects of what typically happens in the business school classroom in particular? How exactly do they work? Can the social and material dimensions of such experiences be intentionally influenced in order to create more catharsis rather than less?

Facilitating catharsis in the classroom: Practical implications

Based on our own experiences as educators and relations to students, we believe that catharsis *can and does* occur within the business school. In response to works of dramatic art, students do have embodied and emotional experiences that are ethically beneficial. These experiences may occur infrequently, and – being part of implicit knowing and learning – they may in any case be very difficult to describe or identify in empirical scientific terms. Yet they can occur – all of us can recall several such instances in our own lives.

But under what conditions exactly do they occur; with what particular enabling or constraining factors? Is there anything that we as educators can do to design and facilitate classroom experiences that trigger more intensive rather than less catharsis? How can the basic pedagogical proposition of the business school be reframed so that educators as well as students would seek out, or at least remain open to, cathartic experiences in the classroom? And importantly: how might the "business school theater" be reproduced in order to "exemplify" the habits of mind and body associated with a more sustainable business practice?

Iterative, pragmatic experimentation and inquiry (following Dewey, 1919) must be sustained within a community of multiple educators over a considerable length of time in order to answer these questions. The first step is simply for business school educators to become more aware of the theatrical dimensions of the classroom, and more intentional about the integration of social and material elements that intensify the drama.

Referring to Figure 2.1, educators who prefer to work in quadrant 1 could seek deliberately to develop and refine their own rhetorical skills. Professors who work in quadrant 2 could seek to choose more poignant case examples, and encourage students to put themselves in the shoes of the people in the case. Professors working in quadrant 3 could include more exercises that force students to interact with each other, explore improv tragedy (Quinn, 2007) as well as improv comedy, and seek to ensure that these interactions include perceptions, emotions, and values that serve the learning objective. Professors working in quadrant 4 could experiment more deliberately with the social and material dimensions of the dramatic processes they employ. Professors could de-emphasize the social and the material, or de-emphasize the social but emphasize the material, and so on, alternating different configurations or sequences of process techniques over time to generate a fuller sense of what is possible and what works best under which conditions. As above, these four options can be presented as a matrix that can guide pragmatic experimentations and specific exercises.

Beyond these generic options, Taylor & Statler (2013) have suggested that the material aspects of business school education can be deliberately influenced to foster

Quadrant 2 Dramatic Process / No Dramatic Contents *Choose poignant case examples, encourage students to empathize with characters*	Quadrant 4 Dramatic Process / Dramatic Contents *Experiment intentionally with social and material dimensions of processes*
Quadrant 1 No Dramatic Process / No Dramatic Contents *Develop and refine rhetorical skills*	Quadrant 3 No Dramatic Process / Dramatic Contents *Include more interactive exercises such as improv comedy and tragedy, focus on perceptions, emotions and values*

Figure 2.2 Pragmatic options for catharsis experimentation.

emotional engagement by students in the learning process. Building on the "Expressive Therapies Continuum" (ETC) that is used by therapists to decide what type of technique to use to achieve particular results with individual patients (Kagin & Lusebrink, 1978), Taylor and Statler identify a series of criteria that can be used to describe particular materials and judge whether they might be appropriate in the classroom, including: fluidity, resistivity, ambiguity of form, boundaries, quantity, mediation, kinesthetics, and sensory awareness (2013: 596–599).

Of course, not all emotions lead to cathartic experiences, and further experimentation is surely necessary to explore what types and levels of emotion can be produced by utilizing these various material properties in the classroom. Still, it seems reasonable to suggest that greater emotional engagement would make it more likely that students would experience catharsis, and so the ETC criteria may be used to refine the other generic options identified above.

But whether these criteria serve or not, the broader point is that as educators and students become increasingly aware of, and intentional about, the design and performance of catharsis in the classroom, they may additionally become more practically wise. The learning objectives associated with particular courses as well as entire curricula or courses of study may be reframed in terms of wisdom. And again, we leave open the question about whether a particular action undertaken by a particular individual – say, Angela Merkel's acceptance of large numbers of refugees into Germany in 2015, or Apple's CEO Tim Cook's affirmation of the value of user privacy over national security in 2016 – exemplifies wisdom or not. The general point about catharsis is that art can help people who deal with similarly ambiguous and difficult situations, and the specific point is that by designing and performing learning processes that trigger cathartic experiences in business schools, we may enable our students to act wisely in the future as business professionals.

Open questions

In this chapter we have responded to a broad set of questions about the purpose and practices of business education by pursuing a line of inquiry that focuses on the development of practical wisdom through catharsis and asks how business educators can facilitate more rather than less catharsis in the classroom. We acknowledge that following these rather preliminary reflections a number of tangled theoretical and methodological issues and implications remain to be addressed. In this final section, we consider several of these issues in more detail because we think that they are crucial for the implementation of catharsis as wisdom-learning and thus a different "re-production" of the business school classroom.

Mirror neurons and the materiality of the social?

Recent neuroscientific research has generated results that appear tantalizing to philosophers and organizational theorists who work within the traditions of phenomenological and hermeneutic research. For example, the recent discovery of the existence and function of "mirror neurons" in the human brain appears to provide empirical "proof" supporting the philosophical conceptualizations of "*in-betweenness*," "being-with," and the ontological primacy of indeterminacy or multiplicity as such.

This situation also brings complications, however, as there is a risk of reducing all psychological, social, and cultural phenomena – all of organizational life – to a set of ultimately physical entities, properties, and processes. Why is this risky? Just as in the case of business education, when empirical sciences (including neurobiology) are taught in schools, then certain values, emotions, and aesthetic perceptions are also being exemplified, and these bodies of knowledge cannot simply be taken for granted as ethically neutral or positive.

Thus there is a need, as organizational theorists making the so-called "material turn" (Barad, 2003; Carlile, Nicolini, Langley, & Tsoukas, 2013; Dale, 2005; Orlikowski, 2007), for us to remain reflexively and self-critically attuned to the affective, ethical, and aesthetic aspects of the knowledge that is exemplified in and through our own research and teaching practices.

The concept of practical wisdom as the result of catharsis?

As we have noted above, Aristotle characterized the normatively positive outcome of such dramatic educational processes in terms of *phronesis* or practical wisdom. There is a well-established and growing stream of contemporary organizational research literature that explores practical wisdom as the desired outcome of business education (Wall, 2003; Nonaka & Toyama, 2007; Eikeland, 2009; Antonacopoulou, 2010; Statler, 2014). Based on our discussion and reflection on the four case illustrations, our own tentative proposition would be that more intense experiences of catharsis will lead toward greater wisdom. But to what extent does this concept effectively serve to describe the results or effects associated with catharsis?

Since we are oriented toward the socio-materiality of the classroom experience, we need a conceptualization of wisdom that similarly integrates social and material dimensions. Psychologists and philosophers tend to conceptualize wisdom as an individual-level phenomenon. Yet even Aristotle acknowledged that the individual cannot thrive or flourish outside of the context of a flourishing household (*oikos*), community (*polis*) and thus culture. Thus we anticipate that organizational researchers can develop a more expansive, holistic, and descriptively accurate conception of (practical) wisdom as it may or may not result from catharsis by conceptualizing it in socio-material terms.

Pedagogical intentionality: The design and facilitation of cathartic processes?

As noted above, experimentation with all of these various dramatic contents and techniques is necessary. The techniques associated with improv appear promising – educational theorists assert that improvisation appeals to the sensibilities of the so-called "net generation," draws on their emotional intelligence, fosters collaboration, and promotes deep learning (Berk & Trieber, 2009). Within the field of business education, we need to engage in cycles of action and reflection in order to develop improvisational as well as other dramatic aspects of our teaching craft.

There is, however, a distinct blind spot at the center of the previously presented concept of "knowledge-by-exemplification" by Chia and Holt. As professors, we can never have perfect and comprehensive knowledge of the normative, affective, and aesthetic lessons our students learn from us. We must acknowledge the severe limitations of our own wisdom, relinquishing the latent fantasy that if only they would do as we have told them to do, they would thrive in life and profit in business. More specifically, the practical "know-how" associated with facilitating catharsis in the classroom cannot itself be fully represented or assessed. Teaching remains an artful craft, one that is best developed through apprenticeship, iterative practice, etc. (Taylor, Ladkin, & Statler, 2015).

This situation – refining a craft practice without much assurance that it can or always will have the effects that we intend – may be familiar to actors, dancers, musicians, and others who perform in the context of theatrical and other artistic productions. It seems therefore likely that we business educators might learn at least a little bit about how to facilitate catharsis in the classroom by engaging in dialogue as well as collaborative practices together with professional artists and theater producers. We may also learn about how to design and perform the educational practices associated with wisdom by collaborating with people working in the various traditions of artistic practice that have direct political, social, and organizational outcomes among their intended effects.

Open questions for the reader

1 What role does the material environment play in educational institutions?
2 How can educators design and facilitate learning experiences that involve catharsis?
3 Can art really help people become more ethical?

References

Antonacopoulou, E. P. (2010). Making the business school more "critical": Reflexive critique based on phronesis as a foundation for impact. *British Journal of Management*, *21*, 6–25.

Barad, K. (2003). Posthumanist performativity: Toward an understanding of how matter comes to matter. *Signs: Journal of Women in Culture and Society*, *28*(3), 801–831.

Barrucand, D. (1970). Catharsis and psychodrama. *Bulletin de Psychologie, 23*(13–16), 736–738.

Berk, R. A., & Trieber, R. H. (2009). Whose classroom is it, anyway? Improvisation as a teaching tool. *Journal on Excellence in College Teaching*, *20*(3), 29–60.

Boal, A. (2006). *The Aesthetics of the Oppressed*. New York: Routledge.

Brown, J. S., & Duguid, P. (2001). Knowledge and organization: A social-practice perspective. *Organization Science*, *12*(2), 198–213.

Carlile, P., Davide, N., Langley, N., & Tsoukas, H. (2013). *How Matter Matters: Objects, Artifacts, and Materiality in Organization Studies*. Oxford: Oxford University Press.

Chia, R., & Holt, R. (2008). The nature of knowledge in business schools. *Academy of Management Learning & Education*, *7*(4), 471–486.

Colby, A., Ehrlich, T., Sullivan, B., & Dolle, J. (2011). *Rethinking Undergraduate Business Education: Liberal Learning for the Profession*. San Francisco, CA: Jossey-Bass.

Da Cunha, J. V., & Orlikowski, W. J. (2008). Performing catharsis: The use of online discussion forums in organizational change. *Information and Organization*, *18*(2), 132–156.

Dewey, J. (1919). *Democracy and Education: An Introduction to the Philosophy of Education*. New York: Macmillan.

Eikeland, O. (2009). *The Ways of Aristotle: Aristotelian Phronesis, Aristotelian Philosophy of Dialogue, and Action Research*. Bern: Peter Lang.

Gabriel, Y. (1991). Turning facts into stories and stories into facts: A hermeneutic exploration of organizational folklore. *Human Relations*, *44*(8), 857–875.

Helin, J., Hernes, T., Hjorth, D., & Holt, R. (Eds.). (2014). *The Oxford Handbook of Process Philosophy and Organization Studies*. Oxford: Oxford University Press.

Huffaker, Sheldon, J., & West, E. (2005). Enhancing learning in the business classroom: An adventure with improv theater techniques. *Journal of Management Education, 29*(6), 852–869.

Humphries, C., & Smith, A. C. T. (2014). Talking objects: Towards a post-social research framework for exploring object narratives. *Organization, 21*, 477–494.

Jarzabkowski, P. (2004). Strategy as practice: Recursiveness, adaptation, and practices-in-use. *Organization Studies, 25*(4), 529–560.

Jones, M. (2013). Untangling sociomateriality. In Carlile, P., Davide, N., Langley, N., & Tsoukas, H. (Eds.) *How Matter Matters: Objects, Artifacts, and Materiality in Organization Studies*. Oxford: Oxford University Press, 197–226.

Kagin, S. L., & Lusebrink, V. B. (1978). The expressive therapies continuum. *Art Psychotherapy*, *5*(4), 171–180.

Kupers, W., & Pauleen, D. (2013). *A Handbook of Practical Wisdom: Leadership, Organization and Integral Business Practice*. London: Gower.

Laditka, S. B., & Houck, M. M. (2006). Student-developed case studies: An experiential approach for teaching ethics in management. *Journal of Business Ethics, 64*(2), 157–167.

Ladkin, D., & Taylor, S. S. (Eds.). (2014). *The Physicality of Leadership: Gesture, Entanglement, Taboo, Possibilities* (Vol. 6). Bingley: Emerald Group Publishing.

Meisiek, S. (2004). Which catharsis do they mean? Aristotle, Moreno, Boal and organization theatre. *Organization Studies, 25*(5), 797–816.

Meisiek, S., & Barry, D. (2007). Through the looking glass of organizational theatre: analogically mediated inquiry in organizations. *Organization Studies, 28*(12), 1805–1827.

Moreno, J. L. (1946). Psychodrama and group psychotherapy. *Sociometry*, 9(2/3), 249–253. http://doi.org/10.2307/2785011

Moshavi, D. (2001). "Yes and...": Introducing improvisational theatre techniques to the management classroom. *Journal of Management Education*, 25(4) 437–449.

Nahapiet, J., & Ghoshal, S. (1998). Social capital, intellectual capital, and the organizational advantage. *Academy of Management Review*, 23(2), 242–266.

Nonaka, I., & Toyama, R. (2007). Strategic management as distributed practical wisdom (phronesis). *Industrial and Corporate Change*, 16(3), 371–394.

Oborn, E., Barrett, M., & Dawson, S. (2013). Distributed leadership in policy formulation: A sociomaterial perspective. *Organization Studies*, 34(2), 253–276.

Orlikowski, W. J. (2007). Sociomaterial practices: Exploring technology at work. *Organization Studies*, *28*, 1435–1448.

Petzold, H. (1972). Situationsanalyse und intensiviertes Rollenspiel in der Industrie. In Petzold, H. (Ed.) *Angewandtes Psychodrama in Therapie, Pädagogik, Theater und Wirtschaft*. Paderborn: Junfermann, 358–372.

Quinn, J. (2007) Improvising our way through tragedy: How an improv comedy community heals itself through improvisation. *America Communication Journal*, 9(1), available http://ac-journal.org/journal/2007/Spring/articles/tragedy.html.

Ropo, A., Sauer, E., & Salovaara, P. (2013). Embodiment of leadership through material place. *Leadership*, 9(3), 378–395.

Salovaara, P. (2013). Embodied learning experience in leadership development. In Melina, L. R., Burgess, G. J., Falkman, L. L., & Marturano, A. (Eds.) *The Embodiment of Leadership*. San Francisco, CA: Jossey-Bass, 193–215.

Salovaara, P. (2014). Video: Leadership in spaces and places. *Organizational Aesthetics*, 3(1), 79.

Sandberg, J., & Tsoukas, H. (2011). Grasping the logic of practice: Theorizing through practical rationality. *Academy of Management Review*, 36(2), 338–360.

Scheff, T. J. (1979). *Catharsis in Healing, Ritual and Drama*. Berkeley: University of California Press.

Shrivastava, P., & Statler, M. (Eds.). (2012). *Learning from the Global Financial Crisis: Creatively, Reliably and Sustainably*. Palo Alto, CA: Stanford University Press.

Spicer, A., Alvesson, M., & Kärreman, D. (2009). Critical performativity: The unfinished business of critical management studies. *Human Relations*, 62(4), 537–560.

Statler, M. (2014). Developing wisdom in a business school? Critical reflections on pedagogical practice. *Management Learning*, 45(4), 397–417.

Taylor, S. S. (2012). *Leadership Craft, Leadership Art*. New York: Palgrave Macmillan.

Taylor, S. S., & Statler, M. (2013). Material matters: Increasing emotional engagement in learning. *Journal of Management Education*, 1052562913489976.

Taylor, S. S., Ladkin, D., & Statler, M. (2015). Caring orientations: The normative foundations of the craft of management. *Journal of Business Ethics*, 128(3), 575–584.

Wall, J. (2003). Phronesis, poetics and moral creativity. *Ethical Theory and Moral Practice*, 6, 317–341.

Westwood, R. (2004). Comic relief: Subversion and catharsis in organizational comedic theatre. *Organization Studies*, 25(5), 775–795.

Whittington, R. (1996). Strategy as practice. *Long Range Planning*, 29(5), 731–735.

Chapter 3

Cultivating practical wisdom through emergent learning

Marilyn M. Taylor

Introduction

In a global context of social, economic, and environmental fragility, and with declining of public trust in business and government (Edelman 2015, 86), leadership wisdom seems an essential requirement for our times. Yet, in practice, it is surprisingly rare. The focus of leaders has been overwhelmingly on the acquisition of knowledge; wisdom has not been a focus. The purpose of this chapter is to illuminate a process of emergent learning through which practical wisdom can be cultivated.

As a context for appreciating that challenge, this chapter begins by distinguishing knowledge and wisdom. While knowledge can be instrumental in solving problems, it comes with a predominantly instrumental mindset that is inadequate for navigating the current uncertainties of a turbulent and unpredictable world. Further, it is not possible to develop the wisdom to do so through learning processes that generate knowledge. We instead require an embodied form of learning. After examining the distinctions between knowledge and wisdom, the chapter illuminates an embodied process of emergent learning through which we can cultivate practical wisdom.

Leadership, knowledge, and wisdom: Paradox and problematic

Leadership and knowledge

Our conventional assumptions about knowledge derive from the Enlightenment era that over 300 years ago gave the Western world rational empiricism as the legitimate foundation for knowledge. Knowledge is understood as an object "outside" us that we acquire as a commodity. A typical metaphor for mind is that of file cabinet in which knowledge is stored and retrieved as needed (Bereiter and Scardamalia 2005). In structure and pedagogical practices educational institutions have been designed on the basis of this objectification of knowledge; as such they not only disseminate knowledge as content but they also foster primarily an instrumental mindset of knowing and knowledge – a commodity to be exchanged and a tool to be used. A somewhat even more subtle but powerful element of our conventional notions about science and knowledge is that they inevitably lead to certainty and, potentially, control. David Peat (2007) reports that in 1900 the President of the Royal Society, Lord Kelvin, stated that "in principle" all that had to be known was already known. "It was to be an era of certainty and knowledge and, thanks to the power of science and technology, a time of limitless progress" (p. 921).

In everyday life, at least tacitly, we have come to expect certainty and control as we become more knowledgeable. By extension, the assumption is that the best leaders are the most knowledgeable and thereby in control. This is less a demonstrable truth than a psychological need. In an age of exponentially accelerating change in operationally relevant conditions, senior leaders are now often among the most removed from specific operational knowledge, related specific skill requirements, and daily challenges. Furthermore, it is impossible for one person to stay current with all domains of knowledge. In complete contradiction to Lord Kelvin, the world's knowledge has been estimated to have doubled every century prior to 1900, by 1945 every quarter century and currently on average every 13 months with doubling daily seen as imminent (Shilling 2013). We are doing so well at knowledge creation speed and, in a digitized world, virtually instantaneous distribution, that the knowledge explosion itself leads to retrieval difficulties with a vast knowledge base, overwhelming and costly management, and an electronic burden of necessary recurrent searches (IBM 2006). While affirming the critical need for relevant knowledge in decisions and actions, it seems obvious that more knowledge alone does not eliminate uncertainty.

Leaders aspiring to meet the expectation of certainty and control through being knowledgeable in the context of constant change and spiralling knowledge creation place themselves in a bind; they must refuse to acknowledge they do not know. Alvesson and Spicer (2012) describe diverse forms of unwillingness and/or incapability to seek, accept, and use knowledge critical to the organization. They call this phenomenon "functional stupidity" defined specifically as "inability and/or unwillingness to use cognitive and reflective capacities in anything other than narrow and circumspect ways" (p. 1201). They note that uncritical reliance on current knowledge and disregard of the wider changing context can paradoxically become an impediment to effective leadership. These themes point to the need to reconsider what knowledge is and its role in leadership. It is suggested here that conventional instrumental notions of knowledge, in and of itself, providing solutions is outdated. In this view, knowledge is necessary but not sufficient.

Leadership and wisdom

The value of wisdom is not widely understood in contemporary Western societies; it has been eclipsed by our instrumental focus on knowledge. Since leadership is a combination of practice and understanding, our concern is what Aristotle called practical wisdom "*phrónêsis*," in contrast to what he called "*epistêmê*" (scientific, analytical knowledge) or "*tékhnê*" (technical knowledge). Bent Flyvbjerg (2004, 284) cites Aristotle's definition of *phrónêsis* directly as "an intellectual virtue that is 'reasoned, and capable of action with regard to things that are good or bad for [people]'." Some have characterized wisdom as a form of advanced knowledge. The view elaborated here is that the two are very distinct. Knowledge can be seen as a constitutive element of wisdom, but wisdom comprises dimensions of human experience well beyond what we believe we know and what we are skilled to do. Six constituent dimensions of practical wisdom that distinguish it from conventional notions of knowledge and conventional knowledge acquisition are:

- *Wisdom is a metacognitive phenomenon.* Wisdom scholar, Robert Sternberg (1990) states: "Wise people know what they know and what they do not know as well as the limits of what can be known and what cannot be. ... Wise people welcome ambiguity, knowing that is an ongoing part of life" (p. 157).
- *Wisdom begins with the particular.* Flyvbjerg (2004) notes that wisdom "focuses on what is variable, on that which cannot be encapsulated by universal rules, on specific cases. ... More than anything else, phrónêsis requires experience" (p. 288).
- *The generation of wisdom comprises creativity.* "The practically wise self ... must, in many respects, be a poet" (Wall 2003). Wisdom is practiced in a dynamic social context where we must constantly evolve new ways of understanding our experience.
- *Wisdom arises through engagement and dialogue in a social context.* Practical wisdom "is understood as dialogical not merely because it can listen as others speak, but also because it recognizes that the concrete situation itself is never exclusively determined by its subjective judgment" (Long 2002, 46); it is "sensation" that "determines the truth through direct encounter" (p. 50).
- *Wisdom derives from reflection on experience.* "An embodied deliberating reflexivity is required for an integral practice of wisdom" (Küpers 2013, 34).
- *The generation of wisdom is an intense experience.* Csikszentmihályi and Rathmunde (1990, 33) argue that the pursuit of wisdom is intrinsically rewarding leading to "intense experiences [that] are felt to be holistic, ethically compelling, and intrinsically motivating" (p. 40).
- *Wisdom is the integration of apparent opposites.* It comprises emotion and thought, engagement and detachment, action and reflection (Birren and Fisher 1990).

Emergent learning is a process in which these features of practical wisdom are posed as challenges through which we develop these capabilities that, in our world are frequently counter-cultural.

Origin and overview of the emergent learning process

Emergent learning is a process that represents a paradigmatic change from an instrumental perspective toward knowledge and leadership to an embodied mindset consonant with the cultivation of wisdom in the practice of leadership. This leadership capability is not learned through contemplation alone or through the acquisition and discussion of ideas; it is certainly not derived in the abstract from logically deduced conclusions from a set of premises. Wisdom is developed and enhanced through active engagement in the conditions and through the events for which it is actually needed.

Emergent learning is a common pattern of experience over time that was first documented nearly 40 years ago among people in an educational setting that replicated the experience of uncertainty we live in and in which the leader refused the role of a leader with all the answers.[1] The participants who generously provided the original data set that were adult educators in diverse contexts – workplaces, other educational settings, communities. Knowledge and learning were central notions in the work and in their motivation for being learners themselves in this particular setting. They brought a conventional instrumental mindset toward knowledge to graduate education setting. The context for the study was a particular course focused on educational leadership as facilitation in which the teacher enacted that form of leadership by creating an environment for self-direction. She invited students to determine themselves how they wanted to focus their own learning, both individually and collectively; she provided a framework of processes and procedures that supported individual students in planning their learning and engaging the class in determining course activities but stopped short of defining the content and assessment criteria for them. She invited them to be leaders in their own learning. Suddenly, these people were faced with an experience that contradicted instrumental assumptions about knowledge, teaching, and learning. Though they subscribed to the *idea* of self-directed learning, the heart of the matter was that their view that knowledge is some*thing*, an object or commodity that is passed from an authority on that knowledge to them as students, was challenged.

The emergent learning process pattern was derived from a very dense phenomenological data set comprising 13 weekly open-ended interviews with each of eight people, who were simply asked what they had experienced each week, with a comparative inductive case analysis designed to identify common patterns using eight of those cases (Taylor 1979). The pattern described here, then, is an "inside-out" perspective on emergent learning, *a narrative constructed from the standpoint of the learner*. The process consists of four phases linked by four transition points as illustrated in Figure 3.1. The quotations throughout are all drawn from the original data set to illustrate the experience from that inside-out perspective. Since this was not a study of people in positional leadership roles, commentary has been drawn from the literature on comparable leader challenges in each "season" of the process.

The emergent learning process model derives from the patterns that were common to all study participants' descriptions of their experiences. In the following description

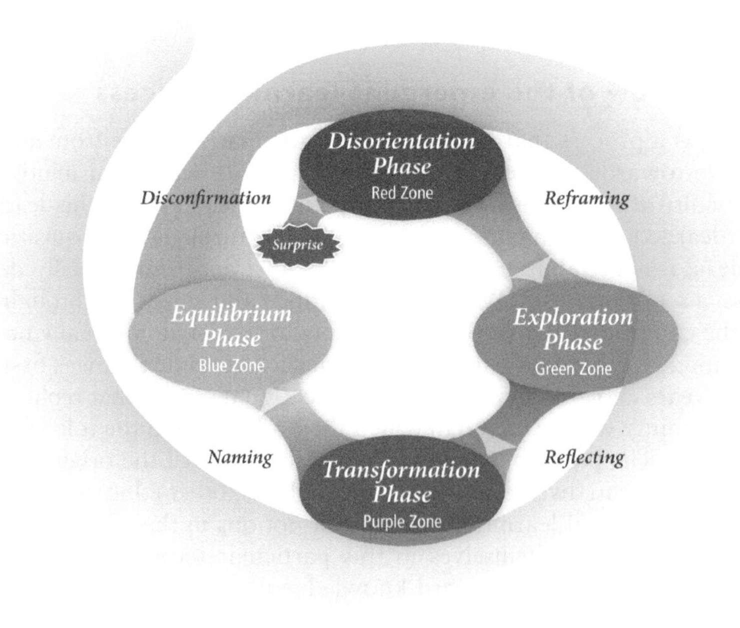

Figure 3.1 Seasons of emergent learning.

these common patterns are described in a subsection entitled "process summary" in each phase and phase transition. It is important to underline that the resulting process pattern was meticulously constructed form the phenomenological descriptions of participants; it was not adapted from any conceptual schema that existed at the time.

Opportunities to cultivate wisdom in the process of emergent learning

Specific moments throughout the emergent learning process provide opportunities to evolve and enhance elements of practical wisdom. Summaries of the defining features of each phase and phase transition are followed by a "wisdom commentary" in each subsection of the process description highlights *what the wisdom-related learning opportunities are at each point in the process.* At the conclusion of the description those elements of wisdom that related to the process as a whole are discussed.

Disconfirmation Transition

Process summary

A university educator stepping out of her conventional role as the origin and *transmitter* of knowledge and the assessor of students" learning, pulled the metaphorical rug out from under their conventional assumptions about knowledge and educational leadership. The familiar student role was not relevant; this was "territory for which their conceptual "maps" were useless. The students felt lost. A typical comment: "It hit to the core of what I believe." Leaders rarely describe their inner experience, especially acknowledge publically their disarray in the face of major unexpected event. Leadership is almost antithetical to the disorder that is associated with the unexpected. Weick and Sutcliffe (2007) observe:

> Organizations often presume that because they have routines to deal with problems, this proves that they understand those problems. ... People tend to look for confirmation that their existing routines are correct. And over time, they come to see more and more confirmation based on fewer and fewer data.
>
> (Chapter 2, Expectations and the search for confirmation, para. 4)

The most challenging cases of the unexpected are those that have implications for the leader's entire approach as a leader. Such an example might be the experience of Ferdinand Piëch, Chairman, and other members of Volkswagen's Supervisory Board, who in September 2015, along with the rest of the world learned that the company had been for six years deliberately deceiving regulators on emissions testing of their diesel vehicles.

Wisdom commentary

We embody unknowing which is likely to be a physical experience, a moment not well understood by those of us who primarily live "in our heads." Referring to a change that is actually happening, Gendlin (1996, 97) defined *felt-shift* as "the body talking back" or as a kind of resonating that occurs when we check with our body about the accuracy of a felt-sense, a carrying forward of the whole, a "symbolic completion" (Gendlin 1964, 10). He regarded bodily felt-sense precedes emotion which implies already an interpretation of the sensation; he spoke of implicit meaning in direct experience that as yet is without conceptual explanation.

Neuroscientific research within the past 25 years has revealed the role of enteric nervous system in the lining of our digestive system – esophagus, stomach, and intestine and colon – in intuitive decision-making. The disconfirming moment launches a process of learning that is completely embodied. To the extent that we may be oblivious or dismissive of physical sensation as signals to us about the significance of our experiences, these moments are opportunities to enhance our awareness and capabilities to expand the range of information sources we have in crucial moments. McKenna et al. (2009) observes: "Wise leaders acknowledge the sensory and visceral as important components of decision-making and judgment" (p. 179). Wise leaders develop sensory literacy.

Disorientation Phase

Process summary

Confusion and anxiety. A significant mismatch between our expectations and what we experience is, by definition, confusion. Not having a conceptual map is both frightening and, in most settings in Western culture, embarrassing. Even in a classroom where people come to learn presumably because they do not yet know, not knowing is seen as unacceptable. One person stated:

> Since I didn't come *armed* with any knowledge, presuppositions, or any assumptions, I was just *there* on my own not knowing what was going on. ... I could feel myself tensing up and getting anxious in a lot of moments.

We become anxious because, in our culture, confusion is not permitted. To the extent that we're embedded in a worldview and mindset that makes no room for not knowing, not being able to name what is going on, having ready answers to problems, we feel vulnerable without answers.

For leaders this experience will be especially intense because we do not hold in high regard leaders who admit to not having answers. Jentz and Murphy (2005) observe that "when faced with disorienting situations most managers deny, hide, or opt for the quick fix, rather than openly acknowledge that they feel confused" (p. 361). They note that there can be a systemic impact from "lost leaders" in denial is that "everyone else learns to hide as well."

Crisis of confidence. We are often unaware of our own dependence on being knowledgeable. In the original study, people blamed themselves for falling short of those expectations. "In some ways it's my own stupidity," exclaimed one person. A diminished sense of self was also generalized to other settings in their lives. These moments draw on every "ounce" of self-esteem we have gathered in ourselves leading up to such a challenge.

Psychological defenses. Left without explanations and ways to rationalize our experience, we frequently invoke other defenses. Intense discomfort and anxiety with our experience of confusion can make us angry and looking for someone to blame for our discomfort. The blame is frequently directed to authorities for their actions or inaction. This pattern is evident in organizational terms when we see someone being forced into taking "the fall" for something. Whatever the circumstances, projection of blame attributing all responsibility to others has two dangerous consequences: it leads to a reduction in the quality of relationships with others and it removes our own capability to act constructively and to learn what we do not yet understand.

Deteriorating relationships. The choice to deny confusion leads down "a slippery slope" of inauthenticity; we become preoccupied with managing our persona. We generally lose our presence with others and our capacity to communicate deteriorates. "I realized I'm in a bad mood; I totally misinterpret what people are feeling and what's going on," one person said. And with our self-confidence sagging, there is the tendency to compete and make comparisons where they show as "better than" or at least not inferior to others.

Negatively focused alliances. Another pattern appearing in this "season" of reaction to a destabilizing surprise is that we can opt to seek relationships with people who are similarly disaffected. In doing so we see uncritical affirmation for our blaming behavior. This pattern has two significantly concerning effects. First, if successful, it can insulate us from what is happening around us. Insulation can lead to isolation. Second, it can create factions that can be institutionalized into long-lasting divisive social structures that limit everyone's possibilities.

An important note is that there are, of course, circumstances when self-protection is necessary. And disconfirming life experiences may well be associated with substantive pain, loss, and sadness. In a leadership context, it may mean employment loss, destruction of what one considers important professional accomplishments, lost opportunities, or lost valued colleagues. The focus here is on patterns of an "inner" fear-based orientation, arising in response to an unexpected experience. The risk of the disorientation experience is that we get stuck in a personally and socially debilitating state of fear that, at very least, limits our individual and collective possibilities and has the potential to become a destructive way of life.

Over years of discussing this experience with people, it has become known as "the Red Zone," season of risk and danger. At the same time, the Disorientation Phase represents an opportunity to reach beyond what has become a limiting perspective. We have to let go of a cherished notion or set of notions in order make room for something radically new. It is to that dimension of the process that we turn next.

Wisdom commentary

The development of practical wisdom begins as we have seen in an experience – a "raw" experience – so new to us that we have no words to describe it, no conceptual framework to "map the territory." Intense emotionality, principally fear and anger, is also preconscious messaging that signals possible threat in an unexpected event. It has the potential of spiraling into deteriorating relationships through blame and deception. The focus in the literature over the past several decades on emotional intelligence can be regarded as expanding the range of leadership and management capabilities to include wisdom-related practices. The emergent learning process underlines emotional literacy as integral to both the development and the practice of wisdom (Statler and Küpers 2008).

It is these challenging experiences also provide the opportunity to appreciate the significance of mindfulness, attention in the moment, in leadership. Wise leadership requires the capability be fully present, self-aware, and contextually conscious. Eckhart Tolle (1999) notes: "To be present in everyday life, it helps to be deeply rooted within yourself, otherwise, the mind, which has incredible momentum, will drag you along like a wild river" (p. 78).

Importantly, few of us can, without fail, avert getting lost and becoming reactive in the midst of crises so a further wisdom-related strength of courage, especially as exemplified in taking responsibility for our behavior and in acting to recover connections with others that have been lost. Palanski et al. (2015) found that behavioral courage is a significant predictor of observers' perceptions of executive leadership performance. Crises provide opportunities to accept responsibility for our misbehaviors in relationship with others and to demonstrate courage to repair any damage that has been caused.

At an organizational level, wise leaders learn to take responsibility in times of crisis and disorientation for accepting the challenge it represents to the organization and the limits of their current knowledge. The operational challenge of managing an organizational disaster, in itself, is not necessarily associated with the development of wisdom. The demand for wisdom and the refinement of wisdom will only evolve if it triggers deep questioning. Picking up from the earlier example, for Piëch or other Board members at Volkswagen, wisdom will only be strengthened by examining their own assumptions and judgment that made a major ethical breech possible "under their watch." In a crisis such as this, as leaders we are plunged into an experience for which we have no ready explanation. "Leaders risk deceit when they seek to tame part of wicked problem for expedience and do not admit that their solutions are limited or that they cannot solve the problem through applying traditional management strategies" (Hutchinson et al. 2015, 3022). Transparency and taking responsibility for unexpected significant events are critical. Bennis et al. (2008) observe, "Transparency and trust are always linked. Without transparency, people don't believe what leaders say" (p. viii). These moments are opportunities for leaders to make big gains or suffer big losses on their credibility that ultimately affects the strength of their influence.

Reframing Transition

Process summary

A critical shift in the unfolding of this process is defined by a re-interpretation of the experience from risk to opportunity, from fear to curiosity, from closed to open, *still without answers*. Each of us in each disconfirming moment has to work from fear to possibility. In the original study there were, however, two elements that participants represented in their commentaries about the experience. One was a positive connection to a person or people, typically an authority identified the source of the disorientation. "I think I was anxious right from the very beginning but talking it over with a couple of other people, I realized I was pleased I was confused about it", said one person. The second defining feature of the transition was a redefinition of "not knowing" from self-as-lacking to self-as-learning; it becomes okay to be without answers. Another's comments underlined the matter of comfort with "not knowing": "I'm strongest when

I show my weakness or when I allow myself not to know. …What I am feeling is *unlocked*. I really feel I have broken out of my chains." The defining features of this transition highlight the *embedded* quality of the process in a social and cultural setting. Connecting with exemplars, representatives, or possibly protagonists of the new and unknown "territory" is, at the same time, a source of stability in uncertainty and a strong indication of their choice to move forward through uncertainty.

Wisdom commentary

The challenge for us in the face of unexpected and significant events is acknowledging and accepting that we didn't know what we didn't know. The added challenge for leaders is acknowledging to their people that they do not have all the answers in the face of a tendency toward fear and projection of blame among others in the midst of change and uncertainty. Both are critical in maintaining personal authenticity and trust by others. Without this acknowledgment, we in a Red Zone state of self-protection and self-preoccupation, a form of at least temporary narcissism in which leaders are focused on defending their own interests and "selling" their own point of view. Greaves et al. (2014) found that leadership that engages others is predicted by only one of five criteria evaluating wisdom used by Baltes and Staudinger (2000), namely, "recognition and management of uncertainty" (p. 335).

While not reported widely in the literature on wisdom, a critical moment in emergent learning is recognition of another person who "knows more than we do" and who, as a credible, trusted other person, affirms us in our state of not knowing. Here we have the opportunity to strengthen our sense of humility. It is a social enactment of acknowledging that we don't know in the presence of a respected person might be expected to know or to be able not to know. We have been considering the challenges of the Red Zone or Disorientation Phase and difficult and risky inner journey of people, particularly leaders as they learn to navigate through this turbulence with wisdom, a metacognitive capability, that enables us to act constructively while in a state of unknowing.

Exploration Phase

Process summary

How do we generate a "map" for a new "territory"? Where do we get new ideas that are nowhere in our current repertoire and, therefore, cannot be logically generated? Where does a completely new understanding come from? There are limited ways in which we can reconfigure our current ideas. The Exploration Phase is an exciting period of excavating insights from the preconscious embodied learning we have been doing to this point in the process. Our relevant knowledge is tacit and unarticulated. As Michael Polanyi (1962) observed, "we can know more than we can tell" (p. 4). Our disorientation arises from an embodied sojourn in a relevant world about which we know little or do not know how to articulate; but it provides us with a raw experience of a new territory.

Relaxation without the answers. A new "season" begins when it is possible to relax with not knowing. "I still don't know what's going to happen [but] … I'm more interested than anxious, more excited than tense," one person observed. We are confident that we will eventually understand and we are satisfied for the moment not to know. This experience is a declaration of the shift from reliance on knowledge alone for self-confidence. With this understanding comes the realization or reminder that safety and ability is not synonymous with having ready answers.

Present-oriented, intuitively guided. Relaxation with an unresolved issue permits a present-oriented focus on our immediate environment. Openness and curiosity create full engagement in what is around us. Rather than have predetermined goals and activities, we gravitate intuitively to people and sources in a sense-making process. Our activity in this phase is not mediated by strategic plans with logically determined outcomes. Rather, we remain open to what evolves one step at a time, "feeling our way" and recognizing relevant conversations and material as we experience them. It is here that we begin to the wisdom practice of *begin with the particular.*

Analogical thinking. Thought and discourse using imagery and metaphor enables us to tap our tacit knowledge and make explicit what we know from experience. Reflecting on her experience, one person commented, "I clicked into being in the middle of things – swimming but not being frightened. A lot of stuff ... isn't quite under control, but it's manageable." Meaning making and creativity are "first cousins"; they draw on the mind in similar ways. Robert Marshak (2009) calls metaphors "the essential bridge between literal and symbolic, between cognition and affect, and between conscious and unconscious" (p. 126). Lakoff and Johnson (1980) and their colleagues at Berkeley have contributed to our appreciation of the significance of metaphor and a surprising new view of the human mind that recognizes that "conceptual knowledge is embodied, that is, it is mapped within our sensory-motor system" (p. 456). Metaphors enable us to bring what we know to consciousness. They further state: "If a new metaphor enters the conceptual system that we base our actions on, it will alter our conceptual system and our perceptions and actions that system gives rise to" (p. 145).

The generative use of ideas. Communications from others, including written resources, are not taken necessarily as definitive answers, but as triggers to meaning-making. This is a subtle but fundamental shift that engages our capability to integrate new ideas with our own thinking. Eleanor Rosch (1999) invites us to a creative use of concepts, "as participating parts of the situation rather than as either representations or as mechanisms for identifying objects" (p. 61).

Collaborative learning and dialogue. Communication and relation patterns consonant with this "season" of experience are dialogue and collaborative exploration of mutual or complementary interests. As with the thoughts of others in the literature, we interact with other people exchanging and developing each other's thinking. In his work on dialogue, Isaacs (2001) in his work on dialogue states, "This kind of exchange entails learning to think and speak together for the creation of breakthrough levels of thought" (p. 38).

Insight episodes. All these features of exploration activity generate a series of different related insights. One person said:

> We got out three or four real 'ah ha's'. ... They hit me as really significant little bits ... that probably don't right now fit together and make a whole but ... little gems of thought that you want to register away.

The process at this point is about generating relevant ways to understand a very new experience, a shared goal of all participants. This discourse configuration matches what David Bohm (2013) has called, dialogue. "

> The object of a dialogue is ... to suspend your opinions and look at the opinions ... to share a common content ... to see what it means .... We can simply share the appreciation of meanings and out of this whole thing, truth *emerges* unannounced ...
>
> (p. 26, emphasis added)

Leaders continue to have two "tracks" in their responsibilities through change. The first track involves a focus on themselves, a searching for understanding of what they have discovered that out-strips their current knowledge. The challenge for leaders is "holding the space" for their own open engagement in inquiry and for open-ended interaction. There will always be the pressure to come up with quick solutions. The second "track" for leaders is that of providing an environment for creative thinking for others in the organization. Such an environment then favors new insights; new ways of seeing that are critical to adaptation and sustainability. Researchers in the leadership and creativity literature offer relevant findings on leaders' vital role in this phase of change. In a literature review on employee creativity, Shalley and Gilson (2004) note that importance of "providing a culture where employees feel psychologically safe such that blame or punishment will not be assigned for new ideas or breaking with the status quo" (p. 44) and "a flatter structure with wider spans of control may be more conducive to employee creativity" (p. 45).

Wisdom commentary

There are profound messages for leaders in the Exploration Phase about human capabilities that have not been regarded as important to learning and leadership. In sharp contrast to strategic thinking we have heuristic thinking – reflection with intention, becoming fully present with others in an open-ended exploration of their "challenge territory." Leaders are challenged to strengthen their intuitive capability now more critical in complex and dynamic contexts.

In organizational terms, leaders are invited to evolve what is usually a cultural innovation, namely, spaces for open-ended, exploratory discussion, social engagement, and dialogue. Implementing these innovations requires courage in an intensively logic-driven Western business culture for immediate results. However, in some organizations, Nonaka and Takeuchi (2011) have identified that wise leaders "constantly create informal as well as formal shared contexts for senior executives and employees to construct new meaning through their interactions" (p. 8). They point to the Japanese concept of *ba* or space, a place of informal interaction where people "talk casually about their immediate concerns or problems, sometimes triggering insights or solutions." Leadership that fosters collaborative inquiry can also shift the organizational culture fundamentally. People are no longer simply employees as conventionally understood, but are directly involved as actors, meaning-makers, and designers of the organization's future. Again, this is another feature of the "season" of exploration that is both an expression of wisdom-related capability and an occasion to develop it.

Michael Polanyi (1962) underlines the importance of a trustworthy social context in the search for fundamentally new knowledge: "No intelligence, however critical or original, can operate outside of such a fiduciary framework ... [that is,] a like-minded community" (p. 266). Long (2002) notes, "the sensation of phrônēsis is never immediate, for it is always mediated by virtue, which is informed by lived experience, and deliberation, which takes time" (p. 51). This emerges through meaningful socially interactive inquiry. In addition to *beginning with the particular,* this season of inquiry provides the opportunities for enhancing our wisdom in its dimensions of *creativity* and *dialogue.*

Reflective Transition

Process summary

There are two possibilities at the close of the Exploration Phase of emergent learning (Taylor 2011). The first is that we are satisfied that our creative insights resolve the issue that precipitated the emergent learning process. This would be second-order learning (Bateson 2000) or double-loop learning (Torbert and Fisher 1992) leading to a *change in the way we do things*. The second alternative is that, if our fundamental assumptions with implication for how we understand ourselves and how we act were found fundamentally inadequate to current experience, the search in the Exploration Phase would have been focused on dialogue with others and symbolic sources that address those more personally and professionally foundational questions. Such an inquiry would lead to Bateson's third-order and Torbert and Fisher's triple-loop learning which involve, not only change in a practical approach, but an "autobiographical awareness" that illuminates *a new perspective on ourselves in the world*, a change in "taken-for-granted purposes, principles, or paradigm" (p. 195). The Reflective Transition marks a withdrawal from social dialogue to significant events of the emergent learning process occurring in solitude.

Reflection that is a critical feature of the Exploration Phase is named here as *primary reflection*, that is, making sense out of a new experience, making the tacit conscious. These insights arise from connecting ideas to direct experience. "I think my head has stopped being blown apart ... I can conceptualize [what] I couldn't have before," observed one person. In the Reflective Transition we are providing the crucible and the conditions for the emergence of a major insight that arises from what is named here as *integrative reflection*. Integrative reflection involves taking a step back from active engagement in the immediate context to understand what the whole experience means. The series of insights from primary reflection provide the springboard to integrative reflection. Again, the initiative to pull back does not result from logical analysis but from a *sense* of completion with the inquiry activity.

Leaders who have engaged in open-ended exploratory discussion with their senior team and employees in search of a solution to an unprecedented challenge may find themselves drawn into solitary reflection as they try to make sense out of the whole experience. Most leaders are not accustomed to giving themselves reflective space, and thus many opportunities to expand their perspective may have been lost. Approaches to leadership coaching that assist leaders to reflect deeply on their experience, their values, and purposes (Lazar and Bergquist 2004; Gunnlaugson and Walker 2014; Whitmore 2009) have undoubtedly assisted in providing a critical reflective space for leaders.

Wisdom commentary

"Whatever else phrönêsis might be, we can safely say that it involves reflection" (Kinsella 2012, 35). In recent decades refined distinctions among forms of reflection have evolved. Building on the work of Schon (1983), Kinsella identifies four domains of reflection on a "continuum of reflection" (p. 36): "intentional reflection," what Schön called "reflection-on-action" in order to improve practice; "embodied reflection," for Schön "knowing-in-action" for the purpose of adaptive sense-making; receptive reflection, "that emerges from receptivity or contemplation" (p. 41); and "reflexivity," critical reflection for "socially informed action." As examined here emergent learning comprises what Kinsella calls "embodied reflection" and "receptive reflection." Both forms have in common their direct connection to experience and personal meaning making; they are distinguished from one another in that the former concerns particulars of the experience and the latter one's place in a context of a fundamentally new experience. This phase transition provides the launch of the key dimension of wisdom as *reflection,* embodied reflexivity, which is the foundation for experience of transformation.

Transformation Phase

Process summary

The Transformation Phase is an extraordinary experience, one that tends to be discussed as rarely in organizational life the depths of confusion in the Disorientation Phase. A defining feature is that a major insight *emerges* suddenly, apparently unbidden, out of a period of deep reflection. It is a time of heightened consciousness in which people describe the capability to simultaneously participate and observe. The *Oxford English Dictionary* definition of "insight" that most closely describes the experience is, "The fact of penetrating with the eyes of the understanding into the inner character or hidden nature of things; a glimpse or view beneath the surface; the faculty or power of thus seeing." Willis (1999, 98) notes that "a receptive stance holds the thinking mind back from closure and returns again and again to behold the object, allowing words and images to emerge from the contemplative engagement."

In the original study described here, the intense nature of the Transformation Phase is best illustrated by selected excerpts of one person's story. Using the analogy of a jigsaw puzzle, she described new pieces "coming in":

> It's not totally active, it's partially passive – partially in the sense I'm letting things in. … I have to be open to them – but I don't try to process them at the moment. … But I let them sit in a passive state somewhere inside me. …It's when I make the connections between them that I get a really big 'ah ha' … I'm broadening my awareness. … All these things started just fell together. I couldn't believe it!

Several weeks later, she described retrospectively the experience as being underwater and being able "to look back up at the light" following:

> If you've looked at the sun from the bottom of some kind of depth, there is a different quality. It's a diffuse, all pervading quality that you don't get when you're on the

> surface of the earth. Then it's more a pin point – darkness and shadows. It's a fully expanding sort of awareness. I don't think I've felt before ... it's a gut level. It's total. It runs from the top of my head and beyond. It almost creates an aura around me. ... It's a way of experiencing learning that I have never experienced before.

Later she spoke of a clear shift of mindset, a paradigmatically new way of seeing the world, associated with her experience.

> My values have changed. My values are [less frequently about] efficiency–getting things done, getting ... totally organized, structured and beautifully arranged [as well as] having exactly the right words to describe it, allowing for no ambiguity. ... And I guess if am honest about it, probably not even listening to people I didn't think of as being smart .... The values that I'm increasingly putting more up front are that these are all people who have ideas and their ideas are very valuable to me. I may not agree with them ... but I want to hear them because, even if I don't agree with them they tell me more about what I do know of myself and how I think, and where I should change or not change.

Later she spoke of how she had come to understand "knowledge" differently:

> I thought of learning in the past in terms of acquisition of knowledge and acquisition of skills. I see it being much broader than that. You get into the whole area of meaning and content, personal meaning ... I used to be a receptacle learner – I spewed it out exactly as it came in. But now it's a more cyclical thing. It's coming in and getting processed in some way that it comes out in a way that is unique to me.

This deeply experienced insight creates a synthesis, a culmination of the inquiry that was precipitated by the knowledge gap experienced at the outset. Others had different stories using different metaphors but all describe what is often called a peak experience. At the end of his career, Maslow (1969) observed in what he called "being cognition" or "B-cognition," features of peak experiences evident in the commentary from the study interview quoted above: "the experience seen as a whole" (p. 74); "a self-validating ... moment that carries its own intrinsic value" (p. 74); "[it] is good and desirable" (p. 81); "[it] is more passive and receptive than active"; and "implies greater openness of perception" (p. 97). More recently, Scharmer (2009) articulated "Theory U," in change processes comparable to that of this participant.[2] Scharmer speaks of "presencing" as a "mode of attention" similar to this Transformation Phase commentary. He describes "I-in-now: what I understand from the source or bottom of my being, that is, from attending with my open will" (p. 11). "It deals with the fundamental happening of letting go and letting come" (p. 41).

Discussion about emotion in reflection on experience has become more acceptable in the workplace over the last 30 years but the intensity of profound insight through experience beyond "normal" consciousness rarely has a place in workplace discussion. On the other hand, values in organizational life and leadership are becoming more focal as values in the wider social context change and as connectivity makes transparency virtually compulsory for leaders especially (Barrett 2014; Mackey and Sisodia 2013;

Sisodia, Wolfe, and Sheth 2007; Linnenluecke and Griffiths 2010; Rogers and Meehan 2007; Schein 2010). We are learning that cultures of organizations are reflections of their leader's values (Schein 2010; Fernández and Hogan 2002; Viinamäki 2012; Dickson et al. 2001; Barrett 2014). Leaders who fortify themselves against their changed and changing environments will foster dysfunction; those who open themselves to fundamental change will experience a pattern of emergent learning in the process as they are challenged to expand their perspective to fully comprehend current dynamic environment.

Again, a prominent innovation in the C-suite that provides space and legitimation for the messy and unconventional inner worlds of leaders is specific forms of coaching oriented to working with people to acknowledge and benefit from the deep and unconventional dynamics of their "inner landscapes." Examples are provided by Gunnlaugson and Walker (2014) who build on the work of Otto Scharmer with "deep presencing." Clarke et al. (2015) note that meditative practices are becoming more prevalent and understood in Western contexts. Gunnlaugson and Walker observe that leaders benefit from learning ways of coming-to-know through stillness as a means for seeing through the past associations and reactions into sensing into what is emerging through the present (p. 132).

Wisdom commentary

An aspect of what McKenna, Rooney, and Boal (2009, 179) see as one of their five criteria of wise leaders is that they "have a metaphysical, even spiritual, quality that does not bind them absolutely to the rules of reason thereby enabling vision, insight and foresight." While we have seen attributes of wisdom distributed throughout the emergent learning process, the depth of insight of the Transformation Phase is almost synonymous with wisdom in scholarly discourse on wisdom, especially the dimension of wisdom – compelling *intensity*. Rosch (1999, 261) observes:

> We are dealing with an entire mode of knowing and of being in the world composed of many interdependent synergistic facets which are simultaneously ways of entering the whole and themselves part of the enlightened awareness itself. These include a relaxation and expansion of awareness, a letting go even into deep states of not knowing, access to wisdom knowing beyond what we think of as consciousness or the mind, and an open hearted inclusive warmth toward all of experience and to the world. It also includes one's deepest intentions toward oneself, other people and the world ...
>
> (p. 261)

Naming Transition

Process summary

The emergent and embodied portion of this learning sequence concludes when we name our new perspective to others who are related in some way to the learning and, therefore, could be expected to understand the discovery and its significance to us. "I didn't know if they'd understand what I was going to say but they got it very well.

People understood where I was coming from," said one person. There are some parallels to be drawn to the transition out of the Red Zone. Both were movements into contact with people after a withdrawn and emotionally intense period and both involved a form of affirmation. The difference is that while the Reframing Transition involves an affirmation of the person, the Naming Transition is about an affirmation of the new perspective. An indication of that this transition point is essential in this process is that in the absence of such relevant colleagues, there was not a sense of closure. By naming the new perspective we are simultaneously developing a way to conceptualize the major insight and its significance. This highlights the centrality of language in thought and the critical social dimension in perspective shift, that of confirming the intelligibility and interest of significant others.

Wisdom commentary

It is important to recognize that a mindset shift amounts to entering a different values perspective. In this case, movement from the centrality of knowledge to practical wisdom in the practice of leadership.

With that shift in values perspective is "membership" in a different circle of interpretation, a different community of shared understanding. The Naming Transition reflects the significance of the social context of practical wisdom. Practical wisdom is situated, embedded community of interpretation; it has relevance in a particular social values context. The capability of the wise leader here is to recognize their necessary community relevant to a new perspective.

Equilibrium Phase

From a period of intense learning, we return to a season of experience that we recognize as ordinary, the everyday world where we have practical goals and responsibilities, and we negotiate the world knowledgeably. We engage the world with an expanded perspective that enables us to relate to the unexpected with a different set of assumptions that enables us to engage a dynamic context more fluidly. While there is high interest in elaborating what this means and relating it to practice, the Equilibrium Phase is less about learning "per se"; it is more about knowing and doing. Having conceptualized the experience, it is possible to proceed more logically, linking plans to explicit goals. One person noted, "Before it was more exploratory, far more open, far more experimental, more interior, relying on my subjective experience than now which is more in my head than my gut." In the workplace takes the form of strategic thinking and planning, conceptualizing a framework for action with goals and priorities. It contrasts in every way from emergent processes. We act primarily independently with preconceived purposes. The one challenge of the learning process at this point is what Scharmer (2007) calls for, that is, keeping "head, heart, and hands" (p. 205) in the action but it is about action beginning with "prototyping and performance." This is a complex matter since it involves integrating apparent opposites. It is a matter of remaining open to the unexpected while focusing strategically on meeting stated goals; it involves relating to people for specific stated purposes without reducing the recognition of them as whole people not functionaries. It means committing to a program of action while acknowledging uncertainty.

Wisdom commentary

Some of conceptions of wisdom that align with this season of human experience are those that highlight capabilities and dispositions that have been established by a leader. For Baltes and Staudinger (2000, 123) wisdom as accomplishment reflected in practice comprises the following:

> an exceptional level of human functioning; ... a state of mind and behavior that includes the coordinated and balanced interplay of intellectual, affective, and motivational aspects of human functioning; a high degree of personal and interpersonal competence, including the ability to listen, evaluate, and to give advice; and used for the well-being of oneself and others.

The transformational journey generates a fundamentally new perspective, a new horizon from which to understand the world. Inherent in that new perspective is shift in focus of attention, what is privileged, what is valued. This is significant in two ways. First, it makes values visible in contrast with those held tacitly in the past. Values, what is really most important, can become explicit in conversation, and authentically integrated in deliberation, planning and decision-making. Values can become more than a brand abstraction. The wise leader can, in contextualizing organizational conversations in values, inspire and foster alignment toward a common goal more powerfully. It is only when leaders understand their own values that they can effectively lead culture change in their organizations. Second, since a new perspective brings a "values divide" in relation to those whose experience is conventional, leaders are challenged, not only to articulate their own values but to identify their differences from others, and to hold those differences as a reality in the workplace. Wise leaders are able to "hear" others" values embedded and reflected in their discourse, and to respect and work with those differences. Wise leaders exemplify values fluency.

The emergent learning process: A holistic perspective of wisdom

The emergent learning process is offered as a helical pattern, as *successive iterations* of the phases in the human experience of learning (Figure 3.2). It is suggested that the seasons of experience recur in this particular sequence, though undoubtedly unfolds somewhat differently for different people in different contexts. The four seasons configure as complementarities – divergence and convergence, engagement and detachment, analytical and analogical, open-ended exploration and goal-directed, collaborative and independent. This complex representation of learning aligns with perspectives on wisdom as dynamic and dialectical – not a state but process comprising complementarities. Central in the literature on wisdom are the themes of balance and dialectic. Gisela Labouvie-Vief (1990, 76) provides an example:

> Wisdom cannot imply a mere return to *mythos* but requires that the individual hold the paradoxical tension of thought being both immanent and transcendent. It is out of that tension that the notion of reflective intelligence needs to be more thoroughly integrated in a theory of organic life ...
>
> (pp. 76, 77)

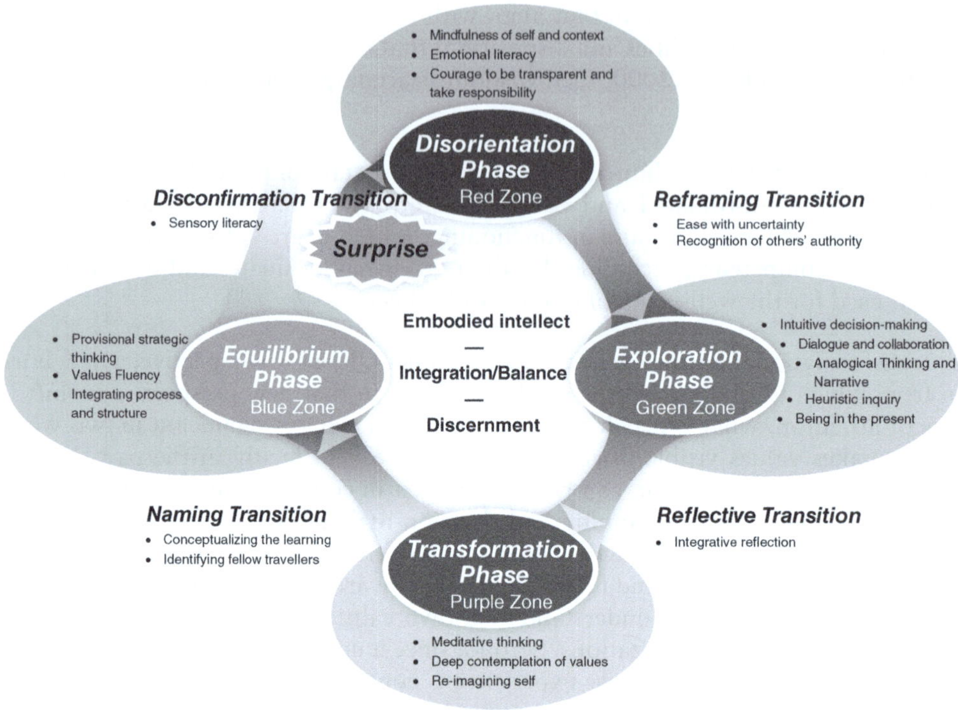

Figure 3.2 Wisdom development opportunities in emergent learning.

Finally, in an unpredictable environment we must infuse decisions with wisdom. Decision-making in the absence of incontrovertible evidence becomes a process of discernment described by Traüffer et al. (2010):

> Discernment, as a decision making process, is a significantly more involving kind of approach to decision making for the leader. It does not rely on precedents, best practices, or benchmarking. Neither does it mean to rely on sweaty palms and gut instincts; for, to do so is to be naïve. It is *to understand the self and organization in a holistic way*, inviting constant self-evaluation and adjustments in order to make good judgments that serve the greater whole.
>
> (Italics added)

Conclusion

This chapter has provided a narrative of a form of learning that develops and enhances capabilities for wise leadership. It is a process that in every way aligns with the precepts of practical wisdom, including that Aristotelian precept that it is in action that we learn. The process considered from the "inside out" perspective highlights moments in a common human experience, successful navigation of which, exemplify the six key dimensions of practical wisdom from the scholarship on wisdom. These moments are simultaneously sites for learning each of these dimensions of wisdom. As such, they offer insight into how wisdom might be not only practiced, but developed, in organizational life. The process model provides a guide for learning toward wisdom in everyday life that reminds us, practical wisdom cannot be taught, but is learned in experience and in action.

Notes

1 The emergent learning process model resulted from an inductive study of learners' weekly reports of their experiences in a course entitled, "Basic Processes of Facilitating Adult Learning," offered in the fall of 1976 in the Department of Adult Education at the Ontario Institute for Studies in Education at the University of Toronto. The course was instructed by Dr. Virginia Griffin. Learners were doctoral and master's students, all midcareer professionals – educators, social workers, librarians, dieticians, public servants, and consultants. Data were gathered in individual minimally structured weekly tape-recorded interviews weekly around their experiences in relation to the course. As descriptions were minimally structure by the interviewer, the data are phenomenological in nature – a chronological set of descriptions from the perspectives of the study participants. The result was 1,600 pages of single-spaced typed transcripts which were studied inductively for 18 months to identify common patterns across the records of participants. The outcome of that work was a dissertation (Taylor 1979) describing a model of learning summarized in this chapter.

2 For a full comparison of the two process representations, see Taylor (2011, 87–120) "Chapter Four: Converging perspectives."

References

Alvesson, Mats, and André Spicer. 2012. "A stupidity-based theory of organizations." *Journal of Management Studies* 49 (7):1194–1220. doi: 10.1111/j.1467-6486.2012.01072.x.

Baltes, Paul B., and Ursula M. Staudinger. 2000. "Wisdom: A metaheuristic (pragmatic) to orchestrate mind and virtue toward excellence." *American Psychologist* 55 (1):122–136. doi: 10.1037/0003-066X.55.1.122.

Barrett, Richard. 2014. *The values driven organization: Unleashing human potential for performance and profit*. New York: Routledge.

Bateson, Gregory. 2000. *Steps to an ecology of mind*. Chicago: University of Chicago Press.

Bennis, Warren G., Daniel Goleman, and James O'Toole. 2008. *Transparency: How leaders create a culture of candor*, Vol. 1. San Francisco, CA: Jossey-Bass.

Bereiter, Carl, and Marlene Scardamalia. 2005. "Beyond Bloom's *Taxonomy*: Rethinking knowledge for the knowledge age." In *Fundamental change: International handbook of educational change,* edited by Michael Fullan, 5–22. Dordrecht: Springer.

Birren, J. E., and Fisher, L. M. 1990. "The elements of wisdom: Overview and integration." In R. J. Sternberg (Ed.), *Wisdom: Its nature, origins, and development* (pp. 317–332). Cambridge, UK: Cambridge University Press.

Bohm, David. 2013. *On Dialogue*. London: Routledge.

Clarke, T., L. Black, B. Stussman, P. Barnes, and R. Nahin. 2015. *Trends in the use of complementary health approaches among adults: United States, 2002–2012*. Hyattsville, MD: National Center for Health Statistics.

Csikszentmihályi, M., and R. Rathmunde. 1990. "The psychology of wisdom: An evolutionary approach." In *Wisdom: Its nature, origins and development*, edited by R. Sternberg, 25–51. New York: Cambridge University Press.

David Peat, F. 2007. "From certainty to uncertainty: Thought, theory and action in a postmodern world." *Futures* 39 (8):920–929. doi: 10.1016/j.futures.2007.03.007.

Dickson, Marcus W., D. Brent Smith, Michael W. Grojean, and Mark Ehrhart. 2001. "An organizational climate regarding ethics: The outcome of leader values and the practices that reflect them." *Leadership Quarterly* 12 (2):197.

Edelman, Richard. 2015. 2015 Edelman Trust Barometer. http://www.edelman.com/insights/intellectual-property/2015-edelman-trust-barometer/ (Accessed Feb 28, 2016).

Fernández, Jorge E., and Robert T. Hogan. 2002. "Values-based leadership." *Journal for Quality and Participation* 25 (4):25.

Flyvbjerg, Bent. 2004. "Phronetic planning research: Theoretical and methodological reflections." *Planning Theory & Practice* 5 (3):283–306. doi: 10.1080/1464935042000250195.

Gendlin, E. 1964. "A theory of personality change." In *Personality change*, edited by P. Byrne and D. Worschel, 100–148. New York: John Wiley & Sons.

Gendlin, E. 1996. *Focusing-oriented psychotherapy*. New York: Guilford.

Greaves, Claire E., Hannes Zacher, Bernard McKenna, and David Rooney. 2014. "Wisdom and narcissism as predictors of transformational leadership." *Leadership & Organization Development Journal* 35 (4):335–358. doi: 10.1108/LODJ-07-2012-0092.

Gunnlaugson, Olen, and William Walker. 2014. "Deep presencing leadership coaching: Building capacity for sensing, enacting, and embodying emerging selves and futures in the face of organizational crisis." In *Perspectives on Theory U: Insights from the field*, edited by Olen Gunnlaugson, Charles Baron and Mario Cayer. Hershey, PA: IGI Global.

Hutchinson, Marie, John Daly, Kim Usher, and Debra Jackson. 2015. "Editorial: Leadership when there are no easy answers: Applying leader moral courage to wicked problems." *Journal of Clinical Nursing* 24 (21–22):3021–3023. doi: 10.1111/jocn.12968.

IBM. 2006. The toxic terabyte. Accessed February 25, 2016.

Isaacs, William. 2001. "Toward an action theory of dialogue." *International Journal of Public Administration* 24 (7):709–748. doi: 10.1081/PAD-100104771.

Jentz, Barry C., and Jerome T. Murphy. 2005. "Embracing confusion: What leaders do when they don't know what to do." *The Phi Delta Kappan* 86 (5):358–366. doi: 10.2307/20441787.

Kinsella, Elizabeth Anne. 2012. "Practitioner reflection and judgment as phronesis." In *Phronesis as professional knowledge: Practical wisdom in the professions*, edited by Elizabeth Anne Kinsella and Allan Pitman, 35–52. Rotterdam: Sense.

Küpers, Wendelin. 2013. "The art of practical wisdom – phenomenology of an embodied, wise inter-practice in organisation and leadership." In *A handbook of practical wisdom: Leadership, organization and integral business practice*, edited by Wendelin Küpers and David Pauleen, 19–45. Ashgate, UK: Gower.

Labouvie-Vief, Gisela. 1990. "Wisdom as integrated thought: Historical and developmental perspectives." In *Wisdom: Its nature, origins, and development*, edited by R. Sternberg, 52–79. New York: Cambridge University Press.

Lakoff, George, and Mark Johnson. 1980. *Metaphors we live by*. Chicago: University of Chicago Press.

Lazar, John, and William Bergquist. 2004. "Alignment coaching [a broader perspective on business coaching]." *Performance Improvement* 43 (10):16–22. doi: 10.1002/pfi.4140431006.

Linnenluecke, Martina K., and Andrew Griffiths. 2010. "Corporate sustainability and organizational culture." *Journal of World Business* 45 (4):357–366. doi: http://dx.doi.org/10.1016/j.jwb.2009.08.006.

Long, Christopher P. 2002. "The ontological reappropriation of phronēsis." *Continental Philosophy Review* 35 (1):35–60. doi: 10.1023/A:1015180421385.

Mackey, John and Raj Sisodia. 2013. *Conscious capitalism: Liberating the heroic spirit of business*. Boston, MA: Harvard Business School Press.

Marshak, Robert J. 2009. *Organizational change: Views from the edge*. Bethel, ME: The Lewin Centre.

Maslow, Abraham H. 1969. "Toward a psychology of being. 1968 (second edition)." *Journal of Extension* 7 (2):124.

McKenna, Bernard, David Rooney, and Kimberley B. Boal. 2009. "Wisdom principles as a meta-theoretical basis for evaluating leadership." *The Leadership Quarterly* 20 (2):177–190. doi: http://dx.doi.org/10.1016/j.leaqua.2009.01.013.

Nonaka, Ikujiro, and Hirotaka Takeuchi. 2011. "The wise leader." *Harvard Business Review*, May.

Palanski, Michael E., Kristin L. Cullen, William A. Gentry, and Chelsea M. Nichols. 2015. "Virtuous leadership: Exploring the effects of leader courage and behavioral integrity on leader performance and image." *Journal of Business Ethics* 132 (2):297–310. doi: 10.1007/s10551-014-2317-2.

Polanyi, Michael. 1962. "Tacit knowing." *Philosophy Today* 6 (4):239.

Rogers, Paul, and Paul Meehan. 2007. "Building a winning culture." *Business Strategy Series* 8 (4):254–261. doi: doi:10.1108/17515630710684420.

Rosch, Eleanor. 1999. "Reclaiming concepts." *Journal of Consciousness Studies* 6 (11–12):61–77.

Scharmer, C. Otto. 2007. *Theory U: Leading from the future as it emerges: The social technology of presencing*. Cambridge, MA: Society for Organizational Learning.

Scharmer, C. Otto. 2009. *Theory U: Learning from the future as it emerges*. San Francisco, CA: Berrett-Koehler Publishers.

Schein, Edgar H. 2010. *Organizational culture and leadership*, fourth edition. San Francisco, CA: Jossey-Bass.

Schon, Donald A. 1983. *The reflective practitioner: How professionals think in action*. New York: Basic Books.

Shalley, Christina E., and Lucy L. Gilson. 2004. "What leaders need to know: A review of social and contextual factors that can foster or hinder creativity." *The Leadership Quarterly* 15 (1):33–53. doi: 10.1016/j.leaqua.2003.12.004.

Shilling, David Russell. 2013. "Knowledge doubling every 12 months, soon to be every 12 hours." Industry Tap into News. Accessed February 25. www.industrytap.com/3950/brainbow_cerebellum.

Sisodia, Rajendra, David B. Wolfe, and Jagdish N. Sheth. 2007. *Firms of endearment: How world-class companies profit from passion and purpose*. Upper Saddle River, NJ: Wharton School Publishing.

Statler, Matt, and Wendelin Küpers. 2008. "Practically wise leadership: Toward an integral understanding." *Culture and Organization* 14 (4):379–400. doi: 10.1080/14759550802489771.

Sternberg, R.. 1990. "Wisdom and its relation to intelligence and creativity." In *Wisdom: Its nature, origins and development*, edited by R. Sternberg. New York: Cambridge University Press.

Taylor, Marilyn M. 1979. *Adult learning in an emergent learning group: Toward a theory of learning from the learner's perspective*. Toronto, ON: University of Toronto.

Taylor, Marilyn M. 2011. *Emergent learning for wisdom*, Vol. 1. New York: Palgrave Macmillan.

Tolle, Eckhart. 1999. *The power of NOW: A guide to enlightenment*. Novato, CA: New World Library.

Torbert, William, and Dalmar Fisher. 1992. "Autobiographical awareness as a catalyst for managerial and organisational development." *Management Education and Development* 23 (3):184.

Traüffer, Hazel C. V., Corné Bekker, Mihai Bocârnea, and Bruce E. Winston. 2010. "Towards an understanding of discernment: A conceptual paper." *Leadership & Organization Development Journal* 31 (2):176–184. doi: 10.1108/01437731011024411.

Viinamäki, Olli-Pekka. 2012. "Why leaders fail in introducing values-based leadership? An elaboration of feasible steps, challenges, and suggestions for practitioners." *International Journal of Business and Management* 7 (9):28. doi: 10.5539/ijbm.v7n9p28.

Wall, John. 2003. "Phronesis, poetics, and moral creativity." *Ethical Theory and Moral Practice* 6 (3):317–341. doi: 10.1023/A:1026063925726.

Weick, Karl E., and Kathleen M. Sutcliffe. 2007. *Managing the unexpected: Resilient performance in an age of uncertainty*, Vol. 2. San Francisco, CA: Jossey-Bass.

Whitmore, John. 2009. *Coaching for performance: GROWing human potential and purpose: The principles and practice of coaching and leadership*, Vol. 4. London: Nicholas Brealey Publishing.

Willis, Peter. 1999. "Looking for what it's really like: Phenomenology in reflective practice." *Studies in Continuing Education* 21 (1):91–112. doi: 10.1080/0158037990210106.

Chapter 4

The seven pillars of paradoxical organizational wisdom[1]

On the use of paradox as a vehicle to synthesize knowledge and ignorance

Filipa Rocha Rodrigues, Miguel Pina e Cunha, Arménio Rego and Stewart Clegg

> Wisdom is the principal thing; therefore get wisdom: and with all thy getting get understanding.
>
> (*Proverbs*, IV, 7)

> Wisdom hath builded her house, she hath hewn out her seven pillars.
>
> (*Proverbs*, IX,1)

> O God, grant us the serenity to accept what cannot be changed. The courage to change what can be changed. And the wisdom to know the difference.
>
> (Reinhold Niebuhr (1892–1971), in Eatock 2009, p. 49)

Introduction

A recent report of Saïd Business School and Heidrick & Struggles (2015) stated, "Faced with competing, yet equally valid, stakeholder demands, CEOs increasingly face paradoxical situations of choosing between 'right ... and right'" (p. 3; bold in the original). The report, whose findings come from interviews with more than 150 CEOs, defends the thesis that "CEOs must constantly balance between personal and organizational paradoxes. Today this is a 'given' of the role. The way CEOs balance their personal paradoxes in the decision making process greatly influences the organization's confidence in their decisions" (p. 25). It has long been a truism that "a first-rate intelligence" can be measured by the ability to hold two opposed ideas simultaneously and maintain functional capacity, ever since F. Scott Fitzgerald (1945) first coined his memorable phrase in *The Crack-up*. In terms of Fitzgerald's maxim, one way that first-rate managers can embrace contradiction is by attending to and appreciating contradiction not as "a signal of defeat but rather the very lifeblood of human life" (Chia & Holt, 2007, p. 512) because of the puzzles it poses to ingenuity. Such an embrace can empower a sense of organizational direction (Chia, 2010; Smith & Lewis, 2011) and facilitate the struggle to thrive in the face of ambiguity, while avoiding preventable errors (Giustiniano, Cunha, & Clegg, 2016). In short, first-rate managers should be able to manage contradiction and draw insights from them (Farjoun, 2016). As Kessler and Bailey (2007, p.lxx) pointed out:

> the seeker and practitioner of OMW [organizational and managerial wisdom] must simultaneously be a realist and an idealist, demonstrating a resilient flexibility (to engage wisdoms) while at the same time exhibiting a broad-mindedness and integrative – perhaps visionary – quality (in pursuing Wisdom).

Different authors have defined wisdom in various ways in management and organization studies. In an influential definition, Kessler and Bailey (2007, p. lxvii) denote it as "the application to professional pursuits of a deep understanding and fundamental capacity for living well." More recently, van Dierendonck and Patterson (2015) noted that (p. 123), although "an exact definition of wisdom is difficult to give," wisdom is usually related to "people who can bridge contradictions" holistically. Ashforth, Rogers, Pratt, and Pradies (2014, p. 1465) also argued that wisdom is the "capacity, in part, to simultaneously acknowledge and embrace opposing orientations, and thereby strive for a course of action that honors both."

The pursuit of organizational and managerial wisdom requires cognitive and behavioral capabilities that most organizations focused on the repetition of routines as the hallmark of efficiency rarely cultivate, capabilities that prioritize judgment rather than rules, despite paradoxical circumstances. Contradictions contribute to the cultivation of wisdom by forcing creative forms of sense-making (Smith & Lewis, 2011), rather than rote application of rules and routines. Inspired by Meacham (1990) and Weick (2007), we extend this reasoning and suggest that paradox can serve to nurture wisdom when used to cultivate a holistic and synthetic relationship between knowledge and ignorance. Weick (2007) associated wisdom with dynamic balancing and synthesis, defending the thesis that wisdom entails the balancing of knowledge and ignorance as an orientation. Paradoxical wisdom is thus the cultivated capacity to use organizational contradictions as sources of good judgment, entailing an appreciation of the duality of knowledge and ignorance.

"Wise scholars," we assume, "should seek to be complexity enhancers" (Pitsis & Clegg, 2007, p. 419). There is a common understanding that wisdom has an important role in management and leadership (Melé, 2010; Nonaka & Takeuchi, 2011; Rego, Cunha, & Clegg, 2012; Small, 2004; Vay, Fleenor, Atwater, Sturm, & McKee, 2014). Moreover, being a manager and aspiring to lead means being confronted by paradoxes. Perhaps Shakespeare's (1998) *Hamlet* first articulated the most famous and classical paradox that managers and leaders frequently confront: the necessity to be cruel and to be kind in the right measure (with acknowledgment of Gomm and Lowe's (1979) appropriation of Hamlet's famous phrase from Act 3, Scene 4). For instance, in the long term, cutting head count now may be kinder for those that remain, as might sacrificing shareholder value for investment in terms of generating sustainable yields. These are examples of wisdom being cultivated through articulating, moving between or synthesizing the poles of paradox in a positive and reinvigorating way.

We organize the chapter in four sections. The first section explores the idea that complex times require complex management, in which wisdom prevails. We introduce the concept of paradoxical wisdom as a way of articulating organizational polarities that align with an Aristotelian virtuous golden mean in a duality (Farjoun, 2010). The next section exposes various approaches to paradox and their implications. It discusses how wisdom displays a central role in the management of paradox and how paradox sustains wisdom. We argue that paradox requires an attitude of flux rather than rigidity between forces that may be contradictory themselves. We finally suggest that paradoxical wisdom may be diffused within organizations via the cultivation of seven pillars of paradoxical wisdom.

Complex times, complex management

Organizing is rich in contradiction, paradox, and ambivalence (Ashforth et al., 2014). The paradoxical lens offers a rich window on the organizational world (Bouchikhi, 1998; Clegg, Cunha, & Cunha, 2002; Farjoun, 2016; Smith & Lewis, 2011). The notion that excellence in management derives from an organization's ability to manage paradox in an integrative way, applying "both/and" solutions, rather than solving tensions through "either/or" approaches, is gaining momentum (Lewis et al., 2014). Paradox refers to the "contradictory yet interrelated elements that exist simultaneously and persist over time" (Smith & Lewis, 2011, p. 382). Paradox is a constitutive feature of organizations, resulting from their essential nature as complex autopoietic systems that generate contradiction as they respond to the challenges resulting from their activity (De Wit & Meyer, 2010). Three main arguments support this observation. First, organizations must respond to different demands from coalitions of multiple and potentially contradictory interests (Küpers & Pauleen, 2013; Saïd Business School & Heidrick & Struggles, 2015). Second, the act of managing *per se*, by responding to fundamental questions, creates boundaries that foster specific tension. By defining what to do, managers define what not to do, creating *performative* tensions between, for instance, the global versus the local, or efficiency versus innovation. By defining how to operate, they trigger *organizing* tensions, such as decentralized versus centralized designs; when defining who does what, *belonging* tensions emerge, such as sharing power versus expressing authority, reflecting contradictions of identity, roles, and values. Finally, as they consider the period of time in which the action takes place, they face tensions between present and future in *learning* from differences that unfold as cognition apprehends the familiar anew and confronts novelty (Smith & Lewis, 2011). Third, management actions produce unanticipated consequences that sometimes reveal themselves to be diametrically opposed to the intended objectives (De Wit & Meyer, 2010), creating new tensions that were not planned or predicted in advance (Clegg et al., 2002).

It is not only that organizations are complex but, increasingly, so are their environments, characterized by instability, volatility, and disruptive change, all of which accentuate the potentiality for paradox, rendering contradictions more salient and persistent (Küpers & Pauleen, 2013; Smith & Lewis, 2011). Consequently, traditional decision-making processes, designed to reduce uncertainty (Tsoukas, 2005) have become inadequate, as decisions must be taken in the face of uncertainty in such dynamic environments (Rowley & Gibbs, 2008; Sull & Eisenhardt, 2015). Traditional decision-making is supported by *probability*, which evaluates outcomes that are finite and expected, whereas *possibility* acknowledges inherent uncertainty, implying not only risk but also opportunity (Stamp, Burridge, & Thomas, 2007). Thus, managing *possibility* rather than *probability* may be increasingly relevant (Hays, 2008; Rowley & Gibbs, 2008). In addition, managers must face uncertainty and complexity ethically; the recent management scandals express the need for virtue-informed behaviors (Rego et al., 2012).

Organizational theorists in current times have started to rediscover and explore the role of *phronesis,* often translated as prudence, practical wisdom, practical intelligence, common sense, or judgment (Flyvbjerg 2006; Bourantas, 2008; Shotter & Tsoukas, 2014). Aristotle distinguished between three types of knowledge: *episteme*, *techne*, and *phronesis*. *Episteme* refers to universal truth, context-independent, and explicit forms of knowledge. *Techne* corresponds to technique, to context-dependent know-how that assumes the shape of practical tacit knowledge. *Phronesis* is the ability to determine and undertake the best action in a specific unknown situation to serve the common good. It is the result of blending knowledge (*episteme*) with experience (*techne*), and adding intuition and character to it. Wisdom is thus a kind of knowledge "beyond knowledge" (Goede, 2011) that results from a deep engagement with lived experience, which comprehends confronting challenging situations and uncertainty in order to act for the common good. These experiences, handled appropriately, assist in "the getting of wisdom" (Richardson, 1910; Izak, 2013). Because it contemplates decisions based on values and judgments, it can be facilitative of a virtuous circle (Flyvbjerg, 2006; Stamp et al., 2007).

The deep relationship between paradoxes and practical wisdom is thus rendered salient, since in moments of "irreducible uncertainty" it is critical to correctly evaluate "complex interdependencies," and to be decisive as others prevaricate (Stamp et al., 2007). Nonaka and Takeuchi (2011) state that knowledge, either tacit or explicit, is not enough but must be enriched with experience, intuition, and the intuitive art of "reading between the lines" upon which interpretation one must act wisely, when dealing with complex rather than merely complicated problems (Stamp et al., 2007). The increasing pressure to meet multiple, often inconsistent demands, raises questions about competitive advantage and sustainability (De Wit & Meyer, 2010). Unsurprisingly, organizations may succeed or fail based on their capabilities to articulate contradictions in a fruitful way (Lado et al., 2006). Organizing and leading with paradox necessarily constitutes an exercise in reflection, knowledge, and action, components of *phronesis*. It can be deducted that it has never been so important to have the ability to articulate the poles of a paradox in an integrative way, generating change for the common good – defined as *paradoxical wisdom*.

Wisdom and paradox

Early theories mainly focused on management in terms of "one best ways," precluding alternative best ways (*A* or *B*). Recent theorizing instead assumes that tensions persist when organizations find some "best way" and that contradictions will ultimately resurface. Hence the need to ask emerges: "how and when to deploy solutions *A* and *B* simultaneously?" Paradox was introduced as a framework to deal with the inherent complexity of organizational life (Cameron & Quinn, 1988). The way organizations approach contradiction defines the build-up of dependences that ultimately push them in the direction of either more virtuous or more vicious circles (Cunha & Tsoukas, 2015; Smith & Lewis, 2011). The capacity of leadership to handle contradictions or conflicting demands *wisely* is key but, before handling ambiguity, contradictions must be appreciated in themselves: they require managers with a "first rate intelligence." If approached as dilemmas, i.e. as competing choices, *A* and *B*, that can be weighed on scales, each with its pros and cons, there may be the tendency to select one pole or the other, losing the potential of their integration in a duality. Rather, in a paradox, contradictions are seen as interdependent, since one pole cannot exist without the other. For example, confidence and doubt, and acting as if one knows while one does not know (Ashford et al., 2014) may be necessary to honor the complexities of the environment and to make better, more timely and informed (i.e., wiser) decisions (see the section "The power of doubt: Finding comfort in discomfort," in Saïd Business School & Heidrick & Struggles, 2015). Paradoxes are often graphically depicted with the Taoist symbol of *ying* and *yang*, which describes how opposite or contrary forces are complementary, interconnected, and interdependent. Cameron and Quinn (1988) explained that while dilemmas can be approached via "either/or" mindsets, paradoxes require richer forms of articulation: the two contradictory notions must work together, craving for some "both/and" strategy. It is when "dilemmas abound with black and white solutions giving way to varying shades of grey" that *phronesis* is most necessary (Stamp et al., 2007, p. 483). The ability to see the paradox in a dilemma, i.e., the "connecting of the dots" between the poles, and searching for "both/and" solutions, involves one in the embrace of paradoxical wisdom.

The tackling of opposites can trigger a number of reactions: arrogance, paralysis, or inertia may be as likely as wisdom in certain circumstances. For instance, when dualisms create emotional anxiety, individuals activate defense mechanisms to avoid inconsistencies (Vince & Broussine, 1996). Organizational members can revise their beliefs or actions to enable integrative responses (Cialdini et al., 1995) or remain stuck in beliefs or behaviors in order to maintain past–future consistency (Weick, 1993). They can adopt a "ready-fire" strategy, selecting one pole and avoiding reflection. Additionally, an attitude of overconfidence or arrogance or inertia may be fatal because they prevent learning, precipitating vicious circles (Sundaramurthy & Lewis, 2003), in which one pole dominates and overrides the other. Vicious circles are reinforced by the increasing focus on one choice while the other is ignored, and the "right" pole is selected. An organization can emphasize systematization *over* creation, power *over* empowerment, stability *over* change – or vice-versa. Enron, for example, offers a salient example of a company in which "performance was stressed over ethics" (Smith & Lewis, 2011, p. 391). Contradictions may be managed via separation in time, space, or work roles. Temporal separation occurs when choosing one pole of a tension at one point in time and then switching. Spatial separation allocates opposing forces across different organizational units (Poole & Van de Ven, 1989). Role separation arises when members of one system split their behaviors in such a way that some members focus on one pole while other members consider the other, in the same space and time. The goal is to increase focus without risking crystallization (Clegg & Cunha, forthcoming).

In any of the previous approaches the attempt to resolve the paradox in a way that may not be sustainable in the long run can prevail. First, because a paradox is made of two forces, where one dominates, sooner or later the dominated pole will resurface. Second, since organizational life is inherently paradoxical, paradox is often better sustained as tension, framing managing rather than being dissolved. When considering a paradox (not a dilemma; see Küpers, 2013), the two poles are seen as interdependent and since they depend on each other, approaches to tension could consist in the integration of the poles. Furthermore, the tension is considered as the source of dynamism rather than conflict: contradiction is a necessity, not an obstacle, for knowledge creation (Nonaka & Toyama, 2002). The organization, in summary, sustains paradox instead of flattening contradiction. Toyota's success has been partly attributed to the company's capacity to create and sustain paradoxes as sources of learning (Takeuchi, Osono, & Shimuzu, 2008). Toyota's employees are mandated to challenge the status quo constantly and to accumulate *chie*. *Chie* consists in challenging the *status quo*, while simultaneously maintaining stability, coming up with innovative solutions while mastering efficiency. The need for stability to optimize efficiency is fueled by the need for innovation (Takeuchi et al., 2008).

Another example of integration can be found in Ferràn Adriá's explanation of the reason behind the success of his radical reinterpretation of *haute cuisine*: "I love anarchy but you need efficiency to be anarchic" (Knott, 2014). Steve Jobs was deemed to be both humble and narcissistic (Owens, Walker, & Waldman, 2015) as a "tempered narcissist." Abraham Lincoln was also described as paradoxically integrative (Brooks, 2015), "deeply engaged" but "able to step back"; "passionate" while able to see opposing points of view; "aware of his own power, but aware of when he was helpless in the hands of fate; extremely self-confident but extremely humble" (see also Goodwin, 2005).

Additional organizations can be premised on the paradoxical gaining of wisdom: Zara, the fast fashion company, "democratized" style via an innovative business model that integrated cost discipline *and* sophisticated design, changing the way companies operate in the industry. Harvey (2014) explained that a consistent pattern of "breakthroughs" at Pixar resulted not from a process of generating divergent perspectives, but from the integration of multiple perspectives under a shared goal. While competitiveness depends significantly on the ability to innovate, at the heart of innovative problem solving is the need continually to recalibrate between, for example, supporting *and* confronting people, promoting improvisation *and* structure, showing patience *and* urgency, and stimulating bottom-up initiatives *and* making top-down interventions (Hill, Brandeau, Sal, & Lineback 2014).

What these examples have in common can be summarized in three main points. First, experience gained in practice is not ossified in such a way that it inhibits the consideration of further possibilities. The context is important to understand the current situation as it is and why but is not constituted as a black box. Wisdom envisions new possibilities, different ways of achieving a specific goal. Second, there is no need for a trade-off: paradoxical approaches can be adopted. This implication is especially important for strategy since for years it was accepted that firms should pursue differentiation *or* cost leadership, avoiding intermediate positions (Porter, 1980). Third, paradoxes function as enablers of change since it generates value for the various stakeholders involved.

A potentially more fruitful way of integrating paradox represents poles not as opposites or even interdependent (Poole & Van de Ven, 1989), but as *forces* vital for organizational renewal. Through *synthesis*, when possible, contradictions may be fused in such a way that a new form of being emerges, transcending the original opposites (Clegg & Cunha, forthcoming). In this case, reality is no longer viewed as "either/or" or "both/and," but "through/through" (Seet, 2007). As Nonaka and Toyama (2002) noted, to "synthesize" is defined as "the dialectic into a higher stage of truth" (*Webster's Dictionary*), implicating an idea of evolution. Terms such as "transcendence" and "breakthroughs" represent a form of deep change that may be supportive of synthesis. Integration refers to finding common ground, a conceptual space beyond the either/or, where something new might emerge. Change is generative of integration, as stated by Mary Parker Follett (in Graham, 1995, p. 189):

> Integration involves invention [...] and the clever thing is to recognize this and not to let one's thinking stay within the boundaries of two alternatives which are mutually exclusive. In other words, never let yourself be bullied by an either-or situation [...] Find a third way.

Integrative approaches are potential enablers of possibilities that transcend the initial alternatives. As previous research has shown, the chance of a breakthrough improves when a greater variety of resources participate in the process (Harvey, 2014). Transcendence thus thrives on complexity and diversity, enabled via paradoxical wisdom, the ability to reconcile two conflicting forces in an integrative way.

Paradoxical wisdom plays a central role in integration and transcendence through synthesis in four main moments (Figure 4.1): (1) it acts as a facilitator in the process of recognizing contradictions without freezing or paralyzing, avoiding overconfidence and over-caution; (2) it supports the dialectical integration of opposites since it allows the articulation of poles by framing and reframing, looking backward and forward; (3) because integration generates innovation, it should benefit different stakeholders and, if based on values, the outcome is more likely to be positive and sustainable; (4) finally, throughout the process, after receiving feedback and having time for reflection, actors may interpret that feedback differently, which will help to open and provoke new contradictions and tensions. Therefore, paradoxical wisdom may function

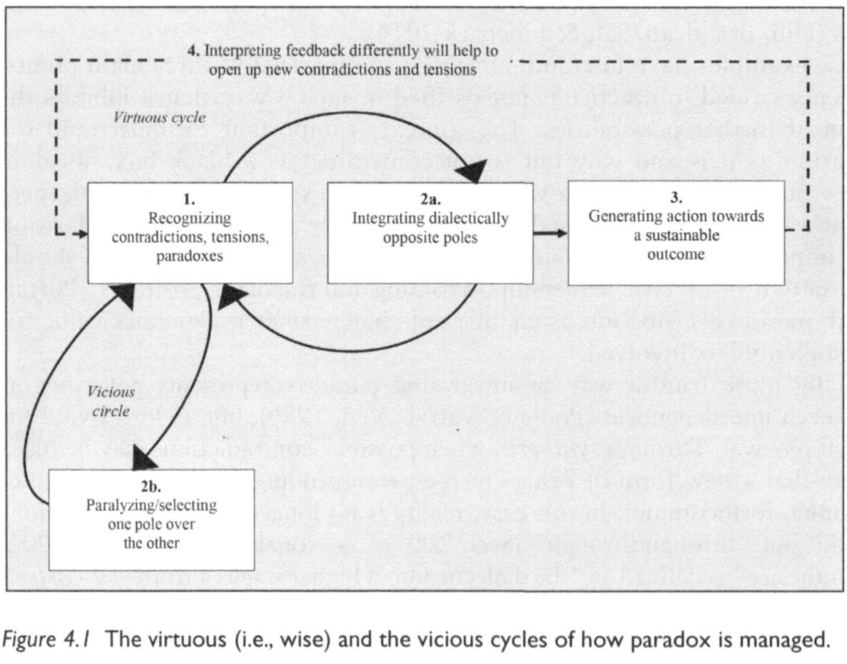

Figure 4.1 The virtuous (i.e., wise) and the vicious cycles of how paradox is managed.

as an enabler that will produce new input to this dynamic process. Paradoxes are thus never fully resolved (Ford & Ford, 1994; Kolb & Putnam, 1992; Murnighan & Conlon, 1991; Poole & Van de Ven, 1989). While paradoxical wisdom influences the processing of paradox, in turn, the paradox process influences wisdom. These dynamics are summarized in Figure 4.1, which suggests that by exposing themselves to paradox, managers cultivate an attitude of wisdom. However, paradoxical wisdom thrives on the ability to handle contradiction.

Orienting to paradoxical wisdom

Managing and organizing paradox implies a continuing tension between opposing forces. It strives not for equilibrium since equilibrium is rooted in stability, but a dynamic stability. In a dialectical process "there is no center, only flux" (Baxter, 2004, p. 8). It is a constant movement from thesis to antithesis to generate synthesis that will sooner or later turn into a new thesis. Therefore, uncertainty and contradictions demand an ongoing "centripetal-centrifugal" flux (p. 8). The orientation toward paradoxical wisdom is thus composed of a constant flux between forces that may be contradictory themselves, but it is the instability that surrounds them that enables a fruitful relationship to paradox (see Küpers, 2013). Instead of letting one pole "ossify" and gain dominance, the organization develops a dynamic movement between forces. Each of the forces influences the paradox process, which includes three phases (Figure 4.2): recognizing the paradox, cultivating an integrative mindset, and acting for the common good. Three forces compose the attitude of paradoxical wisdom: comfort vs. challenge, perception vs. imagination, as well as sense-making vs. sense-giving.

Comfort vs. challenge

Creating comfort with dissonance may reverse the natural tendency for making contradictions familiar by resorting to past practices and perceptions, and adopting modes of either/or solutions, generative of inertia and defensive stagnation (Clegg & Cunha, forthcoming; Lewis, 2000; Vince & Broussine, 1996). Comfort with uncertainty, in turn, necessitates a measure of confidence to seek uncomfortable challenges.

As Weick (1993, 1995a) pointed out, wisdom is the attitude of respect toward that which is known and that which is unknown. It is not a skill or a bundle of information. Wisdom is simultaneously knowing and doubting. As Socrates noticed and Meacham (1983) restated, to know something is also to doubt it, and claims that since the more one knows the more one finds one does not know, learning and development necessarily evolve together. Dialectically, the thesis (what is known) is compared to its antithesis (what is not known) with learning resulting from the synthesis of knowledge and ignorance (Meacham, 1983). Simplicity can be deceptive as the more we learn about a particular domain, the greater the complexity, the number of questions, uncertainties, and doubts that such learning stimulates. The ability to consider complexity and to appreciate it is fundamental for managing paradoxes: "Each bit of knowledge serves as the thesis from which additional questions or antithesis arise" (Meacham, 1983, p. 120). Confidence varies in accordance with what is known and what is not known.

The need for a continuous sense of development by learning is characteristic of *wise people* that embrace the complexity of the world, persistently seeking new challenges to stretch their capabilities to be aware of the paradox of excellence or competency traps. They oscillate between comfort (what is known) and challenge (what is out there to be known). Stamp et al. (2007) pointed out that the willingness to be challenged is functional when in the presence of a challenge and when challenges and life-perspectives match. In this case, wise people engage in a state of "flow" (Csikszentmihalyi, 1990) with such a "mental energy and determination," feeling "energized, confident and competent" to deal with complexity (Stamp et al., 2007). Nonaka and Toyama (2007) consider that confidence and courage work because *wise leaders* accept obstacles and complexity as part of the knowledge creation process, a notion that can be related to a "growth mindset." People with this "growth mindset" believe that their abilities can be developed, and that by learning and developing resilience, they may be able to succeed (Dweck, 2007). It is not that everyone sees challenge as positive, but that *phronetic* wisdom will take on challenge positively as a way to learn, to progress, and to nurture including a sense of familiarity with paradoxes and contradictions. As Lewis et al. (2014, p. 69) pointed out, confidence works as "the antidote of defensiveness, helping individuals work with, rather than against, tensions." Comfort is thus a necessary condition to deal with paradox. However, this comfort to work with tensions is built on confidence gained through the experience of embracing contradiction.

Perception vs. imagination

Past experience may have a negative impact on the handling of paradox since the recall of events that are familiar and that have been tackled in the past, may increase the chance of opting for a tested either/or solutions in an attempt to "solve" the contradiction. Paradoxical wisdom indicates that cultivating doubt stimulates the search for new alternatives, and fosters new interpretations. It requires the ability to navigate between forces of perception and imagination. While perception is the ability to see and comprehend a situation as it is (or supposed to be), imagination refers to the ability to discover and evaluate new possibilities beyond what was experienced or previously known (Abowitz, 2007). Paradoxical wisdom implies perceptiveness (*sunesis*), understanding why a situation is as it is, to "see beyond isolated facts, think beyond linear logic and appreciate the whole" (Bourantas, 2008, p. 5). It further requires affects "to frame" the concrete situation "to the larger context (political-economical-social) which influences local phenomena" (Bourantas, 2008, 10). Since context influences not only emerging paradoxes but also their interpretation (Cunha, Fortes, Rego, Gomes, & Rodrigues, 2015; Shotter & Tsoukas, 2014), it is important to frame contradictions positively.

Paradoxical wisdom implies a certain "distancing of view which enables a multi-perspective interpretation of organizational life" (Bourantas, 2008, p. 9). It requires a constant interplay between looking backward into looking forward, framing and reframing, allowing people to test past experience under new circumstances (Cunha, 2004). Further, because wisdom partly results from intuition, perception, imagination managers are able to "not just join the dots that are not yet joined, but those that are not yet even there" (Stamp et al., 2007, p. 480). As Shotter and Tsoukas (2014, p. 224) put it, "phronetic leaders are people who, in their search for a way out of their difficulties, have developed a refined capacity to intuitively grasp salient features of ambiguous situations and to constitute a landscape of possible paths of response." Organizational environments render the importance of articulating perception and imagination salient. First, they impose a lack of time to conduct detailed analyses or to listen to everyone's perspectives. Second, there is no guarantee that the general rules applied in the past remain valid (Nonaka & Toyama, 2007). The balance between perception and imagination, framing and reframing, looking backward and forward, enables integrative, "both/and" approaches, and increases the chance of achieving paradoxical wisdom.

Sense-making vs. sense-giving

Cultivating paradoxical wisdom involves a measure of reflexivity but also decision and action, as well as a "cultivated predisposition to act in the interest of the greater common good" (Nonaka, Chia, Holt, & Peltokorpi, 2014, p. 367). Since wise leaders and managers express *phronesis*, decision is necessarily drawn on values (Nonaka & Toyama, 2007), on the "right" thing to do. Unsurprisingly, it is in moments of greater uncertainty that people hang on the most to leaders' and the managers' capacity to make sense and to guide the collective in the right direction. Without a clear understanding of purpose and direction, anxiety driven by complexity may inhibit action. The process of reflecting, understanding, envisioning, and creating an order for action, is defined as "sense-making" (Weick, 1995b). Via "sense-making," managers are able to reach complex understandings of the world that will be communicated via "sense-giving" to employees through coherent messages. These in turn will provide a secure and workable ground (Lüscher & Lewis, 2008; Maitlis, 2005). Through "sense-giving," managers will inform subordinates' "sense-making" efforts (Gioia & Chittipeddi, 1991). In this sense, the ability to transform paradoxes into engines of managerial progress depends on the capacity to engage in sense-making and sense-giving as a entwined process of thinking while acting/influencing.

"Sense-making" and "sense-giving" can have an impact on decision-making and implementation, especially when facing change. Strategic change is often designed and envisioned by top managers who, during strategic definition, apprehend external dynamics, defining a new vision and objectives. These will then be materialized in a concrete plan of actions and changes in the organization, offering a sense of order. Middle managers, absent from the strategizing process at its inception, are responsible for implementation by mobilizing teams while still struggling to make sense of change (Gioia & Chittipeddi, 1991; Lüscher & Lewis, 2008). The process thus raises issues of consistency, credibility, and authenticity that interfere with decision and implementation. Making sense and giving sense (understanding and influencing) may enhance wisdom and affect paradoxical wisdom positively: when the targets of the managers' "sense-giving" make their own interpretations, they will be communicated back to the managers, affecting previous sense by changing it or by reinforcing it. Transformative changing should trigger a process of reflection (and an enhancing of wisdom), influencing both what is learned and how such learning takes place (Hays, 2008, p. 14), while energizing the process and fostering implementation, making change happen via learning and improving as the change unfolds (Tichy & Bennis, 2007). Figure 4.2 summarizes the forces that enable paradoxical wisdom.

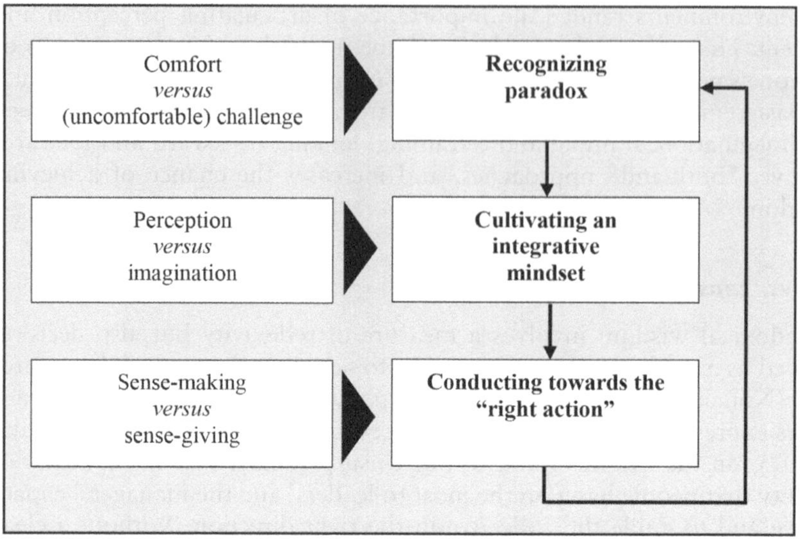

Figure 4.2 Forces of paradoxical wisdom that enable integrative solutions to paradox.

The seven pillars of pardoxical organizational wisdom

Extraordinary results may be obtained when teams and organizations learn to live with paradox and cultivate paradoxical wisdom. Collins and Porras (1994) defend the thesis that organizations that free themselves from the "tyranny of the either/or" approach experience exponential growth through innovation. Similarly, Lewis, Andriopoulos and Smith (2014), drawing from data from five cases, argued that organizational survival depends on strategic agility, dealing with contradictions by seeking creative, "both/and" type solutions. Paul Polman, CEO of Unilever, suggests the importance of an "and mentality":

> The difference between average and outstanding firms is an "AND Mentality". We must find and create tensions – force people into different space for thinking .... This is not just a performance issue but a survival issue, because managing paradox helps foster creativity and high performance.
>
> (Lewis et al., 2014, p. 58)

The capacity to handle oppositions and transcend them must be guaranteed not as an individual asset (i.e., the "wise actor"; Asforth et al., 2014) but as a competence distributed throughout the organization (i.e., the "wise system"). If paradoxical wisdom is embedded in an organization's culture, *wisdom will be shared*, which leads to the question: is it possible to teach and to learn paradoxical wisdom?

Revisiting Aristotle, anything we have to learn we learn through actually doing of it (Shotter & Tsoukas, 2014). Paradoxical wisdom thus may be learned by practising "paradoxification," seeing reality as inherently paradoxical and searching for paradoxes where they can be, i.e. facing paradoxes and gaining comfort with them. Yet, paradoxical thinking goes against the formal linear logic according to which one cause has one effect (Hays, 2008; Lado et al., 2006). Linear vision makes the process of paradoxical wisdom more challenging. Paradoxical wisdom involves the contemplation of multiple events whether they are related or not, rather than a logic of cause and effect. It requires openness to new possibilities, willingness to learn and be challenged. Additionally, it implies the courage to go against the status quo and the confidence to move between poles without the fear of appearing incoherent or weak. Multiple perspectives increase complexity, but also raise the chance of breakthroughs. More importantly, it envisions shared values and acting for the common good which generates more sustainable outcomes. In an attempt to define a portfolio of roles and behaviors that enhance paradoxical wisdom in managers and organizations, we discuss seven guidelines according to the extant literature (Table 4.1).

I. Be curious about contradiction

As Follett remarked, "the first rule for obtaining integration is to put your cards on the table, face the real issue, uncover the conflict" (Graham, 1995, p. 75). To be appreciated and tackled, paradoxes first need to be made rendered explicit and "visible." Having a paradox-friendly mindset and fostering curiosity with regards to contradiction will uncover proactive opportunities to seek oppositions that may be hidden, without freezing or paralyzing while facing them, to ask questions (*what is the reverse way*?), to know what is not known, to increase complexity and to appreciate contradictory evidence. Being curious about contradiction means being able to engage in a *dialectical* exercise: defining the dominant understanding (thesis) and the alternative perspective (antithesis). Paradoxical wisdom means that the more we know, the more we want to know because we know we don´t know. Creating comfort with complexity is necessary to manage paradox through integration (Baxter, 2004; Harvey, 2014; Lewis et al., 2014; Tse, 2013).

II. Synthesize confidence and caution

As pointed out by Weick (1993), extreme confidence and extreme caution are representative of a "closed-mind" which influences the capacity of good judgments and increases the possibility of adoption of "either/or" solutions. Overconfidence may destroy learning opportunities because there is "nothing to be learned." Over-caution may inhibit the embrace of paradox for fear that it will deepen the Pandora's Box of uncertainty and complexity. The attributes of organizational wisdom identified by Weick (1993), as well those explored by Sternberg (2004), define foolishness as knowing everything and assuming that, being so powerful, everything can be done (Isak, 2013). Paradoxical wisdom implies an attitude of humility, in the spirit of prudence toward the world (van Dierendonck & Patterson, 2015), being eager to learn and to unlearn, and open to learn from experience as well as from failure.

III. Promote time for reflection and to deeply engage with context

When there is no time or space for reflection, it is more likely that an easier way is selected and that fruitful crossroads opened by contradiction are ignored, which may lead to vicious circles. As reflection diminishes, opportunities to embrace paradoxes also decrease, minimizing chances of learning through exploration (Hays, 2008). Reflection allows rich articulation of past, present, and future, learning and forgetting. As stated by Lin (2004), organizations should combine *hindsight* (looking back, taking past experience into account), *insight* (perception and perspicacity to deal with current complex problems and situations), and *foresight* (looking forward, imaging, planning, and conceiving implications). When dealing with paradox, issues articulating past, present, and future may arise: How did we manage similar challenges in the past? Why is the current situation as it is? What would be the implications when implementing this path? Promoting moments of reflection is a way to create organizational awareness, which is central for the organization to engage with the context and to appreciate the whole. Otherwise, decision makers will not be able to fully understand the interactions between the environment and the organization, or the implications for stakeholders (Rowley & Gibbs, 2008).

IV. Develop a synthetizing multi-perspectival mindset

Multiple perspectives must be taken into consideration by managers, since diversity of inputs stimulate variety in output and multiply the chance of breakthroughs. Breakthroughs occur not because of multiple perspectives, but because they may result in a shared understanding, in unique syntheses of perspectives (Harvey, 2014). Synthesizing perspectives may make it easier to overcome cognitive and perceptual limitations, since complexity makes it hard for only one person to consider all the variables and process the knowledge needed to evaluate certain circumstances. Personal lenses necessarily color the way one sees reality (Hays, 2008). Therefore, combining lenses may generate a more sustainable outcome.

V. Integrate similarities

Synthesis occurs by building on similarities between perspectives (Harvey, 2014). The dialectical process implies that the opposites are no longer viewed as independent and that interrelated connections may be identified. This is an exercise that finds connections between the tensions, integrating knowledge and ignorance, resulting in something new, not considered beforehand. Harvey (2014) confirmed that extraordinary creativity is built over similarity, positively impacting group members because of the identified similarities between new ideas and their previous ones. The notion of stimulating divergence between perspectives loses ground for the reconciliation of ideas, building on similarity and coherence.

VI. Use experience to support improvisation

Paradoxical wisdom is acquired through experiencing reality and being humble in face of its possibility and its implacability. Rich approaches to paradox potentially have positive effects on wisdom, as paradoxes counter established truths and disturb crystallized assumptions. Paradoxical wisdom prompts a constant flux between looking backward and looking forward, knowing how the organization crafted solutions to deal with paradox in the past, but also being open to consider new possibilities for the present. It requires apperception, that is, the ability to relate new experiences to previous ones, facilitating understanding and resolution (Grint, 2007). Since organizations are dynamic, to build on experience and apperception will enhance the ability to respond quickly to unpredictable situations, to improvise, to acquire knowledge and experience while action unfolds (Clegg et al., 2002; Cunha, Neves, Clegg, & Rego, 2014; Nonaka & Toyama, 2007).

VII. Constantly interrogate the meaning of goodness

People are not "moved to act" on the basis of rationality only. Communicating a vision and moving others to action requires the ability to create emotional rapport. Building a shared vision requires working together toward a common purpose, engaging people in a process of alignment of their ethical models, detaching themselves from their personal goals, and balancing the interests of multiple stakeholders (Rowley & Gibbs, 2008). Decision-making toward action should include constant interrogation about the implications of action for stakeholders, including future generations (Petrick et al., 1999).

Table 4.1 Seven pillars for cultivating paradoxical wisdom

Pillars	*Explanation*	*Representative research*
I. Be curious about contradictions	Open-mindedness and curiosity leads to proactively seeking oppositions, knowing what is not known, increasing complexity, and appreciating contradictory evidence	Baxter (2004); Harvey (2014); Lewis et al. (2014); Tse (2013)
II. Synthesize confidence and caution	Extreme confidence and extreme caution are representative of a "closed-mind." Paradoxical wisdom implies an attitude of humility toward the world	van Dierendonck & Patterson (2015); Weick (1993); Isak (2013)
III. Promote time for reflection and to deeply engage with context	Reflection creates the opportunity to embrace paradoxes, increasing chances of learning and change by allowing the organization to engage with the context	Hays (2008); Lin (2004); Rowley & Gibbs (2008)
IV. Develop a multi-perspectival mindset	Diversity of inputs stimulates variety in output and multiplies the chance of breakthroughs when a shared understanding is possible. Combining lenses may create comfort with paradox	Harvey (2014); Hays (2008)
V. Integrate similarities	The dialectical process implies an exercise of finding connections between the tensions and integrating them, emerging into something that was not considered beforehand	Harvey (2014)
VI. Use experience to support improvisation	To build on experience and apperception will enhance the ability to respond quickly to unpredictable situations, to improvise, acquiring knowledge and experience while action occurs	Clegg et al. (2002); Grint (2007); Cunha et al. (2014); Nonaka & Toyama (2007)
VII. Constantly interrogate the meaning of goodness	The disposition to interrogate the paradoxical consequences of our actions should be deeply embedded in the organization's culture. Asking what is good, as a way of being, may nurture an attitude of wisdom	Rowley & Gibbs (2008); Nonaka & Toyama (2007); Petrick et al. (1999)

Evaluating the implications of one's actions should not represent an occasional exercise, often after some negative occurrence. The disposition to interrogate the paradoxical consequences of our actions should instead be deeply embedded in the organization's culture, fostering the enactment of wisdom as a process, a pursuit that constantly raises formidable obstacles. Asking what is good, as a way of being (Nonaka & Toyama, 2007), may nurture an attitude of wisdom.

Conclusion

Embracing doubt is the attitude of wisdom, Weick (1993) pointed out. This is an organizational version of Socrates' advice to recognize the limits of our "knowability" (Pitsis & Clegg, 2007). We envision no better way to embrace doubt and to test the limits of our knowability, without paralysis, than via deliberately engaging with paradox. Engaging with paradox is an exercise in learning and unlearning, acting and reflecting, doubting and being confident, gaining comfort with contradiction, understanding and influencing. It can thus be an exercise in dialectics. We discussed why and how managers and organizations may cultivate wisdom by exposing themselves to paradox, by synthesizing knowledge and ignorance. Engagement with paradox in search for solutions that transcend habitual dichotomies offers a fertile ground to acquire knowledge and to gain awareness about the limits of the knowledge acquired. The chapter makes three main contributions to the organizational literature. First, it introduces the concept of paradoxical wisdom as an attitude toward contradiction that allows the recognition and articulation of paradox in an integrative way. By referring to an integrative way, we mean synthetizing multiple perspectives resulting in something new and sustainable, since it comprehends shared and ethical goals. Second, it defends that wisdom is necessary to respond to complexity, but it requires complexity itself, as it deals with contradiction. Third, we suggest that paradoxical wisdom may be learned and diffused via the cultivation of seven pillars of paradoxical organizational wisdom. Developing the paradoxical competences of managers seems therefore a promising way to cultivate wisdom. This may be difficult because paradoxical, dialectical, and reflexive work can be politically inconvenient or organizationally perceived as indecisive. Valuing wisdom per se can be difficult when performance becomes the measure of value. Dialectical sophistication, in such a context, can be perceived as limitation rather than as an indicator of conceptual sophistication. In conclusion, successful managing may be more concerned with installing knowledgeable doubt than removing uncertainty or resolving equivocality.

Open questions

- How does wisdom stimulate the handling of paradoxes?
- How can the attitude of wisdom be challenged through paradoxes?
- Can managers develop comfort with paradox and ambivalence?
- How does paradoxical wisdom contribute to avoid organizational vicious circles?
- What are the obstacles to developing paradoxical wisdom?
- What enables the emergence and flourishing of paradoxical wisdom in individuals and organizations?
- Is the idea of "pillars" too static to capture such dynamic processes?
- How can organizations enhance paradoxical wisdom?

Note

1 The title is adapted, we should acknowledge, from the autobiography of T. E. Lawrence (2011) (Lawrence of Arabia).

References

Abowitz, K. K. (2007). Moral perception through aesthetics: Engaging imaginations in educational ethics. *Journal of Teacher Education*, 58, 287–298.

Ashforth, B. A., Rogers, K. M., Pratt, M. G., & Pradies, C. (2014). Ambivalence in organizations: A multilevel approach. *Organization Science*, 25(5), 1453–1478.

Baxter, L. A. (2004). A tale of two voices: Relational dialectics theory. *Journal of Family Communication*, 4(3–4), 181–192.

Bouchikhi, H. (1998). Living with and building on complexity: A constructivist perspective on organizations. *Organization*, 5(2), 217–232.

Bourantas, D. (2008). Phronesis: A strategic leadership virtue. Unpublished article, Athens University of Economics and Business. Available at: www.mbaexecutive.gr/vdata/File/bibliothiki/Arthra/PHRONESIS%202008.pdf

Brooks, D. (2015). What candidates need. *The New York Times*, April 7 (www.nytimes.com/2015/04/07/opinion/david-brooks-what-candidates-need.html?_r=1).

Cameron, K. & Quinn, R. (1998). Organizational paradox and transformation. In R. Quinn & K. Cameron (Eds.), *Paradox and transformation: Toward a theory of change in organization and management* (pp. 1–18). Cambridge, MA: Ballinger.

Chia, R. (2010). Rediscovering becoming: Insights from an oriental perspective on process organization studies. In T. Hernes & S. Maitlis (Eds.), *Process, sensemaking, and organizing* (pp. 112–139). Oxford: Oxford University Press.

Chia, R. & Holt, R. (2007). Wisdom as learned ignorance. In E. H. Kessler & J. R. Bailey (Eds.), *Handbook of organizational and managerial wisdom* (pp. 505–526). Thousand Oaks, CA: Sage.

Cialdini, R., Trost, M., & Newsom, J. (1995). Preference for consistency: The development of a valid measure and the discovery of surprising behavioral implications. *Journal of Personality and Social Psychology*, 69, 318–328.

Clegg, S. R., Cunha, J. V., & Cunha, M. P. (2002). Management paradoxes: A relational view. *Human Relations*, 55(5), 483–503.

Clegg, S. R. & Cunha, M. P. (forthcoming). *Organizational dialectics*. In M. W. Lewis, W. K. Smith, P. Jarzabkowski & A. Langley (Eds.), *The Oxford handbook of organizational paradox: Approaches to plurality, tensions, and contradictions*. Oxford: Oxford University Press.

Collins, C. J. & Porras, I. J. (1994). *Built to last: The successful habits of visionary companies*. New York: HarperCollins.

Csikszentmihalyi, M. (1990). *Flow*. New York: Harper and Row.

Cunha, J. V., Clegg, S. R., & Cunha, M. P. (2002). Management, paradox and permanent dialectics. In S. R. Clegg (Ed.), *Management and organization paradoxes* (pp. 11–40). Amsterdam: John Benjamins.

Cunha, M. P. (2004). Time traveling: Organizational foresight as temporal reflexivity. In H. Tsoukas & J. Shepherd (Eds.), *Managing the future: Foresight in the knowledge economy* (pp. 133–150). Malden, MA: Blackwell.

Cunha, M. P. & Tsoukas, H. (2015). Reforming the State: Understanding the vicious circles of reform. *European Management Journal*, 33(4), 225–229.

Cunha, M. P., Fortes, A., Rego, A., Gomes, E., & Rodrigues, F. (2015). Ambidextrous leadership, paradox, and contingency: evidence from Angola. *The International Journal of Human Resource Management*, 1–26.

Cunha, M. P., Neves, P., Clegg, S., & Rego, A. (2014). Organizational improvisation: From the constraint of strict tempo to the power of avant-garde. *Creativity and Innovation Management*, 23(4), 359–373.

De Wit, B. & Meyer, R. (2010). *Strategy synthesis: Resolving strategy paradoxes to create competitive advantage*. London: Cengage Learning EMEA.

Dweck, C. (2007). *Mindset: The new psychology of success*. New York: Ballantine.

Eatock, G. (2009). *The quest to be human: Myth, truth & science*. Leicester, UK: Matador.

Farjoun, M. (2010). Beyond dualism: Stability and change as duality. *Academy of Management Review*, 35(2), 202–225.

Farjoun, M. (2016). Contradictions, dialectics and paradoxes. In A. Langley and H. Tsoukas (Eds.), *The Sage handbook of process organization studies*. London: Sage.

Fitzgerald, F. S. (1945). *The crack-up*. New York: New Directions.

Flyvbjerg, B. (2006). Making organizational research matter: Power, values and phronesis. In S. R. Clegg, C. Hardy, T. B. Lawrence, & W. R. Nord (Eds.), *The Sage handbook of organization studies* (pp. 370–387). Thousand Oaks, CA: Sage.

Ford, J. D., & Ford, L. W. (1994). Logics of identity, contradiction, and attraction in change. *Academy of Management Review*, 19(4), 756–785.

Gioia, D. A. & Chittipeddi, K. (1991). Sensemaking and sensegiving in strategic change initiation. *Strategic Management Journal*, 12(6), 433–448.

Giustiniano, L., Cunha, M. P., & Clegg, S. (2016). Organizational zemblanity. *European Management Journal*, 34(1), 7–21.

Goede, M. (2011). The wise society: beyond the knowledge economy. *Foresight*, 13(1), 36–45.

Gomm, I. & Lowe, N. (1979) "Cruel to be kind," *Labour of Lust*. London: Radar.

Goodwin, D. K. (2005). *Team of rivals: The political genius of Abraham Lincoln*. New York: Simon & Schuster.

Graham, P. (1995). *Mary Parker Follett, prophet of management: A celebration of writings from the 1920s*. Boston, MA: Harvard Business School Press.

Grint, K. (2007). Learning to lead: Can Aristotle help us find the road to wisdom? *Leadership*, 3(2), 231–46.

Harvey, S. (2014). Creative synthesis: Exploring the process of extraordinary group creativity. *Academy of Management Review*, 39(3), 324–343.

Hays, J. (2008). Dynamics of organizational wisdom. Australian National University, School of Management, Marketing, and International Business, working paper series.

Hill, L. A., Brandeau, G., Sal, E. T., & Lineback, K. (2014). Collective genius. *Harvard Business Review*, June, 94–102.

Izak, M. (2013). The foolishness of wisdom: Towards an inclusive approach to wisdom in organization. *Scandinavian Journal of Management*, 29(1), 108–115.

Kessler, E. H. & Bailey, J. R. (2007). Introduction: Understanding, applying, and developing organizational and managerial wisdom. In E. H. Kessler & J. R. Bailey (Eds.), *Handbook of organizational and managerial wisdom* (pp. xv-lxxiv). Thousand Oaks, CA: Sage.

Knott, B. (2014). What Ferran Adrià did next. *Financial Times*, May 2. Available at: http://howtospendit.ft.com/food/53653-ferran-adrias-pioneering-new-project.

Kolb, D. M., & Putnam, L. L. (1992). The multiple faces of conflict in organizations. *Journal of Organizational Behavior*, 13(3), 341–324.

Küpers, W. (2013). Dilemmas and paradoxes, chiasmic organizing. In W. Küpers *Phenomenology of the embodied organization. The contribution of Merleau-Ponty for organisation studies and practice* (pp. 197–235), London: Palgrave Macmillan.

Küpers, W. & Pauleen, D. (2013). *A handbook of practical wisdom. Leadership, organization and integral business practice*. London: Gower.

Lado, A., Boyd, N., Wright, P., & Kroll, M. (2006). Paradox and theorizing within the resource-based view. *Academy of Management Review*, 31(1), 115–131.

Lawrence, T. E. (2011) *Seven pillars of wisdom: A triumph*. Blacksburg, VA: Wilder.

Lewis, M. (2000). Exploring paradox: Toward a more comprehensive guide. *Academy of Management Review*, 25(4), 750–776.

Lewis, M., Andriopoulos, C., & Smith, W. K. (2014). Paradoxical leadership to enable strategic agility. *California Management Review*, 56(3), 58–77.

Lin, I. (2004). Innovation in the networked world: New corporate mindsets for the cyber age. In C. Barker & R. Coy (Eds.), *Innovation and imagination at work*. Sydney: McGraw-Hill.

Lüscher, L. & Lewis, M. (2008). Organizational change and managerial sensemaking: Working through paradox. *Academy of Management Journal*, 51(2), 221–240.

Maitlis, S. (2005). The social processes of organizational sensemaking. *Academy of Management Journal*, 48(1), 21–49.

Meacham, J. A. (1983). Wisdom and the context of knowledge: knowing that one doesn't know. In D. Kuhn & A. Meacham (Eds.), *On the development of developmental psychology* (pp. 111–134). Basel: Karger.

Meacham, J. A. (1990). The loss of wisdom. In R. J. Sternberg (Ed.), *Wisdom: Its nature, origins, and development* (pp. 181–211). Cambridge: Cambridge University Press.

Melé, D. (2010). Practical wisdom in managerial decision making. *Journal of Management Development*, 29(7/8), 637–645.

Murnighan, J. K. & Conlon, D. E. (1991). The dynamics of intense work groups: A study of British string quartets. *Administrative Science Quarterly*, 35, 165–186.

Nonaka, I., Chia, R., Holt, R., & Peltokorpi, V. (2014). Wisdom, management and organization. *Management Learning*, 45(4), 365–376.

Nonaka, I. & Takeuchi, H. (2011). Are you a wise leader? *Harvard Business Review*, May, 58–67.

Nonaka, I. & Toyama, R. (2002). A firm as a dialectical being: Towards a dynamic theory of the firm. *Industrial and Corporate Change*, 11(5), 995–1009.

Nonaka, I. & Toyama, R. (2007). Strategic management as distributed practical wisdom (phronesis). *Industrial and Corporate Change*, 16(3), 371–394.

Owens, B. P., Walker, A. S., & Waldman, D. A. (2015). Leader narcissism and follower outcomes: The counterbalancing effect of leader humility. *Journal of Applied Psychology*, 100(4), 1203–1213.

Petrick, J., Scherer, R., Brodzinski, J., Quinn, J., & Ainina, M. F. (1999). Global leadership skills and reputational capital: Intangible resources for sustainable competitive advantage. *Academy of Management Executive*, 13(1), 58–69.

Pitsis, T. R. & Clegg, S. R. (2007). "We live in a political world": The paradox of managerial wisdom. In E. H. Kessler & J. R. Bailey (Eds.), *Handbook of organizational and managerial wisdom* (pp. 399–422). Thousand Oaks, CA: Sage.

Poole, M. S. & Van de Ven, A. H. (1989). Using paradox to build management and organization theories. *Academy of Management Review*, 14(4), 562–578.

Porter, M. 1980. *Competitive strategy*. New York: Free Press.

Rego, A., Cunha, M. P. & Clegg, S. (2012). *The virtues of leadership: Contemporary challenge for global managers*. Oxford: Oxford University Press.

Richardson, H. H. (1910) *The getting of wisdom*. London: Heinemann.

Rowley, J. & Gibbs, P. (2008). From learning organization to practically wise organization. *The Learning Organization*, 15(5), 356–372.

Saïd Business School & Heidrick & Struggles (2015). *The CEO Report: Embracing the paradoxes of leadership and the power of doubt*. London: Saïd Business School & Heidrick & Struggles.

Seet, P. (2007). Reconciling entrepreneurial dilemmas: A case study of a Huaqiao entrepreneur in China. *Journal of Asia Entrepreneurship and Sustainability*, 3(3), 74–97.

Shakespeare, W. (1998) *Hamlet*, edited by H. Jenkins. In R. Proudfoot, A. Thompson, & D. S. Kastan (Eds.) *The Arden Shapespeare: Complete Works* (pp. 291–332). London: Bloomsbury Arden.

Shotter, J. & Tsoukas, H. (2014). In search of phronesis: Leadership and the art of judgment. *Academy of Management Learning & Education,* 13(2), 224–243.

Small, M. W. (2004). Wisdom and now managerial wisdom: Do they have a place in management development programs? *Journal of Management Development*, 23(7/8), 751–764.

Smith, W. K. & Lewis, M. W. (2011). Toward a theory of paradox: A dynamic equilibrium model of organizing. *Academy of Management Review*, 36(2), 381–403.

Stamp, G., Burridge, B. & Thomas, P. (2007). Strategic leadership: An exchange of letters. *Leadership*, 3, 479–496.

Sternberg, R. J. (2004). Why smart people can be so foolish. *European Psychologist*, 9(3), 145–150.

Sull, D. & Eisenhardt, K. M. (2015). *Simple rules*. New York: Houghton-Mifflin.

Sundaramurthy, C. & Lewis, M. (2003). Control and collaboration: Paradoxes of governance. *Academy of Management Review*, 28(3), 397–415.

Takeuchi, H., Osono, E. & Shimizu, N. (2008). The contradictions that drive Toyota's success. *Harvard Business Review*, June, 96–104.

Tichy, N. M. & Bennis, W. G. (2007). *Judgment: How winning leaders make great calls*. New York: Penguin.

Tse, T. (2013). Paradox resolution: A means to achieve strategic innovation. *European Management Journal*, 31(6), 682–696.

Tsoukas, H. (2005). *Complex knowledge*. Oxford: Oxford University Press.

van Dierendonck, D. & Patterson, K. (2015). Compassionate love as a cornerstone of servant leadership: An integration of previous theorizing and research. *Journal of Business Ethics*, 128, 119–131.

Vay, D. V., Fleenor, J. W., Atwater, L. E., Sturm, R. E., & McKee, R. A. (2014). Advances in leader and leadership development: A review of 25 years of research and theory. *The Leadership Quarterly*, 25(1), 63–82.

Vince, R. & Broussine, M. (1996). Paradox, defense and attachment: Accessing and working with emotions and relations underlying organizational change. *Organization Studies,* 17(1), 1–21.

Weick, K. E. (1993). The collapse of sensemaking in organizations: The Mann Gulch disaster. *Administrative Science Quarterly*, 38(4), 628–652.

Weick, K. E. (1995a). South Canyon revisited: Lessons from high reliability organizations. *Wildfire,* 4(4), 54–68.

Weick, K. E. (1995b). *Sensemaking in organizations*. Thousand Oaks, CA: Sage.

Weick, K. E. (2007). Foreword. In E. H. Kessler & J. R. Bailey (Eds.), *Handbook of organizational and managerial wisdom* (pp. ix-xiii). Thousand Oaks, CA: Sage.

Chapter 5

Too busy to learn

Wisdom, mindfulness, and grounding learning

Nina Kongsbakk and David Rooney

Introduction

Work life can be frenetic and pose challenges for how we prioritize time and effort. It is therefore useful to ask are we too busy to learn, to be mindful, and to be wise? This chapter explores a knowledge-intensive service sector organization that explicitly states a desire to be wise and examines its curious barriers to learning. Faucher, Everett, and Lawson (2008) correctly say that hierarchical models of data, information, knowledge, and wisdom are flawed and that "messy" social interactions in complex social systems create knowledge. Faucher et al. also say that wisdom develops in these complex interactions when the interactions create higher forms of understanding. We argue that mindfulness is a mechanism in wisdom that turns the messiness into wisdom by grounding learning. Wisdom is an important concept for addressing a wide range of issues around organizational effectiveness (Kolodinsky & Bierly, 2013), and learning. The organization in which this study took place adopted wisdom as one of its core values: its other core values were high competence, enthusiasm, and being hands-on.

To make sense of our data we focus on mindfulness, a component of wisdom. Mindfulness is critical for wisdom's ability to create excellence in a messy and time poor world. Mindfulness is the skill of attending to the present without distractions clouding thought and action. We present a new approach to mindful organizing (Vogus & Sutcliffe, 2012) using a mindful dialogue framework to understand mindfulness in organizational learning. Importantly, this approach does not separate mindfulness from values or wisdom.

Organizational learning

Grounding learning is an intriguing concept in our data and our literature review explores organizational learning research relevant to it. In doing this we create a focus on readiness to learn, values, identity, and time to show how they are linked. Having done this we move to discuss what wisdom and mindfulness are, and how they are linked to each other and to grounding organizational learning. We then demonstrate the importance of dialogue to wisdom and mindfulness in organizational learning.

Organizational learning is understood as a "product of organizational members' involvement in the interaction and sharing of experiences and knowledge" (Curado, 2006, p. 26), and is therefore the process of "acquiring, distributing, integrating, and creating information and knowledge among organizational members" (Wang & Ellinger, 2011, p. 512). Learning takes place as individual learning, learning in teams, and organizational learning (Van Winkelen, 2010). As a multi-level process, organizational learning is both a collective and individual phenomenon occurring at macro and micro levels. Pokharel and Hult (2010) see learning starting at an individual level and developing through people interpreting new information to create actionable knowledge. New knowledge is then integrated with an already existing body of knowledge and is institutionalized as the knowledge is transformed into routines and practices in an organization (Berson, Nemanich, Waldman, Galvin, & Keller, 2006; Phillips, Lawrence, & Hardy, 2004). This approach is consonant with approaches to organizational knowledge that emphasize how knowledge is created and transferred through social interaction (Tsoukas, 2005).

Gärtner (2011a, 2011b) shows that wisdom and mindfulness theory are important means to identify precise micro and embodied practices that are useful for creating positive environments for knowledge sharing and learning. Wisdom and mindfulness deal with the micro and macro aspects of learning simultaneously. However, Gärtner also makes the point that mindfulness has often been incompletely applied by organization scholars. In particular, values and other-oriented aspects of mindfulness (that are also central to wisdom) are least appreciated in contemporary research (Van Doesum, Van Lange, & Van Lange, 2013). Importantly, though, Argote (2011) calls for more mindfulness-based research on organizational learning.

We argue that mindful social processes are needed in organizations because suitable organizational learning contexts are predicated on the ability and willingness of individual organizational members and groups to learn and to convert individuals' knowledge into shared organizational knowledge (Michailova & Sidorova, 2011). Mindfulness builds the skills and willingness to do this (Van Doesum et al., 2013). Readiness means being psychologically and behaviorally prepared to learn (Weiner, 2009). Roland (2005) argues that for an organization to learn it is necessary to foster collective understanding and enthusiasm in employees for learning and knowledge sharing, thus creating readiness to learn. In addition to individual readiness, organizational readiness is a collective commitment that grounds learning through shared beliefs in collective capabilities to learn and execute a course of action based on learning (Weiner, 2009) and shared values. This readiness is created through challenging and evaluating existing mindsets and creating motivation for change and development (Weiner, 2009). Going further, readiness entails direction, persistence, and behavior towards a goal (Ramlall, 2004), and is linked to an individual's feelings and enthusiasm towards an organization (Joo & Lim, 2009; Schnake, 2007). We argue that mindful social processes will create positive experiences that motivate willingness and readiness to learn.

Identity and grounding

Willingness and enthusiasm for social learning processes are grounded in an organization through links to identity. It is important for knowledge-intensive professional organizations to see themselves as learning organizations and in so doing make learning a central part of their identity (Brown & Starkey, 2000). More than this, we argue that knowledge-intensive organizations can improve their learning performance and promote wise practice through mindfully grounding learning. Learning and knowledge sharing interactions need a ground within which to grow and flourish. The absence of a ground and related processes therefore are potential barriers to growing the roots of learning and wise practice.

A person's identity consists of both personal identity and social identity. Personal identity is composed of the unique characteristics of a person that distinguish them from others, while social identity is how people define themselves in relation to membership of different social categories or groups (Hogg & Terry, 2000).

Place identity, which is rarely mentioned in organizational research, is a subcategory of social identity and is important for grounding learning. Proshansky and colleagues (Proshansky, Fabian, & Kaminoff, 1983) explain place identity as a "pot-pourri of memories, conceptions, interpretations, ideas, and related feelings about specific physical settings as well as types of settings" (p. 60) that make one feel a sense of belonging and being grounded in a place. These memories, etc. are experienced as being embodied in a place. In this way, identity is grounded and so too the values, ideas, conceptions, etc. that help form social identities and a sense of belonging somewhere. Part of an individual's professional identity is, therefore, determined by the characteristics that are associated with their organization as a place (Prati, McMillan-Capehart, & Karriker, 2009), including its location, physical characteristics, shared feelings, narratives, interpretations of an organization as a place, and the history of what typically happens in that place (Rooney, Paulsen, et al., 2010).

A ground is also about the reason (and reasoning) about why one does something. The assumptions and patterns of thinking in an organization (culture), and one's values are all part of this ground.

Identity and values

Brown and Starkey (2000) argue that for an organization to become a learning organization it must critically reflect on and change its self-concept. However, such change may threaten an organization's members because it can challenge existing ideas, concepts, and identities that members want to defend (Curado, 2006). Core routines and culture are important aspects of organizational identity, and changing these can change how employees perceive an organization, which in turn can lead to clashes between individuals' identities and organizational identities (Jacobs, Christe-Zeyse, Keegan, & Pólos, 2008).

Yet new approaches to learning may not be perceived as a threat by those who value learning and knowledge. Values therefore are important aspects of identity (Jacobs et al., 2008). Values are standards of importance based on beliefs (Hultman, 2005) that ground a person in a community as community and individual values come to correspond with each other. People prefer to work in an organization that emphasizes the values that are important to them (Dobni, Ritchie, & Zerbe, 2000; Hultman, 2005). Organizational values therefore influence the behavior of employees and also help them make sense of their work environment (Groddeck, 2011).

Time is needed for individuals and organizations to effect meaningful change around identity, values, and organizational learning. Time is not something that is found in abundance in contemporary workplaces. Lack of time and growing work intensification are known to be deleterious to work performance and well-being (Floro, 1995).

Intensifying work is also associated with a management focus on cost reduction rather than employee conditions or service quality (Arrowsmith & Sisson, 2001). Thus, it is germane to this chapter that time pressures on doctors and other health sector workers are shown to be both growing in significance and growing as a problem in maintaining quality of care (Horner et al., 2011; Jacobson Jr et al., 2011).

Argyris (1993, 2004) describes two types of organizational learning. In single-loop learning, errors in an organization are detected and corrected by making incremental changes. However, double-loop learning requires openness to fundamental change including changing assumptions and values. To have this special capacity, organizations need, among other things, to define their values and values conflicts, including values conflicts between the organization and its employees. This kind of reflexive interrogation of grounding identity, knowledge, reasoning, and values to bring about change and coping with time pressure are aspects of the core internal dialogical work of mindfulness and wisdom.

Wisdom and mindfulness

At its best, learning should contribute to wisdom or wise practice. Indeed, our organization, Active, has placed wisdom as one of its core values. As we have said, mindfulness is a component of wisdom and so it is important to show how mindfulness fits in wisdom. We define wisdom using social practice wisdom (SPW) research (Gärtner, 2011b; McKenna, Rooney, & Boal, 2009; Rooney, McKenna, & Liesch, 2010). SPW extends and updates Aristotle's notion of practical wisdom (*phronesis*) and is appropriate for this study because it demonstrates more clearly the collective elements of wise practice and the need to integrate qualities of mind, reasoning, ethics, values, and micro-social practices to achieve wise outcomes. SPW is also informed by Buddhist philosophy and psychology research. SPW sees wisdom as the peak of human social excellence. SPW is defined by the following five nested and integrating principles:

1 *Qualities of mind:* An aware and actively open mind with habituated dispositions that support innate inclinations for virtuous social action. This involves mindfulness, equanimity, and self-knowledge needed to understand uncertainty and situated relativities of life that include conflicting values, identities, cultures, and politics.
2 *Knowledge, insight, and critical reasoning:* Using knowledge (including self-knowledge, social, cultural, economic, and political knowledge), aesthetic knowledge (direct, embodied, sensory-based, and non-rational knowing), and transcendent ability (creativity, insight, foresight, intuition, mindsight, etc.) in reflecting, judging, imagining, and reasoning to create insightful understandings that help achieve social excellence and create well-being.
3 *Ethical and moral skill for pro-social behavior:* This includes ethical skill and courage; ability to understand people's emotional, social, and material needs; magnanimity; and compassion to find the right and ethical (virtuous) thing to do.
4 *Praxis or wise action:* Practical ability using creativity, aesthetics, experience, understanding, mastery, and judgment for responsible and skillful use of knowledge, power, and communication. This involves knowing why, how, and when to adapt to the environment and why, how, and when to change it.

5 *Creating positive and sustainable outcomes for long-term positive change to the conditions of life:* This involves being a galvanizing leader and artful communicator who effects pro-social change with exceptional outcomes. Creating positive, pro-social cultures and communities are central elements of this outcome-orientation.

SPW integrates qualities of mind, reasoning, and ethical skill in praxis to create wise outcomes. The model in Figure 5.1 shows that praxis and qualities of mind are in pivotal positions with bi-directional arrows indicating primary interactions. Because praxis is about wise action the praxis element of the model is surrounded by an illustrative selection of verbs appropriate for it, but readers can add other appropriate verbs. For us the most important quality of mind for wisdom is mindfulness because it conditions the mind's capability to exhibit other important qualities of mind, like openness, and because it links mind to practice.

For this chapter we focus on the mindfulness dynamics in principle 1 of SPW, primarily because of mindfulness's value in coping with dilemmas and stress, and for developing willingness to act wisely. Beyond this, mindfulness is the process that develops the qualities of mind like equanimity and openness that are very important precursors of wise decision making and action. Mindfulness directly links and integrates qualities of mind, which also includes identity, with reasoning (principle 2) and ethics/values/virtues (principle 3), and therefore is a ground for excellent practice (principle 4) that leads to excellent outcomes (principle 5). Mindfulness is indivisible from wisdom (Krafcik, 2015) and is only properly appreciated as part of wisdom's systemic nature that seeks to produce positive outcomes in the world; mindfulness should not therefore be seen as a stand-alone process or an end in itself.

It is useful to review two different models of mindfulness to better understand what mindfulness is and why it contributes to SPW. The Liverpool mindfulness model (Figure 5.2) (Malinowski, 2013) provides a view of the integrating dynamics of mindfulness using a western psychology perspective. This five-level model describes how the messiness of life and minds is integrated to create the right mental stance to underpin wise behavior and outcomes.

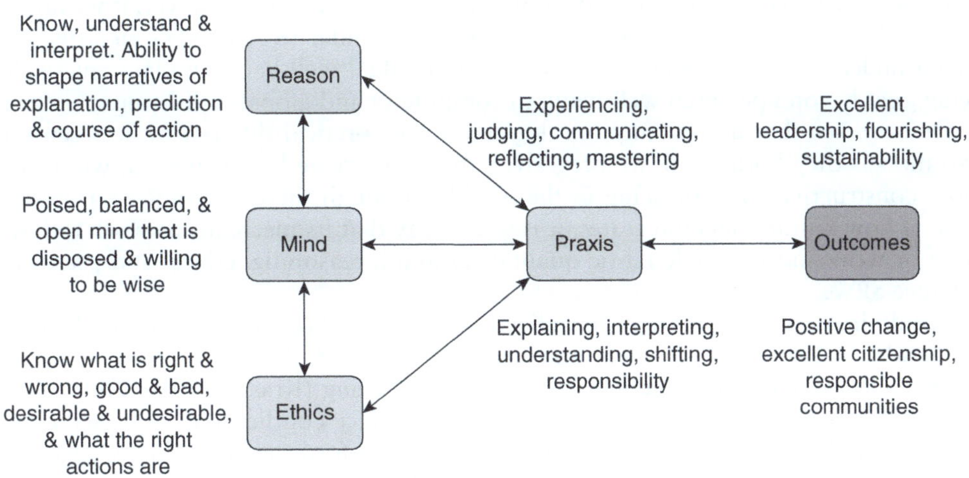

Figure 5.1 Social practice wisdom model.
Source: Rooney (2015).

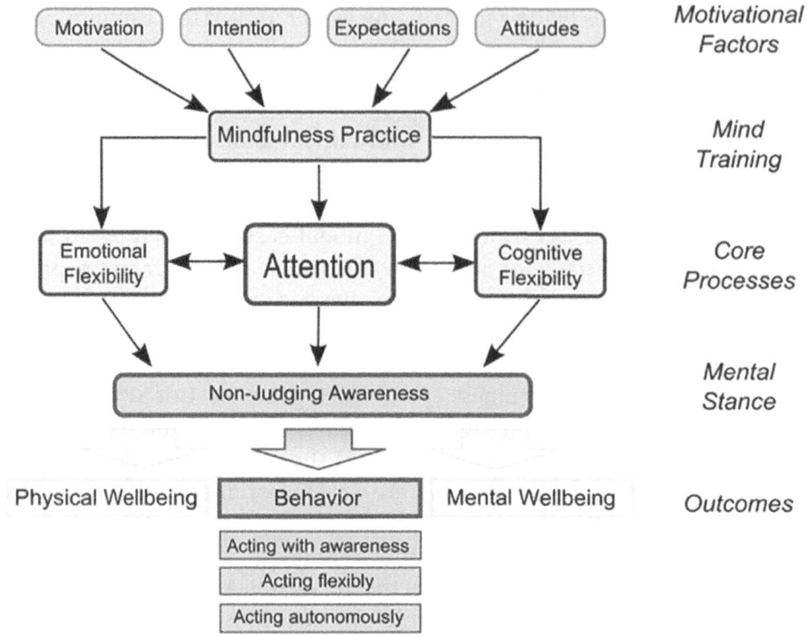

Figure 5.2 Liverpool mindfulness model.
Source: Malinowski (2013).

A more classical, Buddhist psychology view of mindfulness (Grabovac, Lau, & Willett, 2011), identifies ethics as well as (present-oriented) awareness and attention (open and non-attached) flexibility, and (non-judgmental) acceptance to create a mental state that is equanimous and healthy (Figure 5.3). Outcomes of this model include ethical practice, acceptance, and well-being. In this Buddhist psychology model, well-being is similar to the Liverpool model of individual well-being. However, if we take a broader Buddhist philosophical view, well-being is similar to Aristotle's *eudaimonia*, which understands well-being as more than individual well-being. Eudaimonic well-being goes beyond personal well-being to community and global well-being.

One can see that despite any ontological and theoretical differences between the two models they both speak to integrative ability to create better, indeed, wiser and more constructive ways of being in the world. Although there may not be a unified view of how mindfulness integrates, it is safe to say that its mechanisms work to integrate or weave into a single fabric qualities of mind, reasoning, ethics, and praxis to produce SPW.

Mindfulness is known to be beneficial for job satisfaction (Hülsheger, Alberts, Feinholdt, & Lang, 2013), safety and learning (Weick & Putnam, 2006; Weick & Roberts, 1993; Weick & Sutcliffe, 2006), and well-being (Krasner et al., 2009). It is proposed as a way to identify deceit, resolve and reduce conflict, reduce biased communication, develop more creative workforces, and to foster effective knowledge diffusion (Burgoon, Berger, & Waldron, 2000). Although mindfulness has been used in various ways in organizational research (other studies include Beer et al., 2015;

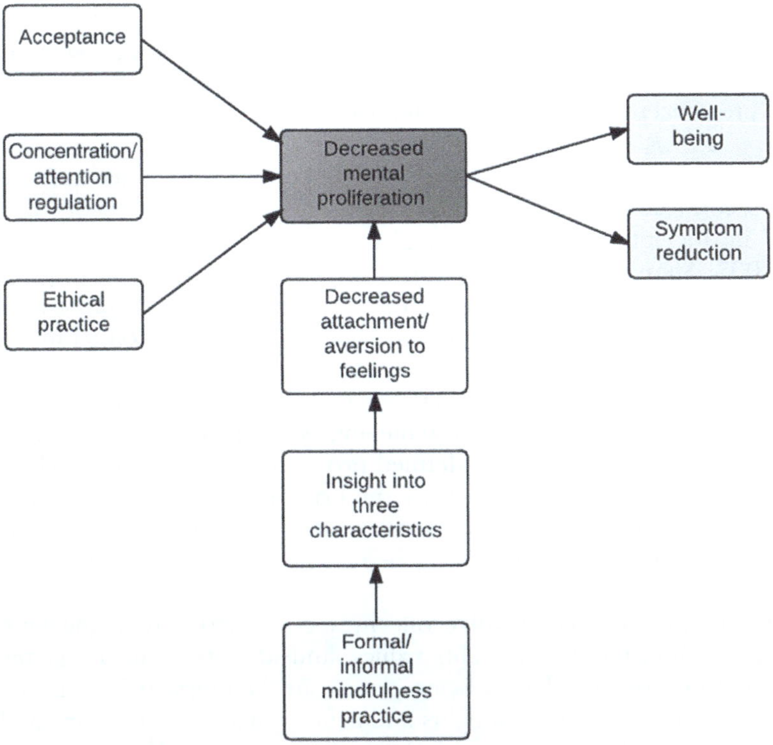

Figure 5.3 Buddhist psychology model of mindfulness.
Source: Grabovac et al. (2011).

Dane, 2011; Hernes & Irgens, 2013; Teo, Srivastava, Ranganathan, & Loo, 2011; Vogus & Sutcliffe, 2012), the research has been criticized for not accurately reflecting authentic mindfulness theory (Gärtner, 2011a). Most often the conceptual failings of such research are related to ignoring or underplaying the roles of values and of being non-judgmental and accepting. Underplaying such things is not only to ignore important aspects of mindfulness but also of learning itself. In mindfulness, non-judgmental means more than simply delaying evaluating what is good and bad. More precisely, non-judgmental acceptance means not processing your thoughts intellectually, it is pre-conceptual (Hülsheger et al., 2013). One tries simply to observe, register, and non-judgmentally acknowledge (accept) what is happening. If one has non-judgmentally accepted the presence of a thought, one can more readily deal constructively with the thought (or feeling, or circumstance). This acceptance prevents, for example, "over-thinking," procrastination, depressive ruminating, and catastrophizing.

Mindfulness can be a difficult concept to understand because knowledge of how to practise it is highly tacit and embodied. As such, mindfulness is about living fully in the moment and being fully aware of what is in the moment, rather than letting the mind constantly wander to thoughts about the past or future. Allowing random thoughts to litter the mind and continually evaluating and judging those thoughts impairs clear thinking in the present (Hafenbrack, Kinias, & Barsade, 2014). A mindful state is therefore one in which unhelpful or extreme (mostly negative) emotions and thoughts that cloud focus, thinking, and judgment are nullified through the skills of being non-judgmental, accepting, and remaining attendant to the present. Hülsheger et al. (2013, p. 311) say that mindfulness requires: (1) awareness and registration of internal experiences and external events; (2) pre-conceptual processing of information; and (3) present-oriented consciousness.

This definition is illuminating, but, like some other contemporary accounts, it elides mindfulness's connection to values. The origins of mindfulness theory and practice are found in ancient Buddhist philosophy and practice where the Eight-Fold Path (Karr, 2007; Shapiro, Carlson, Astin, & Freedman, 2006) and the Ten Precepts (Lawton & Morgan, 2007) that are central to a practical ethical framework for living and working that is focused on pro-social behavior, compassion, elimination of suffering, avoiding egotism, and enlightenment or wisdom. Non-judgmental observation of the moment to create wise social practice is inseparable from mindfulness. In short, mindfulness is a means of achieving wise ends and is anchored by a strong sense of community and a well-defined pro-social values system. Thus, Shapiro, Carlson, Astin, & Freedman (2006) say the primary elements of mindfulness are attention (non-judgmental, pre-conceptual), observing the moment, attitude (acceptance, care, courage, etc.), and intention (the reason for being mindful based on clearly understood positive values).

Importantly, mindfulness practices involve one in a constructive dialogue with one's own, feelings, emotions/moods, thoughts values, and identity to unclutter the mind, rebalance it, and improve its clarity. Being present in the moment is therefore about grounding learning by anchoring thoughts and actions in a particular time and place and insightful reasoning. Given all this, it is appropriate that mindfulness theory has been used to research the continuity of past, present, and future in organizational learning (Hernes & Irgens, 2013), and to consider attention in dynamic environments that require high levels of expertise (Dane, 2011).

Methodology

Sample and data collection

This research uses semi-structured interviews as its data. Our organization, Active, provides occupational health and safety training and educational services to a broad range of companies. Active understands itself as a learning organization and is an example of a Knowledge Intensive Services Sector (KISS) firm (Miles, 2008). KISS firms rely on work done by highly educated professionals whose knowledge is central to the firm's core business and ability to create value. KISS professionals' knowledge is typically informed by research and theory. We had good access to the organization that enabled us to readily engage with almost its entire professional workforce to gather very rich and deep insights about the experience of organizational learning there. Active has twenty-five employees in Bergen, Norway, and twenty of them were interviewed for this study. Five males and fifteen females were interviewed. Interviewees ranged in age from thirty to fifty-six. Interviews were obtained on the basis of availability as two employees were on maternity leave and one was on long-term sick leave. Interviewees have different professional backgrounds; nurses, physical therapists, doctors, psychologists, and engineers and around half have taken additional courses within the fields of organization, business, and leadership studies. All of the interviewees provide occupational health and safety training and educational services to client organizations. According to Beechey (2012), this sample is in keeping with the range of backgrounds and ages, and the gender profile for such an organization. The dominance of female interviewees is not unusual in the human services and health services delivery sectors. Nevertheless, the effect on our data of this feminine dominance is likely to be positive in terms of creating knowledge not distorted by male epistemic privilege and dominance (Alcoff, Alcoff, & Potter, 2013). In addition, one must also consider that contemporary feminist scholars are reconstructing established feminist epistemology that may lead readers to think women are less objective and rational and hence to indulge in neo-Romantic conceptions of feminine emotion and subjectivity-loaded knowledge (Alcoff et al., 2013; Nicholson, 2013). A risk that feminist scholars now see is that we fall into accepting stereotypes and exaggerated epistemological differences between women and men.

In semi-structured interviews topics that should be covered are specified but the interviewee's point of view is of greatest interest. The interview questions are not rigidly outlined and the interviews are flexible (Bryman, 2008). This method was used because the aim of the interviews was to investigate employees' perspectives and lived experiences (Seidman, 2006) of organizational learning, identity, and communication at Active. Semi-structured interviews help develop an understanding of how employees make sense of and create meaning in their environment (Rubin & Rubin, 2005). Through conversation the interviewer can modify and reorder questions to evoke the fullest response, and enable interviewees to provide responses in their own terms (Qu & Dumay, 2011). Interviews ranged from 30 to 45 minutes in duration, and were conducted in the interviewees work location, and were conducted and transcribed in Norwegian, which is the first language of both the interviewees and the interviewer.

This study was designed to examine the relationship between organizational learning and organizational identity. Interview questions therefore were designed to probe both learning and identity to see how (or if) employees connected identity and learning. The questions needed to be specific enough to obtain relevant information and at the same time open enough so that the employees could do their own reasoning. The links to grounding, wisdom, and mindfulness emerged in the analysis; however, our interview questions relate directly to SPW principles 1 (e.g. mind states), 2 (e.g. reasoning), 3 (e.g. ethics and values), 4 (practices), and 5 (outcomes). Interview questions are: What does learning mean to you? How do you best learn? How would you describe a learning organization? Is Active a learning organization? If yes, how does the organization promote learning? Is new knowledge and learning shared in the organization? If yes, how is learning shared? Is Active open to new learning methods? Have you experienced any barriers to learning in the organization? Do you identify with Active? Has this identity changed over time? How would you describe the organizational culture in Active? How does culture affect learning? How does learning affect your identity with Active? Are your own teaching methods affected by the identity and culture in Active?

Analysis and interpretation

Analysis followed an interpretative hermeneutic approach to create an understanding of how individuals make sense of the world around them so that the researcher can grasp some of their reality (Charmaz, 2006; Eikeland, 2008; Flyvbjerg, 2011). Through repeated readings of the source material it is possible to capture the essence, or what is constant in other's experiences and behavior (Miles & Huberman, 1994). Interpretive hermeneutics suggests that analysis aims to interpret a phenomenon and to uncover hidden meanings (Dowling, 2004; Heracleous & Hendry, 2000). Thus the analyst seeks to bring out the meaning of the text from the perspective of the text's author (the interviewee). Such analysis is concerned with the interpretation of human action (Bryman, 2008; Butler, 1998; Flyvbjerg, 2001), and seeks to investigate the producer of the text in context (Bryman, 2008). Hermeneutic analysis of text is built around a core of reading, reflective writing, and interpretation (the hermeneutic cycle) (see for example Schön, 1995). In this study the researchers read and reread the interview texts, each writing interpretations which we discussed, refined, and rewrote repeatedly and collaboratively. Our interpretations were also read primarily in light of the organizational learning, wisdom, and mindfulness literatures. This process also included the reflexive reading-interpretation of other relevant literature such as those in knowledge management and education.

Results and discussion: The ground for organizational learning

We now work through our data analysis and discussion. We begin by setting out our basic data analysis by staying close to the data before more deeply engaging with our interpretation and reengaging with wisdom and mindfulness theory to chart practical action in the form of an eight-step process to create mindful organizational dialogue and learning for wise practice.

Our data shows that Active's employees use terms like grounding learning, acquiring new knowledge, personal and professional development, sharing experiences, mastery, wisdom, values, and competence when they discuss organizational learning. Although there are differences in how Active's employees learn, common methods include attending seminars, reading literature, and dialogical learning. Different interviewees need different kinds of new knowledge, including learning new theories, facts, and methods, as well as extending and relearning what they already know, and developing mastery. As an interviewee said: "Learning is acquiring new knowledge through reading, dialogue, or sharing of knowledge and experiences with co-workers, so that one can be competent to handle and master occupational and personal challenges."

Interviewees relate professional development to learning, which they say is necessary to keep up to date with rapidly changing knowledge. This is also about competence, mastery and (professional and personal) challenges, according to this interviewee. The markets Active operates in are highly competitive, and it is imperative for Active to be up to date with occupational health and safety knowledge and to adjust products and services as knowledge changes. Interviewees also explain that it is important for them as individuals to be challenged and to always focus on achieving higher levels of competence so they can properly train and advise clients. Active's employees are motivated and ready to learn. They enjoy acquiring new knowledge and increasing their competence. Moreover, interviewees say that individual learning is necessary for Active to be a learning organization, and also that individuals' knowledge has to be shared for the organization to learn and develop. However, interviewees also explain that time pressure seriously limits learning and knowledge sharing.

Our interviewees recognize Active as an organization that values learning and its leaders are concerned with educating employees, as far as time and budgets allow. Interviewees say Active's leaders have positive attitudes to knowledge, learning, and competence, but some employees are disappointed that they have to initiate learning processes themselves. Furthermore, as one interviewees say, learning is not grounded.

> The organization absolutely has the premise to be a learning organization. The employees are motivated to acquire new knowledge, but organizational structures, time pressure, and capacity are barriers that hinder organizational learning. Management thinks that competence is important, but the plans to increase this competence are not followed up and not grounded in the organization.

Regardless of any espoused organizational values, learning is limited at Active and so it is interesting that this interviewee considers competence needs to be "grounded" in the organization but structures, time and capacity hinder grounding learning. As we have suggested (above), place identity theory (Proshansky et al., 1983) argues that places or locations provide people who inhabit them with psychological resources that give them a sense of being grounded or belonging, as well as a sense of identity, purpose, values, and efficacy. Recently, place identity has been the subject of research in relation to organizational knowledge and entrepreneurs (Johnson, 2012; Larson & Pearson, 2012; Rooney, Paulsen, et al., 2010). SPW recognizes that wise practice is grounded in a time and place and mindfulness is a specific skill for anchoring oneself in time and place. One implication of place identity research that is consonant with SPW is that learning and knowledge do not rely only on phenomenological resources but also on the physicality of locations as the places where learning happens. Going a step further, how workplaces are organized has to be consonant with any espoused identity-enhancing values of the place. Learning activities that are understood to belong in a place but "are not followed up" fail to ground learning.

Active not only has internal learning needs; its business is to train employees in other companies. Interviewees explain that Active is open to new methods of teaching and for redeveloping already existing methods, but caution that it tends to be "stuck in routines" and to do "what they have always done." However, Active's trainers routinely adjust and develop the content of their seminars to fit particular client needs. Seminar participants often give feedback after a presentation, and this is taken into account for further improvement.

Relationship between identity, values, and learning

All our interviewees identify with Active. When describing what promotes this feeling of identity terms like "values," "wisdom," "quality," and "knowledge and competence" are used. The majority of interviewees therefore strongly identify with Active's values, which are publically stated on their website as: high competence, enthusiasm, wisdom, and being hands-on. Previously, Active had not explicitly articulated a set of values. Interviewees explain that they relate to these values because they are similar to their personal values. It is important for interviewees that organizational values and personal values do not conflict.

Furthermore, when asked if their ability to identify with Active has changed over time, interviewees reply that as they learnt more about the organization; its vision, its values, and how the organization works, the more strongly they identified with it. As one employee explains:

> I like being identified with the organization. Not everything is perfect, but the values are attractive to me and they go together with my personal values. It took some time to feel this identity, but as the values became more stable and more similar to my personal values, the identity has grown.

Our interviewees know Active's values well because they had participated in defining them. In the interviews, the core values of "high quality" and "competence" are repeatedly mentioned as important organizational and personal values, and it is important to interviewees that the training and other services that Active provides bear such qualities. Interviewees also emphasize the importance of having the time and resources to gain new knowledge and be "up to date" with relevant research. Time is also required before one comes to "feel this [organizational] identity." Significantly, wisdom and mindfulness both also require growth, which takes time to realize.

Interviewees recognize that lack of time is a challenge in the organization and explain that time limits, work intensification, and resulting stress stop learning from occurring. Expectations related to learning are therefore not always met, and interviewees are frustrated by not having the time to better engage in learning activities like reading research literature, attending seminars, and discussing and sharing knowledge with co-workers. Despite the lack of time for learning activities, management still expects employees to have a high level of competence and to deliver quality products.

Knowing that learning is a part of Active's identity and values stimulates employees to develop readiness to learn and predisposes them to welcome change related to learning. Interviewees also explain that knowledgeable and competent colleagues are important stimulants for their motivation to learn. Being surrounded by such colleagues promotes a positive learning environment:

> [A]s I got to know my colleagues, their competence, and the value of learning in the organization, I could focus on learning and increasing my own level of competence. I needed to match the quality and competence of my co-workers.

For Active to improve, learning processes need to be grounded in values and the micro-sociology of interactions between colleagues. Part of this is being able to "match the qualities and competences of my co-workers." Matching in this case is about aligning, meshing, and harmonizing with the organization and ones colleagues. To better understand what the data says about the grounded nature of learning it is important to consider interviewees' thoughts on knowledge sharing.

Sharing knowledge

Sharing knowledge and experience is seen as central to learning by Active's employees. However, the pressures of demands linked to maximizing billable hours make it difficult for employees to spend time engaging in learning dialogues with each other to share knowledge. Moreover, the billable hours dilemma prevents wise learning values being anchored in Active and prevents the integrated grounding of learning. Specifically, creating time to ground, share, and communicate information is not a management priority, and interviewees express a great deal of frustration about this.

> The idea has been to carry out regular internal seminars and knowledge transfer, but it is not always doable because of the great amount of work pressure and invoicing. The organization does not have routines or strategies for knowledge sharing.

The idea that learning needs to be grounded is put in the context of seminars, routines, and strategies. Routines, seminars, and strategies are important because the interviewee wants learning to be structured by them, as part of being grounded in time and place. Grounding includes processes for learning through face-to-face communication. Grounding involves communication intimacy: this learning is very personal and local. Knowledge and learning routines therefore need to be grounded in specific social processes in time and space to actively facilitate learning and knowledge sharing. These processes give learning and learners, a location, focus, certainty, intimacy or closeness, and priority.

Because of time pressures in Active, information is usually shared by sending power point presentations to each other via e-mail. Our interviewees find this method superficial and inadequate. They explain that having internal seminars used to be a priority in the organization, but as other demands and time pressure increased this was no longer so. Interviewees indicate that Active does not have a strategy for shifting learning from the individual level to the organizational level. Keeping learning at the individual level appears easier for management in terms of time and resources than it is for knowledge and learning to be taken to the organizational level.

We argue that organizational learning requires carefully crafted and grounded communication processes, particularly dialogue. Active is clearly taking a risk by leaving learning and knowledge sharing to chance and the good intentions of employee. The process of allowing other matters like maximizing billable hours to push learning down the priority list is shortsighted and incommensurate with Active's core values.

Wisdom and mindfulness for practical action

Our analysis shows what understandings and experiences Active's employees have of the way learning, values and identity interact in their workplace. In this section our findings are discussed to further consider barriers to organizational learning. Much literature related to organizational learning focuses on the importance of developing readiness to learn within employees, but this does not seem sufficient based on our data. Our data suggests that Active takes its employees readiness and motivation for granted. Our data also says that learning must be grounded in an organization rather than simply existing in the minds of employees. It is important for organizations to spend time investing thoughtfully in people, helping employees unlearn and relearn, and to map out learning and development plans for individuals, groups, and the organization (Roland, 2005). Beyond this, our data suggests that bringing people together in particular ways, places, and spaces for learning is important. Learning tacit and abstract knowledge is known to require intimate communication (Nonaka & Takeuchi, 1995; Rooney, Mandeville, & Kastelle, 2013; Tappeiner, Hauser, & Walde, 2008).

Active places high demands on employees in terms of how many billable hours they produce. This is stressful for employees as their work intensifies, reducing opportunities to learn. As organizations want to learn, be more effective, and adjust more quickly to changing environments, time must be invested in learning. Time pressure is a challenge for both employees and managers (Thomas, Fugate, & Koukova, 2011). Managers may focus more on costs than on learning and communication (Spillan, Mino, & Rowles, 2002). Employees may cope by working faster and reducing communication quality but this negatively affects learning and knowledge sharing (Thomas et al., 2011). Rooney, McKenna, et al. (2010) see this kind of scenario as a failure of organizational discursive structures and culture to provide the space for learning, wisdom, and excellence to flourish. It is not surprising, then, that interviewee's feel their expectations are not met, creating a conflict of personal and organizational values because the clear time and space for learning has not been created. Our data therefore provides little evidence of mindful organizing for learning at Active. Indeed, there is a poor fit between mindful social process and organizational practices and values in Active. There are shortcomings at Active in terms of each of the five SPW principles. Active:

1 lacks the capacity for mindful organizing;
2 is at risk of its knowledge being out of date;
3 has a gap between its espoused and enacted values and the values of employees;
4 has a service delivery that is potentially compromised by inadequate learning;
5 is at risk of providing health and safety advice that is damaging to well-being.

Lack of mindful organizing is a root cause of these problems. It is fair to say that our data shows critical aspects of learning at Active to be disjointed, or at least in need of harmonizing (cf. Intezari & Pauleen, 2014). The time, identity, and values barriers to learning that our data indicates exists at Active can be overcome by promoting mindful organizing through developing appropriate social processes.

Practical implications: creating social learning processes and mindful organizing

The clutter, agitation, and inability for effective and focused organizational learning that Active experiences can be countered by adapting mindfulness techniques. A mindful learning environment can realign disjointed processes, values, and identities. Our earlier discussion of mindfulness theory indicates that mindful organizing for learning would enable: (1) awareness and non-judgmental acceptance or registering of events; (2) focusing on the present and moment-to-moment experience; and (3) the use of these abilities to align identities, values, and practices to create positive social value. Importantly, a fundamental element of mindfulness practice, then, is creating an internal accepting and open dialogue that changes the relationship that one has with one's thoughts and emotions by non-judgmentally focusing on the present.

Dialogical wisdom

If mindfulness is fundamentally a constructive dialogue within oneself, dialogue is a good starting point for considering how to create mindful organizing. Dialogical communication and constructing life narratives are also important for developing wisdom (Barge & Little, 2002; Eikeland, 2008; Ferrari, Weststrate, & Petro, 2013; Flyvbjerg, 2001). Communication is central to social learning because it is necessary in tasks like learning from others, i.e., transferring knowledge (Curado, 2006). Communication is the "process by which people interactively create, sustain, and manage meaning" (Bambacas & Patrickson, 2008, p. 52). Communication and learning, then, are related to the process of creating meaning (Pace, 2002). When individuals receive information, mental models and cognitive maps affect how this information is interpreted (Berson et al., 2006), and how knowledge is shared (Mazutis & Slawinski, 2008). Interpretive mental models are used as frameworks for more complete understandings, and are influenced by individual values, beliefs, experiences, culture, and identities (Spicer, 1998); hence different individuals will have different mental models when interpreting messages. Mindfulness enhances this process by bringing clarity, focus, parsimony, calmness, and the ability to better act in accord with one's values. The clarity that mindfulness brings also contributes to the integrity of knowledge because it is based in sound values and intentions. We argue that clarity, focus, parsimony, and calmness can be brought to an organization's knowledge work and learning if organizational dialogue has the qualities of mindfulness. Our interviewees' strong identification with Active is linked to Active's espoused organizational values. Yet interviewees experience a sense of values conflict between their own personal values and Active's enacted organizational values. Employees feel that they are caught in a conflict between what they perceive as genuine quality and what is just good enough as far as time and resources allow. They are effectively questioning if Active can guarantee the integrity of its knowledge and act with genuine professionalism (cf. Schwartz & Sharpe, 2010).

In this scenario, attention, intention, and attitude are misaligned and in conflict at Active and this precludes mindful organizing. Although Active and its employees have many good intentions, the organization cannot attend properly to organizational learning because there is no coherence between attention, intention, and attitude. If we take values, identities, and knowledge as important components of the collective mind at Active, its mind is an agitated, cluttered, and conflicted one.

Developing mindful organizing

Knowledge, identities, and values are organizational analogues in this chapter for the thoughts, intentions, and emotions that are dealt with in personal mindfulness practices. Although any knowledge-intensive organization should be busy, it should not be too busy or unmindful to learn well. But this begs the question, how can Active become a mindful knowledge-intensive organization? It is useful to look at what could be done to improve mindful organizing and learning by developing constructive dialogues. We develop a dialogical mindfulness and acceptance-based framework based on Roemer and Orsillo (2009). The framework is developed from mindfulness theory and adheres to and integrates with the principles in SPW such that none of them is ignored, thus maximizing the chances of generating better outcomes and wise practice. This guide is particularly useful for Active because of its focus on values.

At Active, dialogue (and action) can take an eight-step approach (Roemer & Orsillo, 2009):

1 understanding how avoidance limits performance;
2 reorientation (reassessment) of values;
3 identifying confusion between values and goals;
4 balancing across multiple domains to avoid "values perfection" (absolutist) traps;
5 increasing awareness of action and inaction on things that matter;
6 promote mindful, valued action;
7 making effective commitments and increasing willingness to commit;
8 evaluating progress.

We start with (1) avoidance, noting that Active has avoided (and not accepted) dealing adequately with its learning barriers. Not making time or space and not attending to the present to ground learning in specific processes, despite how busy the organization is and how much billable hours matters, is a trap that managers must not get caught in. Convincing management to focus attention on the problem in the present may require an external facilitator. It is important for management to talk about values and learning barriers without immediately deflecting thoughts to the future or past or by making hasty judgments. Importantly, managers should understand why it matters to have dialogues about how the contingencies of commercial reality (mostly future oriented in our data) have distracted them from grounding learning. Having done this, an organization can benefit from acceptance and acknowledge the scope of the problem rather than continuing the adverse effects of avoidance.

(2) Reviewing, reassessing, and reorienting (again) values that are central to an organization is important and should also be done as a dialogue across the organization. Of course, such processes may even lead to complete transformations of organizational values. A participative approach is best so that the formalized values are ones that everyone can embrace to a reasonable extent. Having done this kind of review and reassessment, (3) conflicts and confusion between values, goals, and behavior can be identified and resolved so that values, goals, and behavior are consistent with each other. An important next step is to make sure that values are (4) balanced across all aspects of the organization and its work. Some compromise may be needed here, and part of this process is avoiding what is called the perfection trap. Overly idealized and rigid commitment to an absolute value is often unworkable because of competing interests and incommensurable work demands. Taking absolute positions is called all-or-nothing thinking in cognitive behavior therapy and is regarded as a cognitive distortion. Competing and incommensurate demands could come from regulatory or legal restrictions that must be met but which are not an easy fit with the organizations values. Other "contingencies of life" like limited resources could also be complicating factors.

(5) Increasing awareness of action and inaction on things that matter is important for Active. It is easy to forget to act consistently in accord with our values. Being non-judgmentally aware of what is happening in the present is central to mindfulness; and for an organization it means (among other things) being aware of how well

it is keeping its current actions in line with its values. If talk of learning, values, and mindfulness is part of the organization's discourse this awareness can be maintained. With this awareness is the possibility of rewarding activities that are consonant with values to (6) promote mindful and valued actions. It would be useful to map learning and knowledge growth and how knowledge is applied so that management can "see" its value and thus feel rewarded. Over time this will embed values-consistent behavior in culture.

(7) Making effective commitments is important and is linked to intentions, as much as to outcomes. This also links to organizational culture and discourse. People's intentions will align with the organization's values and goals and vice versa if the talk and behavior within an organization reinforces defined and agreed upon organizational values and this, in turn, will shape or reinforce intentions. Part of this "talk" should not only be about what the values are and why they matter but should also be about being appropriately committed and engaged. People should feel free to openly discuss commitment, including when they feel management's commitment is waning. These processes will produce increasing willingness to commit to valued action, including from managers. Evaluating progress is important and so regular (say, half yearly) checkups are advisable. Dialogue is important in these checkups too, and these dialogues might best be informed by, for example, a values survey, interviews, and observational study.

Vervaeke and Ferraro (2013) argue that social, political, cultural, and economic conditions can work for or against wisdom. An important aspect of SPW in a work setting is that it says managers must create the space (the ground) for mindfulness and wisdom to flourish (Rooney, McKenna, et al., 2010). This can include changing organizational structures and cultures, but also physical spaces, how spaces are used, and what activities they are associated with. Management can create favorable environments for learning by, for example, setting strategic learning goals linked to the organization's vision and direction (Milway & Saxton, 2011; Roland, 2005). When an organization's direction and vision are communicated to employees it provides psychological resources that may enhance their ability to identify with learning in their organization (Prati et al., 2009). Consistent leadership and communication through social interaction and shared experiences can generate a shared sense of readiness (Weiner, 2009). A strong participatory approach will motivate learning (Prati et al., 2009), and this is emphasized in social learning theory (Coghlan & Jacobs, 2005; Tahir, Naeem, Sarfraz, Javed, & Ali, 2011).

Active does not look like a mindful place because it is too busy and agitated to focus on and attend to learning in the present in a calm, non-judgmental, accepting, skilled, and disciplined way. What is fascinating about our study is that despite the fact that there is agreement that organizational learning is important, learning barriers persist. Organizations can begin by clearing out clutter and distraction using the eight steps above and thereby provide space for a disciplined and wise focus on learning. Billable hours is an important concept in our data and is a factor that hinders a clearer focus on learning and creating the space to ground learning in Active. In our data, billable hours distracts attention and keeps focus on a limited picture of the future rather than on doing learning in the here and now; it also clutters work time, limits disciplined attention, and may hinder the organizations intellectual resilience and integrity.

Conclusion

Managers, employees, and others often see the value and importance of effective learning, but may be unsure of how to reach their learning and knowledge goals. The eight-step mindfulness dialogue approach is useful to enhance performance through grounding learning and knowledge sharing (Spillan et al., 2002). Leaders have to be clear about the best approaches to achieve effective and mindful dialogues for learning and knowledge sharing (Spillan et al., 2002). When organizational learning and knowledge are important to a busy professional workplace, our data says a mindfulness dialogue and learning plan that is grounded in mindful organizing, values, and place is important. Wise communication and mindful dialogue structured around the eight steps set out above offer ways to understand how to create such plans (see Barge & Little, 2002 for wise dialogue). As Krieger says, mindful communication is a shared state of mindfulness:

> [W]hereby, in the communicative interaction, the individuals involved are in an active state of attending, responding, and perceiving information correctly. As a result, they are continually updating, attuned, and open to incoming data that are unexpected, disconfirming, improbable, implicit, and/or contested.
>
> (Krieger, 2005, p. 138)

This perspective is important because learning is about opening up to the new, including that which challenges and surprises. The non-judgmental acceptance of mindfulness is part of the ground that can make this kind of learning and wise organizations more likely to occur. Finally, wisdom research offers new potential by giving insight into integrating such things as mindfulness, reason, transcendence, subjectivity, virtue, aesthetics, and social practice in organizations. Mindfulness is an aspect of wisdom that has integrative power. Wisdom is the art of living mindfully to produce deliberative excellence and well-being; therefore, wisdom is something that one does. Wise organizational agents are necessarily mindful; open to new ideas, experiences, and critique; they can skilfully work with any situated relativities of values; and they have practiced predispositions to strive for excellence. These are ideal conditions for fostering organizational learning and knowledge for social practice wisdom. It is possible for Active to move significantly closer to operationalizing all its core values, including wisdom. Moreover, it is likely that learning and wise practice can be facilitated by mindful dialogue in any organisation and that the basic principles and process presented in this chapter are useful in any organizational context. Finally, wisdom and its mindfulness component are underpinned by processes that are learnable and because they have this process component they can be embodied by organizations to ground learning.

Reflective questions

If readers want questions to reflect on having read this chapter it makes sense to reflect on the questions about the eight steps we asked on behalf of Active. The same questions can be asked of any organization.

- Do you understand how avoidance limits performance?
- Do you need to reorient (or reassess) your values?
- Have you identified confusions between your values and goals?

- Do you achieve balance across multiple domains to avoid "values perfection" (absolutist) traps?
- Will you increase awareness of action and inaction on things that matter?
- Will you promote mindful, valued action?
- When will you next make effective commitments and increase your willingness to commit?
- Will you evaluate your progress?

References

Alcoff, L., Alcoff, L. M., & Potter, E. (2013). *Feminist Epistemologies*. London: Routledge.

Argote, L. (2011). Organizational learning research: Past, present and future. *Management Learning, 42*(4), 439–446.

Argyris, C. (1993). *On Organizational Learning*. Cambridge, MA: Blackwell Business.

Argyris, C. (2004). *Reasons and Rationalizations: The Limits to Organizational Knowledge*. New York: Oxford University Press.

Arrowsmith, J., & Sisson, K. (2001). International competition and pay, working time and employment: Exploring the processes of adjustment. *Industrial Relations Journal, 32*(2), 136–153.

Bambacas, M., & Patrickson, M. (2008). Interpersonal communication skills that enhance organizational commitment. *Journal of Communication Management, 12*(1), 51–72.

Barge, J. K., & Little, M. (2002). Dialogical wisdom, communicative practice, and organizational life. *Communication Theory, 12*(4), 375–397.

Beechey, V. (2012). Women and production: A critical analysis of some sociological theories of women's work. In A. Kuhn & Wolpe (Eds.), *Feminism and Materialism: Women and Modes of Production*, 155–197. London: Routledge & Kegan Paul.

Beer, L. E., Rodriguez, K., Taylor, C., Martinez-Jones, N., Griffin, J., Smith, T. R., . . . Anaya, R. (2015). Awareness, integration and interconnectedness contemplative practices of higher education professionals. *Journal of Transformative Education, 13*(2), 161–185.

Berson, Y., Nemanich, L. A., Waldman, D. A., Galvin, B. M., & Keller, R. T. (2006). Leadership and organizational learning: A multiple levels perspective. *The Leadership Quarterly, 17*, 577–594.

Brown, A. D., & Starkey, K. (2000). Organizational identity and learning: A psychodynamic perspective. *Academy of Management Review, 25*(1), 102–120.

Bryman, A. (2008). *Social Research Methods*, 3rd edition. New York: Oxford University Press.

Burgoon, J. K., Berger, C. R., & Waldron, V. R. (2000). Mindfulness and interpersonal communication. *Journal of Social Issues, 56*(1), 105–127.

Butler, T. (1998). Towards a hermeneutic method for interpretive research in information systems. *Journal of Information Technology, 13*, 285–300.

Charmaz, K. (2006). *Constructing Grounded Theory: A Practical Guide Through Qualitative Analysis*. London: Sage.

Coghlan, D., & Jacobs, C. (2005). Sound from silence: On listening in organizational learning. *Human Relations, 58*(1), 115–138.

Curado, C. (2006). Organizational learning and organizational design. *The Learning Organization, 13*(1), 25–42.

Dane, E. (2011). Paying attention to mindfulness and its effects on task performance in the workplace. *Journal of Management, 37*(4), 997–1018.

Dobni, D., Ritchie, J. R. B., & Zerbe, W. (2000). Organizational values: The inside view of service productivity. *Journal of Business Research, 47*(2), 91–107.

Dowling, M. (2004). Hermeneutics: An exploration. *Nurse Researcher, 11*(4), 30–39.

Eikeland, O. (2008). *The Ways of Aristotle: Aristotelian Phronesis, Aristotelian Philosophy of Dialogue, and Action Research*. Bern: Peter Lang.

Faucher, J.-B. P. L., Everett, A. M., & Lawson, R. (2008). Reconstituting knowledge management. *Journal of Knowledge Management, 12*(3), 3–16.

Ferrari, M., Weststrate, N. M., & Petro, A. (2013). Stories of wisdom to live by: Developing wisdom in a narrative mode. In M. Ferrari & N. M. Weststrate (Eds.), *The Scientific Study of Personal Wisdom: From Contemplative Traditions to Neuroscience* (pp. 137–164). Dordrecht: Springer.

Floro, M. S. (1995). Women's well-being, poverty, and work intensity. *Feminist Economics, 1*(3), 1–25.

Flyvbjerg, B. (2001). *Making Social Science Matter: Why Social Inquiry Fails and How it Can Succeed Again* (S. Sampson, Trans.). Cambridge: Cambridge University Press.

Flyvbjerg, B. (2011). Case study. In N. K. Denzin & Y. S. Lincoln (Eds.), *The Sage Handbook of Qualitative Research*, 4th edition (pp. 301–316). Thousand Oaks, CA: Sage.

Gärtner, C. (2011a). Putting new wine into old bottles: Mindfulness as a micro-foundation of dynamic capabilities. *Management Decision, 49*(2), 253–269.

Gärtner, C. (2011b). Wisdom in the flesh: Embodied social practices of wisdom in organizations. *Philosophy of Management, 10*(1), 29–42.

Grabovac, A. D., Lau, M. A., & Willett, B. R. (2011). Mechanisms of mindfulness: A Buddhist psychological model. *Mindfulness, 2*(3), 154–166.

Groddeck, V. (2011). Rethinking the role of value communication in business corporations from a sociological perspective: Why organizations need value- based semantics to cope with societal and organizational fuzziness. *Journal of Business Ethics, 100*(1), 69–84.

Hafenbrack, A. C., Kinias, Z., & Barsade, S. G. (2014). Debiasing the mind through meditation mindfulness and the sunk-cost bias. *Psychological Science, 25*(2), 369–376.

Heracleous, L., & Hendry, J. (2000). Discourse and the study of organization: Towards a structurational perspective. *Human Relations, 53*(10), 1251–1286.

Hernes, T., & Irgens, E. J. (2013). Keeping things mindfully on track: Organizational learning under continuity. *Management Learning, 44*(3), 253–266.

Hogg, M. A., & Terry, D. J. (2000). Social identity and self-categorization processes in organizational contexts. *Academy of Management Review, 25*(1), 121–140.

Horner, R. D., Szaflarski, J. P., Ying, J., Meganathan, K., Matthews, G., Schroer, B., . . . Raphaelson, M. (2011). Physician work intensity among medical specialties: emerging evidence on its magnitude and composition. *Medical care, 49*(11), 1007–1011.

Hülsheger, U. R., Alberts, H. J. E. M., Feinholdt, A., & Lang, J. W. B. (2013). Benefits of mindfulness at work: The role of mindfulness in emotion regulation, emotional exhaustion, and job satisfaction. *Journal of Applied Psychology, 98*(2), 310–325. doi:doi: 10.1037/a0031313

Hultman, K. (2005). Evaluating organizational values. *Organizational Development Journal, 23*(4), 32–44.

Intezari, A., & Pauleen, D. (2014). Management wisdom in perspective: Are you virtuous enough to succeed in volatile times? *Journal of Business Ethics, 120*(3), 393–404.

Jacobs, G., Christe-Zeyse, J., Keegan, A., & Pólos, L. (2008). Reactions to organizational identity threats in times of change: Illustrations from the German police. *Corporate Reputation Review, 11*(3), 245–261.

Jacobson Jr, C. J., Bolon, S., Elder, N., Schroer, B., Matthews, G., Szaflarski, J. P., . . . Horner, R. D. (2011). Temporal and subjective work demands in office-based patient care: An exploration of the dimensions of physician work intensity. *Medical Care, 49*(1), 52–58.

Johnson, V. (2012). Identity, sustainability, and local setting at U.S. botanical gardens. *Organization and Environment, 25*(3), 259–285. Retrieved from www.scopus.com/inward/record.url?eid=2-s2.0-84867675620&partnerID=40&md5=569b5013500dcf036123334f502be0ca

Joo, B. K., & Lim, T. (2009). The effects of organizational learning culture, perceived job complexity, and proactive personality on organizational commitment and intrinsic motivation. *Journal of Leadership and Organizational Studies, 16*(1), 48–60.

Karr, A. (2007). *Contemplating Reality: A Practitioner's Guide to the View in Indo-Tibetan Buddhism*. Boston: Shambhala.

Kolodinsky, R. W., & Bierly, P. E. (2013). Understanding the elements and outcomes of executive wisdom: A strategic approach. *Journal of Management & Organisation, 19*(1), 1–24.

Krafcik, D. (2015). Words from the wise: Exploring the lives, qualities, and opinions of wisdom exemplars. *Integral Review, 11*(2), 7–35.

Krasner, M. S., Epstein, R. M., Beckman, H., Beckman, H., Suchman, A. L., Chapman, B., . . . Quill, T. E. (2009). Association of an educational program in mindful communication with burnout, empathy, and attitudes among primary care physicians. *Journal of the American Medical Association, 302*(12), 1284–1293.

Krieger, J. L. (2005). Shared mindfulness in cockpit crisis situations an exploratory analysis. *Journal of Business Communication, 42*(2), 135–167.

Larson, G. S., & Pearson, A. R. (2012). Placing identity: Place as a discursive resource for occupational identity work among high-tech entrepreneurs. *Management Communication Quarterly, 26*(2), 241–266.

Lawton, C., & Morgan, P. (2007). *Ethical Issues in Six Religious Traditions*. New York: Oxford University Press.

Malinowski, P. (2013). Neural mechanisms of attentional control in mindfulness meditation. *Frontiers in Neuroscience, 7*, 8.

Mazutis, D., & Slawinski, N. (2008). Leading organizational learning through authentic dialogue. *Management Learning, 39*(4), 437–456.

McKenna, B., Rooney, D., & Boal, K. (2009). Wisdom principles as a meta-theoretical basis for evaluating leadership. *The Leadership Quarterly, 20*(2), 177–190.

Michailova, S., & Sidorova, E. (2011). From group- based work to organizational learning: The role of communication forms and knowledge sharing. *Knowledge Management Research and Practice, 9*, 73–83.

Miles, I. (2008). Patterns of innovation in service industries. *IBM Systems Journal, 47*(1), 115–128.

Miles, M. B., & Huberman, A. M. (1994). *Qualitative Data Analysis*, 2nd edition. Thousand Oaks, CA: Sage.

Milway, K. S., & Saxton, A. (2011). The challenge of organizational learning. *Stanford Social Innovation Review, 9*(3), 44–50.

Nicholson, L. (2013). *Feminism/Postmodernism* London: Routledge.

Nonaka, I., & Takeuchi, H. (1995). *The Knowledge Creating Company: How Japanese Companies Create the Dynamics of Innovation*. New York: Oxford University Press.

Pace, R. W. (2002). The organizational learning audit. *Management Communication Quarterly, 15*(3), 458–465.

Phillips, N., Lawrence, T. B., & Hardy, C. (2004). Discourse and institutions. *Academy of Management Review, 29*(4), 635–652.

Pokharel, M. P., & Hult, K. M. (2010). Varieties of organizational learning: Investigating learning in local level public sector organizations. *Journal of Workplace Learning, 22*(4), 249–270.

Prati, L. M., McMillan-Capehart, A., & Karriker, J. H. (2009). Affecting organizational identity. *Journal of Leadership & Organizational Studies, 15*(4), 404–415.

Proshansky, H. M., Fabian, A. K., & Kaminoff, R. (1983). Place-identity: Physical world socialization of the self. *Journal of Environmental Psychology, 3*(1), 57–83. Retrieved from http://www.sciencedirect.com/science/article/B6WVC-446B4MW-2J1/2/408c83bdf4d5244edd7ba85f626e1d03

Qu, S. Q., & Dumay, J. (2011). The qualitative research interview. *Qualitative Research in Accounting & Management, 8*(3), 238–264.

Ramlall, S. (2004). A review of employee motivation theories and their implications for employee retention within organizations. *Journal of American Academy of Business, 5*, 52–63.

Roemer, L., & Orsillo, S. M. (2009). *Mindfulness and Acceptance-Based Behavioral Therapies in Practice*. New York: Guilford.

Roland, Y. (2005). Implementing organizational learning initiatives. *Development and Learning in Organizations, 19*(2), 5–7.

Rooney, D. (2015). The knowledge economy, knowledge policy, & wisdom site. Retrieved from https://sites.google.com/site/davidrooneyknowledge/ (2/5/15).

Rooney, D., Mandeville, T., & Kastelle, T. (2013). Abstract knowledge and reified financial innovation: Building wisdom and ethics into financial innovation networks. *Journal of Business Ethics, 118*, 447–459.

Rooney, D., McKenna, B., & Liesch, P. (2010). *Wisdom and Management in the Knowledge Economy*. London: Routledge.

Rooney, D., Paulsen, N., Callan, V. J., Brabant, M., Gallois, C., & Jones, E. (2010). A new role for place identity in managing organizational change. *Management Communication Quarterly, 24*(1), 44–73.

Rubin, H. J., & Rubin, I. S. (2005). *Qualitative Interviewing: The Art of Hearing Data*, 2nd edition. Thousand Oaks, CA: Sage.

Schnake, M. (2007). An integrative model of effort propensity. *Human Resource Management, 17*(3), 274–289.

Schön, D. (1995). *The Reflective Practitioner: How Professionals Think in Action*. Aldershot, UK: Ashgate.

Schwartz, B., & Sharpe, K. E. (2010). *Practical Wisdom: The Right Way to Do the Right Thing*. New York: Riverhead Books.

Seidman, I. (2006). *Interviewing as Qualitative research: A Guide for Researchers in Education and the Social Sciences*, 3rd edition. New York: Teachers College Press.

Shapiro, S. L., Carlson, L. E., Astin, J. A., & Freedman, B. (2006). Mechanisms of mindfulness. *Journal of Clinical Psychology, 62*(3), 373–386. doi:DOI: 10.1002/jclp.20237

Spicer, D. P. (1998). Linking mental models and cognitive maps as an aid to organizational learning. *Career Development International, 3*(3), 125–132.

Spillan, J. E., Mino, M., & Rowles, M. S. (2002). Sharing organizational messages through effective lateral communication. *Communication Quarterly, 50*(2), 96–104.

Tahir, A., Naeem, H., Sarfraz, N., Javed, A., & Ali, R. (2011). Organizational learning and employee performance. *Interdisciplinary Journal of Contemporary Research in Business, 3*(2), 1506–1514.

Tappeiner, G., Hauser, C., & Walde, J. (2008). Regional knowledge spillovers: Fact or artifact? *Research Policy, 37*(5), 861–874.

Teo, T. S., Srivastava, S. C., Ranganathan, C., & Loo, J. W. (2011). A framework for stakeholder oriented mindfulness: Case of RFID implementation at YCH Group, Singapore. *European Journal of Information Systems, 20*(2), 201–220.

Thomas, R. W., Fugate, B. S., & Koukova, N. T. (2011). Coping with time pressure and knowledge sharing in buyer–supplier relationships. *Journal of Supply Chain Management, 47*(3), 22–42.

Tsoukas, H. (2005). *Complex Knowledge: Studies in Organizational Epistemology*. Oxford: Oxford University Press.

Van Doesum, N. J., Van Lange, D. A., & Van Lange, P. A. (2013). Social mindfulness: Skill and will to navigate the social world. *Journal of Personality and Social Psychology, 105*(1), 86.

Van Winkelen, C. (2010). Deriving value from inter-organizational learning collaborations. *The Learning Organization, 17*(1), 8–23.

Vervaeke, J., & Ferraro, L. (2013). Relevance, meaning and the cognitive science of wisdom. In M. Ferrari & N. M. Weststrate (Eds.), *The Scientific Study of Personal Wisdom: From Contemplative Traditions to Neuroscience*. Heidelberg: Springer.

Vogus, T. J., & Sutcliffe, K. M. (2012). Organizational mindfulness and mindful organizing: A reconciliation and path forward. *Academy of Management Learning & Education, 11*(4), 722–735.

Wang, Y. L., & Ellinger, A. D. (2011). Organizational learning: Perception of external environment and innovation performance. *International Journal of Manpower, 32*(5), 512–536.

Weick, K. E., & Putnam, T. (2006). Organizing for mindfulness Eastern wisdom and Western knowledge. *Journal of Management Inquiry, 15*(3), 275–287.

Weick, K. E., & Roberts, K. H. (1993). Collective mind in organizations: Heedful interrelating on flight decks. *Administrative Science Quarterly, 38*, 357–381.

Weick, K. E., & Sutcliffe, K. M. (2006). Mindfulness and the quality of organizational attention. *Organization Science, 17*(4), 514–524.

Weiner, B. J. (2009). A theory of organizational readiness for change. *Implementation Science, 4*, 1–9.

Chapter 6

Is practical wisdom and learning literature actually wise on its "right to speak"?

Vincenzo Mario Bruno Giorgino and Xabier Renteria-Uriarte

Introduction

In the literature on practical wisdom, especially related to economics and business, there is an advocation for seeing it as wisdom as transformative power in daily activities, and its translation to modern times and parameters is of foremost concern, like in business ethics (e.g., Moberg, 2007) or business schools (e.g., Roca, 2008). Its meaning is in line with the *phrónêsis* (*φρόνησις*) developed by Aristotle in his *Nichomaquean Ethics*, which can be defined as the "ancient Greek practical wisdom virtue" (Jeannot, 1989), in the Thomist sense of "prudence" (Bartunek & Trullen, 2007, p. 91). In any case, the concept must be reinterpreted for our world and time. For example, it cannot be the same as at the times of Aristotle, with his heroic, one-man (male), his hierarchical leadership, and a clear immobile univocal morality, with one moral truth (Küpers & Pauleen, 2013, pp. 3–7). The existing scholarship on practical wisdom and its updating involves already a remarkable collective effort of researchers, yet we think that some important aspects can still be further developed and improved. Our proposal concerns the first ground of the research: why is practical wisdom so advisable in response to the increasingly complex and uncertain global business environment? This ontological and epistemological foundation implies – in the first instance – the "right to speak" of any knowledge. The question is, in this sense: can the practical wisdom scholarship and its literature face reflectively its own sense, especially according to its epistemic coherence with its ontological vision of the reality? Or more directly: are studies of practical wisdom actually "wise'?

It is obvious that "practical wisdom" works, regardless of what "scholarly practical wisdom literature" or "worldviews of ancient wisdom traditions" say on the subject. Professional and everyday activity differentiate from science as they are more experience-based; tacit knowledge prevails (Polanyi, 1958; 1966; Schein, 1987; 2010; Schön, 1983), and wisdom is closely related to those "daily practices." However, the assessment of the coherency of academic knowledge needs to go beyond, from its ontology to its final rethoric; and this should be reflected in its learning.

The "ethical righteousness" of practical wisdom

A major argument in the literature on practical wisdom in a foundational sense, supporting its consideration in different situations and more specifically in organizational studies and management theory, is the ethical or moral. Frequently this stems from the understanding of Aristotle's *phrónêsis* (φρόνησις) as underlying source of the concept (Townley, 1999; Tsoukas & Cummings, 1997). It was even labeled as "phronesiology" (Intezari, Pauleen, & Rooney, 2014), and has its roots in the "Neo-Aristotelian revival" fostered by the consequentialist virtue ethics of Anscombe (1958). For example, Jeannot (1989), after defining *phrónêsis* as "ancient Greek practical wisdom virtue," proposes, with the help of some contemporary moralists, "a certain kind of wisdom in relation to character" for the modern leadership and practical wisdom. The *phrónêsis* concept has also been applied, in this regard, in practices of school leadership (Dalton, 2002; Halverson, 2004).

However, the vast heritage of ancient wisdom traditions of humanity is not reduced to a strictly located source, although it has been valued high, such as in Angel Falls in Venezuela (the world's highest waterfall, which consists of a main plunge). It is more like the *Iguazu* of Argentina and Brazil; a conjunction of many separate waterfalls and cataracts. Other works of practical wisdom literature cover this gap: for example, Blomme & Hoof (2014) reviewed the ancient traditions (Humanism, Confucianism, or Taoism), wise writings (Confucius, Rumi, Dogen, Spinoza, or Camus), and key cultural characteristics (of China, Japan, India, Nigeria, or Western societies). They all aim at deriving the implications for contemporary leadership and organization. Whether by Aristotelian or Humanist traditions of the West, or other non-Western approaches, the ethical dimension seems inevitable because "management is never neutral" and, therefore, its learning "should focus on the development of both virtues and techniques" (Roca, 2008).

The "practical strength" of wisdom virtues

Aristotelian *phrónêsis* is directly related to the virtue of practical strength, in the sense of "prudence" and "correct action" necessary to address the daily decisions. This "practical desirability" or "practical strength criterion" of wise virtues is present in various forms of practical wisdom. For example, Aubrey & Cohen (1995) propound that "working wisdom" should be a strategy in learning organizations, review what organizations are doing to enhance it, and specify how one's own learning strategies can be assessed by different tactics defined by practical wisdom in the past. Overall, *phrónêsis* should be seen as "professional knowledge" with implications in education (Kinsella & Pitman, 2012). In short, according to the argument implied by these proposals, an action with wisdom works in the real world more effectively than an action without it, and this practical strength – beyond "scholastic debates" on its realism – becomes its main support.

The multidimensionality in reality/wisdom

Some works on practical wisdom rely more on the notion of "ethical righteousness," while others prefer to focus more on "practical desirability of wisdom virtues," but both involve the idea that a multidimensional reality demands, in its management, a multidimensional perspective. In the first case, "ethics" is reasoned because an ethical side is supposed to be undoubtedly present in daily activities. Therefore, any action must be ethical to fit adequately and faithfully to reality. In the second case, reality is complex and heterogeneous, thus, a wise person is one who acts accordingly; because practical wisdom involves "the ability to draw upon knowledge selectively and apply it successfully in specific situations" (Dalton, 2002).

We have not brought to the fore anything new in the arguments, but we want to elaborate now their most epistemic nuances. Ethics is not to be followed only "because it is right," and practical strength is not to be highlighted only "because it operates." The ultimate reason of those aspects is that, as assumed in contemporary Western society, they reflect better the reality, that is, the multidimensionality of the real world (not "apart from the context," according to Halverson, 2004). For example, the impact of organizational learning on competitive advantage needs wisdom as an understanding of the complexity of a situation and as the ability to make sense and simplify the actions to be taken (Bierly, Kessler, & Christensen, 2000); this shift from abstract episteme to practical *phrónêsis* has important implications in education (Kessels & Korthagen, 1996); and the collective integration of organizational people and purpose should emerge from learning together (Blockley, 2015).

Ethics, practical strength, and multidimensionality at stake

The correctness of a theory based on ethics, that is, this ontological foundation, has been has been dismissed largely in the orthodoxy of Philosophy of Science, especially for the "Analytic Philosophy" that dominates the English-speaking countries. And even more for its origin, for the Logical Positivism of the first half of the twentieth century. For their authors, ethical and aesthetic judgments cannot be objectively verified or falsified, and therefore are unreal, meaningless, unscientific, and not cognitive: their knowledge is not real (Moore, 1903; Sorell & Rogers, 2005; Soames, 2009; Beaney, 2013).

In addition, the context-dependent essence of ethics can become a problem for the argumentation of wisdom's suitability. In this issue, perhaps the most radical are the anthropologists, likely because of their interest in the diversity of cultures. Overall, they agree that universalist proposals are "oppressive cultural imperialism," that is, the imposition of the values of the dominant culture's values (Fowers & Richardson, 1996, p. 610). It is the risk highlighted by Küpers & Pauleen (2013, pp. 3–7) when they remind us that Aristotle's wisdom is grounded on slavery and subordination of women. Thus, wisdom exists in different persons and cultures, but if it is linked to ethical considerations, can some concept of wisdom be intersubjective or universal when ethics is not?

The practical strength seems less objectionable: if something works in the real world, how could we dismiss it? This criterion reflects the *instrumentality* as ontological foundation in science methodology, one of great importance in modern times (Reiss, 2012; Hu, 2004; Cacioppo, Semin, & Berntson, 2004; Alekseev, 1999; Keita, 1983; Doody, 1974), specially around Duhem (1906), Toulmin (1972), and van Fraassen (1980). According to it, the aim of scientific theories is not to discover truth, but to provide adequate predictions for facts, answers to questions and solutions to problems, in a given domain (van Fraassen, 2002). The value of arousal theory in psychology, rational choice theory in economics, and Newtonian mechanics in physics, is that they predict or describe in more abstract terms observable data (Cacioppo et al., 2004, p. 217); and if they describe real structures in the world or not, it becomes other debate (propositions "are neither true nor false ... only convenient or inconvenient" according to Duhem, 1954, p. 334).

Nevertheless, if we seek the most essential and coherent ontological foundation for the literature, it is unsatisfactory as such. And the reason is an old friend of science: the "simplicity" in choosing theories; that is, the so-called "Razor of Ockham" with which we circumvent any "superfluous ontological apparatus" in the confidence that Nature operates in the simplest possible way (Baker, 2013). In addition, here we will focus on another, which is more typical of the wisdom traditions: the "consistency" with the central ontology of wisdom, in what we might call "the *kusala* criterion."

The ontology of wise persons and wisdom traditions

Despite the virtues, attitudes and sayings of wise persons, and the concepts, metaphors, and worldviews of ancient wisdom traditions are widely varied, they point to a somewhat vague but well-known assumption: *we are able to unravel the essence and sense of our complex and heterogeneous world, and act accordingly.* Wisdom is "expert knowledge and inference of important, difficult, and ambiguous problems connected to the meaning and organization of life" (Kunzmann & Baltes, 2003), and "a thought leader ... is able to understand the larger historical scene in terms of its meaning for both the inner life and the life trajectory of a variety of individuals" (Gumede, 2014, p. 2). This implies certain ontology which cannot be ignored: *ordinary reality hides some "sense," "logic" or "meaning," that is, some mystery or some sort of "secret" that can be deciphered.*

This is not an "essentialist" view in the sense of "some common essence" of the ordinary world, but in a trans-ordinary and trans-conceptual level beyond our rational understanding, because "what is impenetrable to us really exists, manifesting itself as the highest wisdom" (Einstein, quoted in Mitchell, 1991). Unfortunately, this "non-explicit sense" or "hidden meaning" is usually just an intuition or an operational and unconscious principle to the contemporary people who are considered as "wise," and who are taken as documentary sources in Western empirical research. Furthermore, they used to lack, in their culture tradition, the appropriate words or metaphors to make possible an adequate report of their experience. However, and now fortunately, ancient wisdom traditions have produced enough literature on this matter, and we also have examples of contemporary wise persons who follow their path (and therefore have the concepts and metaphors to communicate their experience). Thanks to them, "wisdom ontology" has been systematized for centuries, and it is still in action, in different cultures and languages.

The core of ancient wisdom traditions has been called *Perennial Philosophy* (since Huxley, 1945), and its ontological side has been systematized mostly, no doubt, by what is known as "Asian," "Oriental," or "Eastern" philosophies, mainly Hinduist and Buddhist. As briefly as possible: the meaning of reality is something that cannot be conceptualized, and that can only be approached as *deep consciousness, happiness, compassion, unity, wisdom.*

In this ontology, the perceivable existences are separated (in an illusory manifestation) and – at the same time – are united (in their inner meaning) by this deep consciousness (what differentiates existences is the level of awareness achieved or "realized" by them). This consciousness cannot be known conceptually, it can only be approached by metaphors (like the "deep consciousness" and the "happiness, compassion, unity, wisdom" above), but it is possible to know it immediately and straightaway by direct experience (by "realization," "liberation," or "illumination"). All the processes and phenomena of the reality are movements of this deep consciousness: movements "out" from (or "unfolding") their source; or movements "into" (or "folding") it (for more description and nuances see Renteria-Uriarte, 2013).

In modern Western culture there are two well-known examples. One is more accessible, because it recurs more to ordinary emotions and concepts: the Hinduist *Satcitānanda*. For this kind of text we depend on translators and intepreters from Sanskrit, Pali, or Chinese, so nothing can be taken with certainty (Batchelor, 2015), but *Satcitānanda* may be explained in English as follows. *Sat* is the pure essence of reality; in Shaivism the *svarupa* ("the real nature of reality") are *Cit* and *Ananda*: *Cit* or the power of self-revelation is the changeless principle of all changes, an aspect in which the "Supreme" is known as *Siva*; and *Ananda* or *Svatantrya* is the "Absolute bliss," an aspect in which it is known as *Sakti* (Singh, 1979, pp. XIX–XXI). We can choose as a conceptual approach, between the various translations of the concept, that: *Sat*, or "the essence of reality," is *Cit*, or "consciousness directly realizable," by *Ananda*, or "perfect bliss."

Another well-known approach, more intricate because it points to the innermost meaning of reality, is the Chinese *Tao* aphorism: "the *Tao* that can be expressed is not the enduring and unchanging *Tao*" (*Tao Te King*, 1). Halfway between them, *Pratītya-samutpāda*, "dependent-origination" or "co-arising," is one of the most fundamental principles of Buddhism. It is generally understood as a description of all existence: mental as well as physical phenomena are believed to come into existence only in relation to, and conditioned by, other phenomena. But it is not a statement about the perceptible surface of phenomena, but about their "inner awareness origin" (Shulman, 2008, p. 297).

Please note that those concepts, terms, and sentences are approaches to a mystery that can be seen as "something different," as up to now, or not. Because another constant in wisdom traditions is that, whatever "this" is, it is not different from our ordinary world (in a Hindu saying attributed to Śaṅkarācārya, "the world is illusory, only Brahman is real, but Brahman is the world"). These approaches have oriental expressions, but the earnest reader of different wisdom traditions might note the common reference of any of them, either Eastern or Western or another. It was called "the Only Tradition," a "worldwide system of belief that would restore value and meaning" for modern times (Quinn, 1997). Let us summarize its ontology as a *conscientism* (consciousness as the only reality) which implies *unity* (veiled unity of deep consciousness explains the existences and their processes), *dialectic* (objects are separated, but also united), and *relationships* (objects are determined by their relationships, not by their identities) (Renteria-Uriarte, 2013).

The empiria of wisdom traditions: The contemplative turn

Empiria or "experience" (Greek *empeiria* or ἐμπειρία) is, for the dominant Western view, any data about the world as perceived by our mind. But ancient wisdom traditions follow the insight that "external world," "sensory experiences," and even a "shallow rationality," do not guarantee a reliable basis on which existence can be understood; as we said before, some "mystery" or "secret" is presumably hidden.

Thus, a different "access to reality" is needed. And everywhere in the world where any human has felt this "existential question," and also in major cultural traditions, be it in the East (Abbhidharma, Prajnaparamita ...) or in the West (Meister Eckhart, Teresa of Avila, John of the Cross, Thomas Merton ...), "*contemplation*," "*meditation*," "*interiorization*," or "*immersion*" in the present moment has been seen an adequate way of knowledge.

According to the conventional operationalization of the American Psychological Association provided by Shapiro (1982, p. 268), "contemplation" or "meditation" is a "family of techniques which have in common a conscious attempt to focus attention in a nonanalytical way, and an attempt not to dwell on discursive, ruminating thought." The numerous techniques that have been developed by different wisdom traditions are not easy to taxonomize, but a complex "structured tree of different practices" is operational (Duerr, 2015).

In fact, the true meditation is best understood not as a technique or process, as it is customary in Western semantics, but as the real core of consciousness and reality, as some known Eastern advocates remind us (Krishnamurti, 1989; Osho, 1977, Ch. 7). This is, for instance, why, in the most profound steps of meditation techniques, the technique (to realize a reality) and the reality (realized by the technique) become just the same. In the Zen technique of *shikan taza* or "just sitting," as the ancient master Eihei Dogen (1231/2009, Ch. 7) used to say: *shushô-itto,* "practice and realization are one and the same."

What does it mean? If contemplation or meditation is practiced seriously, with discipline and rigor, a concise awareness would finally emerge and it would "realize" the reality; that is, it would "know by direct experience" the knowledge, and this apparent "inner meaning" of the reality. The "shared meaning" (conceptually approached as "consciousness, happiness, compassion, unity, wisdom") of all existences (be it mental/human, living/animal/vegetal, or physical/object) is just the deepest layer of our mind (although that will not be known until it is realized by rigorous techniques of introspection).

Metaphors may vary, but the reference of the metaphors is the same. Ancient Chinese Lao-tzu (2009), medieval German Eckhart (1998; see also Turner, 2002), and contemporary Basque Orixe (1934) lived very different sociocultural and historic environments, but described the inner meaning of the reality and the process or path to experience it with the same words. Outer levels of mind can vary greatly, but the more we interiorize them, eventually they match the common essence of all existences.

This has two important methodological implications. First, contemplation is the empiria according to which wisdom ontology can be confirmed. "[W]e need wisdom to understand wisdom" (Ferrari & Weststrate, 2013, p. 332) but, more concisely, "we need contemplative wisdom to understand wisdom." Second, the best way to understand an object of study (no its external features but its inner logic) is *to delve into the mind of each, into the existence of each, until the meaning and logic that explains the outer existence under study is encountered.* In an important heuristic potential of contemplative Science; if Flyvbjerg (2001) argues that all social science must be "phronetic" and not "epistemic" as the natural sciences, human self-knowledge demonstrates that meditative perspective and practices are appropriate for all scientists (either natural or social scientists). Then, *we need contemplative wisdom* not only to understand wisdom, but also *to better understand any object of study.*

Implications on usual foundational reasonings of the literature

In science it is customary to deny any ontological role to ethics, assuming it is something on the reality, ex-post, and not from the reality, of its phenomenal characteristics. Conversely, wisdom's essential ontology appreciates this role. But it is not due to a primal ethical criterion on "what it is right and wrong" (this is, certainly, an ex-post argument), but because the unity or rapprochement function of ethical actions (this is the key ontological ex-ante argument). Ethics unites us, and this is what it is right: it brings us closer to the underlying reality of the common bond.

This way, the "ethical righteousness or rectitude" is not dissociated from the fundamental ontology of wisdom, and it is not on a moral secondary criterion "on" the reality. In short, ethics is not desirable because it tells us what is right, but because it unites us (and this is the right and "true" thing). A good example is the basic ethics of Buddhism, the "*kusala* ethics": actions are never "right or wrong," or "true or false"; they are only "wise" (when they decrease suffering, bringing us closer to unity), or "ignorant" (on the contrary). Perhaps the best-known case is the *Abhidharma* literature (Frauwallner, 1995), in which *dharmas* (or "experiential factors") are subdivided into those conducive to liberation (*kusala*); unconducive (*akusala*); and neutral (more on the "*kusala* criterion" in Harvey, 2012; Haag, Peterson, & Spezio, 2012, p. 299; Adam, 2005).

What about "practical strength" arguments? In our case above, Blomme & Hoof (2014) cannot resist the temptation to ensure the practical desirability of ancient wisdom traditions with cases of "respected" top leaders (nobody is poor or middle-class) and "globally successful" companies (no one has low or intermediate position in benefits and market). Is this consistent with which it is considered "successful" or "rich" in other cultures? For example,

> One of the surprising things we found in the village [in Zambia] was the idea of well-being . . . the money meant very little . . . the poorest person was the only person with a salary . . . . Welfare criteria emphasized the education of children, health and good humor . . . . The less affluent group included the richest person of the people, an unhappy, moody type, placed . . . with drunks and the sick.
>
> (Delia Paul, cited in Chambers, 1997, p. 179)

> [In primitive cultures] the accumulation is one of the biggest differences, [for example,] the greedy person is the worst one, who will not enter into the Kingdom of the Afterlife.
>
> (Pancorbo, 2000, p. 6)

> [In traditional societies,] income, the reductionist criterion of normal economists, has never been given an explicit priority.
>
> (Chambers, 1997, p. 179)

In other terms: a contemporary Western view, where "value" means "economic (value)," and "economic" means "monetary (economic value)," is hidden by the concept of "creation of value" in practical wisdom literature. We clothe our monetary logic with successive layers of wisdom, but we continue referring to "monetary and economic success"; what we want are "Wisdom Paradigms" for "the Enhancement of Profitable Business Practices" (Jones, 2005). And this is not the case for (at least a number of) non-western social and philosophical views. It is not the case, also, for ancient wisdom's traditions.

Thus, "simplicity" or "parsimony" is not perfect. By contrast, in ancient traditions, the ontology of wisdom is the same as that of the practical actions of wisdom. Wise actions are appropriate by definition, because they are more close to the essential meaning of reality. Would the way in which modern research argues (why common wisdom is practical) be accepted by the ontology of the ancient traditions of wisdom? It is hard to admit it; the style of reasoning has another focus.

Consequently, in multidimensionality argument, the duality of universes of discourses remains. For example, when Flyvbjerg (2001) argues that social science should embody practical reason in terms of Aristotle, rather than Socrates, we must wonder which of these views is more accurate with wisdom traditions. If we want to support the economic practicality of the wise actions, then Aristotle is the key, but if we want to understand the rationale for those actions, then Socrates (e.g., in Plato, 1980) is the key.

In sum, practical wisdom's best rationale (in terms of simplicity and coherence) derives from its own ontology (as proposed by wisdom traditions): *wisdom has many positive effects in individuals and societies*. These effects are independent of what may be the mechanisms, *because wise persons become closer to the inner reality of unity*, and to the disappearance of their separations with the rest of the existences (the so-called "non-duality"). For example, the *Prajñāpāramitāsūtra* (1960) simultaneously shows the "stages of the path of wisdom" and "the nature of the reality or vacuity," as they are just the same (Kelsang Gyatso, 2000). The essential ontology of wisdom is the necessary and sufficient foundation for practical wisdom literature. And inevitably we must consider this in its learning, as in our proposal below.

The holographic paradigm

The so-called *holographic paradigm*, also under the label of *integral studies*, brings together different authors and gathers their proposals with an explicit intention: to turn the ancient wisdom tradition's epistemology into a new heuristics able to be applied in all distinct scientific disciplines. inspired by the perennial philosophy that synthesizes the core of ancient wisdom traditions, applying the hologram as research image, and fostering the contemplative methods, the holographic paradigm (the term became widely known mostly thanks to Wilber, 1982) tries to be, thus, a "wisdom-based-science": the heart of wisdom, now a guide for scientific practice.

This heuristic image (which is applied in the structure of the object of study by the researcher) is the optical *hologram* or *holography*, reflecting the "whole-universe-is-in-its-existences" perennial criterion according to this metaphor. It can be applied in different disciplines with conceptual constructions like the *All-Quadrant, All-Level* model (introduced in Wilber, 1995; see also Wilber, 2005; and an overview in Esbjörn-Hargens, 2010) or the *Nature's Realms Holographic Structure* (Renteria-Uriarte, 2013), in research structures that treat their different levels as "holons," and they function as "holarchy," putting into practice what it is supposed to happen in the real world, as Koestler (1968) indicated.

This ontoepistemic framework has also different applications or reflections in practical wisdom, leadership, and learning literature. Unicity manifests itself in different life aspects, such as empathy, compassion and compassionate relationships remarked on in many proposals (Birren & Fisher, 1990; Clayton & Birren, 1980; Taranto, 1989). Overall, wise people are "not self-centered, ... concerned with the whole world" (Montgomery, Barber, & McKee, 2002, p. 154). In addition, strict methodological applications of the holographic principle are the AQAL models, with explicit essays in the leadership side (Best, 2014) and the learning side (Haigh, 2013) of practical wisdom. The above-mentioned Integral Studies is the scientific area with greater relevance to this aspect, seeing "integrality" as life practice (Wilber, Patten, Leonard, & Morelli, 2008). Overall aplication of these ideas to the business world can be found in the emerging field of *Integral Leadership* (Forman & Ross, 2013; Keizer & Nandram, 2010; Küpers & Weibler, 2008; S. Nandram & Borden, 2011; S. S. Nandram, 2010; Reams, 2005; Volckmann, 2014) with journals like *Integral Review*.

The unity of the existence is reflected in its separate beings and phenomena as a dialectic. This is why life is "a contradiction-ridden, tension-filled unity of two embattled tendencies, . . . the centripetal and the centrifugal" (Bakhtin, 1981, p. 272). In this sense, "problems of life" are frequently referenced in accounts of wisdom (Baltes & Smith, 1990) and, to manage them, different ways of "non dualist thinking" need to be developed in organizations (Cayer & Minkler, 1998), with a learning with the *dynamic unity of the opposites* as a challenge (Subbiondo, 2015). Considering that any dialectical ontology in social realms includes agency, holism, contradiction, and synthesis (Kuczynski & Mol, 2015), the reflections are varied. For example, organizational leaders must balance a dialectic of inspiration and control in striving to create models of organizing that disrupt the subjugation of the spiritual in organizational life (Goodier & Eisenberg, 2006).

Holographic emergence has also had different reflections in the literature, for example because the process toward wisdom is a "self-transcendence" in which love, as an experience of unity, has an important role (Le & Levenson, 2005). Jaworski (2012) applies the idea explicitly. Leadership rests on the "inner wisdom" which is "the deeper region of consciousness," and entrepreneurial impulse's first origin is located in "the creative source of infinite potential enfolded in the universe."

The enactive contemplative-based turn

The translation of contemplative methods in lay terms is in part the legacy of the 1960s, a decade in which the counterculture, fighting the basic values of capitalism in Western Countries, met Eastern philosophies and meditation practices (with Alan Watts, 1957, The Esalen Institute, The San Francisco Zen Center of Shunryu Suzuki, etc.). In social sciences the dialogue with those traditions has been witnessed by two sociologists, Malhotra Valerie Bentz and Jeremy Shapiro (1998). Focusing on methodology, they were able to integrate Buddhist methods (meditation) within the toolcase of social sciences. In the same years, from the contemplative side, Alan B. Wallace (2000; 2007) proposes principles of contemplative science as a science of consciousness able to avoid scientific materialism. But at the end of the 1980s the neurobiologist Francisco Varela had begun to question the foundations of cognitive science, following his previous work on autopoiesis with his mentor Humberto Maturana, in an important contribution for the later essay with Thompson and Rosch (1991).

In their view, living entities are formed by a "creative interaction" of their components, both among themselves and with the environment, in a phenomenon known as *emergence*; the cognition arises when the organism changes or *enacts* its world (see also Stewart, Gapenne, & Di Paolo, 2010; Noë, 2004; Thompson, 2007; Luciani & Cadoz, 2007). Psychological activity is viewed not as occurring within the individual organism, but within the engagement between the motivated and active autonomous agent and its contexts, including the social one (McGann, De Jaegher, & Di Paolo, 2013).

The reflections of those phenomena in wisdom, leadership, and learning are varied; let us see some examples. Wisdom of a person cannot be explained by itself or by the person, because it arises by an iterative process of learning from life experiences and also management practices (this process has been described in a number of cases, e.g., Taylor, 2010); "interactive minds" form a context which significantly enhances performance on wisdom-related tasks (Staudinger & Baltes, 1996); the balance side of wisdom is based on intrapersonal, interpersonal, and extrapersonal interests in order to achieve a balance among adaptation to, shaping of, and selection of, environments (Sternberg, 1998); and, in entrepreneurial world, "not-yet-embodied or self-transcending" knowledge, "not-yet-embodied and embodied" tacit knowledge, and explicit knowledge require a different type of organizational environment and learning infrastructure (Scharmer, 2001). In leadership, major model is the "distributed leadership," with growing literature and intense debates and applications (Ali & Yangaiya, 2015; Spillane, 2012; Leithwood, Mascall, & Strauss, 2009; Harris, 2008; Duignan & Bezzina, 2006; Gronn, 2002), also on the learning side (Camburn, Rowan, & Taylor, 2003; Klar, Huggins, Hammonds, & Buskey, 2015; Timperley, 2005). An autopoietic perspective has been also explicitly proposed for leadership capability, including case studies (Sice, Koya, & Mansi, 2013).

From the empirical side, and followed by an intense collective work on first -person approaches (Varela & Shear, 1999), ten years later (Petitmengin, 2009) it is clear that the original discussion within the epistemology of cognitive sciences has gone fast forward to integrate first-person approaches to the lived experience with specific attention to methodologies and methods. The personal implications for the researcher to investigate the intra-subjective empiricality, that allow her to understand better the object of study, are an inspiration for or is present in proposals. Examples of these propositions are the "Theory U" (Scharmer, 2009); the "integral pheno-practice" based on Merleau-Ponty (Küpers, 2007, 2009); and practical wisdom developed through enquiry appropriate for the workplace, with *phrónêsis* and Heidegger (Gibbs, 2007). And this leads us to the common place, in this type of branch of science, which is what could be called "contemplative empiria."

Contemplative empiria's meeting point

Contemplative practices are the main or an important method for the branches of contemporary science that try to translate wisdom traditions to modern parameters or, at least, to reflect them more than mainstream science. Before all, wisdom inevitably implies a "soul-searching" to find "underlying values and principles" and to see "[w]hat other people don't see" (Reporters in Montgomery et al., 2002). Therefore, wisdom is characterized by a concern to dig "beneath surface appearances" and find the "deeper meanings" in things (Sternberg, 1990). Accordingly, becoming wise includes a looking-within-oneself component (Beck, 2006), and this seems necessary to be "wise organizational researchers" (Rooney, 2013).

Interestingly, the usual intra-subjective and individual dynamic of contemplative logic has been translated to inter-subjective collective dynamics: wisdom has been seen as the discovery of "inner truths," with Bohmian dialogue as a tool (Bohm, 2013; Cayer, 1997; Cayer, 2005). An example of this kind of contribution is the application of the AQAL Model as a tool of "generative dialogue" for this collective thinking (Gunnlaugson, 2007), and "presencing" as a collective generative tool in holistic organizational frameworks (Scharmer, 2000; Senge, Scharmer, Jaworski, & Flowers, 2005; Senge & Scharmer, 2008). We cannot fail to mention other intriguing contributions: a dynamics based on emptiness as tools for organizations and work (Mirvis, 1997).

In proposals for learning, the contemplative literature is also emerging (Coburn et al., 2011; Gunnlaugson, Sarath, Scott, & Bai, 2014; Miller, 2013; O'Reilly, 1998; Rockefeller, 2006), with special attention to higher education and concise cases (Barbezat & Bush, 2013; Gunnlaugson, 2009; Kroll, 2010; S. L. Shapiro, Brown, & Astin, 2011; Thurman, 2006), and specially active is the *Association for Contemplative Mind in Higher Education* (ACHME). Similar pedagogical lines oriented to second-person inquiry during curricula courses in traditional disciplines are also followed by Giorgino (2010).

Conclusion and future study

"Wisdom has been legitimatised in the science of psychology by operationalising it into a knowledge system framework, i.e., borrowing from an established scientific approach" (Blanchard-Fields & Norris, 1995, p. 105). Here we tested if this legitimation is the same as, or at least consistent with, which would be derived from wisdom's worldview. And the answer is that, unfortunately, the "right-or-wrong-ethics," the "economic-value-pragmatism," and the inferred "multidimensional realism," which are the basis of this established framework, are not consistent with wisdom's inner logic.

In wisdom's worldview, to say it figuratively, *"practical" wisdom and learning, as the pragmatic side of wisdom*, and *"wisdom" itself, as the virtues, character and attitudes of wise people*, stem from *wisdom as the primal meaning and ontological essence of ordinary reality*; and not from those arguments that relate to practical wisdom's effectiveness in ordinary life. In any case, wisdom's "non-ordinary" ontology explains more consistently, and furthermore more parsimoniously, the effectiveness of "ordinary" or "daily" wise activities.

After its ontology's argumentative phases, practical wisdom research can be assessed as sufficiently and significantly founded. And this implies that, in terms of scholarship consistency, the interested writers have "all the right to speak." However, practical wisdom and learning literature may benefit from more implications and deductions. We will discuss it in three parts: increasing the presence of this aspect in the literature; the need for "wisely consistent" knowledge techniques; and the materialization of these aspects in wisdom learning programs.

First of all, this issue has a weak presence in the scholarly literature. Management development programs where practical wisdom is aimed at developing the "whole person" (Small, 2004); university and on-the-job learning programs for managers with a model of the process of becoming wise in organizations (Bigelow, 1992); managerial wisdom learning routes like executive coaching (Kilburg, 2000); procedures for developing practical wisdom in novice managers (Gibson, 2008); or wisdom principles for learning effective leadership (McKenna, Rooney, & Boal, 2009), show methods and techniques to help executives develop wisdom and gain insight into the chaotic organizational life, but the key question is missed even in their introductory sections: Why is practical wisdom and learning so effective? What is the reason, from wisdom's ontology?

For example, Sternberg (2001) proposes the fostering of wisdom in modern societies through learning, with contents like "wisdom-related skills" (e.g., "how to think") in appropriate spaces (to reflect on fulfillment, community, values, and interests), class discussions with dialogical thinking (encompassing multiple perspectives) and dialectical thinking (considering knowledges as contextual processes), and materials of "the wisdom of the sages" as special cases (p. 283). Note that the latter are not proposed or explained as the key foundation giving consistency to all the full effective power of practical wisdom.

This is in line with an assumed specific analytic behavior. Practical wisdom literature often focuses on descriptive analyses of wise people and actions, and most of the wisdom learning courses – as a review of the Web shows – present some ancient wisdom tradition, or a series of "wise features" examined by the literature, as materials and tools for the student. However, that different wisdom traditions share a specific focus on existence, that this "wise ontology focus" explains the practical application of wise actions, and that, accordingly, it should be considered more broadly in analytic and learning proposals, is frequently missed.

Even some "Eastern-style proposals" aimed at developing managerial effectiveness show this lack (see as a case Muniapan & Satpathy, 2010): they are more mechanistic than explanatory, and not so practical from wisdom's worldview, because they do not notice the importance of self-knowledge. Other proposals better reflect wisdom's ontology, as when wise leadership comes from "the ability to perceive the indivisible whole and this ability is not a function of the … reasoning mind but of the inner mind," and "a … model of man [comes from] the unfoldment of unitive SELF-awareness" (Chakraborty, 1995). Other models depict a six-fold path of "Jnan" or Knowledge (Bhattacharjee, 2012) or seven holistic and integrated "pillars" (Chatterjee, 2009) under the same logic.

In conclusion on this scholarly dimension, any practical and learning side of wisdom literature (see a broad spectrum of learning alternatives in Ferrari & Potworowski, 2008) should consider the common unitive ontology of different traditions. For example, wisdom as "a multidimensional construct" that connects a "number of desired learning outcomes" has been proposed (Brown, 2004, p. 134), and this "ancient unitivism" has much to help us here. Not in vain, "Chinese and Japanese intellectuals … coined the neologism 'wisdom learning' (Ch. *zhexue*, J. *tetsugaku*) to translate the Western concept of "philosophy'" (Denecke, 2010, p. 4). The performance of wisdom figures as the primary essence or engine of the existence (like with the *Satchidānanda* or the *Dharmakāya*, or even in Western approaches with the *Monad* of the Pythagoreans and Leibniz, or *The One* of Plotinus) is still awaiting recognition in modern Western society, including wisdom literature.

Second, and beyond this conceptual explanation likely of interest mainly to scholars, wisdom's ontology has a larger pragmatic scope. It poses us a particular system of approaching to practical issues, which is not "outerly" reached, but "innerly." As Couture (1991, p. 61) synthesizes for indigenous knowledge, "reality is experienced by entering deeply into the innerbeing of the mind, and not by attempting to break through the outer world to a beyond." Direct self-knowledge and self-transcendence is an ongoing requirement of wisdom traditions; "[a]ll the mystics and sages affirm the Delphic oracle's admonition, 'Know thyself'" (Hart, 2001, p. 6). Unfortunately, it is somewhat striking how different features of wisdom appear in its scholarly explanations widely, but being almost absent just its key epistemic method. It is a lack only remedied by the holographic, integral and enactive proposals reviewed above, with which fields like Transpersonal Psychology, "whether or not they use the terminology of wisdom, ... have something relevant to say about it" (Curnow, 1999, p. 14).

Wise knowledge will not be fully consistent, and indeed "wise," until the researcher delves into this *intra-subjective empiricality*, in order to better understand existence and, within it, any object of study. "Meditation," "Mindfulness," or "Contemplation" (see a good explanation of concept and techniques in McCown, Reibel, & Micozzi, 2011) fosters transcendence of self-centered patterns and unity of wisdom (Rosch, 2008). In more speculative words, the "encounter with the Transcendent One" is the basis of all wisdom traditions (with this term, e.g., in the Near Eastern traditions reviewed by Crenshaw, 1987), but, regardless of the term used, a consistent scholar should not avoid this pragmatic implication of wisdom.

Therefore, organizations should acquire wisdom based on reflective activities (as Yan, 2009; or Zheng, 2010 propose to wise teaching), and the most "wisely consistent" reflection technique is contemplation, with which "Wisdom is cultivated by learning to use the mind rather than being used by it" (Hart, 2001, p. 25). Meditation gives the researcher the possibility to test directly the heart of wisdom, and to date it involves the most coherent and effective way to research wisdom, its practical effects, and its transformative leadership and learning approach.

Third, and finally, practical and managerial wisdom learning programs would benefit, accordingly, with both the conceptual explanation of wisdom's pragmatic effectiveness and the praxis of knowledge techniques. We have "effective ways to transfer and express the practical wisdom in words" (Meihong, 2008), but wisdom learning cannot be reduced to "the learning of moral skills" to make "tough decisions in uncertain times" (as in Schwartz & Sharpe, 2010); to an ability to alternate between different modes of teaching as the only factor that earns teachers the designation of "wise practitioner" (as Wineburg & Wilson, 1991 suggest); or even to some "inter-relational teaching style" like the Socratic one (Ebertz, 1996; Lum, 1996). Broader frameworks closer to wisdom ontology's implications (like the principles of indigenous education systemized by Sanford, Williams, Hopper, & McGregor, 2013) are easily applicable to learning organizations, and show possible ways to materialize it.

In conclusion, wisdom learning should not lack those aspects, like a table with the following legs: (a) wisdom's worldview and ontology as consistency of the framework (like the proposal here or some formulation of an ancient tradition); (b) wise people's virtues, character, and other features (from person-based scholar literature or tradition-based ancient literature); (c) wisdom-based science (with examples of the application in the operative and heuristic scientific practice); and (d) wisdom-based learning of life skills (with contemplative and meditative techniques). According to this proposal, this platform involves the actual "Wisdom of Teaching Wisdom" (in terms of Zhen-sheng, 2007).

References

Adam, M. T. (2005). Groundwork for a metaphysic of Buddhist morals: A new analysis of puñña and kusala, in light of sukka. *Journal of Buddhist Ethics, 12*, 62–85.

Alekseev, B. T. (1999). Realism and instrumentalism in the methodology of science. *Vestnik Sankt-Peterburgskogo Universiteta. Seriia 6 Filosofiia, Politologiia, Sotsiologiia, Psikhologiia, Pravo, Mezhdunarodnye Otnosheniia, 3*(20), 16–18.

Ali, H. M., & Yangaiya, S. A. (2015). Distributed leadership and empowerment influence on teachers organizational commitment. *Academic Journal of Interdisciplinary Studies, 4*(1), 73–85.

Anscombe, G. E. M. (1958). Modern moral philosophy. *Philosophy, 33*(124), 1–19.

Aubrey, R., & Cohen, P. M. (1995). *Working wisdom: Timeless skills and vanguard strategies for learning organizations*. ERIC.

Baker, A. (2013). Simplicity. In E. N. Zalta (Ed.), *Stanford encyclopedia of philosophy*. Stanford University (http://plato.stanford.edu/archives/fall2013/entries/simplicity/)

Bakhtin, M. M. (1981). *The dialogic imagination: Four essays*. Austin: University of Texas.

Baltes, P. B., & Smith, J. (1990). Toward a psychology of wisdom and its ontogenesis. *Wisdom: Its Nature, Origins, and Development, 1*, 87–120.

Barbezat, D. P., & Bush, M. (2013). *Contemplative practices in higher education: Powerful methods to transform teaching and learning*. San Francisco, CA: Jossey-Bass.

Bartunek, J. M., & Trullen, J. (2007). The virtue of prudence. In E. H. Kessler, & J. R. Bailey (Eds.), *Handbook of organizational and managerial wisdom* (pp. 91–108). London: Sage.

Batchelor, S. (2015). After Buddhism: A new idiom for a pragmatic, ethical culture based on the teaching of Gotama (interview). *Insight Journal*, 2.

Beaney, M. (2013). *The Oxford handbook of the history of analytic philosophy*. Oxford: Oxford University Press.

Beck, S. (2006). *Confucius and Socrates: Teaching wisdom*. Goleta, CA: World Peace Communications.

Bentz, V. M., & Shapiro, J. J. (1998). *Mindful inquiry in social research*. London: Sage.

Best, J. (2014). An integral theory analysis of complexity leadership. *Integral Leadership Review, 9*(24).

Bhattacharjee, A. (2012). Modern management through ancient Indian wisdom: Towards a more sustainable paradigm. *Purushartha: A Journal of Management Ethics and Spirituality, 4*(1), 14–37.

Bierly, P. E., Kessler, E. H., & Christensen, E. W. (2000). Organizational learning, knowledge and wisdom. *Journal of Organizational Change Management, 13*(6), 595–618.

Bigelow, J. (1992). Developing managerial wisdom. *Journal of Management Inquiry, 1*(2), 143–153.

Birren, J. E., & Fisher, L. M. (1990). The elements of wisdom: Overview and integration. In R. J. Sternberg (Ed.), *Wisdom: Its nature, origins, and development* (pp. 120–141). New York: Cambridge University Press.

Blanchard-Fields, F., & Norris, L. (1995). The development of wisdom. In M. A. Kimble, S. H. McFadden, J. W. Ellor, & J. J. Seeber (Eds.), *Aging, spirituality, and religion: A handbook* (pp. 102–118). Minneapolis, MN: Fortress Press.

Blockley, D. (2015). Finding resilience through practical wisdom. *Civil Engineering and Environmental Systems, 32*(1–2), 18–30.
Blomme, R., & Hoof, B. v. (2014). *Another state of mind: Perspectives from wisdom traditions on management and business*. New York: Palgrave.
Bohm, D. (2013). *On dialogue*. London: Routledge.
Brown, S. C. (2004). Learning across the campus: How college facilitates the development of wisdom. *Journal of College Student Development, 45*(2), 134–148.
Cacioppo, J. T., Semin, G. R., & Berntson, G. G. (2004). Realism, instrumentalism, and scientific symbiosis: Psychological theory as a search for truth and the discovery of solutions. *The American Psychologist, 59*(4), 214–223.
Camburn, E., Rowan, B., & Taylor, J. E. (2003). Distributed leadership in schools: The case of elementary schools adopting comprehensive school reform models. *Educational Evaluation and Policy Analysis, 25*(4), 347–373.
Cayer, M. (1997). Bohm's dialogue and action science: Two different approaches. *Journal of Humanistic Psychology, 37*(2), 41–66.
Cayer, M. (2005). The five dimensions of Bohm's dialogue. In J. Banathy (Ed.), *Dialogue as a means of collective communication* (pp. 161–191). New York: Kluwer Academic.
Cayer, M., & Minkler, L. (1998). Dualism, dialogue and organizations: Reflections on organizational transformation and labor-managed firms. *The Journal of Socio-Economics, 27*(1), 53–77.
Chakraborty, S. (1995). Wisdom leadership: Leading self by the SELF. *Journal of Human Values, 1*(2), 205–220.
Chambers, R. (1997). *Whose reality counts?* London: Intermediate Technology Publ.
Chatterjee, S. R. (2009). Managerial ethos of the Indian tradition: Relevance of a wisdom model. *Journal of Indian Business Research, 1*(2/3), 136–162.
Clayton, V. P., & Birren, J. E. (1980). The development of wisdom across the life span: A reexamination of an ancient topic. In P. B. Baltes, & O. G. J. Brim (Eds.), *Life-span development and behavior* (pp. 103–135). New York: Academic Press.
Coburn, T., Grace, F., Klein, A. C., Komjathy, L., Roth, H., & Simmer-Brown, J. (2011). Contemplative pedagogy: Frequently asked questions. *Teaching Theology & Religion, 14*(2), 167–174.
Couture, J. E. (1991). Explorations in native knowing. In J. W. Friesen (Ed.), *The cultural maze: Complex questions on native destiny in Western Canada* (pp. 53–73). Calgary: Detselig.
Crenshaw, J. L. (1987). The acquisition of knowledge in israelite wisdom literature. *Word & World, 7*(3), 245–252.
Curnow, T. (1999). *Wisdom, intuition and ethics*. Aldershot, UK: Ashgate.
Dalton, J. C. (2002). The art and practical wisdom of student affairs leadership. *New Directions for Student Services, 98*, 3–9.
Denecke, W. (2010). *The dynamics of masters literature: Early Chinese thought from Confucius to Han Feizi*. Cambridge, MA: Harvard University.
Dōgen, E. D. Z. (1231/2009). *Bendowa: A talk on exerting the way*. Ottawa: Great Matter.
Doody, J. A. (1974). *Scientific realism and instrumentalism: An analysis of the concepts of description and explanation*. Available from University of Notre Dame (10446189).
Duerr, M. (2015). *The tree of contemplative practices*. Retrieved from www.contemplativemind.org/practices/tree.
Duhem, P. (1906). *La théorie physique, son objet et sa structure*. Paris: Chevalier et Rivière.
Duhem, P. (1954). *The aim and structure of physical theory*. Princeton, NJ: Princeton University Press.
Duignan, P., & Bezzina, M. (2006). Distributed leadership: The theory and the practice. Paper presented at the *CCEAM Annual Conference*, Hilton Cyprus Hotel, Lefkosia, Cyprus, 12–17.

Ebertz, R. P. (1996). Socratic teaching and the search for coherence. In K. Lehrer, B. J. Lum, B. A. Slichta & N. D. Smith (Eds.), *Knowledge, teaching and wisdom* (pp. 71–81). New York: Springer.

Eckhart, M. (1998). *El fruto de la nada y otros escritos*. Madrid: Siruela.

Esbjörn-Hargens, S. (2010). *Integral theory in action: Applied, theoretical, and constructive perspectives on the AQAL model*. New York: SUNY.

Ferrari, M., & Potworowski, G. (2008). *Teaching for wisdom: Cross-cultural perspectives on fostering wisdom*. New York: Springer.

Ferrari, M., & Weststrate, N. M. (2013). *The scientific study of personal wisdom*. New York: Springer.

Flyvbjerg, B. (2001). *Making social science matter: Why social inquiry fails and how it can succeed again*. Cambridge: Cambridge University.

Forman, J. P., & Ross, L. A. (2013). *Integral leadership: The next half-step*. New York: SUNY Press.

Fowers, B. J., & Richardson, F. C. (1996). Why is multiculturalism good? *American Psychologist, 51*(6), 609.

Frauwallner, E. (1995). *Studies in abhidharma literature and the origins of Buddhist philosophical systems*. New York: SUNY Press.

Gibbs, P. (2007). Practical wisdom and the workplace researcher. *London Review of Education, 5*(3), 223–235.

Gibson, P. S. (2008). Developing practical management wisdom. *Journal of Management Development, 27*(5), 528–536.

Giorgino, V. (2010). *Flexible strategies to develop a contemplative perspective in HED* (2nd ACMHE Conference "The Contemplative Academy" ed.). Amherst: University of Massachusetts.

Goodier, B. C., & Eisenberg, E. M. (2006). Seeking the spirit: Communication and the (re)development of a "spiritual" organization. *Communication Studies, 57*(1), 47–65.

Gronn, P. (2002). Distributed leadership as a unit of analysis. *The Leadership Quarterly, 13*(4), 423–451.

Gumede, V. (2014). *Thought leadership, thought liberation, and critical consciousness for Africa's development and a just world* (inaugural professorial lecture). Unisa: Thabo Mbeki African Leadership Institute.

Gunnlaugson, C. O. (2007). Exploratory perspectives for an AQAL model of generative dialogue. *Integral Review, 4*, 44–58.

Gunnlaugson, C. O. (2009). *Exploring presencing as a contemplative framework for inquiry in higher education classrooms*. Available from University of British Columbia.

Gunnlaugson, C. O., Sarath, E., Scott, C., & Bai, H. (2014). *Contemplative learning and inquiry across disciplines*. New York: SUNY Press.

Haag, J. W., Peterson, G. R., & Spezio, M. L. (2012). *The Routledge companion to religion and science*. London: Routledge.

Haigh, M. (2013). AQAL integral: A holistic framework for pedagogic research. *Journal of Geography in Higher Education, 37*(2), 174–191.

Halverson, R. (2004). Accessing, documenting, and communicating practical wisdom: The phronesis of school leadership practice. *American Journal of Education, 111*(1), 90–121.

Harris, A. (2008). Distributed leadership through the looking glass. *Journal of Educational Administration, 46*(2), 31–34.

Hart, T. (2001). Teaching for wisdom. *Encounter: Education for Meaning and Social Justice, 14*(2), 3–16.

Harvey, P. (2012). An analysis of factors related to the kusala/akusala quality of actions in the pāli tradition. *Journal of the International Association of Buddhist Studies, 33*(1–2), 175–209.

Hu, G. (2004). Struggle between realism and instrumentalism in modern western philosophy of science. *Dalian Ligong Daxue Xuebao Shehui Kexue Ban/Journal of Dalian University of Technology (Social Sciences), 25*(2), 61–64.

Huxley, A. (1945). *The perennial philosophy*. London: Harper.

Intezari, A., Pauleen, D. J., & Rooney, D. (2014). Is knowledge enough? The case for research that leads to a better world. In *28th ANZAM Conference, "Reshaping Management for Impact"*, Sydney, Australia.

Jaworski, J. (2012). *Source: The inner path of knowledge creation*. San Francisco, CA: Berrett-Koehler.

Jeannot, T. M. (1989). Moral leadership and practical wisdom. *International Journal of Social Economics, 16*(6), 14.

Jones, C. A. (2005). Wisdom paradigms for the enhancement of ethical and profitable business practices. *Journal of Business Ethics, 57*(4), 363–375.

Keita, L. (1983). The instrumentalism-realism debate. *Crítica, 15*(43), 79.

Keizer, W. A., & Nandram, S. S. (2010). Integral transformational coaching. In S. S. Nandram & M. E. Borden (Eds.), *Spirituality and business* (pp. 129–140). Heidelberg: Springer.

Kelsang Gyatso, G. (2000). *Heart of wisdom: The essential wisdom teachings of Buddha*. Delhi: Motilal Banarsidass.

Kessels, J., & Korthagen, F. (1996). The relationship between theory and practice: Back to the classics. *Educational Researcher, 25*(3), 17–22.

Kilburg, R. R. (2000). *Executive coaching: Developing managerial wisdom in a world of chaos*. Washington, DC: American Psychological Association.

Kinsella, E. A., & Pitman, A. (2012). Phronesis as professional knowledge. In E. A. Kinsella & A. Pitman (Eds.), *Phronesis as professional knowledge* (pp. 163–172). New York: Springer.

Klar, H. W., Huggins, K. S., Hammonds, H. L., & Buskey, F. C. (2015). Fostering the capacity for distributed leadership: A post-heroic approach to leading school improvement. *International Journal of Leadership in Education*, (ahead-of-print), 1–27.

Koestler, A. (1968). *The ghost in the machine*. New York: Macmillan.

Krishnamurti, J. (1989). *El último diario*. Barcelona: Edhasa.

Kroll, K. (2010). *Contemplative teaching and learning: New directions for community colleges*. San Francisco, CA: Jossey-Bass.

Kuczynski, L., & De Mol, J. (2015). Dialectical models of socialization. In W. F. Overton & P. C. M. Molenaar (Eds.), *Theory and method*. Volume 1 of the *Handbook of Child Psychology and Developmental Science* (7th ed., pp. 326–368). Hoboken, NJ: Wiley.

Kunzmann, U., & Baltes, P. B. (2003). Wisdom. *The Psychologist, 16*(3), 131–133.

Küpers, W. M. (2007). Phenomenology and integral pheno-practice of wisdom in leadership and organization. *Social Epistemology, 21*(2), 169–193.

Küpers, W. M. (2009). The status and relevance of phenomenology for integral research: Or why phenomenology is more and different than an "Upper left" or "Zone# 1" affair. *Integral Review, 5*(1), 51–95.

Küpers, W. M., & Pauleen, D. (2013). Introducing a handbook of practical wisdom for our times. In *A handbook of practical wisdom* (pp. 1–18). London: Gower.

Küpers, W. M., & Weibler, J. (2008). Inter-leadership: Why and how should we think of leadership and followership integrally? *Leadership, 4*(4), 443–475.

Lao-Tzu (2009). In Hohne K. (Ed.), *Tao te ching: The poetry of nature*. Carnelian Bay: Way of Tao Books.

Le, T. N., & Levenson, M. R. (2005). Wisdom as self-transcendence: What's love (& individualism) got to do with it? *Journal of Research in Personality, 39*(4), 443–457.

Leithwood, K., Mascall, B., & Strauss, T. (2009). *Distributed leadership according to the evidence*. London: Routledge.

Luciani, A., & Cadoz, C. (2007). *Enaction and enactive interfaces: A handbook of terms*. Grenoble: ACROE.

Lum, B. J. (1996). The teaching of wisdom: The platonic model of teacher as learner and teaching as inquiry. In K. Lehrer, B. J. Lum, B. A. Slichta & N. D. Smith (Eds.), *Knowledge, teaching and wisdom* (pp. 85–99). New York: Springer.

McCown, D., Reibel, D., & Micozzi, M. S. (2011). *Teaching mindfulness: A practical guide for clinicians and educators*. New York: Springer.

McGann, M., De Jaegher, H., & Di Paolo, E. (2013). Enaction and psychology. *Review of General Psychology, 17*(2), 203.

McKenna, B., Rooney, D., & Boal, K. B. (2009). Wisdom principles as a meta-theoretical basis for evaluating leadership. *The Leadership Quarterly, 20*(2), 177–190.

Meihong, X. (2008). Can the teacher's practical wisdom be transferred and expressed in words? *Research in Educational Development, 20*, 27–30.

Miller, J. P. (2013). *The contemplative practitioner: Meditation in education and the workplace*. Toronto: University of Toronto Press.

Mirvis, P. H. (1997). Crossroads: "Soul work" in organizations. *Organization Science, 8*(2), 192–206.

Mitchell, S. (1991). *The enlightened mind: An anthology of sacred prose*. New York: Harper Collins.

Moberg, D. J. (2007). Practical wisdom and business ethics. *Business Ethics Quarterly, 17*(3), 535–561.

Montgomery, A., Barber, C., & McKee, P. (2002). A phenomenological study of wisdom in later life. *The International Journal of Aging and Human Development, 54*(2), 139–157.

Moore, G. E. (1903). *Principia ethica*. Cambridge: Cambridge University Press.

Muniapan, B., & Satpathy, B. (2010). Ancient Indian wisdom for managers: The relevance of valmiki ramayana in developing managerial effectiveness. *International Journal of Indian Culture and Business Management, 3*(6), 645–668.

Nandram, S. S. (2010). Synchronizing leadership style with integral transformational yoga principles. In S. S. Nandram, & M. E. Borden (Eds.), *Spirituality and business* (pp. 183–203). New York: Springer.

Nandram, S., & Borden, M. E. (2011). Leading with wisdom: The development of an integral leadership model. In M. J. Thompson & J. Eynikel (Eds.), *Leading with wisdom* (pp. 57–77). Antwerp: Maklu.

Noë, A. (2004). *Action in perception*. Cambridge, MA: MIT Press.

O'Reilly, M. R. (1998). *Radical presence: Teaching as contemplative practice*. Portsmouth, NH: Boynton/Cook.

Orixe, O. N. (1934). *Barne-muinetan*. Zarautz: Itxaropena.

Osho (1977). *Ancient music in the pines: Talks on zen stories*. Poona: Rajneesh Foundation.

Pancorbo, L. (2000). *Sobre la última vuelta al mundo en 80 días*. Barcelona: Ediciones B.

Petitmengin, C. (2009). *Ten years of viewing from within: The legacy of Francisco Varela*. Exeter: Imprint Academic.

Plato (1980). *The symposium (συμπόσιον)* (Greek text with commentary by Kenneth Dover, Ed.). Cambridge: Cambridge University Press.

Polanyi, M. (1958). *Personal knowledge: Towards a post-critical philosophy*. Chicago: University of Chicago Press.

Polanyi, M. (1966). *The tacit dimension*. Chicago: University of Chicago Press.

Prajñāpāramitāsūtra. (1960). In Oonze E. (Ed.), *The prajnaparamita literature*. Mouton: Gravenhage.

Quinn, W. W. (1997). *The only tradition*. New York: SUNY Press.

Reams, J. (2005). What's integral about leadership? A reflection on leadership and integral theory. *Integral Review, 1*, 118–131.

Reiss, J. (2012). Idealization and the aims of economics: Three cheers for instrumentalism. *Economics and Philosophy, 28*(03), 363–383.

Renteria-Uriarte, X. (2013). *Hacia una Economía Holográfica. Una revisión de la ciencia económica desde la ontoepistemología oriental*. Bilbao: University of the Basque Country.

Roca, E. (2008). Introducing practical wisdom in business schools. *Journal of Business Ethics, 82*(3), 607–620.
Rockefeller, S. (2006). Meditation, social change, and undergraduate education. *The Teachers College Record, 108*(9), 1775–1786.
Rooney, D. (2013). Being a wise organizational researcher: Ontology, epistemology and axiology. In W. M. Küpers, & D. J. Pauleen (Eds.), *Handbook of practical wisdom* (pp. 79–99). London: Gower.
Rosch, E. (2008). Beginner's mind: Paths to the wisdom that is not learned. In M. Ferrari, & G. Potworowski (Eds.), *Teaching for wisdom* (pp. 135–162). New York: Springer.
Sanford, K., Williams, L., Hopper, T., & McGregor, C. (2013). Indigenous principles decolonizing teacher education: What we have learned. *In Education, 18*(2), 18–34.
Scharmer, C. O. (2000). *Presencing: Learning from the future as it emerges.* Cambridge, MA: MIT Sloan School of Mangement.
Scharmer, C. O. (2001). Self-transcending knowledge: Sensing and organizing around emerging opportunities. *Journal of Knowledge Management, 5*(2), 137–151.
Scharmer, C. O. (2009). *Theory U: Learning from the future as it emerges.* San Francisco, CA: Berrett-Koehler.
Schein, E. H. (1987). *The clinical perspective in fieldwork.* London: Sage.
Schein, E. H. (2010). *Organizational culture and leadership.* London: Wiley & Sons.
Schön, D. A. (1983). *The reflective practitioner: How professionals think in action.* New York: Basic Books.
Schwartz, B., & Sharpe, K. (2010). *Practical wisdom: The right way to do the right thing.* New York: Riverhead.
Senge, P. M., & Scharmer, C. O. (2008). *Community action research: Learning as a community of practitioners, consultants and researchers.* London: Sage.
Senge, P. M., Scharmer, C. O., Jaworski, J., & Flowers, B. S. (2005). *Presence: An exploration of profound change in people, organizations, and society.* New York: Crown Business.
Shapiro, D. H. (1982). Overview: Clinical and physiological comparison of meditation with other self-control strategies. *American Journal of Psychiatry, 139*(3), 267.
Shapiro, S. L., Brown, K. W., & Astin, J. (2011). Toward the integration of meditation into higher education: A review of research evidence. *Teachers College Record, 113*(3), 493–528.
Shulman, E. (2008). Early meanings of dependent-origination. *Journal of Indian Philosophy, 36*(2), 297–317.
Sice, P., Koya, K., & Mansi, S. (2013). Leadership capability: An autopoietic perspective. *Human Systems Management, 32*(2), 95–103.
Singh, J. (1979). Introduction: The main sources of the non-dualistic saiva system of philosophy and yoga. In Vasugupta (Ed.), *Śiva sūtras: The yoga of supreme identity* (pp. xv–xix). Delhi: Motilal Banarsidass.
Small, M. W. (2004). Wisdom and now managerial wisdom: Do they have a place in management development programs? *Journal of Management Development, 23*(8), 751–764.
Soames, S. (2009). *Philosophical analysis in the twentieth century* (Vols 1 and 2). Princeton, NJ: Princeton University Press.
Sorell, T., & Rogers, G. A. J. (2005). *Analytic philosophy and history of philosophy.* Oxford: Oxford University Press.
Spillane, J. P. (2012). *Distributed leadership.* London: Wiley & Sons.
Staudinger, U. M., & Baltes, P. B. (1996). Interactive minds: A facilitative setting for wisdom-related performance? *Journal of Personality and Social Psychology, 71*(4), 746.
Sternberg, R. J. (1990). Wisdom and its relations to intelligence and creativity. *Wisdom: Its nature, origins, and development* (pp. 142–159). Cambridge: Cambridge University Press.
Sternberg, R. J. (1998). A balance theory of wisdom. *Review of General Psychology, 2*(4), 347–365.

Sternberg, R. J. (2001). Why schools should teach for wisdom: The balance theory of wisdom in educational settings. *Educational Psychologist, 36*(4), 227–245.

Stewart, J. R., Gapenne, O., & Di Paolo, E. A. (2010). *Enaction: Toward a new paradigm for cognitive science*. Cambridge, MA: MIT Press.

Subbiondo, J. L. (2015). The dynamic unity of the opposites: Haridas chaudhuri's integral method and higher education. *Integral Review, 11*(1), 11–16.

Taranto, M. A. (1989). Facets of wisdom: A theoretical synthesis. *The International Journal of Aging and Human Development, 29*(1), 1–21.

Taylor, C. (2010). *The experiential process of acquiring wisdom: How wise individuals report learning life lessons*. Master Thesis, Queen's University, Kingston, Ontario.

Thompson, E. (2007). *Mind in life: Biology, phenomenology, and the sciences of mind*. Cambridge, MA: Harvard University Press.

Thurman, R. (2006). Meditation and education: India, Tibet, and modern America. *The Teachers College Record, 108*(9), 1765–1774.

Timperley, H. S. (2005). Distributed leadership: Developing theory from practice. *Journal of Curriculum Studies, 37*(4), 395–420.

Toulmin, S. E. (1972). *Human understanding*. Princeton, NJ: Princeton University Press.

Townley, B. (1999). Practical reason and performance appraisal. *Journal of Management Studies, 36*(3), 287–306.

Tsoukas, H., & Cummings, S. (1997). Marginalization and recovery: The emergence of Aristotelian themes in organization studies. *Organization Studies, 18*(4), 655–683.

Turner, D. (2002). *The darkness of God: Negativity in western Christian mysticism*. Cambridge: Cambridge University Press.

van Fraassen, B. C. (1980). *The scientific image*. New York: Clarendon Press.

van Fraassen, B. C. (2002). *The empirical stance*. New Haven, CT: Yale University Press.

Varela, F. J., & Shear, J. (1999). *The view from within: First person approaches to the study of consciousness*. Exeter: Imprint Academic.

Varela, F. J., Thompson, E., & Rosch, E. (1991). *The embodied mind: Cognitive science and human experience*. Boston: MIT Press.

Volckmann, R. (2014). Generativity, transdisciplinarity, and integral leadership. *World Futures, 70*(3–4), 248–265.

Wallace, A. (2000). *The taboo of subjectivity*. Oxford: Oxford University Press.

Wallace, A. B. (2007). *Contemplative science where Buddhism and neuroscience converge*. New York: Columbia University Press.

Watts, A. (1957). *The way of zen*. New York: Vintage Books.

Wilber, K. (1982). *The holographic paradigm and other paradoxes: Exploring the leading edge of science*. Boulder, CO: Shambhala.

Wilber, K. (1995). *Sex, ecology, spirituality: The spirit of evolution*. Boston: Shambhala.

Wilber, K. (2005). Introduction to integral theory and practice. *AQUAL, 1*(1), 1–38.

Wilber, K., Patten, T., Leonard, A., & Morelli, M. (2008). *Integral life practice*. Boston: Shambhala.

Wineburg, S. S., & Wilson, S. M. (1991). Models of wisdom in the teaching of history. *History Teacher, 24*(4), 395–412.

Yan, Y. (2009). Listening to the voice of "wisdom": Examining the "teaching wisdom" with another thinking mode. *Theory and Practice of Education, 22*, 19–25.

Zheng, D. (2010). On the generation of reflective teachers' teaching wisdom. *Journal of Zhejiang Education Institute, 5*, 4–13.

Zhen-sheng, G. (2007). The wisdom of teaching wisdom: An appreciation of an American philosophical lesson plan. *Journal of Teachers College Qingdao University, 3*, 18–24.

Part II

Empirical and practical contributions for wisdom learning, teaching and education

Chapter 7

Practical wisdom and professional development

Engagement for the next generation of business

Charles Oden and Monika Ardelt

> When wisdom is the priority for an individual or a team passionate about a purpose, they create what seem like miracles.
>
> (Paul David Walker, 2010)

Introduction

We live in a time of unprecedented change. The digital revolution that we are only beginning to experience will soon change occupations and industries as well as the way we work and live. Disruptive innovations, such as 3D printing, computer–brain interfaces, robots, drones, driverless vehicles, and others are rapidly transforming business processes, requiring new skills and mindsets (Bojanova, 2014). The new Airbus A350 XWB, for example, contains over 1,000 parts that were 3D printed from lightweight materials (Simmons, 2015). Newer technologies have allowed for digitization of non-routine tasks, enabling autonomous robots to perform tasks that may even require subtle judgment usually reserved for individuals (Frey & Osborne, 2015). Cars have driven themselves over millions of miles in the last ten years, recognizing the difference between trees and pedestrians, without causing a single accident. Certain computers can now see, hear, write, recognize, and understand nuances better than humans (Howard, 2014). They are better than human pathologists at detecting cancer, defining treatments, and predicting survival rates and are even teaching humans new lessons as they work together (Howard, 2014; Rometty, 2015). IBM CEO Ginni Rometty (2015, p. 2) predicts that "in the future, every decision mankind makes is going to be informed by a cognitive system and as a result our lives are going to be better for it." However, not everyone agrees with this optimistic outlook. Stephen Hawkins, Elon Musk, and Bill Gates are all concerned about artificial intelligence (AI) getting out of human control (McMillan, 2015). According to Bill Gates, "we should be worried about the threat posed by artificial intelligence" (Rawlinson, 2015). "Google, Facebook, Microsoft, and Baidu, to name a few, are hiring artificial intelligence researchers at an unprecedented rate and putting hundreds of millions of dollars into the race for better algorithms and smarter computers" (McMillan, 2015, p. 2).

Yet, economic benefits from advancements in technology have not been evenly distributed, causing concerns about capitalism (Frey & Osborne, 2015; Jones, 2015). Corporations' laser-like focus upon profits, share prices, and quarterly earnings have resulted in large profit margins, high income disparity, and low emphasis on sustainability and charitable giving, all of which are potentially destroying the basis of our innovative capitalist society, which has brought about many new products and saved many lives (Jones, 2015).

Though the new generation of Millennials includes approximately 90 million workers, by 2030 there will be a global workforce shortage of nearly 20 percent in most of the world's largest economies primarily due to baby-boomer retirements (Frey & Osborne, 2015; Moon, 2014). Up to 47 percent of US jobs, including the low-skill and low-income sector, may become automated, and this rapid growth in technology will create a large skills mismatch (Frey & Osborne, 2015). This will have a particularly large impact on the manufacturing and the services industry, as well as social and economic structures (Howard, 2014; Strack, 2014).

The need for personal and organizational wisdom

Rapid advances in technology are indicative of the increased complexities involved in organizational decision-making. Leaders need to be able to make sound decisions that include both explicit and tacit factors during complexity and times of rapid technological changes, without being reactive and unreflective (Kaipa, 2014). Managers are called upon to handle conceptual complexity, make informed decisions, and utilize their ability to read and understand emotions. The uncertain, unpredictable, and highly political global business environment requires both cognitive and social expertise (Sparrow, 1999). Practical wisdom, first discussed by Aristotle, assists managers with understanding and integrating the technical, social, cultural, relational, and ethical complexity of global business environments to develop creative solutions (McKenna, Rooney, & Boal, 2009). Practical wisdom helps in the decision making process under the conditions of uncertainty and ambiguity "where cause and effect may not be clear cut – and where the result of an act or decision cannot be predicted with any certainty" (Grint, 2007, p. 237). Wise leaders understand what needs to be done to obtain a certain goal, but they also ask whether the goal is desirable and who might be the winners and losers if the goal is attained (Grint, 2007). Practical wisdom improves managers' decision-making capabilities based on reflection, emotional understanding, intuition, values, virtues, as well as knowledge and analytic ability (Ardelt, 2003; Roca, 2008). In 1954, Bertrand Russell noted that "the world needs wisdom as it has never needed it before; and if knowledge continues to increase, the world will need wisdom in the future even more than it does now" (Russell, 1997, p. 4).

Practical wisdom goes beyond scientific understanding. It includes a holistic understanding of how things work and are organized, a comprehension of the written and unwritten rules of the situation, and the ability to make expert and virtuous decisions (Bloomfield, 2000; Kessels & Korthagen, 1996). It also involves the development of character and virtues and a consideration of what is good for society (Flyvbjerg, 2001; Huigens, 1995). Wisdom includes the ability to clearly understand a situation and discern the best course of action according to the values of the organization (Nonaka & Toyama, 2007).

Practical wisdom is a comprehensive capacity that goes beyond predetermined or discrete answers. It bridges the category of cognitive knowledge to include necessary emotional elements and behavior (Halverson, 2004; Phelan, 2005; Schwarzenbach, 1996). Wisdom also includes perceptiveness, understanding, intuition, judgment, and the ability to analyze and assess consequences (Church, 1999; Halverson, 2004; Holliday & Chandler, 1986; Kramer, 1990). Wise individuals have the ability and willingness to look at phenomena and events from different perspectives and view problems from a broader and long-term perspective (Ardelt, 2004; Baltes & Staudinger, 2000).

With major technological and business challenges and changes in progress, there is a strong need for both individuals and organizations to focus on increasing practical wisdom in order to resolve complex and practical company problems (Bierly, Kessler, & Christensen, 2000; Minsky, 1985) and to increase both efficiency and effectiveness (Pinheiro, Raposo, & Hernandez, 2012). Wisdom encompasses a myriad of capabilities including seeing the big picture (Baltes & Staudinger, 2000), understanding complexity from multiple vantage points (Ardelt, 2004), recognizing our limitations (Ardelt, 2003), a desire to know the truth (Ardelt, 2003), and serving the greater good (Clayton & Birren, 1980; Webster, 2003). Sternberg (1990) suggested that wisdom has five functions, including resolving dilemmas and making decisions, advising others, management and guidance, self-reflection, and theoretical and philosophical thinking. All of these functions can be developed and are relevant to business environments.

The promotion of wisdom within individual employees of an organization can assist in reframing problems, provide goal orientation and context, develop trust and relationships, incorporate values, and provide new perspectives (Rowley, 2006). Providing professional development geared towards increasing practical wisdom might not only improve individuals' and organizations' cognitive and relational capabilities, but the ability to learn from past and current situations as well. This kind of training should be organization-wide and not solely reliant on the wisdom of a few select leaders (Hays, 2008).

Practical wisdom as the goal of professional development

In a 2013 study by PricewaterhouseCoopers, 65 percent of Millennials reported that personal development was the most important factor in their current job (Kuhl, 2014). Millennials favor professional development and guidance from leaders to be innovative and creative within an organization's framework (Moon, 2014). The requirements of many jobs today are partly undefined, and people skills are more expected than cultivated. Providing professional wisdom-related development and mentoring opportunities are likely to assist Millennials to build trust, confidence, and relationships, increase interpersonal and leadership skills to handle difficult situations, and gain organizational knowledge (Chaudhuri & Ghosh, 2012; Murphy, 2012). Encouraging professional development of practical wisdom among individuals within an organization is also likely to enhance moral and ethical decision-making (Hays, 2008; Moberg, 2008; Roca, 2008). Furthermore, it is strengthening the ability to focus on the big picture when faced with difficult decisions and potential loss, and increase understanding of complex situations to arrive at creative solutions (McKenna et al., 2009).

Fostering practical wisdom within organizations is likely to provide clarity for leaders to enhance business vision, values, purpose, goals and objectives, and the courage and justice needed for global leadership (Gottlieb, 1994; Hays, 2008; Jacobs, 1989; McKenna et al., 2009; Nonaka & Toyama, 2007). It will assist leaders in facing rapidly changing technology and global competition and promote greater concern for moral character and personal integrity, rather than positional power (Staudinger & Baltes, 1996; Sternberg, 1998). Developing wisdom will enhance leaders moral and ethical decision-making, enabling them to do the right thing instead of just following written rules for doing things right (Hays, 2008; Moberg, 2008; Roca, 2008). Wise leaders are more likely to go beyond replication of others' ideas to utilize their own creativity, intelligence, experience, and judgment (Sternberg, 2003).

We propose that practical wisdom should be the goal of professional development, because it is expected to strengthen interpersonal trust and team cohesiveness, which appear to be important workplace factors to the rising Millennial generation.

The Millennial workforce

The Millennial generation is creative, innovative, and passionate about technology (Moon, 2014). They are team-oriented and high achieving (Howe & Strauss, 2007). Baby boomers are beginning to retire and Millennials, with their digital talent, will lead businesses, making up the largest part of the US workforce within five years and three quarters of the global workforce within fifteen short years (Kuhl, 2014). Millennials also bring some changes, for example, a desire for expectations to be set up front, both rapid feedback and rapid gratification, job flexibility, and a better work/life balance. Many young talented professionals are looking at unconventional and innovative cultures like Google and Xiaomi and have rated them as the best places to work (Lee, 2014). Millennials are digitally and socially connected and have high expectations for trust in the workplace, especially with supervisors (Ito, 2011). They are more interested in doing meaningful work and making a difference than in earning a high salary (Kuhl, 2014; Moon, 2014). Fostering practical wisdom within organizations will help these individuals to handle increasingly complex social situations and develop interpersonal relationships that are characterized by cooperation and conflict resolution and the giving and receiving of advice (Bray & Howard, 1983; Kramer, 1990; Labouvie-Vief, 1980). The pursuit of practical wisdom among employees of the Millennial generation is likely to enhance their intuitive, intellectual, motivational, and relational capabilities (Curnow, 2011) and further their professional development.

Practical wisdom

The Three-Dimensional Wisdom Model (Ardelt, 1997, 2003, 2004) defines and operationalizes wisdom as an *integration of cognitive, reflective, and compassionate dimensions*. All three dimensions are considered necessary, but also sufficient for wisdom to emerge. The increasing number of managerial/leadership challenges and the growing need to meet social as well as corporate obligations require increased wisdom rather than mere intellectual knowledge for their solution (Goede, 2009; Leduc, 2004). Wise individuals and wise leaders have the maturity to understand people's actions and the discernment to make moral and ethical choices, particularly if circumstances are not clear-cut (Baltes & Staudinger, 2000; Holt, 2006). Wisdom includes the ability to withhold judgment and engage in reflective thinking (Clayton & Birren, 1980; Sternberg, 1990) but also to provide expert judgment and advice concerning difficult life situations (Baltes & Staudinger, 2000; Mickler & Staudinger, 2008).

Wise people know when to give and when to withhold judgment and advice, depending on the concrete situation and circumstances. The cognitive, reflective, and compassionate dimensions of wisdom work together to produce wise judgment, advice, decisions, and actions. For example, for Walsh (2015, p. 282), "Practical wisdom is skillful benevolent responsiveness to the central existential issues of life."

Both intelligence and wisdom include reasoning and problem-solving capabilities. However, intelligence alone has only a marginal effect upon a person's level of wisdom (Glück et al., 2013; Staudinger, Lopez, & Baltes, 1997). The *cognitive dimension of wisdom* includes a desire to know the truth, knowledge of extraordinary scope and depth, and the ability to apply intelligence, experience, and reason to solve life's problems (Ardelt, 2004; Baltes & Staudinger, 2000; Clayton & Birren, 1980). Wise individuals are able to understand the deeper meaning of life, particularly its interpersonal and intrapersonal aspects and the many facets of human nature, and can accept life's ambiguities and uncertainties (Ardelt, 2003). Yet they also know and understand that human knowledge is limited (Ardelt, Achenbaum, & Oh, 2013).

Wisdom is related to discernment and in-depth understanding (Staudinger et al., 1997). Discernment is the ability to deeply perceive and distinguish the right course of action (Scholl, 2001). Information becomes wisdom-related knowledge through discernment. When information has been processed through discernment, the knowledge can then be shared throughout the organization for effective problem-solving. Sharing insights from reflection upon these vital decisions increases wisdom-related knowledge throughout the organization and reinforces shared values and goals. Choosing the appropriate goals through creativity and insight and designing the strategy for achieving them are vital functions of strategic management (Nonaka & Toyama, 2007). This situational knowledge is known as practical wisdom (Baltes, 1992).

To obtain greater insight and in-depth understanding, individuals need to engage in reflection and self-reflection. The *reflective dimension of wisdom* represents the ability to look at life events from many different perspectives, self-awareness and self-insight, transcendence of subjectivity, and the avoidance of blame and bitterness (Ardelt, 2003). It also includes the ability to maintain a balanced and realistic outlook on life and to accept responsibility for one's actions (Ardelt, 2004).

There is a call in the academic literature for improved "retrospective sense-making" by managers to avoid repeated mistakes (Sparrow, 2000, p.16). The reflective dimension of wisdom includes intuition, reflective thinking, and the ability to withhold judgment to reflect on available options and understand why things happened or why decisions were chosen (Clayton & Birren, 1980; Sternberg, 1990). Greater reflection within organizations is needed to "deepen the analytic and collaborative dimensions" (Ranjan Chatterjee, 2009, p.158). Wisdom, especially the reflective wisdom dimension, is crucial for guiding the long-term future of an organization (Rowley, 2006).

Reflecting on one's experiences and life situation mindfully and objectively leads to a reduction in self-centeredness and, therefore, greater insight into one's own person and life in general, fostering the cognitive dimension of wisdom. Simultaneously, a reduced self-centeredness and greater insight and understanding of oneself and others lead to increased tolerance, sympathy, and compassion toward oneself and others, which characterize the compassionate dimension of wisdom (Ardelt et al., 2013). Hence, the development of the reflective wisdom dimension is pivotal for the development of the cognitive and compassionate wisdom dimensions.

The *compassionate dimension of wisdom* refers to sympathy, compassion, and honest concern for others, the motivation to foster the well-being of others, and the absence of negative and indifferent attitudes and feelings toward others (Ardelt, 2003). It includes tolerance, open-mindedness, and empathy of others' emotions (Kramer, 1990; Staudinger, Maciel, Smith, & Baltes, 1998). Wise individuals are less interested in seeking a pleasant life than being affectively involved in society and with friends. They tend to resolve work conflicts through cooperation and mutual agreement rather than dominance and nurture the personal growth and well-being of their teammates (Kunzmann & Baltes, 2003).

The development of wisdom is related to ego development and requires awareness of repressed emotions and the acknowledgment of struggles (Labouvie-Vief, Hakim-Larson, & Hobart, 1987). Wisdom involves overcoming immature coping mechanisms and self-centeredness to become empathetic and compassionate toward others (Kramer, 1990). Individuals choosing to work in helping professions, which deal frequently with struggles, such as divorce, death, abuse, addiction, and mental and physical illness, are likely to learn many valuable life lessons to gain greater wisdom if they are able to overcome their subjectivity and projections through the practice of reflection and self-reflection (Baltes & Staudinger, 1993).

Taken together, wisdom appears to be positively related to interpersonal trust and team cohesiveness, given that wise individuals have developed tolerance, understanding, sympathy, and compassion for others and are concerned with the well-being of all rather than only themselves.

Interpersonal trust

In general, trust within organizations is essential for effectiveness (Tschannen, 2004). Interpersonal trust is an individual's willingness to be open and vulnerable to another based on confidence in the other's competence, reliability, and concern (McAllister, 1995). Interpersonal trust results in improved behaviors, attitudes, processes, and performance (Dirks, 2000; Dirks & Ferrin, 2002; Jones & George, 1998). Trusting relationships are built upon experience and perception and can increase employee job satisfaction, organizational commitment, and financial profits while reducing job-related stress (Dirks & Ferrin, 2001; Flaherty & Pappas, 2000; Robinson, 1996; Staples & Ratnasingham, 1998). Teams who lack trusting relationships waste time establishing rapport and monitoring others' quality and progress (Serva & Fuller, 2004). When operating or trading outside the United States, trust is considered a necessary precursor to operations and may be more important than pricing considerations. Within a single organization, an individual's level of trust in the organization is also correlated with the level of trust among members of the organization (DeTienne, Dyer, Hoopes, & Harris, 2004).

Webber (2008) studied 78 teams and found that affective trust developed when individuals were willing to help, take a personal interest in, and perform additional tasks for other team members. The cognitive aspect of trust, where an individual decides who to trust, is dependent upon consistent and reliable performance (Lewis & Weigert, 1985; Webber, 2008). Assessment of competence, reliability, and dependability are also necessary for development of interpersonal trust. Interpersonal trust is demonstrated by limited self-centeredness, concern for others, a willingness to be open and accessible, and the belief that other team members share the same interests (Mishra, 1996). Interpersonal trust is developed from the assessment of previous events and prior performance of team members. Wisdom provides a synergy of mind and character, knowledge, and virtues (Baltes & Staudinger, 2000), which are likely to strengthen interpersonal trust, particularly if wise individuals actively further the personal growth and well-being of their teammates (Kunzmann & Baltes, 2003).

Team cohesiveness

Though specific empirical studies concerning Millennials and team cohesiveness are lacking, the Millennial generation tends to be socially and collaboratively oriented (Howe & Strauss, 2000). In addition, Millennials who are more idealistic tend to have stronger ethical values and more commitment to teamwork (VanMeter, Grisaffe, Chonko, & Roberts, 2013). In a previous study, we found that practical wisdom was inversely related to an individual's willingness to engage in questionable ethical business conduct (Oden, Ardelt, & Ruppel, 2015). Hence, greater wisdom might also be associated with the desire to work as members of a cohesive team.

Team cohesiveness is the level to which individual team members have affinity for each other and the team (Chidambaram, 1996). Team cohesiveness includes the acceptance of roles, norms, orientations, and the general direction of the group (Schriesheim, 1980). Cohesive teams are more cooperative and willing to assist each other, which is positively related to team success and employee job satisfaction (Dobbins & Zaccaro, 1986; Robbins & Fredendall, 2001; Sanders & Schyns, 2006). It also enhances decision-making, communication, cooperation, morale, motivation, sensitivity, and creativity (Chidambaram, 1996).

Working in teams has become a matter of common practice, resulting in increased productivity, effectiveness, quality, creativity, and problem-solving ability (Northouse, 2007). Effective teams understand their strengths and weaknesses, develop the ability to take the necessary action, and are focused upon the group's goals. In settings like healthcare, teams must be able to communicate well, work with conflicting and incomplete information, accept unpredictability and disagreement, and make wise decisions collectively (Edmondson & Pearce, 2007). In an industrial environment, team cohesiveness reduces the workplace anxiety of team members, yet team members also feel pressure from other team members to perform well (Seashore, 1977). Teams that are characterized by respect and interpersonal trust allow members to take risks and encourage them to ask questions, voice concerns and ideas, and receive constructive feedback (Adams et al., 2002; Edmondson, 1999). The ability of team members to listen, explore alternatives, and become mutually dependent, greatly affects team effectiveness and productivity (Adams et al., 2002).

Teamwork enhances the organization's ability to combine strengths and overcome weaknesses. Employees who operate as part of a team have the ability to learn more effectively and deal with more complex concepts by sharing experiences, engaging together in reflective thinking, and developing insights in the process that go beyond the current issues or needs of the organization (Lee, Bonk, Magjuka, Su, & Liu, 2006; McEvoy & Buller, 1997). Members of truly effective teams exemplify the cognitive, reflective, and compassionate dimensions of wisdom. Team cohesiveness requires the ability to assess past group and personal performances in both tasks and social settings.

This assessment necessitates reflection from multiple perspectives and the ability to provide balanced constructive feedback. Team members must be able to work around emotion and moods of others to express concerns and receive constructive feedback, which requires social skills, respect, and the ability to listen (Kessler & Bailey, 2007). Wise individuals have an acute understanding of both themselves and others, engage in reflective thinking, and demonstrate compassion and concern for their team members, customers, and those outside the organization (Ardelt, 2004, Bartolome, 1989).

Testing the relations of practical wisdom on interpersonal trust and team cohesiveness

Interpersonal trust and team cohesiveness have each shown to improve organizational decision-making and, therefore, enhance an organization's performance and productivity. By potentially increasing interpersonal trust and team cohesiveness, wisdom might indirectly and cumulatively improve organizational performance.

This study assessed practical wisdom within individuals as an integration of the previously presented cognitive, reflective, and compassionate wisdom dimensions (Ardelt, 2003) rather than general wisdom (Baltes & Staudinger, 2000) or transcendent wisdom (Levenson, Jennings, Aldwin, & Shiraishi, 2005). We assumed that it is possible to examine the effect of employee wisdom on organizations, because organizations are made up of groups of individuals working toward a common goal. As wisdom tends to have a positive impact on interpersonal relationships (Ardelt, 2000), it is likely to result in improved interpersonal relationships with all stakeholders. The study tested whether practical wisdom of individuals in a business setting is predictive of the needed team cohesiveness and interpersonal trust required for businesses to be successful throughout the arising changes. In particular, the following four hypotheses were tested:

- *Hypothesis 1*. Practical wisdom of individuals in a business setting, as measured by the integration of cognitive, reflective, and compassionate wisdom dimensions, is positively related to team cohesiveness.
- *Hypothesis 2*. Practical wisdom of individuals in a business setting is positively related to cognitive-based interpersonal trust.
- *Hypothesis 3*. Practical wisdom of individuals in a business setting is positively related to compassionate-based interpersonal trust.
- *Hypothesis 4*. Practical wisdom is expected to be more strongly related to team cohesiveness and cognitive-based and affect-based interpersonal trust than the individual dimensions of wisdom.

Methods

Procedure

After conducting a pilot study with 104 employees at two North Florida community colleges to validate the instruments, 535 surveys were distributed by mail to non-instructional employees from both a traditional university setting and numerous branch offices in six states. A total of 232 surveys were returned, resulting in a

43 percent return rate. Only non-instructional employees were targeted based on their service-orientation and emphasis on customer service. Study participants were told that the survey concerned several different aspects of business. It was not mentioned, however, that the survey included a wisdom scale to prevent contamination of the data. Names were not requested or recorded to allow for participant anonymity.

Of the 232 surveys returned, two surveys had missing data on 13–14 variables which included at least four of the five demographic questions. These two surveys and one survey that was clearly marked in haste, with all answers being scored three, were eliminated from the data analysis. This provided 229 usable surveys.

Sample

The 229 study participants ranged in age from 20 to 69 years, with a median and mean age of 45 years ($SD = 12.51$). Women constituted 64 percent of the sample. Seventeen percent of the participants had a high school degree, 28 percent a Bachelor's degree, 40 percent a Master's degree, and 14 percent a Doctorate or equivalent. Forty-six percent of the sample members were staff, 39 percent professionals, 9 percent senior professionals, and 6 percent executives. The time respondents worked for their current employer ranged from 4 months to 30 years, with an average of 6 years ($SD = 5.53$) and a median of 5 years.

Measures

Practical wisdom

To assess practical wisdom, Ardelt's (2003) Three-Dimensional Wisdom Scale (3D-WS) was used. This instrument measures wisdom as an integration of cognitive, compassionate, and reflective dimensions. The multi-dimensional wisdom scale has been found to be a valid and reliable instrument (Ardelt, 2003). The 3D-WS contains 39 items with 14 items measuring the cognitive dimension (e.g., I prefer to just let things happen rather than try to understand why they turned out that way), 12 items gauging the reflective dimension (e.g., When I look back at what's happened to me, I feel cheated), and 13 items assessing the compassionate dimension (e.g., Sometimes when people are talking to me, I find myself wishing they would leave). Two 5-point Likert scales are used to assess the 39 items, ranging from 1 = *strongly agree* to 5 = *strongly disagree*, and 1 = *definitely true of myself* to 5 = *not true of myself*, with all items scored in the direction of greater wisdom. Computing the average of the scale items yielded Cronbach's alpha reliability values of 0.74, 0.81, and 0.73 for the cognitive, reflective, and compassionate wisdom dimensions, respectively. The composite wisdom score was created by taking the average of the three dimensions (rather than the 39 items), resulting in a Cronbach's alpha value of 0.74 (0.85 for the 39 items). The correlations of the three dimensions ranged from 0.42 ($p < 0.001$) for the cognitive and compassionate wisdom dimensions to 0.55 ($p < 0.001$) for the reflective and compassionate dimensions. A factor analysis demonstrated that the three dimensions loaded on a single factor, with factor loadings of 0.78, 0.85, and 0.81 for the cognitive, reflective, and compassionate dimensions of wisdom, respectively.

Team cohesiveness

The most widely utilized instrument for team cohesiveness was developed by Seashore (1977). It has been modified and utilized in many varied studies. The instrument was developed for an industrial environment and utilized in 1950 to assess employee morale, relationships, and practices. This study utilized Chidambaram's (1996) Cohesiveness Scale, shown in Appendix A, which was adapted from Seashore's Index of Group Cohesiveness. It contains four items (e.g., I feel that I am a part of the team) with scores ranging from 1 = *strongly disagree* to 5 = *strongly agree*. Cronbach's alpha was 0.92.

Interpersonal trust

The measure to assess interpersonal trust consists of 11 items developed by McAllister (1995), shown in Appendix B. Six items assess the cognitive-based dimension (e.g., This person approaches his/her job with professionalism and dedication) and five items the affect-based dimension (e.g., I would have to say that we have both made considerable emotional investments in our working relationship). All scale items range from 1 = *strongly disagree* to 5 = *strongly agree* with one item being reverse scored. Cronbach's alpha was 0.91 and 0.90, respectively, for cognitive-based and affect-based interpersonal trust.

Some of the respondents did not respond to all of the items of the 3D-WS and the team cohesiveness scale. Twenty-one respondents failed to answer one item of the 3D-WS, six participants failed to respond to two items of the 3D-WS or the team cohesiveness scale, and one respondent did not answer three items of the 3D-WS. Therefore, the mean of all valid scale items was computed to construct the scales and subscales. No values were missing for the interpersonal trust subscales.

Demographic control variables

We controlled for gender (0 = male, 1 = female), age (in years), education, organizational position, and number of years employed by the current organization. Education was assessed as the highest degree completed and measured by four dichotomous variables: High School, Bachelor's Degree, Master's Degree, Doctorate or equivalent. Organizational position was also assessed by four dichotomous variables: Staff, Professional, Senior Professional, and Executive. Two values were missing for gender, 20 for age, 15 for years with employer, eight for education and six for organizational position. Mean substitution was used to replace missing values for gender, age, and years with employer, following Schumacker and Lomax's (2004) suggestion that mean substitution is appropriate when handling a proportionately small amount of missing data. The missing values for education and organizational position were assigned to the dichotomous variable representing the median of the ordinal variables (i.e., Master's Degree and Professional).

Results

Bivariate analysis

The bivariate correlations between variables and their means and standard deviations are shown in Table 7.1. As hypothesized, the composite measure of wisdom was positively and significantly related to perceptions of team cohesiveness as well as cognitive-based and affect-based interpersonal trust. All three wisdom dimensions were positively associated with the two interpersonal trust scales, but only the reflective wisdom dimension was significantly correlated with team cohesiveness. Team cohesiveness and the two interpersonal trust scales correlated positively with each other, indicating that team cohesiveness strengthens interpersonal trust in a business setting and vice versa.

Among the demographic variables, female gender was positively associated with the compassionate wisdom dimension. An independent sample *t*-test resulted in significantly higher average scores on the compassionate wisdom dimension for women ($M = 3.63$, $SD = 0.43$) than for men ($M = 3.49$, $SD = 0.49$; $t(225) = -2.30$, $p = 0.022$). A high-school degree and staff organizational position were negatively correlated with wisdom, specifically the cognitive and reflective dimensions of wisdom, whereas a doctorate or equivalent was positively associated with wisdom, specifically the cognitive wisdom dimension. A professional organizational position was positively related to the cognitive wisdom dimension, and an executive position was positively correlated with the reflective wisdom dimension. None of the demographic control variables was associated with team cohesiveness or interpersonal trust.

Table 7.1 Bivariate correlations between wisdom dimensions, ethical attitudes scales, and demographics; Pearson's *r*

	1	*2*	*3*	*4*	*5*	*6*	*7*	*m*	*sd*
1 3D-Wisdom	–							3.73	0.39
2 Cognitive wisdom dimension	0.79**	–						3.71	0.48
3 Reflective wisdom dimension	0.85**	0.51**	–					3.91	0.50
4 Compassionate wisdom dimension	0.80**	0.42**	0.55**	–				3.58	0.46
5 Team cohesiveness	0.17**	0.04	0.26**	0.12	–			3.82	0.90
6 Cognitive-based interpersonal trust	0.25**	0.15*	0.26**	0.19**	0.45**	–		3.97	0.86
7 Affect-based interpersonal trust	0.20**	0.15*	0.17**	0.17*	0.38**	0.56**	–	3.72	0.85
8 Gender (0 = male, 1 = female)	0.05	−0.04	0.02	0.15*	−0.01	0.03	0.03	0.64	0.48
9 Age	0.08	0.12	0.09	−0.02	0.06	0.01	−0.01	45.16	12.51
10 High-school degree	−0.18**	−0.28**	−0.13*	−0.03	0.07	0.02	0.04	0.17	0.38
11 Bachelor's degree	−0.06	−0.06	−0.08	0.00	0.03	0.05	−0.04	0.28	0.45
12 Master's degree	0.06	0.06	0.08	−0.00	−0.03	−0.02	0.04	0.40	0.49
13 Doctorate or equivalent	0.19**	0.30**	0.12	0.03	−0.06	−0.06	−0.06	0.14	0.35
14 Staff	−0.20**	−0.27**	−0.19**	−0.04	0.02	0.03	−0.06	0.46	0.50
15 Professional	0.08	0.15*	0.06	−0.02	−0.09	−0.09	0.03	0.39	0.49
16 Senior professional	0.12	0.10	0.10	0.09	0.04	0.07	0.03	0.09	0.28
17 Executive	0.13	0.13	0.15*	0.02	0.09	0.04	0.01	0.06	0.24
18 Years with employer	0.03	0.06	−0.01	0.01	0.12	−0.11	−0.07	6.07	5.53

Note: $n = 229$; ** $p < 0.01$; * $p < 0.05$.

Multivariate regression analyses

Ordinary least squares (OLS) regression analyses showed that composite wisdom was positively related to team cohesiveness and both interpersonal trust scales, even after controlling for demographic characteristics, as predicted in Hypotheses 1 and 2 (see Table 7.2). In addition, respondents with a Doctorate or equivalent had significantly lower average scores on team cohesiveness than respondents who had earned only a high-school degree, possibly due to the nature of their work, with high-school graduates being more dependent on team member support than respondents with a doctoral degree. Yet, no significant differences emerged between the staff of the organization and other organizational positions. Years with employer was negatively related to cognitive-based trust. However, the variables in the model explained only 4 percent, 7 percent, and 2 percent, respectively, of the variation in team cohesiveness, cognitive-based interpersonal trust, and affect-based interpersonal trust.

Table 7.3 displays the separate effects of the three wisdom dimensions on the dependent variables. As expected, the effects of the three individual wisdom dimensions on the two interpersonal trust scales were weaker than the effects of the three dimensions combined in a composite wisdom measure. In fact, none of the three individual wisdom dimensions was significantly related to affect-based interpersonal trust, whereas the significant relation between the reflective wisdom dimension and cognitive-based interpersonal trust was somewhat weaker than the association between the composite wisdom measure and cognitive-based interpersonal trust in Table 7.2. This indicates an important synergistic effect of the integration of the cognitive, reflective, and compassionate wisdom dimensions, which is lost when the individual wisdom

Table 7.2 Results of OLS regression analyses with composite wisdom and controls as predictors of team cohesiveness and interpersonal trust

Independent variables	*Dependent variables*								
	Team cohesiveness			*Cognitive-based trust*			*Affect-based trust*		
	b	*β*	*SE*	*b*	*β*	*SE*	*b*	*β*	*SE*
3D-Wisdom (overall)	0.48	0.21**	0.16	0.61	0.27***	0.15	0.48	0.22**	0.15
Control variables									
Gender (1 = female)	−0.08	−0.04	0.13	−0.02	−0.01	0.12	−0.01	−0.01	0.13
Age	0.00	0.01	0.01	0.01	0.07	0.01	0.00	0.01	0.01
High-school degree (reference)									
Bachelor's degree	−0.20	−0.10	0.19	−0.01	−0.01	0.18	−0.21	−0.11	0.18
Master's degree	−0.33	−0.18	0.19	−0.14	−0.08	0.18	−0.18	−0.10	0.18
Doctorate or equivalent	−0.63	−0.25*	0.25	−0.39	−0.16	0.23	−0.39	−0.18	0.24
Staff (reference)									
Professional	−0.04	−0.02	0.15	−0.10	−0.06	0.14	0.11	0.06	0.14
Senior professional	0.06	0.02	0.25	0.29	0.10	0.23	0.22	0.07	0.24
Executive	0.37	0.10	0.28	0.15	0.04	0.27	0.14	0.04	0.27
Years with employer	0.02	0.13	0.01	−0.02	−0.15*	0.01	−0.01	−0.07	0.01
Model fit									
Adjusted R^2		0.04*			0.07**			0.02	

Note: $n = 229$; ***$p < 0.001$; **$p < 0.01$; *$p < 0.05$.

Table 7.3 Results of OLS regression analyses with dimensions of wisdom and controls as predictors of team cohesiveness and interpersonal trust

Independent variables	*Dependent variables*								
	Team cohesiveness			*Cognitive-based trust*			*Affect-based trust*		
	b	*β*	*SE*	*b*	*β*	*SE*	*b*	*β*	*SE*
Cognitive wisdom dimension	−0.14	−0.08	0.15	0.14	0.08	0.15	0.20	0.11	0.15
Reflective wisdom dimension	0.63	0.35***	0.15	0.36	0.21*	0.15	0.13	0.08	0.15
Compassionate wisdom dimension	−0.08	−0.04	0.16	0.09	0.05	0.15	0.16	0.08	0.16
Control variables									
Gender (1 = female)	−0.06	−0.03	0.13	−0.01	−0.01	0.12	−0.01	−0.00	0.13
Age	−0.00	−0.01	0.01	0.00	0.06	0.01	0.00	0.01	0.01
High-school degree (reference)									
Bachelor's degree	−0.16	−0.08	0.19	−0.01	−0.00	0.18	−0.22	−0.11	0.18
Master's degree	−0.31	−0.17	0.19	−0.14	−0.08	0.18	−0.19	−0.11	0.19
Doctorate or equivalent	−0.52	−0.20*	0.25	−0.37	−0.15	0.24	−0.46	−0.19	0.25
Staff (reference)									
Professional	−0.04	−0.02	0.14	−0.10	−0.06	0.14	0.10	0.06	0.14
Senior professional	0.03	0.01	0.24	0.28	0.09	0.23	0.23	0.08	0.24
Executive	0.29	0.08	0.28	0.12	0.03	0.27	0.15	0.04	0.27
Years with employer	0.03	0.16*	0.01	−0.02	−0.14	0.01	−0.01	−0.08	0.01
Model fit									
Adjusted R^2		0.08**			0.07**			0.01	

Note: $n = 229$; ***$p < 0.001$; **$p < 0.01$; *$p < 0.05$.

dimensions are analyzed separately. Yet for team cohesiveness as dependent variable, the reflective wisdom dimension had greater predictive power than the composite wisdom measure, suggesting that the abilities to take the perspective of another person and to overcome subjectivity and projections are most important for team cohesiveness. Among the control variables, years with employer was positively related to team cohesiveness, while the negative relation between years with employer and cognitive-based trust just failed, with a p-value of 0.052, to be significant at the 0.05-level of statistical significance in Table 7.3.

Multicollinearity tests indicated that the variance inflation factor (VIF) for the three wisdom dimensions ranged from 1.60 to 1.73, which is well within acceptable limits, and makes it unlikely that the results were affected by multicollinearity. The variables in the model explained 8 percent, 7 percent, and 1 percent, respectively, of the variation in team cohesiveness, cognitive-based interpersonal trust, and affect-based interpersonal trust. Notably, none of the variables was significantly related to affect-based trust in Table 7.3.

Discussion and conclusions

Wisdom is a complex construct with significant potential to increase organizational success. The empirical results presented indicate that helping individuals in a business setting grow in wisdom, consisting of the integration of cognitive, reflective, and compassionate wisdom dimensions, might strengthen team cohesiveness and cognitive-based and affect-based interpersonal trust among co-workers. Interestingly, the longer respondents worked for the same employer, the lower their cognitive-based trust tended to be. This suggests that long-term employees might be in danger of burnout if they do not develop wisdom. Wisdom, in turn, can counteract the erosion of cognitive-based interpersonal trust.

Wisdom has long been considered the pinnacle of human development and may serve well as the highpoint for leadership training and business development. With the growth of global business, and China and India playing a larger role in the world market, understanding wisdom from both the Eastern and Western traditions (Takahashi, 2000) should enhance business functions (Ranjan Chatterjee, 2009). "Management is wise to the extent that it uses a blend of intelligence, creativity, experience, and virtue to achieve a common good through balancing intrapersonal, interpersonal, and extrapersonal organizational/institutional/spiritual interests over both the short and long terms" (McKenna & Rooney, 2005, p. 4).

With the retirement of older workers, with their experience and knowledge, from many organizations, a growing need arises for leaders capable of strategic planning, perspective-taking, and values-based decision making. Though the Millennial generation might score higher in terms of raw intelligence (Greenfield, 1998) and gather information more quickly, while sharing it more collaboratively (Howe & Strauss, 2000), they are still in need of practical wisdom, which can be developed through shared experience. "Wisdom represents the synthesis of knowledge-based potential with higher order visioning and practical implementation" (Pinheiro et al., 2012, p. 1466). In addition to strategic thinking and decision making, wise leaders are capable of connecting processes, perspective-taking, anticipating reactions, understanding how concerns are linked, self-restraint, and maintaining the unwritten obligations between an employee and employer (McKenna & Rooney, 2005). Wisdom has the ability to achieve deeper organizational harmony through the reduction in selfishness and the introduction of tolerance, sympathy, and compassion for others and includes the courage and justice needed for ensuring moral, social, and ethical global leadership (Gottlieb, 1994; Jacobs, 1989; Ranjan Chatterjee, 2009).

In the social environment of business, the dimensions and components of practical wisdom can be developed in individuals and teams, enhancing their creativity and innovative thinking, encouraging them to share their experience and to develop a deeper understanding, and increasing a team's and an organization's willingness to learn and to become vision-oriented and virtuous (Hays, 2008; Rowley & Gibbs, 2008; Sternberg, 1990). Balanced growth in all three dimensions of wisdom (cognitive, reflective, and compassionate) is likely to increase intellectual, emotional, and spiritual maturity, resulting in more even-temperedness, open-mindedness, and sociability and reduced emotional liability in the workplace (Clayton & Birren, 1980). Wisdom provides the ability to direct behaviors and to address legitimate concerns of the organization (Rowley, 2006). Increased wisdom provides for better decision-making, greater team cohesiveness, more interpersonal trust, and lessened emotional liability, providing the company a strong competitive advantage. Practical wisdom might lead to a more balanced, inspired, perceptive, discerning, and engaged organization, better suited for international competition as well as the promotion of the common good (Kunzmann & Baltes, 2003; Sternberg, 1985, 1998).

Limitations and Implications

Participants in this study were from six states and included staff from both a traditional university setting and numerous branch offices. Yet, the study was conducted within a single university and therefore might not be representative of other business organizations or even other universities. Moreover, the study suffers from well-known limitations of survey research, conducted at a single point in time, which makes it impossible to determine the causality of the variable relationships. Further longitudinal studies in other similar settings or within other types of organizations will be required to validate the findings. This study indicates that the practical wisdom of individuals in a business setting has important organizational outcomes in the specific areas of teamwork and trust. Future research should be conducted to examine the relationship between wisdom and other important organizational outcomes, as well as personal and interpersonal outcomes beyond the scope of business.

Summary

Organizations must utilize the knowledge, experience, emotional understanding, and intuition of its managers and employees to understand and operate in the increasingly complex business environment (Sparrow, 2000). Practical wisdom within an organization enables individuals to make decisions based not only on intellectual knowledge and analytic ability, but also upon emotional understanding, reflection, and compassion. Wisdom enables individuals to handle increasingly complex social situations, develop trusting interpersonal relationships, foster cooperation and conflict resolution, overcome disillusionment, give and receive advice, and accept change more readily (Bray & Howard, 1983; Kramer, 1990; Labouvie-Vief, 1980). Understanding the function, interrelation, and growth of practical wisdom among individuals within organizations can help businesses face rapidly changing technology, the challenges faced by the retirement of the baby-boomer generation and rise of the Millennial generation, and the interdependence of globalization and increasing global competition. Therefore, the growth in practical wisdom will not only help individuals to lead more harmonious and satisfying lives that benefit them and those around them (Ardelt & Ferrari, 2014) but also should be the goal of organizational professional development to attain more harmonious business relationships between all stakeholders and to advance sustainable business practices that save the planet (Ranjan Chatterjee, 2009; Rowley & Gibbs, 2008).

References

Adams, S., Simon, L., & Ruiz, B. (2002). A pilot study of the performance of student teams in engineering education. Paper presented at the Session 1017 Proceedings of the American Society for Engineering Education Annual Conference, Montreal.

Ardelt, M. (1997). Wisdom and life satisfaction in old age. *Journal of Gerontology: Psychological Sciences, 52B*(1), P15-P27. doi: 10.1093/geronb/52B.1.P15.

Ardelt, M. (2000). Antecedents and effects of wisdom in old age: A longitudinal perspective on aging well. *Research on Aging, 22*(4), 360–394. doi: 10.1177/0164027500224003.

Ardelt, M. (2003). Empirical assessment of a three-dimensional wisdom scale. *Research on Aging, 25*(3), 275–324. doi: 10.1177/0164027503025003004.

Ardelt, M. (2004). Wisdom as expert knowledge system: A critical review of a contemporary operationalization of an ancient concept. *Human Development, 47*(5), 257–285. doi: 10.1159/000079154.

Ardelt, M., & Ferrari, M. (2014). Wisdom and emotions. In P. Verhaeghen & C. Hertzog (Eds.), *The Oxford handbook of emotion, social cognition, and problem solving in adulthood* (pp. 256–272). New York, NY: Oxford University Press.

Ardelt, M., Achenbaum, W. A., & Oh, H. (2013). The paradoxical nature of personal wisdom and its relation to human development in the reflective, cognitive, and affective domains. In M. Ferrari & N. M. Weststrate (Eds.), *The scientific study of personal wisdom: From contemplative traditions to neuroscience* (pp. 265–295). New York, NY: Springer.

Baltes, P. B. (1992). Wise, and otherwise: Our mental hardware declines with age, but our software sometimes improves. *Natural History, 2*, 50–51.

Baltes, P., & Staudinger, U. (1993). The search for a psychology of wisdom. *Current Directions in Psychological Science, 2*(3), 75–80. Retrieved from www.jstor.org/stable/20182206.

Baltes, P. B., & Staudinger, U. M. (2000). Wisdom: A metaheuristic (pragmatic) to orchestrate mind and virtue toward excellence. *American Psychologist, 55*(1), 122–136. doi: 10.1037/0003-066X.55.1.122.

Bartolome, F. (1989). Nobody trusts the boss completely – Now what? *Harvard Business Review, 67*(2), 135–142.

Bierly, P. E., III, Kessler, E. H., & Christensen, E. W. (2000). Organizational learning, knowledge and wisdom. *Journal of Organizational Change Management, 13*(6), 595–618. doi: 10.1108/09534810010378605.

Bloomfield, P. (2000). Virtue epistemology and the epistemology of virtue. *Philosophy and Phenomenological Research, 60*(1), 23–43. doi: 10.2307/2653426.

Bojanova, I. (2014). The digital revolution: What's on the horizon? *IT Professional, 16*(1), 8–12. doi: 10.1109/MITP.2014.11.

Bray, D. W., & Howard, A. (1983). The AT&T longitudinal studies of managers. In K. W. Schaie (Ed.), *Longitudinal studies of adult psychological development* (pp. 266–312). New York, NY: Guilford Press.

Chaudhuri, S., & Ghosh, R. (2012). Reverse mentoring: A social exchange tool for kleping the boomers engaged and millennials committed. *Human Resource Development Review, 11*(1), 55. doi: 10.1177/1534484311417562.

Chidambaram, L. (1996). Relational development in computer-supported groups. *MIS Quarterly, 20*(2), 143–165. doi: 10.2307/249476.

Church, R. P. (1999). The breakdown of the constitutional tradition: MacIntyrian and theological responses. *Journal of Law and Religion, 14*(2), 351–389. doi: 10.2307/3556575.

Clayton, V. P., & Birren, J. E. (1980). The development of wisdom across the life-span: A reexamination of an ancient topic. In P. B. Baltes & O. G. Brim, Jr. (Eds.), *Life-span development and behavior* (Vol. 3, pp. 103–135). New York: Academic Press.

Curnow, T. (2011). *Sophia* and *phronesis*: Past, present, and future. *Research in Human Development, 8*(2), 95–108. doi: 10.1080/15427609.2011.568849.

DeTienne, K. B., Dyer, G., Hoopes, C., & Harris, S. (2004). Toward a model of effective knowledge management and directions for future research: Culture, leadership, and CKOs. *Journal of Leadership & Organizational Studies, 10*(4), 26–43. doi: 10.1177/107179190401000403.

Dirks, K. T. (2000). Trust in leadership and team performance: Evidence from NCAA basketball. *Journal of Applied Psychology, 85*(6), 1004–1012. doi: 10.1037/0021-9010.85.6.1004

Dirks, K. T., & Ferrin, D. L. (2001). The role of trust in organizational settings. *Organization Science, 12*(4), 450–467. doi: 10.1287/orsc.12.4.450.10640.

Dirks, K. T., & Ferrin, D. L. (2002). Trust in leadership: Meta-analytic findings and implications for research and practice. *Journal of Applied Psychology, 87*(4), 611–628. doi: 10.1037/0021-9010.87.4.611.

Dobbins, G. H., & Zaccaro, S. J. (1986). The effects of group cohesion and leader behavior on subordinate satisfaction. *Group & Organization Studies, 11*(3), 203–219. doi: 10.1177/105960118601100305.

Edmondson, A. (1999). Psychological safety and learning behavior in work teams. *Administrative Science Quarterly, 44*(2), 350–383. doi: 10.2307/2666999.

Edmondson, R., & Pearce, J. (2007). The practice of health care: Wisdom as a model. *Medicine, Health Care and Philosophy, 10*(3), 233–244. doi: 10.1007/s11019-006-9033-3.

Flaherty, K. E., & Pappas, J. M. (2000). The role of trust in salesperson-sales manager relationships. *Journal of Personal Selling & Sales Management, 20*(4), 271–278. doi: 10.1080/08853134.2000.10754247.

Flyvbjerg, B. (2001). *Making social science matter: Why social inquiry fails and how it can succeed again*. New York, NY: Cambridge University Press.

Frey, C. B., & Osborne, M. (2015). Technology at work: The future of innovation and employment. *Citi GPS: Global Perspectives & Solutions*, from www.oxfordmartin.ox.ac.uk/downloads/reports/Technology%20at%20Work.pdf.

Glück, J., König, S., Naschenweng, K., Redzanowski, U., Dorner-Hörig, L., Strasser, I., et al. (2013). How to measure wisdom: Content, reliability, and validity of five measures. *Frontiers in Psychology, 4*(405), 1–13. doi: 10.3389/fpsyg.2013.00405.

Goede, M. (2009). Can Curaçao become a creative economy? A case study. *International Journal of Social Economics, 36*(1/2), 47–69. doi: 10.1108/03068290910921181.

Gottlieb, P. (1994). Aristotle on dividing the soul and uniting the virtues. *Phronesis, 39*(3), 275–290. doi: 10.1163/156852894321052081.

Greenfield, P. M. (1998). The cultural evolution of IQ. In U. Neisser (Ed.), *The rising curve: Long-term gains in IQ and related measures* (pp. 81–123). Washington, DC: American Psychological Association.

Grint, K. (2007). Learning to lead: Can Artistotle help us find the road to wisdom? *Leadership, 3*(2), 231–246. doi: 10.1177/1742715007076215.

Halverson, R. (2004). Accessing, documenting, and communicating practical wisdom: The phronesis of school leadership practice. *American Journal of Education, 111*(1), 90–121. doi: 10.1086/424721.

Hays, J. M. (2008). Dynamics of organisational wisdom. *School of Management, Marketing, and International Business Working Paper Series 3*(3).

Holliday, S. G., & Chandler, M. J. (1986). *Wisdom: Explorations in adult competence*. Basel, New York: Karger.

Holt, R. (2006). Principals and practice: Rhetoric and the moral character of managers. *Human Relations, 59*(12), 1659–1680. doi: 10.1177/0018726706072867.

Howard, J. (2014, December). The wonderful and terrifying implications of computers that can learn. *TEDxBrussels*, from www.ted.com/talks/jeremy_howard_the_wonderful_and_terrifying_implications_of_computers_that_can_learn?utm_source=email&source=email&utm_medium=social&utm_campaign=ios-share.

Howe, N., & Strauss, W. (2000). *Millennials rising: The next great generation*. New York, NY: Vintage.

Howe, N., & Strauss, W. (2007). *Millennials go to college*. Great Falls, VA: American Association of Collegiate Registrars and Admissions Offices (AACRAO) and Life Course Associates.

Huigens, K. (1995). Virtue and inculpation. *Harvard Law Review, 108*(7), 1423–1480. doi: 10.2307/1341807.

Ito, M. (2011). *Millennials' expectation of trust for supervisors and coworkers in the workplace.* MA Thesis, University of Kansas, Lawrence, KS.

Jacobs, J. (1989). Practical wisdom, objectivity and relativism. *American Philosophical Quarterly, 26*(3), 199–209.

Jones, G. R., & George, J. M. (1998). The experience and evolution of trust: Implications for cooperation and teamwork. *The Academy of Management Review, 23*(3), 531–546. doi: 10.2307/259293.

Jones, P. T., II. (2015, March). Why we need to rethink capitalism. *TED2015*, from www.ted.com/talks/paul_tudor_jones_ii_why_we_need_to_rethink_capitalism.

Kaipa, P. L. (2014). Making wise decisions: Leadership lessons from Mahabharata. *Journal of Management Development, 33*(8–9), 835–846. doi: 10.1108/jmd-06-2014-0061.

Kessels, J. P. A. M., & Korthagen, F. A. J. (1996). The relationship between theory and practice: Back to the classics. *Educational Researcher, 25*(3), 17–22. doi: 10.2307/1176664.

Kessler, E. H., & Bailey, J. R. (2007). *Handbook of organizational and managerial wisdom.* Los Angeles, CA: Sage.

Kramer, D. A. (1990). Conceptualizing wisdom: The primacy of affect-cognition relations. In R. J. Sternberg (Ed.), *Wisdom: Its nature, origins, and development* (pp. 279–313). New York: Cambridge University Press.

Kuhl, J. S. (2014). Investing in millennials for the future of your organization. *Leader to Leader, 2014*(71), 25–30. doi: 10.1002/ltl.20110.

Kunzmann, U., & Baltes, P. B. (2003). Wisdom-related knowledge: Affective, motivational, and interpersonal correlates. *Personality and Social Psychology Bulletin, 29*(9), 1104–1119. doi: 10.1177/0146167203254506.

Labouvie-Vief, G. (1980). Beyond formal operations: Uses and limits of pure logic in life-span development. *Human Development, 23*(3), 141–161. doi: 10.1159/000272546.

Labouvie-Vief, G., Hakim-Larson, J., & Hobart, C. J. (1987). Age, ego level, and the life-span development of coping and defense processes. *Psychology and Aging, 2*(3), 286–293. doi: 10.1037/0882-7974.2.3.286.

Leduc, L. (2004). Corporate governance with a difference: Fiduciary duty for a wisdom economy. *International Journal of Business Governance and Ethics, 1*(2–3), 147–161. doi: 10.1504/IJBGE.2004.005251.

Lee, S.-H., Bonk, C. J., Magjuka, R. J., Su, B., & Liu, X. (2006). Understanding the dimensions of virtual teams. *International Journal on E-Learning, 5*(4), 507–523.

Lee, Y.-F. L. (2014). When Google meets Xiaomi: Comparative case study in western and eastern corporate management. *Journal of International Technology and Information Management, 23*(3–4).

Levenson, M. R., Jennings, P. A., Aldwin, C. M., & Shiraishi, R. W. (2005). Self-transcendence: Conceptualization and measurement. *International Journal of Aging & Human Development, 60*(2), 127–143. doi: 10.2190/XRXM-FYRA-7U0X-GRC0.

Lewis, J. D., & Weigert, A. (1985). Trust as a social reality. *Social Forces, 63*(4), 967–985. doi: 10.2307/2578601.

McAllister, D. J. (1995). Affect- and cognition-based trust as foundations for interpersonal cooperation in organizations. *Academy of Management Journal, 38*(1), 24–59. doi: 10.2307/256727.

McEvoy, G. M., & Buller, P. F. (1997). The power of outdoor management development. *Journal of Management Development, 16*(3), 208–217. doi: 10.1108/02621719710164355.

McKenna, B., & Rooney, D. (2005). Wisdom management: Tensions between theory and practice in practice. Paper presented at the Knowledge Management in Asia Pacific Conference on

Building a Knowledge Society, Wellington, New Zealand. http://espace.library.uq.edu.au/view/UQ:8839/KMAP_Tensions_be.pdf.

McKenna, B., Rooney, D., & Boal, K. B. (2009). Wisdom principles as a meta-theoretical basis for evaluating leadership. *Leadership Quarterly, 20*(2), 177–190.

McMillan, R. (2015, January 16). AI has arrived, and that really worries the world's brightest minds. *Wired*, from www.wired.com/2015/01/ai-arrived-really-worries-worlds-brightest-minds/.

Mickler, C., & Staudinger, U. M. (2008). Personal wisdom: Validation and age-related differences of a performance measure. *Psychology and Aging, 23*(4), 787–799. doi: 10.1037/a0013928.

Minsky, M. (1985). *The society of mind*. New York, NY: Simon & Schuster.

Mishra, A. K. (1996). Organizational responses to crisis: The centrality of trust. In R. M. Kramer & T. R. Tyler (Eds.), *Trust in organizations: Frontiers of theory and research* (pp. 261–287). Thousand Oaks, CA: Sage.

Moberg, D. (2008). Mentoring and practical wisdom: Are mentors wiser or just more politically skilled? *Journal of Business Ethics, 83*(4), 835–843. doi: 10.1007/s10551-008-9668-5.

Moon, T. M. (2014). Mentoring the next generation for innovation in today's organization. *Journal of Strategic Leadership, 5*(1), 23–35.

Murphy, W. M. (2012). Reverse mentoring at work: Fostering cross-generational learning and developing millennial leaders. *Human Resource Management, 51*(4), 549. doi: 10.1002/hrm.21489.

Nonaka, I., & Toyama, R. (2007). Strategic management as distributed practical wisdom (phronesis). *Industrial and Corporate Change, 16*(3), 371–394. doi: 10.1093/icc/dtm014

Northouse, P. G. (2007). *Leadership: Theory and practice*. Thousand Oaks, CA: Sage.

Oden, C., Ardelt, M., & Ruppel, C. (2015). Wisdom and its relation to ethical attitude in organizations. *Business and Professional Ethics Journal, 34*(2), 141–164. doi: 10.5840/bpej2015111032.

Phelan, A. M. (2005). A fall from (someone else's) certainty: Recovering practical wisdom in teacher education. *Canadian Journal of Education, 28*(3), 339–358. doi: 10.2307/4126474.

Pinheiro, P., Raposo, M., & Hernandez, R. (2012). Measuring organizational wisdom applying an innovative model of analysis. *Management Decision, 50*(8), 1465–1487. doi: 10.1108/00251741211262033.

Ranjan Chatterjee, S. (2009). Managerial ethos of the Indian tradition: Relevance of a wisdom model. *Journal of Indian Business Research, 1*(2/3), 136–162. doi: 10.1108/1755 4190911005336.

Rawlinson, K. (2015, January 29). Microsoft's Bill Gates insists AI is a threat. *BBC News*, from www.bbc.com/news/31047780.

Robbins, T. L., & Fredendall, L. D. (2001). Correlates of team success in higher education. *Journal of Social Psychology, 141*(1), 135–136. doi: 10.1080/00224540109600534.

Robinson, S. L. (1996). Trust and breach of the psychological contract. *Administrative Science Quarterly, 41*(4), 574–599. doi: 10.2307/2393868.

Roca, E. (2008). Introducing practical wisdom in business schools. *Journal of Business Ethics, 82*(3), 607–620. doi: 10.1007/s10551-007-9580-4.

Rometty, G. (2015, May 6). IBM's Watson supercomputer to speed up cancer care. *BBC News*, from www.bbc.com/news/technology-32607688.

Rowley, J. (2006). Where is the wisdom that we have lost in knowledge? *Journal of Documentation, 62*(2), 251–270. doi: 10.1108/00220410610653332.

Rowley, J., & Gibbs, P. (2008). From learning organization to practically wise organization. *Learning Organization, 15*(5), 356–372. doi: 10.1108/09696470810898357.

Russell, B. (1997). *Collected Papers of Bertrand Russell, 1954*. Retrieved from: http:// high erintellect.info/texts/thought_and_writing/philosophy/Russell,%20Bertrand/ Bertrand%20 Russell%20-%20Knowledge%20And%20Wisdom.pdf.

Sanders, K., & Schyns, B. (2006). Leadership and solidarity behaviour. *Personnel Review, 35*(5), 538–556. doi: 10.1108/00483480610682280.

Scholl, E. (2001). The mother of virtues: Discretio. *Cistercian Studies Quarterly, 36*(3), 389–402.

Schriesheim, J. F. (1980). The social context of leader-subordinate relations: An investigation of the effects of group cohesiveness. *Journal of Applied Psychology, 65*(2), 183–194. doi: 10.1037/0021-9010.65.2.183.

Schumacker, R. E., & Lomax, R. G. (2004). *A beginner's guide to structural equation modeling* (2nd ed.). Mahwah, NJ: Lawrence Erlbaum.

Schwarzenbach, S. A. (1996). On civic friendship. *Ethics, 107*(1), 97–128. doi: 10.2307/2382245.

Seashore, S. E. (1977). *Group cohesiveness in the industrial work group*. New York, NY: Arno Press.

Serva, M. A., & Fuller, M. A. (2004). The effects of trustworthiness perceptions on the formation of initial trust: Implications for MIS student teams. *Journal of Information Systems Education, 15*(4), 383–395.

Simmons, D. (2015, May 6). Airbus had 1,000 parts 3D printed to meet deadline. *BBC News*, from www.bbc.com/news/technology-32597809.

Sparrow, P. R. (1999). Strategy and cognition: Understanding the role of management knowledge structures, organizational memory and information overload. *Creativity and Innovation Management, 8*(2), 140–148. doi: 10.1111/1467-8691.00128.

Sparrow, P. R. (2000). Strategic management in a world turned upside down: The role of cognition, intuition and emotional intelligence. In P. Flood, T. Dromgoole, & S. Carroll (Eds.), *Managing strategy implementation* (pp. 15–30). Malden, MA: Blackwell.

Staples, D. S., & Ratnasingham, P. (1998). Trust: The panacea of virtual management? Paper presented at the Proceedings of the International Conference on Information Systems.

Staudinger, U. M., & Baltes, P. B. (1996). Interactive minds: A facilitative setting for wisdom-related performance. *Journal of Personality and Social Psychology, 71*(4), 746–762. doi: 10.1037//0022-3514.71.4.746.

Staudinger, U. M., Lopez, D. F., & Baltes, P. B. (1997). The psychometric location of wisdom-related performance: Intelligence, personality, and more? *Personality and Social Psychology Bulletin, 23*(11), 1200–1214. doi: 10.1177/01461672972311007.

Staudinger, U. M., Maciel, A. G., Smith, J., & Baltes, P. B. (1998). What predicts wisdom-related performance? A first look at personality, intelligence, and facilitative experiential contexts. *European Journal of Personality, 12*(1), 1–17. doi: 10.1002/(SICI)1099-0984(199801/02)12:1%3C1::AID-PER285%3E3.0.CO;2-9.

Sternberg, R. J. (1985). Implicit theories of intelligence, creativity, and wisdom. *Journal of Personality and Social Psychology, 49*(3), 607–627. doi: 10.1037/0022-3514.49.3.607.

Sternberg, R. J. (1990). Understanding wisdom. In R. J. Sternberg (Ed.), *Wisdom: Its nature, origins, and development* (pp. 3–9). New York, NY: Cambridge University Press.

Sternberg, R. J. (1998). A balance theory of wisdom. *Review of General Psychology, 2*(4), 347–365. doi: 10.1037/1089-2680.2.4.347.

Sternberg, R. J. (2003). WICS: A model of leadership in organizations. *Academy of Management Learning & Education, 2*(4), 386–401. doi: 10.5465/amle.2003.11902088.

Strack, R. (2014, October). The workforce crisis of 2030 – and how to start solving it now. *TED@BCG Berlin*, from www.ted.com/talks/rainer_strack_the_surprising_workforce_crisis_of_2030_and_how_to_start_solving_it_now?utm_source=email&source=email&utm_medium=social&utm_campaign=ios-share.

Takahashi, M. (2000). Toward a culturally inclusive understanding of wisdom: Historical roots in the East and West. *International Journal of Aging and Human Development, 51*(3), 217–230.

Tschannen, D. (2004). The effect of individual characteristics on perceptions of collaboration in the work environment. *Medsurg Nursing, 13*(5), 312–318.
VanMeter, R. A., Grisaffe, D. B., Chonko, L. B., & Roberts, J. A. (2013). Generation Y's ethical ideology and its potential workplace implications. *Journal of Business Ethics, 117*(1), 93–109. doi: 10.1007/s10551-012-1505-1.
Walker, P. D. (2010). Leadership Insights: Is wisdom the first priority in your life? *Huffington Post*, from www.huffingtonpost.com/paul-david-walker/leadership-insights-is-wi_b_786417.html.
Walsh, R. (2015). What is wisdom? Cross-cultural and cross-disciplinary syntheses. *Review of General Psychology, 19*(3), 278–293. doi: 10.1037/gpr0000045.
Webber, S. S. (2008). Development of cognitive and affective trust in teams: A longitudinal study. *Small Group Research, 39*(6), 746–769. doi: 10.1177/1046496408323569.
Webster, J. (2003). An exploratory analysis of a self-assessed wisdom scale. *Journal of Adult Development, 10*(1), 13–22. doi: 10.1023/A:1020782619051.

Appendix A

Chidambaram's (1996) Cohesiveness Scale

Adapted from Seashore's Index of Group Cohesiveness; measured using a 5-point Likert scale, ranging from 1 = *strongly disagree* to 5 = *strongly agree*.

1. I feel that I am a part of the team.
2. My team works together better than most teams on which I have worked.
3. My teammates and I help each other better than most other teams on which I have worked.
4. My teammates and I get along better than most other teams on which I have worked.

Appendix B

Interpersonal Trust Measures (McAllister, 1995)

Measured on a 5-point Likert scale, ranging from 1 = *strongly disagree* to 5 = *strongly agree*.

Cognitive-based trust

1. This person approaches his/her job with professionalism and dedication.
2. Given this person's track record, I see no reason to doubt his/her competence and preparation for the job.
3. I can rely on this person not to make my job more difficult by careless work.
4. Most people, even those who aren't close friends of this individual, trust and respect him/her as a coworker.
5. Other work associates of mine who must interact with this individual consider him/her to be trustworthy.
6. If people knew more about this individual and his/her background, they would be more concerned and monitor his/her performance more closely. (Reverse-coded.)

Affect-based trust

1 We have a sharing relationship. We both freely share our ideas and hopes.
2 I can talk freely to this individual about difficulties I am having at work and know that (s)he will want to listen.
3 We would both feel a sense of loss if one of us was transferred and we could no longer work together.
4 If I shared my problems with this person, I know (s)he would respond constructively and caringly.
5 I would have to say that we have both made considerable emotional investments in our working relationship.

Chapter 8

A wise course

Educating for wisdom in the twenty-first century

Jay Martin Hays

Introduction: Orientation and context

This chapter covers a number of issues relating to wisdom learning, or, more specifically, educating for wisdom. Three main points are emphasised: (a) greater wisdom is needed in the world; (b) wisdom can be learned; and (c) institutions of higher learning are obligated to foster the development of wisdom, though have been remiss in doing so.

The centrepiece is a proposed curriculum for wisdom learning called RJRA: Reasoning, Judgement and Reflective Action. RJRA is a model of wisdom comprising capabilities, dispositions and contexts that work in concert to enable wise thought and action, as individuals, teams and organisations develop greater sophistication and discipline in applying them (see Figure 8.2). The curriculum proposed here draws on suggestions from the literature regarding the teaching and learning of wisdom (Adams, 2011; Rosch, 2008; Sternberg, 2001) and others.[1]

Exploiting RJRA capabilities and dispositions can improve solution finding and decision making, and thus might reasonably be expected to produce more effective individuals and organisations. The model also might help us account for behaviour that appears unwise or produces undesirable results by highlighting strategies and considerations that were neglected in the process or dealt with superficially. Further, the RJRA model of wisdom comprises a set of skills, knowledge areas and dispositions that can be systematically developed. This allows us to chart progress over time and to identify particular strengths and areas where further development is needed.

Given these propositions, it would be a logical extension to suggest that universities and other tertiary education institutions could and should be teaching RJRA in some form. However, higher education is not consistently producing graduates who possess the skills and habits demanded by the complex, global world of the twenty-first century (Adams, 2011; Hays, 2015a; Madsen and Turnbull, 2006; Thomas, 2009).

What makes the model of particular value is that it simplifies and makes concrete various dimensions of wisdom, which can often seem idealistic, abstract and intangible. The reinforcing and synergistic nature of the model's elements working in concert – systemic and holistic – suggest the power of an integrating curriculum and its contribution to wisdom. Blatner (2010, n. p.) has noted that 'wisdom is something one *does* [emphasising that its] component activities [are] skills that need to be exercised in concert'.

Wisdom, here, is defined simply as *doing the right thing for the greater good, all things considered* (Hays, 2008a),[2] as depicted in Figure 8.1.

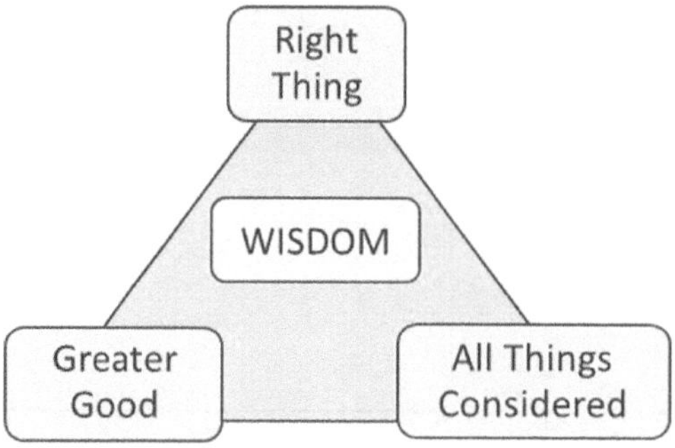

Figure 8.1 The three elements of wisdom (wisdom triangle).

In laying the groundwork for a possible wisdom curriculum, or what might be called *a wise course,* the chapter 'unpacks' the three elements of this definition – right thing, greater good, all things considered. Explicating these elements reveals the philosophy, aspirations and attributes of one possible wisdom curriculum that redress a range of shortcomings found amongst university graduates and meets at least some of the criteria of wisdom and expectations held of those entering and thriving in the professions (Hays, 2015a).

Inherent and implicit in this definition is that 'a wise course' is, by nature, sustainable. To be sustainable, a wise course would be extensible and evolvable into the future, widely benefiting stakeholders, accommodating new and diverse challenges and opportunities, and neither damaging the environment, nor drawing unnecessarily on its natural resources (Sterling, 2001; Warburton, 2003).

A wise course and its need

Educating for wisdom should not be dismissed as idealistic, impractical, irrelevant or impossible (Bassett, 2011). It is feasible, reasonable and desirable, if not critical (Bierly et al., 2000; Hays, 2013c; Rosch, 2008). The fact that educating for wisdom has not gained much traction in mainstream university or professional development programmes does not mean that it should not be pursued more assiduously. Amongst reasons for neglecting educating for wisdom is a focus on utility and accountability, as cogently portrayed by Wilhelm and Novak (2011) and referred to as the 'audit culture' by Gidley (2009). Jacobs (2007), too, underscores the insidious effects of a utilitarian bias with which students arrive to study, demanding knowledge and skill that will assure success and promotion. Such narrow focus produces fragmented individuals and views of the world, and contributes to vicious cycles that perpetuate the instructional status quo and its limitations (Adams, 2011; Hays, 2012).

Wisdom may be getting lost in higher education, either pushed aside by an emphasis on generic skills and preparing a ready and competent workforce (see Star and Hammer, 2008), or as a result of perceived insufficiencies and criticism. Duke (1999) writes with respect to universities:

> The case for *wisdom* is seldom put with great force these days: partly from loss of confidence and credibility suffered by universities in the eyes of the 'establishment' and of the broad community from the seventies in various societies; also because of continuing hostility to academic pretensions on the part of some governments in modern times.
>
> (p. 26; emphasis in the original)

These scholars would no doubt join with Maxwell (2014) who asserts that universities can and should help create a wiser world and that an academic revolution is necessary to enable and ensure universities fulfil that mandate.

Topping the list of reasons why wisdom may not figure prominently in university and tertiary curricula is that many people believe that wisdom cannot be taught, a view supplemented by the belief that wisdom comes with maturity and age (Hays, 2008a; Sternberg, 2005). A casual read of the extant academic wisdom literature suggests that wisdom scholars generally support the view that wisdom can be learned and that there are learning strategies that can be employed to build wisdom or accelerate its development. Reams (2015) summarises some of this supporting literature and presents a rich and compelling example of how wisdom learning may be orchestrated. There are contrary cautions, typified by the remark from Biloslavo (2009; p. 13) confessing that: 'I acknowledge that it is not possible to teach wisdom, but do claim that it is possible to teach *for* wisdom'. If we accept that wisdom is both possible and desirable, our challenge then becomes how best to achieve it.

A large part of the problem is a general lack of awareness of what wisdom education is and that educating for wisdom is possible and needed (Maxwell, 2014). Fortunately, we are seeing evidence of increasing acceptance, appreciation and application (Bassett, 2011; Hays, 2013c; Reams, 2015; Reznitskaya and Sternberg, 2004). Wisdom can be learned *and* institutions of higher learning can and should play a role in developing wisdom. Nevertheless, the complication remains that a basic, shared understanding and acceptance of what wisdom is may never be entirely possible.[3]

There do seem to be some convergences in the literature relevant to the contentions of this chapter. Specifically, these concern the understanding that wisdom is not merely an individual but collective phenomenon (Bierly et al., 2000; Hays, 2010; Rooney and McKenna, 2008; Rowley, 2006a), that it is not a destination but an ongoing journey (Baltes and Staudinger, 2000; Parse, 2004; Warm, 2011) and that it is not a unitary capability or virtue but an amalgam of a range of competencies, aptitudes and dispositions (Bassett, 2011; Küpers, 2007; Staudinger and Glück, 2011; Sternberg, 1998, 2001).

Wisdom is doing (1) the right thing for (2) the greater good, (3) all things considered

1 The right thing

The right thing implies an ethical dimension to wisdom but does not 'push' a particular set of values and ideals. Wise individuals are conscious of what they care about and what their motives are for acting as they do (Bassett, 2011; Jacobs, 2007). They remain true to their values in all their acting. Thus, there is strength and consistency in their beliefs and aspirations and congruent authenticity between thought and action. At times, this may require considerable courage because 'the right thing to do' may be unpopular, unprecedented or daunting (Eriksen, 2009). The right thing may be perceived as complicated, risky and 'expensive', particularly by individuals or organisations driven to improve efficiencies and reduce cost (Ackoff, 1993; Giluk and Rynes-Weller, 2012). To make matters worse, there are likely to be competing options on offer that appear easier, cheaper or otherwise more attractive, including doing nothing.

So, the wise are courageous (Bassett, 2011; Blatner, 2005; Hays, 2015a). They act on their convictions, if only to speak out when they see lack of wisdom around them (Bierly et al., 2000). Lack of wisdom is evident, for example, in waste, injustice, avarice and abuse – generally behaviour that undermines the current and future health and well-being of people and planet. This is one of the key links to sustainability. Biloslavo (2009, p. 4) notes: 'The wise person realizes the importance of long-term outcomes of actions taken today'.

The right thing implies more than ethical considerations and character virtues, however. It encompasses 'intellectual fortitude'. Not intelligence, per se (as in cleverness and traditional views of IQ), but habits of mind that pose and pursue answers to important questions – those that challenge the way things are, explore impediments and seek betterment and transformation (Jacobs, 2007). These include dispositions and qualities such as curiosity, discipline, critical thinking and complex problem-solving (Biloslavo, 2009; Gidley, 2009). The capabilities of and dedication toward wise reasoning, judgement and reflective and mindful actions are particularly important.

2 The greater good

The greater or common good essentially demands of the wise that they work to improve themselves and change the world for the better, overcoming the limitations and motives of self-interest (Bennet and Bennet, 2008a). Whilst altruism may be difficult to attain or sustain, the wise always seek to at least balance self-interest with general betterment and improvement of collective interests (Baltes and Staudinger, 2000). As above, they must first know themselves and remain conscious of the desires, fears and beliefs that influence their thinking, decisions and ultimate action in the world (Blatner, 2010). At the minimum, the greater good causes us to ask questions such as the following before we make final decisions or elect a given course of action:

- How will this decision or strategy impact all stakeholders today and in the long term?
- Who *are* all the stakeholders that might be touched by or should have a say in this decision or course of action?
- What is my (or our) personal 'stake' in this decision or strategy? How might gain or fear of loss be motivating thinking or limiting options?
- What are the 'trade-offs' (upsides and downsides) of this decision or course of action; and, on balance, do they favour the greater good and long-term consequences?

A course of action that neglects, undermines, negatively impacts or obscures any stakeholders or other issues and concerns is *probably* unwise and unsustainable.

3 All things considered

All things considered is, perhaps, the crux of wisdom – its challenge and its charge. One may never know all: some things remain unknowable (Barnett, 2004; Bonnett, 2009; Davidson, 2010; Stacey, 1992); technology and time may constrain what we can discover. We may not have all the information and answers; we may not even know what best questions to ask. But the mandate maintains: as much should be understood in any given circumstance as possible before rash conclusions are drawn, decisions made, actions embarked upon (Hays, 2008a). Again, we ask: Who are the stakeholders involved and how will they be affected? What are the variables or influencing factors, and how are stakeholders likely to respond to intervention? What are the potential 'costs' or implications of a proposed remedy or solution? How might our assumptions, biases, beliefs, values, perceptions and attitudes undermine our ability to 'objectively' see things as they are and accurately assess the circumstances and context within which we are working (Blatner, 2010; Hastie, 2001; Mezirow, 1997)?

Wisdom takes time as it considers various angles and takes different perspectives on an issue in question. Multi-perspectivity and the capability and disposition to consider the implications and possibilities of a plurality of issues and agendas is a key aspect of wisdom (Bassett, 2011; Gidley, 2009; Staudinger and Glück, 2011). It is complex as it accepts that all things hang together in intricate and complex fashion, and that problems, issues and opportunities are linked. Accordingly, any course of action will have consequences and implications, some subtle, some dramatic – perhaps not immediately felt, but inevitable. Wise people down through the ages have always understood this, possessing an implicit if 'non-technical' more intuitive appreciation for systems thinking (Hays, 2008a, 2010), balance, harmony, integration and wholism. The *unwise* have *never* known these dimensions or have cared little, placing self-interest, immediate gratification and short-term value ahead of future outcomes; taking short-cuts and preferring and pursuing cheap, quick and ostensibly obvious solutions to problems that cannot possibly be sufficiently addressed by such superficial or one-dimensional approaches. Sustainability forbids such profligate, irresponsible behaviour.

Thus, wisdom may not appear decisive, clever, popular, politically correct, economical, efficient or 'sexy'. It is, by contrast, reasoned, deliberative, encompassing and inclusive, and will demonstrate principled judgement and acute foresight. More than anything, this way of thinking, and attendant tools and techniques for heightening the reasoning, problem-solving, decision-making and planning processes are what wisdom is and depends upon. A wise course would equip learners with and require them to demonstrate effective use of systemic, complex and holistic strategies for exploring issues thoroughly, evaluating encompassing solution alternatives, and proposing reasoned decisions exhibiting deep understanding of and attention to context, including the breadth of stakeholder perspectives, ethical and sustainability considerations, trade-offs, likely outcomes, implications, risks and other factors.

Higher-order capabilities and dispositions – the matrix and constituents of wisdom – can be developed and encouraged, but, to date, we have not done very well at eliciting them at the tertiary level (Hays, 2013c). There are rare exceptions, and calls for progress are increasing.[4] While evidence is scant, there appears to be even less attention to these higher-order skills, abilities and orientations in professional development and education, despite the fact that they are in high demand, with emphasis on reflective practice a notable exception (see Conlon, 2004, or van Woerkom et al., 2002). Other attention to higher-order skills, abilities and orientations demanded in professional practice has been drawn by Buckley and Monks (2004), Meldrum and Atkinson (1998) and Shelton and Darling (2003).

Adult professionals are expected to possess or have developed them at university or through some combination of previous work and life experiences. Little appears to be written on the subject and less on how, where and when these higher-order skills are specifically developed and how they are used. It may be that lack is considered a character flaw, an individual responsibility, or to be sought in formal study rather than an institutional or corporate duty. A related possible explanation for lack of corporate and industry attention to development of higher-order capabilities is that they are sometimes, and inappropriately, considered 'soft' or generic skills. By this they are placed outside the parameters of operational and technical training, where needs for them might be more immediately apparent and specifiable.

Institutions of higher learning and providers of advanced professional development can and should be doing more to educate for wisdom (Bassett, 2011; Kuhn and Udell, 2001; Reznitskaya and Sternberg, 2004; Sternberg et al., 2007). To accomplish this, they must themselves 'wise up', which implies a transformation at individual and institutional levels, for how could anyone undertake to educate for wisdom meaningfully and authentically without evincing attributes of the same? Thus they would have to embody principles, values and virtues beyond rationality, expertise, practicality and efficiency, demonstrating greater conscience and consciousness, and stewardship for the greater good (Griffey, 1998; Hays, 2010).

Why educate for wisdom?

Given the argument as laid-out so far, it stands to reason that greater wisdom should lead to a better world. It could reduce the kinds of problems that are produced and perpetuated by inadequately understood issues, and short-sighted, poorly thought-through goals, decisions, solutions and implementation strategies. While there are no guarantees, greater wisdom may actually help us solve or ameliorate some of the intractable challenges of our time. This is because wisdom strives to see the bigger picture, to understand phenomena more fully, to think through the consequences of action (and inaction), and to take responsibility for it (Bierly et al., 2000; Carraccio et al., 2008; Nonaka and Toyama, 2007). Since wisdom is concerned with justice, equality and flourishing (Grant, 2012), greater wisdom is likely to lead to a more equitable distribution of wealth around the globe and a better balance of health and well-being amongst the peoples of the planet. In many respects, wisdom and sustainability are the same thing (Sivaraksa, 2011). Both strive to reduce harm and continually do things that benefit the world and its inhabitants.

This may sound as if wisdom and educating for wisdom are idealistic, touted as the panacea to the world's ills. Well, even with progress, both wisdom and its education will never be entirely perfect, total or completely 'sustainable'. But, they *have* to offer more than what we are currently achieving. Despite swelling numbers of university graduates (Keeling and Hersh, 2011), most societies and economies remain surprisingly dull, parochial and susceptible to empty and even destructive seductions. We are failing to educate the next generation of citizens ready, willing and able to assume capable stewardship of our communities, organisations and, indeed, planet. On the contrary, we continue to mismanage, underutilise and abuse each other, our resources and the environment (Mohamed, 2014). We fail to act in concerted ways to fight disease, end hunger, stem widespread corruption or stamp out genocide. The list is painfully endless.

One of the advantages of wisdom is that it leads individuals to accept responsibility for their actions as well as demanding of them to step in where others have caused problems or failed to resolve them. To the extent that such a culture can be fostered, blaming becomes irrelevant, as does expecting others to fix things. In this respect, wisdom exhibits a sense of civic, social, even global citizenship (Colby et al., 2003) that includes service to the greater good, and this as a task for everyone and not just some select few or preferred class (Hays, 2015b).

As individuals, communities, businesses and globally, we have to take notice and act proactively and wisely. We need to be more than clever. Institutions of higher learning fail if all they do is produce knowledgeable and skilled graduates that have acquired no sense of desire, interest and capability to contribute to making the world a better place for their communities and global neighbours (Shek, 2010; Sibbel, 2009).

What makes educating for wisdom difficult?

Educating for wisdom confronts numerous challenges. Two related prime impediments are a belief that wisdom cannot be taught and, even if it can be fostered, that it is not the role of institutions of higher learning to undertake such instruction. Wisdom does occupy a niche in certain institutions and in disciplines such as theology and philosophy. But there is far to go in achieving mainstream acceptance that wisdom is a legitimate subject of study or curriculum framework (McKenna and Rooney, 2005), much less agreeing on where and how it should be taught. Wisdom, with its attention to big picture over narrow considerations, concern for effectiveness rather than efficiency, and devotion to long-term as well as present well-being should be of particular interest to leadership and management educators. Yet, in the author's experience, attempts to integrate wisdom into the management curriculum are frequently obstructed or dismissed.

Two additional hurdles are worth mentioning. First, as there is considerable dispute in what wisdom is and what it comprises, agreeing upon a core set of material and instructional strategies will always be 'fraught'. Second, given that many programmes and curricula are already strained to capacity, there is little room or flexibility to add or change units and contents and direction of courses (Barnett, 1994).

The breadth of wisdom and its amorphous nature do pose challenges with which many courses and disciplines must not contend. Take accounting, for example; most of its procedures are finite and straightforward. The basics of many respective fields are more or less standard. Despite the extensive preparation needed by and esteem conferred on them, much of the work of professionals is governed by established rules, formulas and procedures. These ensure a measure of consistency and accountability across typical and predictable problems and tasks.

However, the complex and unpredictable world of the twenty-first century often demands a level of expertise that is beyond mere knowledge and skill, a level of competence more a matter of *being* or embodiment than proficiency (McKenna and Rooney, 2005; see also Benner's, 2004, research on the highest levels of expertise). At higher levels of challenge, recipes, formulas, rote knowledge, basic skills training, procedural routines, textbook problems, close supervision, and reliance on expert authority and direction fall short or disappear, and, in some cases, may become counterproductive. Higher levels of challenge, such as posed by never-before-encountered problems, is the realm of the unknown, replete with risk, perplexity, disorientation and possibilities, but with few corresponding rules, guideposts or clues as to what best to do. In a complementary view, Rowley and Gibbs (2008) indicate that mastery implies something greater than mastery of self, others, or knowledge and skill. It is concerned with making ethically balanced contributions, rather than achieving personal gain, meaning, in organizational terms, 'seeking and developing individuals whose virtue is not solely in their ability to perform, but also whose disposition to others enables them to understand the consequences of their own and the organization's action' (p. 366).

Unknown territory is where creativity, initiative and independent thinking, wonder, adaptation, invention, intuition and courage are called for – all judged intangible and difficult if not impossible to teach, yet so necessary. When rules no longer apply, basic skills and standard procedures are insufficient and the limits of knowledge are reached, what is needed are confidence and competence that transcend the basics of what one knows and can do: the agility to combine, reassemble, adapt to purpose and unlearn (Akgün et al., 2007; Becker, 2005; De Meuse et al., 2010, DeRue et al., 2012). New, diverse and complex, wicked problems and the agile, learning mind they require are the province of wisdom. Here we can find its potential for extending, deepening, becoming more, evolving, renewing, transforming and creating solutions or entirely new approaches (Cheetham and Chivers, 1996).

A wise course will cultivate the potential of all participating, and develop skills and strategies for exploiting it – getting the most out of resources, ourselves and each other, but sustainably, which requires constant attention and investment (investment not in dollar terms, necessarily, but in enduring and encompassing health and well-being, represented in the author's homeland, New Zealand, by the Maori term *hauora*). Some of the words that embody a sustainable and beneficent culture and environment of health and well-being include respect, stewardship, service, reciprocity, community, altruism and contribution. Not surprisingly, these are terms often ascribed to wisdom and the wise (Hays, 2010; Spiller et al., 2011). None of this is to assert that skills and capabilities such as complex problem-solving or strategic decision-making are not essential – they most certainly are – but to remind us that they really only matter in the context of the greater good, and that more than technical expertise is needed to survive and thrive in the challenging and complex world of the twenty-first century (McKie et al., 2012; Rowley and Gibbs, 2008).

What is the nature of educating for wisdom?

Wisdom seeks harmony, balance, authenticity and integration, while appreciating that much in existence is inharmonious and out of balance. In practical terms, wisdom accepts that forces of imbalance and disharmony such as contention, provocation and competition may provide the impetus for change, learning and innovation (Hays, 2015a; Sterling, 2001).

While such forces may propel individuals and societies toward action, there is no guarantee that resultant action will be progressive in a qualified sense, that is, sustainable and toward betterment. Short-sighted progress does more harm than good in the long run. An example would be an innovation that unnecessarily consumes resources in its manufacture or use, pollutes the environment, or is otherwise destructive of health and well-being. A wise course provokes while channelling the tensions and energies that such provocation produces towards positive outlets. It converts chaos to creativity and capability (see Hays, 2015a). Think of wisdom and educating for wisdom less as harmony-oriented peace-keeping and more as disrupting, destabilising and conflicting.

The nature of educating for wisdom must be different than conventional education. At best, conventional education provides modest incremental improvements on learning. It is, as Sterling (2001) agrees, conservative and slow to change. Slight modifications to content and refinements in instruction shape what is learnt and how, but, basically, produce more of the same. In fact, there are often insidious and unwitting forces at work to keep things in higher education as they are or change only safely and predictably (Hays, 2012, 2013c). Thus, something unconventional is needed.

Energy is needed to excite change (and promote learning); and dilemmas, ambiguities, contradictions, paradoxes and pokings, proddings, pullings and tenuous proppings of all sorts provide the fuel for and much of the process of wisdom learning (Jacobs, 2007; Tisdell, 2011). What is needed is a continuous stimulus for critical and sustainable learning and growth. This might be thought of as a finish line that becomes progressively further in a race whose course is constantly changing. The competitor must be always vigilant to the direction, pace and intensity of effort whilst realising that the race need not necessarily be won, but *the running* is consequential in terms of its impact on a flourishing future, that is to say, its contribution to the greater good.

Calls for unconventionality do not inevitably mean that educating for wisdom necessitates more material or even dramatically different contents. Skills and knowledge designated by the professions as required must still be taught. It is *how* they are taught that is more the concern. A reinvention of education is needed to interrupt and supplant conventional and conservative ways of fostering learning that essentially perpetuate the status quo and, ultimately, undermine the getting of wisdom.

Most essential is that skills, knowledge and understandings imparted or conveyed should to the fullest extent possible be integrated and combined. While it may seemingly be easier or more efficient to teach individual skills and knowledge bits, without sufficient integration and contextualising, the learning remains fragmented, likely to quickly decay (Arthur et al., 1998), and unable to transfer, that is, to be applied in novel circumstances (Star and Hammer, 2008). Such learning is superficial or shallow, what is referred to in 'eduspeak' as surface learning (Beattie et al., 1997; Hay, 2007).

What a wise course seeks is deep learning (Vos et al., 2011; Warburton, 2003; Weigel, 2002). Deep learning is not just knowledge and skills that are reproducible in controlled and predictable situations on problems that conform to typical classroom, textbook and laboratory environments (like an examination). It is understanding how and why the knowledge and skills or insights are used in certain situations and not others, their limitations and contestability, alternatives available, and what to try if they don't work. An individual who has learned something deeply can take it into diverse situations, apply it to new problems and adapt or supplant it as appropriate. This is often referred to as learning-transfer or transfer of learning (Haskell, 2000; McKeough et al., 1995). Sterling (2001) equates deep learning and change with sustainability. He asserts:

> At a deeper level still, when *third-order learning* happens we are able to see things differently. It is creative, and involves a deep awareness of alternative worldviews and ways of doing things. It is, as Einstein suggests, a shift in consciousness, and it is this *transformative* level of learning, both at individual and whole society levels, that radical movement toward sustainability requires.
>
> (p. 15; emphasis in the original)

Of course there is more to this portability than just the requisite germane knowledge and skill. It is those capabilities and dispositions within which knowledge and skill are couched that enable knowing and effective performance in unknown circumstances. These are the targets of a wise course, and they include various dimensions; the following list includes only some of them:

- will and discipline to experiment; openness to new ideas and perspectives;
- propensity to share, collaborate and collectively create;
- dedication to exploring (and re-exploring) options and alternatives;
- commitment to and capability to continually learn, relearn and unlearn;
- belief in the value of life and devotion to creating conditions for universal flourishing;
- capacity to take the 'long view' and show restraint today for the benefit of tomorrow;
- courage to take stands and courage to revise them when needed.

Notably, these same passions and practices are necessary for and characterise sustainability (Bagheri and Hjorth, 2007; Hammond and Churchman, 2008; Sterling, 2001), highlighting again, as have others (see, for example, McKenna et al., 2014), parallels between wisdom and sustainability.

Towards a curriculum for wisdom

One of the challenges confronting educators of wisdom is that wisdom is both everything and nothing. As a subject, it embraces a wide breadth of capacities, values and dispositions, with no little disagreement as to what it might include and possible inclusions virtually infinite. McKie et al. (2012), for example, identify four major frames through which wisdom has been viewed: philosophical, religious, psychological and clinical, each with its own set of assumptions and emphases. Whether a separate distinction or not, it appears that organisational or management wisdom is emerging as distinct application or field of study, as seen in works by Dickie (2011), Rowley (2006a) and others. Of particular relevance to the RJRA model, McKenna and Rooney (2005) reveal nine characteristics of management wisdom, many if not all relating to the model's elements and their dynamic, holistic interaction. These contribute to such leadership and organisational imperatives as strategic thinking, visioning, decision-making, anticipating reactions and dialogue – each a sophisticated capability in its own right, and, as McKenna and Rooney (2005) maintain, in short supply.

The extent to which wisdom is, then, encompassing poses practical complications to the wisdom curriculum designer. How could one educate so widely? How thoroughly could any number of potential topics and capabilities be meaningfully addressed in a university or professional development programme, much less in a particular unit or course? And, given that some agreement as to core content could be obtained, how could this be added to programmes that are already full and for which core prescriptions permit little flexibility?

Such questions apply to the magnitude of wisdom – its potential 'everythingness'. Before attempting to answer them, let's return to the other side of the paradox: wisdom is nothing. How can wisdom be both everything and nothing? The nothing argument alludes to a number of assumptions concerning wisdom of relevance to education – that wisdom is intangible; cannot be defined or measured; cannot be taught (though may be learned); and dare not be trivialised (as might be the case in breaking it down into competencies or discrete topic areas; and, relatedly, that its essence or vital and vibrant nature might be lost were it to be 'unpacked'), points alluded to in McKenna and Rooney (2005). If wisdom is everything, and everything cannot be taught, then what's the point? If wisdom is nothing, then how and why should it be added to existing curricula?

These questions and assumptions considered, it is clear that proceeding towards a curriculum for wisdom must sufficiently contend with them. It has got to address the issues of:

1 *Content* – a defensible and generally acceptable set of knowledge, capabilities and dispositions.
2 *Size* – a content set that, taken together, comprises manageable breadth and depth.
3 *Fit* – suitability and integratability of content to existing and evolving programmes.
4 *Tangibility and measurability* – defining wisdom knowledge, capabilities and dispositions such that they are more concrete and can be broken down and structured (the unpacking) as discrete competencies for which learning strategies and commensurate assessments of learning can be developed and reasonably applied.
5 *Sustainability* – extensibility and adaptability over time that continues to deliver relevant material and process as context shifts, and doing this in ways that contribute to the greater good while minimising resource demands and negative impacts on people and planet.
6 *Wholism* – the notion that even 'unpacked' and narrowed in scope, the distilled content remaining encapsulates wisdom and wise acting in the world, embodying a complex of knowledge, capabilities and dispositions that are conceivable and believable as a whole and representing wisdom and enabling wise acting in the world (Miller, 2007; Spector and Anderson, 2000).

Taken together, and drawing on Sterling (2001) and Thomas (2009), points 1–6 raised in the previous paragraph – content, size, fit, concreteness, sustainability and wholism – suggest that 'a wise course', that is, educating for wisdom, is not likely to be (or be achieved through) a stand-alone, adjunct or replacement unit or course. Rather, it will be a holistic programme, a comprehensive framework and an integrated curriculum (Embong et al., 2013; Miller, 2007). What is meant by integration here is not just about alignment, as important as that is. It is more about a virtuous harmony and synergy amongst educative components that generate a quality of learning greater than courses, per se, might be expected to produce. It might be likened to university curricula already that specify desired graduate attributes and key generic skills (Barrie, 2006; Clanchy and Ballard, 1995). These are meant to permeate all majors and degrees and assure that all graduates possess such capabilities and dispositions as cultural competence, leadership, critical thinking and civic-mindedness. In an integrated curriculum, programmes (majors), if not individual courses, have to document how and where key learning outcomes with respect to the graduate profile are developed and demonstrated.

However, a curriculum for wisdom must exceed the aspirations of existing integrated curricula. While laudatory, such intents are not always met. Little guidance exists as to how to translate and incorporate generic skills and graduate attributes into unit instructional strategies (Hays, 2015a). As an exception, Barrie (2007) provides a helpful framework for positioning strategies for the development of generic skills and graduate attributes. To date, there are few proven and accepted means of assessing and demonstrating students have developed them appreciably by graduation time. It could be argued, for example, that requiring group projects builds teamwork skills, probably develops communication skills and useful habits, and may even cultivate leadership. Little is known, however, about what is specifically learnt and who is learning what, which mechanisms best promote the learning, or how many such projects are enough and how different they must be to add value. Concerning assessment, what is usually evaluated is the project itself, not the team, communication, or leadership competence. There is little regard for their contribution to the project's success or otherwise (Kearns and Hays, 2015).

Given the above, a wise course must be integrative, encompassing, sophisticated and unconventional. Yet, it must be definable, practicable and target a finite range of capabilities and dispositions that are part of a basic common core of wisdom. The RJRA model of wisdom put forward here incorporates and integrates a set of capabilities, knowledge areas and dispositions that have been linked to wisdom. None of the elements individually ensures or suggests wise thought and action, but taken together can reasonably be assumed to produce more viable solutions and decisions than might otherwise be the case. The model, then, is complex but workable, and unconventional, while based in established practice and theory.

Attempting to achieve both the lofty and the mundane – the idealistic and the realistic – sounds contradictory, paradoxical or just unlikely. However, if we agree that wisdom learning is possible and desirable, as numerous scholars profess, and little is being done in that regard (McKenna and Rooney, 2005; Rowley, 2006b), then we need to start somewhere. The paradoxical, dialectical and 'wicked' nature of educating for wisdom – inferred from the kind of thinking demanded by the complex, dynamic environment in which professionals find themselves, identified by scholars such as Biloslavo (2009), Hays (2013c) and Staudinger and Glück (2011) – may provide tensions and possibilities founded on 'both-and' thinking, rather than 'either-or' or, then, 'neither' thinking (see Lewis and Smith, 2014, or Chen, 2002).

A wise course must transcend business as usual or it will not promote transformation (Hays, 2008b, 2013b). Yet, it must take place in a world that requires some measure of planning, organisation and day-to-day operation, albeit in a form that flexes and evolves, and accommodates complexity, ambiguity and the unexpected, an individual or organisational capability that might be called ambidextrous (Hartman, 2008; McKenzie and Aitken, 2012; Nonaka et al., 2014).

The results of a wise course, built on the premises just outlined, taken together and in sufficient supply, would be shown in individuals (and, presumably, teams) through greater incidence and / or depth of wisdom in pertinent, palpable ways. In other words, it would enable wise action and produce richer solutions more often than not at practical and professional levels. Problem-solving, decision-making, planning, implementation and evaluation processes would be sustainable and lead to sustainability because they would be better informed, more inclusive of the range of factors and stakeholder concerns, and attentive to the future. Implicit is that these processes produce and respond to continuous learning – at each individual step along the way and collectively, thus can be continually improved (Bennet and Bennet, 2008b; O'Toole, 2004).

From both a research and applied practice point of view, this agreed common core must be assessable. The material and the instructional approaches taken must be shown to make a substantive difference in ways that are relevant and significant to educators, wisdom scholars and practitioners in the field. Moreover, students themselves should be mindful and cognisant of what they've learned and how they've learned it (and what the limitations are). They should appreciate and be able to articulate how these capabilities and dispositions equip them for professional careers and, more generally, how they contribute to the quality of their lives. Finally, to find any level of acceptance, our nascent wise course cannot burden programmes and instructors with vast new material or demand skills and tools needing much investment. Perceived extra work, complication or challenge to capability will result in rejection of or resistance to the model unless offset by recognised benefit. Thus, the model needs to comprise elements that teachers and trainers appreciate, understand and see relevant and applicable in their courses and programmes. One solution would be to provide a wisdom package replete with resources, activities, tools, assessments, instructor's guide and teaching notes, all built around agreed core content and approach, and, perhaps, deployable on Learning Management Systems, such as Moodle or Blackboard.

One set of common core capabilities, knowledge areas and dispositions that has been assembled is the RJRA model of wisdom (Figure 8.2), which represents an attempt to amalgamate a complex set of skills generally believed to be extremely important in industry and demanded of university graduates (Hays, 2012, 2013c). In addition to reasoning, judgement and reflective action, the RJRA model includes critical thinking, complex problem-solving, creative problem-solving (CPS), decision-making and planning.[5]

Particularly strong support for the RJRA model is found in the interesting article by Rowley and Gibbs (2008) concerning the practically wise organisation. Amongst other things the authors cover with respect to organisational learning and wisdom, they discuss the relationships amongst experience, deliberation, reasoning, judgement, decision-making and the importance of contextual understanding, and practical and ethical action. They argue that more than rational, technical analysis is needed to make decisions in uncertain environments. A more dimensional wisdom is needed to understand complex, dynamic situations – the context – and generate solutions that are practicable. Further, they emphasise that the practically wise organisation is also a sustainable one, not just in terms of its own survival but in its responsibility and contribution to society.

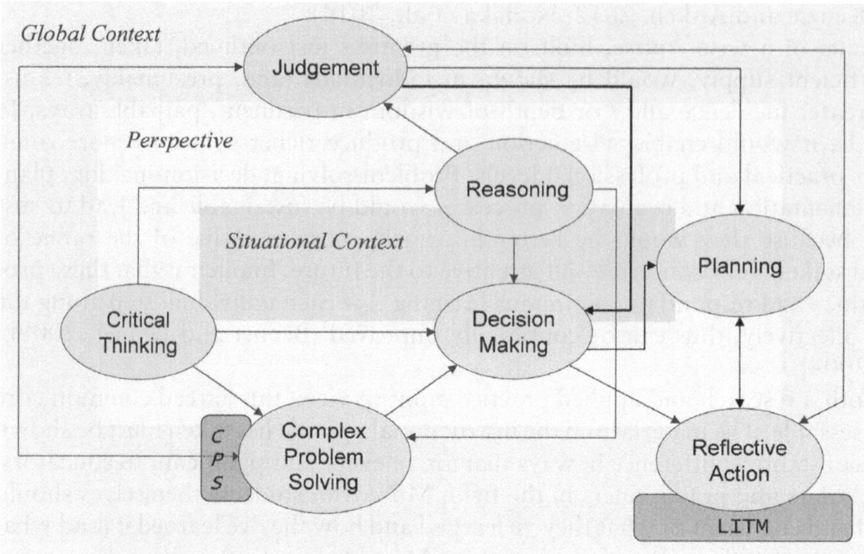

Figure 8.2 The RJRA model, showing the elements comprising a proposed wisdom curriculum (the 'wise course'), and their relationships.

Referring again to Figure 8.2, LITM, adjoining Reflective Action, is described as *Learning in the Moment.* This idea is consistent with Blatner's (2010) view that wisdom 'isn't something one has or achieves, but rather what is done moment by moment' (n.p.). It also invokes the idea of continuous learning, and highlights the significant contribution of reflecting and self-correcting in the midst of action (judicious action being one of the most agreed-upon indicators of wisdom (Bierly et al., 2000; Reams, 2015; Rowley and Gibbs, 2008).

As a starting point, RJRA offers a set of topics and associated skills and tools that might comprise a possible wisdom curriculum, what is referred to here as 'a wise course'. To meet the criteria outlined previously, a wisdom curriculum would embrace, permeate and integrate an entire major or programme. This is a daunting and, at least initially, an unlikely task. There would be few programmes and programme administrators flexible, equipped and courageous (or foolhardy) enough to undertake such an ambitious and risky challenge. It would also be next to impossible to determine which specific aspects of the curriculum actually produced wisdom behaviour in its graduates. For these reasons, a single unit (course) is proposed. This might be a one- or two-semester offering. Many programmes could accommodate one more elective, especially if it built knowledge and skills needed in other units or that they have trouble developing or demonstrating. And, non-tertiary versions are also possible, for professional development practitioners and programmes capable of instructing the complete set of capabilities and dispositions.

In design, the wise course is similar to a survey course that covers a range of topics, such as an HR unit might cover recruitment, benefits, performance management and appraisal, arbitration, succession planning, termination, and so on. The topics are rather like individual puzzle pieces. Unlike most survey courses, however, a wise course links the topics together, and leads the learner to a deep understanding of the pieces and how they fit together – integrated to encompass a complete whole, in keeping with the holistic nature of wisdom (Reams, 2015; Waddock, 2014; see also Trowbridge, 2011). Akin to a capstone unit, assessment would require learners to demonstrate facility in assembling and applying the topics and skills appropriately and explicatively to create a meaningful whole picture (like parts in a puzzle) in unique and creative ways – unprescribed, but meeting agreed-upon criteria indicative of wisdom. This is important as learners should appreciate that there is no textbook solution, no one right answer to many real-world problems (Baker and O'Malley, 2008; Nonaka and Toyama, 2007).

Such assessment would require evidence that the individual has reasoned through a complex and vexing problem posing one or more dilemmas, critically examined the data available and interrogated the assumptions, beliefs, biases, values and attitudes that influence understanding of the problem and possible solutions. The learner would have to articulate and defend a decision or conclusion. Moreover s/he would outline how that would be put into effect, and what the risks, likely consequences, implications and repercussions might be and how they could be best mediated. This all depends on the ability to demonstrate recognition of and attention to multiple perspectives and stakeholder interests. All of this may all sound rather basic and present nothing new to the teacher or trainer. At the same time, it embraces a complex of capabilities and dispositions identified as indicative of wisdom.

Further, the learner would have to demonstrate good judgement in deliberating on solution and corresponding implementation strategies, reflecting understanding and appreciation for local and global contexts, including stakeholders involved, environmental impacts, constraints and sustainability, and show a cross-disciplinary approach. Finally, evidence of reflective action must be present in the problem-solving, decision-making and planning processes. This may be easier and more telling in a real project, as conscious 'Learning in the Moment' transpires and feeds back into the process. In a test situation or simulation, the learner would be expected to make his or her implicit knowing, feeling and thinking explicit in order to explain, describe and elaborate on intuitive moments, insights, reactions, aversions, seductions, uncertainties and the like, and how they influenced the process and its results. The latter is indicative of mindfulness and meta-cognition, thought to be essential aspects of self-directed learning and continuous improvement, effectiveness in complex problem-solving, and interpersonal competence, as noted by various scholars including Blatner (2010), Kuiper and Pesut (2004) and Reams (2015). Mindfulness and meta-cognition are also held to be critical management skills, and there exists some evidence that they are being introduced into management curricula with positive effect (Boyatzis, 2008; Fenton-O'Creevy et al., 2006; Sadler-Smith and Shefy, 2007).

Using the RJRA model of wisdom as a framework, for instance, suggests that each domain (reasoning, critical thinking, planning and the others) could provide an individual section of an assessment inventory or battery. Such an assessment could reveal respective strengths as well as overall achievement, and could be used formatively as well as summatively (Harlan and James, 1997; William and Black, 1996; Yorke, 2003). Hypothetically, an individual might demonstrate critical thinking facility though be less proficient in complex problem-solving. Likewise, an individual might exhibit heightened intuitive or reflective thinking, but struggle to articulate the process or method leading to decision or plan or be unable to defend it with compelling data or reasoning. Importantly, such capability and critical awareness are likely to be required in professional life.

A wise course and sustainability

There is a direct relationship between wisdom and sustainability (McKenna et al., 2014; Sivaraska, 2011; Sterling, 2001) and a wise course is a sustainable one. They both require and demonstrate concern for the greater good and the long-term implications of action.

A wise course is one with staying power, but not one that statically or stubbornly persists despite changing context and environment. It remains viable and continues to contribute to the greater good, as it responsively and responsibly evolves and adapts to contend with changing demands, and, in fact, inspires and enables a continuing challenging of the way things are and a re-imagining of how things might be and co-creating new ways of acting (Jacobs, 2007; Rowley and Gibbs, 2008). In this sense, a wise course is a creative one, creative not merely to be novel and different – though that could be helpful; rather, creative as always entertaining impermanence and mutability, that things don't have to be the way they are and can usually be bettered (Lozano, 2014; Palmer et al., 2007), but that betterment is not just improvement or change because it's possible or popular, but within the context of its contribution to the greater good. Such a contribution comes at little cost to the planet and its inhabitants and causes no harm. It intentionally produces health, well-being and flourishing, rather than progress or profit at any cost.

A course in wisdom is a wise course, and thus a sustainable one, if it embodies and produces graduates who demonstrate certain values, such as concern for long-over short-term benefit or a more altruistic and universal orientation rather than one of self-interest, and exhibit behaviours relevant to practical wisdom and living life well in a world worth living in (see Csikszentmihalyi and Csikszentmihalyi, 2006, or Ryan, Huta, and Deci, 2008). These include a strong commitment to courageously and open-mindedly challenge and question, propose sustainable solutions and act on results of inquiry and consultation in ways that best serve the greater good around such themes as:

1 How can we remain current and relevant in …?
2 How can we best serve *all of* our stakeholders and extend our reach towards them?
3 Of all the concerns and issues confronting us today, which are the most important to tackle? (These would be the ones that would reduce harm the most and provide the greatest return in terms of health and well-being now (widely) and in the long run.)
4 What are we doing right now that is unnecessarily wasteful or destructive, and how can we do it more sustainably?
5 How can we design and organise ourselves such that we reduce our dependence on external provision of resources and capitalise on our own inherent potential and capabilities?
6 How can we 'learn forward', that is, prepare for challenges and opportunities over the horizon (Hays, 2013a, 2015a)?

7 How can we move forward, reinventing ourselves, whilst taking the best of what we are and shedding the attitudes, beliefs, biases, values, motives, assumptions, perspectives and behaviours that might impede us now or in the future (Blatner, 2010)?
8 Particularly in New Zealand (though the principles may apply elsewhere), how can we best embody Kaupapa Maori philosophy, values, principles and practices of dialogue, collaboration and engagement in working with our communities and stakeholders to create change and build vibrant, robust organisations and society?

The bottom line is that a wise course is one that asks (and sustainably answers and promotes this discipline in graduates): *What must we learn, relearn and unlearn to remain a viable and positive contributor in a complex, chaotic and confusing world?*

Conclusion

This chapter puts forward a wisdom model that has been temporarily named RJRA – Reasoning, Judgement and Reflective Action. As outlined, this model also contains other elements, all within context that includes local-situational, global and ethical considerations. RJRA is proposed as foundation for a wisdom curriculum, in this case 'a wise course'. It is assuredly not a course *about* wisdom, though diverse conceptions of and approaches to the understanding and 'getting' of wisdom would be covered. It is primarily an applied and practical course to build capabilities and dispositions that will contribute to wise sensing, thinking and acting.

Our world needs wisdom, at least as much now as in any time in the past, and quite likely more so, a point underscored by many of the noted scholars cited herein, including and particularly Biloslavo (2009), Bierly et al. (2000), Hays (2015a), Küpers (2007), Küpers and Pauleen (2013), McKenna et al. (2014), McKie et al. (2012), and Rowley and Gibbs (2008), and alluded to by many of the others referenced. While there may be a shortage of wisdom displayed in the world, especially the world of business and leadership, there is great potential amongst human beings to develop and demonstrate wisdom (Bassett, 2011).

Developing demonstrable wisdom amongst engaged citizenry and, particularly, in leaders and professional practitioners is one of the greatest challenges for professional education and development. Irrespective of great investment, effort, organisational efficiency and sophisticated tools to educate and train more knowledgeable students graduating and entering professional life, many lack wisdom. They may be technically savvy and possess deep discipline knowledge and skill, but are deprived of the will, understanding and capability to do the right thing for the greater good all things considered.

For Jacobs (2007), doing 'right things' is imminently more important than 'doing things right'; and wisdom knows the difference between the two, or at least continually challenges what may be at risk to the greater good in blindly pursuing a course of doing things right. That graduates are entering the workforce and civic life rather one-dimensional, where they might otherwise be more multi-faceted and capable of seeing the bigger picture through a range of alternative perspectives, is not their fault or shortcoming. This is an unnecessary, though highly predictable failure of the education systems that produce them (Hays 2012, 2013c).

No doubt, many individuals will develop wisdom with the passing of time, seasoning and accumulation of professional and life-experiences. And some seem to find their way successfully in the world with no particular additional training in wisdom. These individuals, endowed with 'natural' ingenuity, drive, curiosity, or creativity, become leaders and leading lights. However, where the clever succeed (often for themselves), the wise contribute to the common good.

From an educational point of view, there is no reason why we can't do more to bring out and 'capitalise' upon wisdom by activating its potentials. Institutions of higher learning are obligated to do more for their students, communities and the local and global greater good (Biloslavo, 2009; Jacobs, 2007; Star and Hemmer, 2008). As educators, trainers and mentors, we can do more to foster the development of wisdom by acting more wisely ourselves in the first place and serving as role models for wisdom. One way of acting more wisely lies in the choices and practices of what and how we teach and learn.

A 'wise course', built around the proposed RJRA wisdom model, seems to offer an effective way forward. It helps to build professional competencies and capabilities crucial in the complex challenging world of the twenty-first century. Such a 'wise course', though, begins with learning critical thinking, problem-solving and decision-making. Significantly, it frames and seeks to apply these practical and much-needed competencies in micro- and macro-contexts, while considering ethical considerations and sustainability concerns.

Although presented here as new and different, the 'wise course' and RJRA model on which it is founded rest solidly on concepts, principles and capabilities that are familiar and recognised as essential. It is *if* and *how* they are integrated in higher and professional education that will make a distinct difference between technically competent and wise being and doing (Adams, 2011; Biesta, 2015; Meldrum and Atkinson, 1998; Tisdell, 2011).

To foster integration, holism and complex, systemic thinking, then, a wise course must be equally whole and integrated. It must strive to bind knowledge, competencies, skill, will and practices together with a fabric of altruism, ethics and sustainability, blending foresight, insight and reflection and building awareness, responsiveness and responsibility. Such a course will instil a spirit of inquiry and a passion for deep, transformative learning. Furthermore, it will equip learners with tools and strategies of evolution and renewal and embody and enliven these attributes and practices.

The 'contents' of such a course – its parts – are all essential though may change as context does and new methods, knowledge areas and competencies or solutions are called for. Taking the RJRA model as our starting point, all the elements outlined before are not itself wisdom, but functions or enablers of it, each playing a vital role. Independently, these elements or parts cannot account directly for wisdom, though as enablers and processed together they mediate it. Wisdom resides more implicitly and throughout the model, more in its spirit or soul than as a function or even an outcome. Thus, wisdom arises and emanates in the model from applying it, while attending and integrating all aspects.

As a final thought, pondering the merits of having to always articulate how a given proposal, decision or course of action might diminish or contribute to the greater good – and to do this honestly and as thoroughly as possible – is called for. This is a guiding evaluative question asked throughout a wise course, and it is the kind of question its graduates will hopefully ask themselves throughout their lifetimes.

Prompts for reflection, exploration and extension

1 Do you agree with the author of this chapter that (greater) wisdom is needed by leaders, managers and professional practitioners in today's organisations and communities? Why or why not?
2 What evidence do you see in the workplace (or elsewhere) of wisdom or lack of it?
3 What are some of the main differences you see between wisdom (for example, in a wise leader) and other dimensions of exceptional performance?
4 With reference to this chapter or other sources and understandings, what are your wisest capabilities and dispositions needed? Where do you feel you need to develop most and how?
5 What is your overall reflection on the RJRA model advanced in this chapter? Does it 'speak' to you and resonate with your understandings of wisdom?
6 What elements of the RJRA model seem most relevant to you? Why is this? What value might one or more of the elements of the model contribute to the preparation of your study or other students for professional practice or the further professional development of practitioners and managers?
7 What seems missing for you from the RJRA model in terms of wisdom? Where and how might you fit this in?
8 The chapter 'unpacks' the definition of wisdom put forward (*doing the right thing for the greater good all things considered)*. How well does this definition accord with your own understandings of wisdom? How might you add to or revise it?
9 Do you believe wisdom can be taught or at least learned through facilitated and structured lessons and experience?

   (a) If so, do you believe the RJRA model and the notion of 'a wise course' as proposed in this chapter provide a useful way forward? How and why?
   (b) If you believe wisdom can be taught or at least learned through facilitated and structured lessons and experience, but the RJRA model and wise course seem lacking, what would you offer as supplementary or alternative approaches?
   (c) If you do *not* believe wisdom can be taught or at least learned through facilitated and structured lessons and experience, what are some of the most important capabilities and dispositions than *can* be furthered that need greater attention?

10 Do you think wisdom (or some aspects of it) is being sought by leaders, organisations and institutions today, that is, considered as selection criteria by potential employers? Should it be? What indicators of wisdom would you notice or seek in an aspiring candidate for a professional position?

Notes

1 Staudinger and Glück (2011) identify, for example, some of the components of wisdom and briefly outline how they might be addressed in families and schools. These include practising reflection and understanding context, two important parts of the RJRA model. Jacobs (2009) stresses the posing of provocative questions that challenge the status quo and introducing perplexity as part of building critical thinking and wise decision-making, also aspects of the RJRA model. Likewise, Tisdell (2011) posits that the use of paradoxes and multiple ways of knowing in learning environments can lead to improved critique and creativity and better judgement, all features of wisdom and the RJRA model. Finally, Hays (2013c) has

argued strongly that educating for complexity and wisdom demand a 'wicked' approach. This would be one that intentionally complicates the learning environment and thinking of learners. Implied is that the curriculum should be as complex as the world graduates will inhabit and every bit as challenging as the roles they will occupy in professional practice. Wisdom scholars, however, agree that all this provocation, disruption, and tension take place best in a climate of safety and caring. Such an environment is one where suspension of judgement, openness and tolerance for ambiguity and uncertainty are encouraged and where learners and teachers see themselves as on the journey together (Gidley, 2009; Jacobs, 2009; Pizzolato, 2006).

2 Devotion to the greater or common good is a pervasive theme across wisdom literature (e.g. Bassett, 2011; Bierly et al., 2000; Biloslavo, 2009). Baltes and Staudinger (2000) assert that wisdom includes a balanced attending to the good or well-being of self and others. Other scholars explain that wisdom involves multi-perspectivity and an ability to integrate diverse and sometimes conflicting or apparently contradictory themes and agenda (Staudinger and Glück, 2011; Tisdell, 2011).

3 Disagreement and wide diversity in interpretation are rife, as a review of some of the literature cited herein reveals (see, as examples, Baltes and Staudinger (2000), Hays (2008a), Jones and Culliney (1998), Kitchener and Brenner (1990), Korac-Kakabadse et al. (2004), Lynch (1999), McKenna et al. (2009), Nonaka and Toyama (2007), Smith (2007) and Sternberg (1998).

4 Positive indications that wisdom can and should be a focus for education (and general agreement that it is lacking) are found in Bassett (2011), Brown (2004), Miller (2005), Reznitskaya and Sternberg (2004), Roca (2007), Rosch (2008) and Sternberg (2001), as well as more recently McKenna et al. (2014).

5 Support for the inclusion of these elements in the implicit wisdom model underpinning 'a wise course' is found in the sources cited above, and others such as Baltes and Staudinger (2000) – judgement, context; Bierly et al. (2000) – judgement and decision-making, context; Biloslavo (2009) – critical thinking, systems thinking, context, long view; Blatner (2010) – reflection, creativity, discernment; Gidley (2009) – problem-solving, creativity, perspective; McKie et al. (2012) – reflective judgement; Tisdell (2011) – judgement, critique and creativity, integrating mind.

References

Ackoff, R. (1993). Beyond total quality management. *The Journal for Quality and Participation*, Vol. 16, No. 2, pp. 66–78.

Adams, A. (2011). Integral intelligence: a 21s century necessity. *Integral Review,* Vol. 7, No. 1, pp. 75–85.

Akgün, A., Byrne, J., Lynn, G., and Keskin, H. (2007). Organizational unlearning as changes in beliefs and routines in organizations. *Journal of Organizational Change Management*, Vol. 20, No. 6, pp. 794–812.

Arthur, W., Bennett, W., Stanush, P., and McNelly, T. (1998). Factors that influence skill decay and retention: a quantitative review and analysis. *Human Performance*, Vol. 11, No. 1, pp. 57–101.

Bagheri, A., and Hjorth, P. (2007). Planning for sustainable development: a paradigm shift towards a process-based approach. *Sustainable Development*, Vol. 15, No. 2, pp. 83–96.

Baker, W., and O'Malley, M. (2008). *Leading with Kindness: How Good People Consistently get Superior Results*. AMACOM.

Baltes, P., and Staudinger, U. (2000). Wisdom: a metaheuristic (pragmatic) to orchestrate mind and virtue toward excellence. *American Psychologist,* Vol. 55, No. 1, pp. 122–136.

Barnett, R. (1994). *The Limits of Competence: Knowledge, Higher Education and Society*. Buckingham: Open University Press.

Barnett, R. (2004). Learning for an unknown future. *Higher Education Research & Development,* Vol. 23, No. 3, pp. 247–260.

Barrie, S. C. (2006). Understanding what we mean by the generic attributes of graduates. *Higher Education*, Vol. 51, No. 2, pp. 215–241.

Barrie, S. C. (2007). A conceptual framework for the teaching and learning of generic graduate attributes. *Studies in Higher Education*, Vol. 32, No. 4, pp. 439–458.

Bassett, C. (2011). Understanding and teaching practical wisdom. *New Directions for Adult and Continuing Education,* No. 131, pp. 35–44.

Beattie, V., Collins, B., and McInnes, B. (1997). Deep and surface learning: a simple or simplistic dichotomy? *Accounting Education,* Vol. 6, No. 1, pp. 1–12.

Becker, K. (2005). Individual and organisational unlearning: directions for future research. *International Journal of Organisational Behaviour,* Vol. 9, No. 7, pp. 659–670.

Benner, P. (2004). Using the Dreyfus model of skill acquisition to describe and interpret skill acquisition and clinical judgment in nursing practice and education. *Bulletin of Science, Technology & Society*, Vol. 24, No. 3, pp. 188–199.

Bennet, A., and Bennet, D. (2008a). Moving from knowledge to wisdom, from ordinary consciousness to extraordinary consciousness. *VINE: The Journal of Information and Knowledge Management Systems,* Vol. 38, No. 1, pp. 7–15.

Bennet, A., and Bennet, D. (2008b). The fallacy of knowledge reuse: building sustainable knowledge. *Journal of Knowledge Management*, Vol. 12, No. 5, pp. 21–33.

Bierly, P., Kessler, E., and Christensen, E. (2000). Organizational learning, knowledge and wisdom. *Journal of Organizational Change Management,* Vol. 13, No. 6, pp. 595–618.

Biesta, G. (2015). How does a competent teacher become a good teacher? On judgement, wisdom and virtuosity in teaching and teacher education. *Philosophical Perspectives on the Future of Teacher Education.* Oxford: Wiley Blackwell.

Biloslavo, R. (2009). Management education and wisdom: what they can do for promoting sustainable development. Paper presented at the 23rd annual conference of the Australian and New Zealand Academy of Management, *Sustainable Management and Marketing,* Melbourne, Australia, 1–4 December.

Blatner, A. (2005). Perspectives on wisdom-ing. *ReVision: A Journal of Consciousness and Transformation,* Vol. 28, No. 1, pp. 29–33.

Blatner, A. (2010). Wisdom-ing. Blog post, downloadable at www.blatner.com/adam/consctransf/wisdom-ing.html. This reference is largely based on Blatner (2005).

Bonnett, M. (2009). Systemic wisdom, the 'selving' of nature, and knowledge transformation: education for the greater whole. *Studies in Philosophy and Education,* Vol. 28, No. 1, pp. 39–49.

Boyatzis, R. (2008). Competencies in the 21st century. *Journal of Management Development,* Vol. 27, No. 1, pp. 5–12.

Brown, S. (2004). Learning across the campus: how college facilitates the development of wisdom. *Journal of College Student Development,* Vol. 45, No. 2, pp. 134–148.

Buckley, F., and K. Monks. (2004). The implications of meta-qualities for HR roles. *Human Resource Management Journal,* Vol. 14, No. 4, pp. 41–56.

Carraccio, C., Benson, B., Nixon, L., and Derstine, P. (2008). From the educational bench to the clinical bedside: translating the Dreyfus developmental model to the learning of clinical skills. *Academic Medicine*, Vol. 83, No. 8, pp. 761–767.

Cheetham, G., and G. Chivers. (1996). Towards a holistic model of professional competence. *Journal of European Industrial Training,* Vol. 20, No. 5, pp. 20–30.

Chen, M. (2002). Transcending paradox: the Chinese 'middle way' perspective. *Asia Pacific Journal of Management,* Vol. 19, pp. 179–199.

Clanchy, J., and Ballard, B. (1995). Generic skills in the context of higher education. *Higher Education Research and Development*, Vol. 14, No. 2, pp. 155–166.

Colby, A., Ehrlich, T., Beaumont, E., and Stephens, J. (2003). *Educating Citizens: Preparing America's Undergraduates for Lives of Moral and Civic Responsibility.* San Francisco, CA: Jossey-Bass.

Conlon, T. (2004). A review of informal learning literature, theory and implications for practice in developing global professional competence. *Journal of European Industrial Training*, Vol. 28, Nos. 2/3/4, pp. 283–295.

Csikszentmihalyi, M., and Csikszentmihalyi, I. (2006). *A Life Worth Living: Contributions to Positive Psychology*. New York: Oxford University Press.

Davidson, S. J. (2010). Complex responsive processes: a new lens for leadership in twenty-first-century health care. *Nursing Forum,* Vol. 45, No. 2, pp. 108–117.

De Meuse, K., Dai, G., and Hallenbeck, G. (2010). Learning agility: a construct whose time has come. *Consulting Psychology Journal: Practice and Research*, Vol. 62, No. 2, pp. 119–130.

DeRue, A., Ashford, S., and C. Myers. (2012). Learning agility: in search of conceptual clarity and theoretical grounding. *Industrial and Organizational Psychology*, Vol. 5, pp. 258–279.

Dickie, C. (2011). Coordinating knowledge hierarchies in management: re-conceptualising organisational wisdom. *Philosophy of Management*, Vol. 10, No. 1, pp. 79–94.

Duke, C. (1999). Lifelong learning: implication for the university of the 21st century. *Higher Education Management,* Vol. 11, No. 1, pp. 19–35.

Embong, R., Hashim, R., Yusoff, W., and Mohamad, M. (2013). Holistic integrated curriculum and its theoretical framework: implications for contemporary educational System. *The Social Sciences*, Vol. 10, No. 1, pp. 31–40.

Eriksen, M. (2009). Authentic leadership: practical reflexivity, self-awareness, and self-authorship. *Journal of Management Education,* Vol. 33, No. 6, pp. 747–771.

Fenton-O'Creevy, M., Knight, P., and Margolis, J. (2006). A practice-centered approach to management education. *New Visions of Graduate Management Education*, pp. 103–123.

Gidley, J. (2009). Educating for evolving consciousness: voicing the emergenc-y for love, life and wisdom. In *International Handbook of Education for Spirituality, Care and Wellbeing* (pp. 553–561). Dordrecht: Springer.

Giluk, T., and Rynes-Weller, S. (2012). Research findings practitioners resist: lessons for management academics from evidence-based medicine. *The Oxford Handbook of Evidence-Based Management*, pp. 130–164.

Grant, C. (2012). Cultivating flourishing lives: a robust social justice vision of education. *American Educational Research Journal*, Vol. 49, No. 5, pp. 910–934.

Griffey, S. (1998). Conceptual frameworks beyond the learning organisation. *The Learning Organization*, Vol. 5, No. 2, pp. 68–73.

Hammond, C., and Churchman, D. (2008). Sustaining academic life: a case for applying principles of social sustainability to the academic profession. *International Journal of Sustainability in Higher Education,* Vol. 9, No. 3, pp. 235–245.

Harlan, W., and James, M. (1997). Assessment and learning: differences and relationships between formative and summative assessment. *Assessment in Education: Principles, Policy & Practice,* Vol. 4, No. 3, pp. 365–379.

Hartman, F. (2008). Preparing the mind for dynamic management. *International Journal of Project Management*, Vol. 26, No. 3, pp. 258–267.

Haskell, R. (2000). *Transfer of Learning: Cognition, Instruction, and Reasoning.* San Diego, CA: Academic Press.

Hastie, R. (2001). Problems for judgment and decision making. *Annual Review of Psychology*, Vol. 52, No. 1, pp. 653–683.

Hay, D. (2007). Using concept maps to measure deep, surface and non-learning outcomes. *Studies in Higher Education,* Vol. 32, No. 1, pp. 39–57.

Hays, J. (2008a). Dynamics of organisational wisdom. *The Business Renaissance Quarterly*, Vol. 2, No. 4, pp. 77–122.

Hays, J. (2008b). Threshold and transformation. *European Journal of Management,* Vol. 8, No. 3, pp. 24–46.

Hays, J. (2010). The ecology of wisdom. *Management & Marketing Journal*, Vol. 5, No. 1, pp. 71–92.

Hays, J. (2012). Wicked problem: educating for complexity and wisdom. Paper presented at the Wise Management in Organisational Complexity Conference, 23–24 May 2012, Shanghai, China.

Hays, J. (2013a). Theory U and team performance: presence, participation, and productivity. *Perspectives on Theory U: Insights from the Field: Insights from the Field*, 138.

Hays, J. (2013b). Transformation and transcendence for wisdom: the emergence and sustainment of wise leaders and organisations (Ch. 7; pp. 133–154). In Küpers, W. and D. Pauleen (Eds.), *Handbook of Practical Wisdom: Leadership, Organization and Integral Business Practice*. London: Gower.

Hays, J. (2013c). Wicked problem: educating for complexity and wisdom (Ch. 6; pp. 134–150). In Thompson, M., and D. Bevan (Eds.), *Wise Management in Organisational Complexity*. Basingstoke: Palgrave Macmillan.

Hays, J. (2015a). *Chaos to Capability: Educating Professionals for the 21st Century*. Monograph Series, Vol. 1. Auckland: Unitec.

Hays, J. (2015b). Citizenship, democracy, and professionalism for a sustainable future. Paper presented at the Unitec Community Development Conference, Auckland, New Zealand, 18–20 February.

Jacobs, R. (2007). Navigating learning and teaching in educational administration: educating aspiring principals in wisdom. In Lemasters, L., and R. Papa (Eds.), *At the Tipping Point: Navigating the Course for the Preparation of Educational Administrators. The 2007 Yearbook of the National Council of Professors of Educational Administration* (pp. 371–379). Lancaster: DEStech/Proactive.

Jones, D., and Culliney, J. (1998). Confucian order at the edge of chaos: the science of complexity and ancient wisdom. *Zygon*, Vol. 33, No. 3, pp. 395–404.

Kearns, N., and Hays, J. (2015). Student teams: promises, problems and paradoxes. Paper presented at the National Tertiary Learning and Teaching Conference 2015, *Te Tipuranga – Growing Capability*. Bay of Plenty, New Zealand, 30 Sep–2 Oct.

Keeling, R., and Hersh, R. (2011). *We're Losing Our Minds: Rethinking American Higher Education*. New York: Palgrave Macmillan.

Kitchener, K., and Brenner, H. (1990). Wisdom and reflective judgment: knowing in the face of uncertainty. In Sternberg, R. (Ed.), *Wisdom: Its Nature, Origins, and Development*. Cambridge: Cambridge University press.

Korac-Kakabadse, N., Korac-Kakabadse, A., and Kouzmin, A. (2004). Leadership renewal: towards the philosophy of wisdom. *International Review of Administrative Sciences*, Vol. 67, pp. 207–227.

Kuhn, D., and Udell, W. (2001). The path to wisdom. *Educational Psychologist*, Vol. 36, No. 4, pp. 261–264.

Kuiper, R., and Pesut, D. (2004). Promoting cognitive and metacognitive reflective reasoning skills in nursing practice: self-regulated learning theory. *Journal of Advanced Nursing*, Vol. 45, No. 4, pp. 381–391.

Küpers, W. (2007). Phenomenology and integral phenol-practice of wisdom in leadership and organization. *Social Epistemology*, Vol. 21, No. 2, pp. 169–193.

Küpers, W., and Pauleen, D. (2013). Introduction, In Küpers, W. and D. Pauleen (Eds.), *A Handbook of Practical Wisdom: Leadership, Organization and Integral Business Practice* (pp. 1– 18). London: Gower.

Lewis, M., and Smith, W. (2014). Paradox as a metatheoretical perspective: sharpening the focus and widening the scope. *The Journal of Applied Behavioral Science*, pp. 1–23.

Lozano, R. (2014). Creativity and organizational learning as means to foster sustainability. *Sustainable Development*, Vol. 22, No. 3, pp. 205–216.

Lynch, R. (1999). Seeking practical wisdom. *Business and Economic History*, Vol. 28, No. 2, pp. 123–135.
Madsen, S., and Turnbull, O. (2006). Academic service learning experiences of compensation and benefit course students. *Journal of Management Education*, Vol. 30, No. 5, pp. 724–742.
Maxwell, N. (2014). *How Universities Can Help Create a Wiser World: The Urgent Need for an Academic Revolution*. Exeter: Imprint Academic.
McKenna, B., and Rooney, D. (2005). Wisdom management: tensions between theory and practice in practice. In *KMAP 2005 Knowledge Management in Asia Pacific Conference: Building a Knowledge Society*. Victoria University, Wellington.
McKenna, B., Rooney, D., and Boal, K. (2009). Wisdom principles as a meta-theoretical basis for evaluating leadership. *Leadership Quarterly*, Vol. 20, No. 2, pp. 177–190.
McKenna, B., Sigurjonsson, O., Arnardottir, A., Biloslavo, R., Bulut, C., Bagnoli, C., and Dibben, M. (2014). The relationship between concern for environmental sustainability and the capacity for wisdom and other factors among postgraduate business students: an international comparison. In *Proceedings of the 17th Irish Academy of Management Conference*, Limerik, Ireland, 3–5 Sep.
McKenzie, J., and Aitken, P. (2012). Learning to lead the knowledgeable organization: developing leadership agility. *Strategic HR Review*, Vol. 11, No. 6, pp. 329–334.
McKeough, A., Lupart, J., and Marini, A. (Eds.). (1995). *Teaching for Transfer: Fostering Generalization in Learning*. Mahwah, NJ: Lawrence Erlbaum.
McKie, A., Baguley, F., Guthrie, C., Jackson, C., Kirkpatrick, P., Laing, A., O'Brien, S., Taylor, R., and Wimpenny, P. (2012). Exploring clinical wisdom in nursing education. *Nursing Ethics*, Vol. 19, No. 2, pp. 252–267.
Meldrum, M., and Atkinson, S. (1998). Meta-abilities and the implementation of strategy: knowing what to do is simply not enough. *Journal of Management Development*, Vol. 17, No. 8, pp. 564–575.
Mezirow, J. (1997). Transformative learning: theory to practice. *New Directions for Adult and Continuing Education*, Vol. 74, pp. 5–12.
Miller, J. (2005). *Educating for Wisdom and Compassion: Creating Conditions for Timeless Learning*. Thousand Oaks, CA: Corwin.
Miller, J. (2007). *The Holistic Curriculum*, 2nd ed. Toronto: University of Toronto Press.
Mohamed, N. (2014). Capturing green curriculum spaces in the Maktab: implications for environmental teaching and learning. In Chapman, J., McNamara, S., Reiss, M. and Waghid, Y. (Eds.), *International Handbook of Learning, Teaching and Leading in Faith-Based Schools* (pp. 335–351). Dordrecht: Springer.
Nonaka, I., and Toyama, R. (2007). Strategic management as distributed practical wisdom (phronesis). *Industrial and Cultural Change*, Vol. 16, No. 3, pp. 371–394.
Nonaka, I., Kodama, M., Hirose, A., and Kohlbacher, F. (2014). Dynamic fractal organizations for promoting knowledge-based transformation – a new paradigm for organizational theory. *European Management Journal*, Vol. 32, No. 1, pp. 137–146.
O'Toole, L. J. (2004). Implementation theory and the challenge of sustainable development: the transformative role of learning. *Governance for Sustainable Development: the Challenge of Adapting Form to Function*, Ch. 2, pp. 32–60. Cheltenham: Edward Elgar.
Palmer, J., Smith, T., Willetts, J., and Mitchell, C. (2007). Creativity, ethics and transformation: key factors in a transdisciplinary application of systems methodology to resolving wicked problems in sustainability. In *Institute for Sustainable Futures, University of Technology, Proceedings from the Australia and New Zealand Systems Conference*.
Parse, R. (2004). A human becoming teaching-learning model. *Nursing Science Quarterly*, Vol. 17, No. 1, pp. 33–35.
Pizzolato, J. (2006). Complex partnerships: self-authorship and provocative academic-advising practices. *NACADA Journal*, Vol. 26, No. 1, pp. 32–45.

Reams, J. (2015). The cultivation of wisdom in the classroom. *Integral Review*, Vol. 11, No. 2, pp. 103–134.

Reznitskaya, A., and Sternberg, R. (2004). Teaching students to make wise judgments: the teaching for wisdom program. In *Positive Psychology in Practice* (Ch. 11), details unavailable, downloaded at: www.shkodraonline.com/e107_files/public/1264164501_514_FT216478_positive_psychology_in_practice.pdf#page=205.

Roca, E. (2007). Introducing practical wisdom in business schools. *Journal of Business Ethics*, Vol. 82, pp. 607–620.

Rooney, D., and McKenna, B. (2008). Knowledge, wisdom and intellectual leadership: a question of the future and knowledge-based sustainability. *International Journal of Learning and Intellectual Capital*, Vol. 6, Nos. 1–2, pp. 52–70.

Rosch, E. (2008). Beginner's mind: paths to the wisdom that is not learned. In Ferrari, M., and G. Potworoski (Eds.), *Teaching for Wisdom: Cross-Cultural Perspectives on Fostering Wisdom*. Dordrecht: Springer.

Rowley, J. (2006a). What do we need to know about wisdom? *Management Decision*, Vol. 44, No. 9, pp. 1246–1257.

Rowley, J. (2006b). Where is the wisdom that we have lost in knowledge. *Journal of Documentation*, Vol. 62, No. 2, pp. 251–270.

Rowley, J., and Gibbs, P. (2008). From learning organization to practically wise organization. *The Learning Organization*, Vol. 15, No. 5, pp. 356–372.

Ryan, R., Huta, V., and Deci, E. (2008). Living well: a self-determination theory perspective on eudaimonia. *Journal of Happiness Studies*, Vol. 9, No. 1, pp. 139–170.

Sadler-Smith, E., and Shefy, E. (2007). Developing intuitive awareness in management education. *Academy of Management Learning & Education*, Vol. 6, No. 2, pp. 186–205.

Shek, D. (2010). Nurturing holistic development of university students in Hong Kong: where are we and where should we go? *The Scientific World Journal*, Vol. 10, pp. 563–575.

Shelton, C., and J. Darling. (2003). From theory to practice: using new science concepts to create learning organizations. *The Learning Organization*, Vol. 10, No. 6, pp. 353–360.

Sibbel, A. (2009). Pathways towards sustainability through higher education. *International Journal of Sustainability in Higher Education*, Vol. 10, No. 1, pp. 68–82.

Sivaraksa, S. (2011). *The Wisdom of Sustainability: Buddhist Economics for the 21st Century*. London: Souvenir Press.

Smith, C. (2007). Working from the inside out: management and leadership through the lens of the perennial wisdom tradition. *Journal of Management Development*, Vol. 26, No. 5, pp. 475–483.

Spector, J., and Anderson, T. (Eds.). (2000). *Integrated and Holistic Perspectives on Learning, Instruction and Technology*. Dordrecht: Springer.

Spiller, C., Pio, E., Erakovic, L., and Henare, M. (2011). Wise up: creating organizational wisdom through an ethic of Kaitiakitanga. *Journal of Business Ethics*, Vol. 104, No. 2, pp. 223–235.

Stacey, R. (1992). *Managing for the Unknowable: Strategic Borders between Order and Chaos in Organizations*. San Francisco, CA: Jossey-Bass.

Star, C., and Hammer, S. (2008). Teaching generic skills: eroding the higher purpose of universities, or an opportunity for renewal? *Oxford Review of Education*, Vol. 34, No. 2, pp. 237–251.

Statler, M. (2014). Developing wisdom in a business school? Critical reflections on pedagogical practice. *Management Learning*. Vol. 45, No. 4, pp. 397–417.

Staudinger, U., and Glück, J. (2011). Psychological wisdom research: commonalities and differences in a growing field. *Annual Review of Psychology*, Vol. 62, pp. 215–241.

Sterling, S. (2001). *Sustainable Education: Re-visioning Learning and Change*. Schumacher Briefing No. 6. Cambridge: Green Books.

Sternberg, R. (1998). A balance theory of wisdom. *Review of General Psychology*, Vol. 2, No. 4, pp. 347–365.

Sternberg, R. (2001). Why schools should teach for wisdom: the balance theory of wisdom in educational settings. *Educational Psychologist*, Vol. 36, No. 4, pp. 227–245.
Sternberg, R. (2005). Older but not wiser? The relationship between age and wisdom. *Ageing International*, Vol. 30, No. 1, pp. 5–26.
Sternberg, R., Reznitskaya, A., and Jarvin, L. (2007). Teaching for wisdom: what matters is not just what students know, but how they use it. *London Review of Education*, Vol. 5, No. 2, pp. 143–158.
Thomas, I. (2009). Critical thinking, transformative learning, sustainable education, and problem-based learning in universities. *Journal of Transformative Education*, Vol. 7, No. 3, pp. 245–264.
Tisdell, E. (2011). The wisdom of webs a-weaving: adult education and the paradoxes of complexity in changing times. *New Directions for Adult and Continuing Education*, No. 131, Fall, pp. 5–13.
Trowbridge, R. (2011). Waiting for Sophia: 30 years of conceptualizing wisdom in empirical psychology. *Research in Human Development*, Vol. 8, No. 2, pp. 149–164.
van Woerkom, M., Nijhof, W., and Nieuwenhuis, L. (2002). Critical reflective working behaviour: a survey research. *Journal of European Industrial Training*, Vol. 26, No. 8, pp. 375–383.
Vos, N., van der Meijden, H., and Denessen, E. (2011). Effects of constructing versus playing an educational game on student motivation and deep learning strategy use. *Computers & Education*, Vol. 56, No. 1, pp. 127–137.
Waddock, S. (2014). Wisdom and responsible leadership: aesthetic sensibility, moral imagination, and systems thinking. In *Aesthetics and Business Ethics* (pp. 129–147). Dordrecht: Springer.
Warburton, K. (2003). Deep learning for sustainability. *International Journal of Sustainability in Higher Education*, Vol. 4, No. 1, pp. 44–56.
Warm, R. (2011). *Leading Deeply: A Heroic Journey Toward Wisdom and Transformation* (Doctoral dissertation, Antioch University).
Weigel, V. (2002). Deep *Learning for a Digital Age: Technology's Untapped Potential to Enrich Higher Education*. San Francisco, CA: Jossey-Bass.
Wilhelm, J., and Novak, B. (2011). *Teaching Literacy for Love and Wisdom: Being the Book and Being the Change*. New York: Teachers College Press.
William, D., and Black, P. (1996). Meanings and consequences: a basic for distinguishing formative and summative functions of assessment? *British Educational and Research Journal*, Vol. 22, No. 5, pp. 537–548.
Yorke, M. (2003). Formative assessment in higher education: movements toward theory and the enrichment of pedagogic practice. *Higher Education*, Vol. 45, pp. 477–501.

Chapter 9

How managers understand wisdom in decision-making

A phronetic research approach

Mike J. Thompson

Introduction

In this chapter I explore the nature of wisdom and provide research insights into the way in which practical wisdom is understood and practised by senior managers. The research for this chapter is drawn from the Wisdom Project inaugurated in 2010 by the Euro China Centre for Leadership and Responsibility at the China Europe International Business School (CEIBS). The objective of the Wisdom Project was to assess the way in which wisdom was understood by 181 senior managers and applied in the managerial decision-making process. A subsidiary objective was to test the extent to which the descriptions collected through the research survey could be aligned with the five principles of social practice wisdom (SPW) (McKenna, Rooney and Boal, 2009, pp. 178–180). I first set out the academic and research context for phronetic research and then proceed to set out the survey method, an analysis of results and comparisons with the five SPW principles.

The phronetic research approach

In recent years a small group of social science research scholars have put forward a case for organisational wisdom-based research methods; notably David Rooney and Bernard McKenna (McKenna et al., 2009; Rooney, 2013a, 2013b; Rooney, McKenna and Liesch, 2010); Bent Flyvbjerg (2001) and Wendelin Küpers and Matt Statler (Küpers, 2007; Küpers and Statler, 2008). The need for a wisdom research methodology becomes apparent when behavioural and management researchers investigate the way in which a person leads with wisdom and develops what McKenna and Rooney (2008, p. 2) call ontological acuity: 'wise leaders with insights beyond the isomorphic tendencies of organizational discourse by which they are able to clearly render visible the ontological foundations of the opaque epistemic bases and relations of power within organizations'. The research task is thus set 'to theoretically and empirically show the important connections among discourse, schema, context, and agency' (McKenna and Rooney, 2008, p. 544).

In a formative essay entitled 'Empirical Wisdom Research: A Community Approach', Rooney (2013a) calls for the creation of a community of organisational wisdom researchers. Integral to this call is the need for 'wise universities' since, according to Rooney, universities use

> Misconceived Key Performance Indicators that drive institutional and researcher behaviour, research that universities value primarily as a PR opportunity, and a conservative, even reactionary, scholarly journal system that is not working are also symptomatic of problems in need of a wisdom-based solution.
>
> (Rooney, 2013a, p. 47)

Rooney argues that 'wisdom's potential is profound as a research approach focus, as a research methodology and as business practice' (Rooney, 2013a, p. 37). To this end, Rooney with McKenna have developed a 'social practice wisdom' (SPW) model (McKenna, Rooney and Boal, 2009; Rooney, McKenna and Liesch, 2010) described by Rooney on his website as

> the ability to live coherently and appropriately according to the situation to produce excellence for oneself and others .... Wise practitioners do this by integrating intellectual and ethical virtues in praxis (including in specific cultural, social, political, and economic contexts) to create deliberative excellence that has positive long-term impacts for humanity.
>
> (Rooney, 2016)

SPW focuses on social practices in management and workplace contexts and embraces philosophical traditions, as well as psychology, neuroscience, and other disciplines that further enrich our knowledge of integrating values in workplace practice (Zhu, Rooney and Phillips, 2015). The five principles of SPW are illustrated in Figure 9.1 and in further detail, later, in Table 9.2.

Kinsella and Pitman (2012) have reinforced the phronetic research approach in their significant collection of papers by eleven scholars in this field entitled: *Phronèsis as Professional Knowledge: Practical Wisdom in the Professions*. Kinsella and Pitman (2013, p. 1) explore Aristotlean *phronèsis* as a source for reconceptualising professional knowledge and challenges the trend in the social sciences in which value rationality has given way to instrumentalist rationality. The simplest translation of *phronèsis* is practical wisdom but, in context, *phronèsis* may be linked to virtuous practices and the goal of *eudaimonia* (wellbeing or human flourishing). *Phronèsis* is the practical common sense needed to develop *eudaimonia* through 'a true and reasoned state of capacity to act with regard to the things that are good or bad for man' (Aristotle, *Nichomachean Ethics* VI.5). Correspondingly, *phronèsis* concerns practical judgement, the ability to act virtuously and for the common good in difficult and uncertain situations (McKenna, 2013, p. 15; Grint, 2007, p. 237). It concerns the *practice* and *praxis* of life and, in both Aristotelian and Confucian thought, *phronèsis* is inseparable from the practice of virtue which, in turn, becomes the axiom of wisdom, and potentially, for wise management in the midst of organisational complexity (Thompson and Bevan, 2013).

Phronèsis might be regarded as the process of drawing from *episteme*, which is context-independent intelligence or scientific knowledge (Grint, 2007, p. 237) and *nous*, 'the insightfulness that makes up for the imprecision of rationality' (Dunne, 1993, p. 15). *Phronèsis* should be distinguished from *sophia*, a metaphysical or transcendent quality derived intuitively in contemplation (Trowbridge, 2011, p. 151) and, following Socrates, a contemplative, esoteric or philosophical wisdom (Robinson 1990, p. 14).

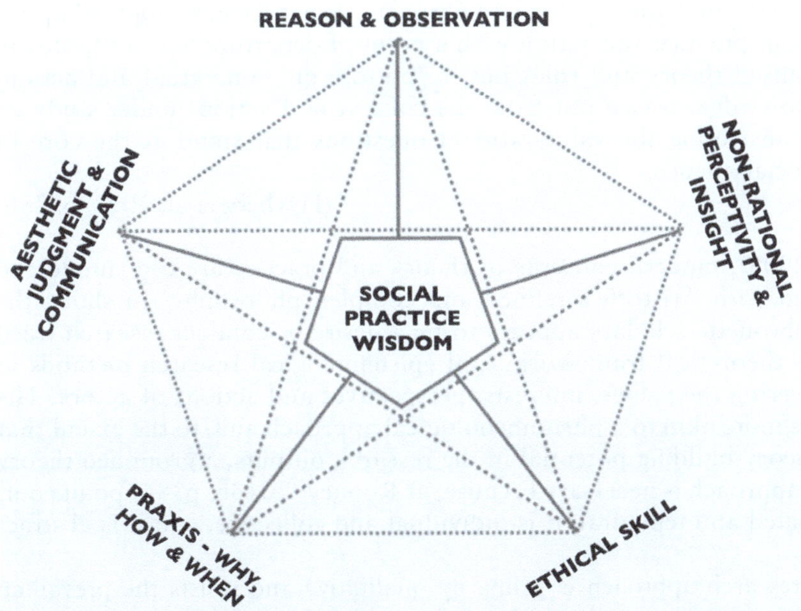

Figure 9.1 Social practice wisdom principles: McKenna and Rooney.
Source: Adapted from McKenna et al. (2009) and Rooney (2016).

In returning to Aristotelian *phronèsis*, a number of social sciences scholars have drawn from the contemporary philosophical movement inspired by MacIntyre (1984) and Dunne (1993) to challenge the scientific assumptions that have dominated the means by which professional domains of knowledge have been conceived, practised and institutionalised (Kinsella and Pitman, 2012). Phronetic research takes a praxeological and axiological approach resonant with MacIntyre's interpretation of practice as the 'arena in which the virtues are exhibited and … receive their primary … definition' (MacIntyre, 1981, p. 218). The focus is on human agency and intentionality shaped within particular narratives and, following MacIntyre, a 'telos' or a sense of future goals or ends within particular narratives (Brewer, 1997, p. 828).

The proponents of phronetic research incorporate personal narrative accounts, case knowledge, context, praxis and power relations to balance instrumental rationality (*episteme*) with value-rationality (Flyvbjerg, 2001). Flyvbjerg, Landman and Schram (2012) explain how phronetic research/social science differ from the conventional social scientific approach:

> The conventional view holds that theory precedes action in a top-down movement where one arrives at the right action by first choosing the right theory and then applying that theory properly to the practical question at hand, for example, like engineers applying the laws of physics to construct a bridge. Phronetic social scientists are sceptical of this view; at least as it pertains to social and

> political action, as such action requires a knowledge of context that is simply not accessible through theory alone. In phronetic social science, 'applied' means thinking about practice and action with a point of departure not in top-down, decontextualised theory and rules but in 'bottom-up' contextual and action-oriented knowledge, teased out from the context and actions under study by asking and answering the value-rational questions that stand at the core of phronetic social science.
>
> (Flyvberg et al, 2012, p. 286)

For Eikeland (2008), modern concepts of theory and practice are too simple and coarse compared with Aristotle's refined and complex philosophy. In short, the plea from the phronetic scholars appears to be a desire to conduct research freed from normative theoretical frameworks and epistemological research methods in search of discovering the values, interests, perspectives and actions of actors. The approach is thus more akin to a phenomenological approach and, to the extent that there may be theory-building potential in the research outputs, a grounded theory approach. This approach is necessary because, as Rooney (2013b, p. 84) points out, 'Wisdom is situated and temporal, it is individual and collective, and it is abstract and concrete'.

A phronetic research approach is primarily qualitative and resists the prevailing dominance of quantitative research which requires a high degree of interpretation and suffers from a number of interpretive shortcomings which have been well-rehearsed by Yuki (1989), Alvesson (1996), Conger (1998) and Barker (2001).

More recently, and following a phronetic research approach, Macklin and Whiteford (2012) have proposed 'interpretive qualitative research' that is 'interpretive, flexible, participatory, and reflexive', unlike quantitative methods which they characterise as restricting knowledge creation to objective techniques (Macklin and Whiteford, 2012, p. 86).

In the leadership research field, Gardner et al. (2010) have expressed the potential for concern over the trend towards a heavier mix of quantitative methods (Gardner et al., 2010, p. 943), whilst Conger (1998) has claimed that qualitative research 'can be the richest of studies, often illuminating in radically new ways, phenomena as complex as leadership' (Conger, 1998, p. 7). Knowledge management and leadership scholars, Nonaka and Takeuchi (2011) suggest that a phronetic research approach is required in their view that social and business phenomena require an axiological and praxeological context:

> Dependence only on explicit knowledge prevents leaders from coping with change. The scientific, deductive, theory-first approach assumes a world independent of context and seeks answers that are universal and predictive. However, all social phenomena – including business – are context dependent, and analyzing them is meaningless unless you consider people's goals, values, and interests.
>
> (Nonaka and Takeuchi, 2011, p. 60)

In short, the phronetic research approach may also be regarded as a return to Weberian interactionism and *Verstehen* in which an interpretation of meaning from the perspective of the actor/s is paramount.

Wisdom Project survey method

The intent of the survey stage of the Wisdom Project was to explore managers' self-understanding of practical wisdom and to identify the ontological acuity present in their managerial decision-making. This was done in order to 'evaluate normative practice and its underlying episteme to provide alternative ways of knowing, deciding, and acting' (McKenna and Rooney, 2008, p. 538). Rooney (2013a, pp. 38–39) argues for close observance of cases, contexts and practice using dialogical and empathetic approaches to ask 'how' and to analyse both the narrative and the tacit elements such as emotions, habits, skills and actions. SPW as articulated by Rooney (2013a, p. 38) requires the integration of epistemology (knowledge creation) and ontology (ways of being and becoming) with the methodologies of axiology (values and value), praxeology (enactment or application of knowledge) and *eudaimonia* (wellbeing or human flourishing) in order to contribute to wise social research. But SPW is not only a research approach, it is also a re-articulation of Aristotelian *phronèsis* enabling its application to contemporary financial (Rooney, Mandeville and Kastelle, 2013), entrepreneurial and educational challenges (Rooney, 2015b). This contemporary grounding of *phronèsis* is described by Rooney (2013b, p. 86):

> Within practical wisdom, the word practical does not mean short-term convenience or ease, or simple instrumentality, as it tends to mean in contemporary parlance. Practical, in a practical wisdom sense, is linked to a philosophy of wisdom that is about learning to live, see, experience, value, participate, and create (Maxwell, 1984). To be practical is to be able to navigate the challenges of thoughtfully and mindfully acting in social life; it means creating long-term well-being through praxis. In this sense, practical wisdom is a way of being that is often far from easy and convenient.

The Wisdom Project research outputs and findings thus aim to be praxeological, ontological, axiological and epistemological. Specifically they help to:

1. assess the alignment between the self-understanding of practical wisdom by senior managers with the five SPW principles as originally described by McKenna, Rooney and Boal (2009);
2. identify the values and personal development dimensions in the survey data;
3. suggest ways in which the research findings might be enacted and applied in management and education.

Other than the five SPW principles, no other theories or models were used as normative constructs of practical wisdom. Therefore, the leading psychological and psychometric models of wisdom by Sternberg (1998), Ardelt (2004) and Baltes and Staudinger (2000a, 2000b), for example, are beyond the purview of this study.

The Wisdom Project enquiry might be summarised and framed in one simple question: 'How do you, as a manager, understand and apply wisdom in making decisions?' No a priori definitions are stated, descriptive or normative categories, or theories. Whilst there are elements of a grounded theory approach in illuminating boundaries and categories within the data, there is no theoretical sampling involved in the analysis.

An advisory panel of two strategic consultants and one executive coach designed three survey questions for senior level business leaders defined as C-Suite leaders (or organisational equivalents) and company owners. The selection process for respondents was not random but was drawn from the networks of the advisory panel and a CEIBS executive education network. During 2010, 85 Western leaders from 21 countries were surveyed and during 2011, 96 Chinese leaders based in mainland China were surveyed. The majority of the Chinese respondents held senior management positions in mid-sized enterprises (RMB 400m to RMB 600m annual turnover). Of the Western survey participants, 63.5 per cent served companies with annual turnover exceeding €60 million. Participant responses were largely captured via email or hard-copy forms, although 11 participants were interviewed.

Participants were asked to respond to three questions:

1 What does wisdom mean for you?
2 Management decisions are generally acknowledged as requiring fact informed knowledge and a rational approach. In your experience, can you describe how wisdom might add something more to the decision-making process?
3 How might someone acquire wisdom?

Question one was posed to understand how respondents in senior managerial positions defined wisdom and therefore no definitions were constructed prior to the survey or provided to the participants. However, in seeking to establish the role that wisdom played in decision-making it was decided to define the meaning of knowledge in this context to avoid any potential confusion with the notion of wisdom. For the purpose of knowledge in the decision-making process the definition of knowledge used in question two was: 'technical expertise, data, facts'. Management decision-making was defined as a combination of knowledge and 'a rational approach'. Most of the responses to question one indicated that wisdom concerns knowledge, reason and judgement but that it also incorporated other attributes such as experience, intuition and values. Question two therefore developed the idea of wisdom being 'something more' and explicitly referred to the central capacities of management decision-making being knowledge and rationality. Question three was set to allow respondents to reflect on the acquisition of wisdom, implying that wisdom might be acquired and cultivated.

Analysis of the Wisdom Project findings

Through a textual analysis of the language used by participants, similarities of expression were grouped to identify broad constructs. The initial textual analysis of the data (approximately 18,000 words) was carried out by Leximancer software. Leximancer analysis achieves the validity much sought after by qualitative researchers including face validity, stability (sampling of members), and reproducibility including structural validity (sampling of representatives), predictive validity, and correlative validity (McKenna & Waddell, 2007). Figure 9.2 is a Leximancer concept map which associates the concepts derived from the textual data to the three questions asked of participants. The textual corpora of the responses made by the 181 survey participants in answering the three questions were placed into files that match these three questions.

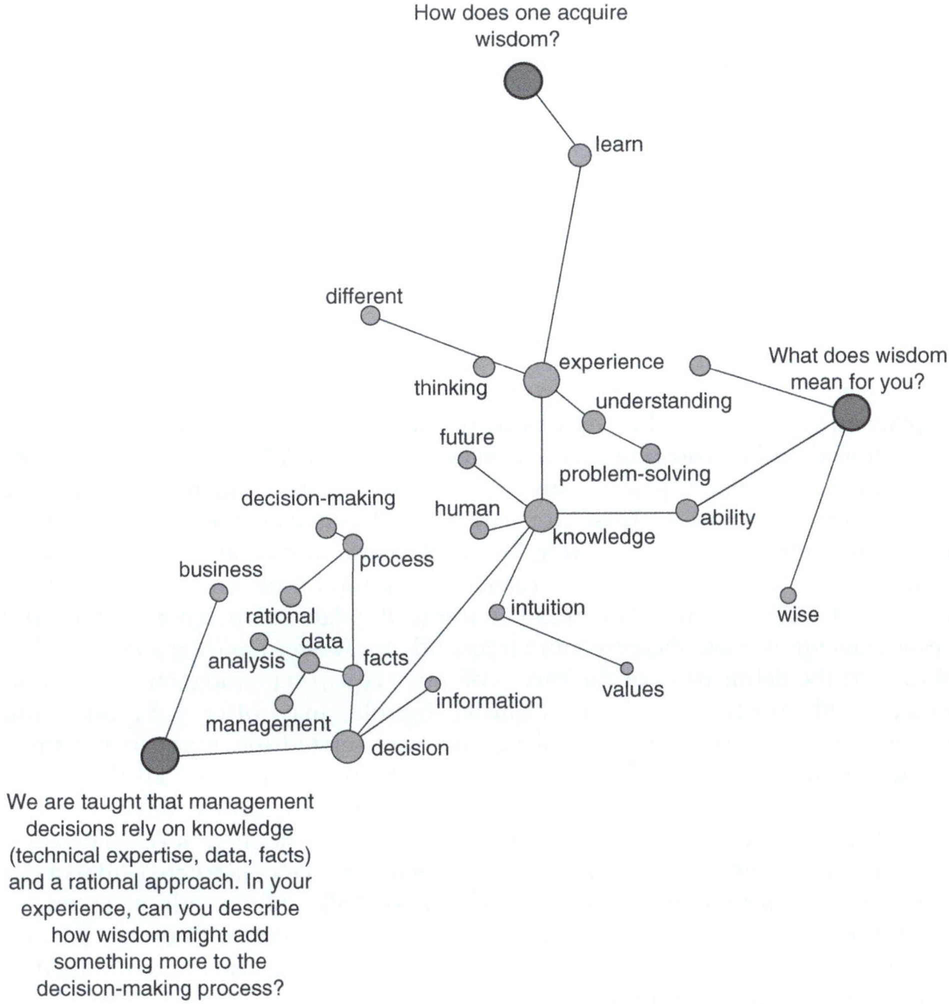

Figure 9.2 Leximancer concept map.

The map spatially represents how the three questions link to what the participants said in their responses to the three questions.

To proceed with further analysis, the researcher is in need of what Küpers and Pauleen (2013, p. 9) call a more critical delineation of wisdom from closely related yet distinct constructs. The initial wave analysing similar concepts are identified as five broad constructs: (1) judgement / decision-making; (2) intuition; (3) values; (4) problem-solving; and (5) smart/knowledgeable. The latter three constructs are closely related with potential for overlap in meaning.

The number of references to concepts in the participants' narratives have been grouped by the five broad constructs and set out in Table 9.1 which also displays the differences in the number of references by construct between Western and Chinese respondents.

Table 9.1 Number of participants who referred to the broad constructs of wisdom

Broad constructs	*Number of participants*	*Percentage of all participants*	*Percentage references by Chinese*	*Percentage references by Western*
Judgement/ decision-making	75	41.4	29.8	55.3
Intuition	58	32.0	13.8	50.6
Values	51	28.2	13.8	44.7
Problem-solving	34	18.8	26.6	10.6
Smart/ knowledgeable	32	17.7	23.4	11.8

There was a significant difference between the number of times concepts were mentioned by Chinese and Western participants and these are shown by the percentages of concept mentions by each of the five constructs. The percentage of Chinese participants who mentioned problem-solving was 2.6 times greater than Western participants and the percentage of Chinese participants who mentioned being smart/knowledgeable was double the percentage of Western participants. The association of intuition with wise decision-making is comparatively low by Chinese participants compared with over half of the Western participants referring to intuition or 'gut instinct' in relation to wise decision-making. The broad concepts of judgement/decision-making and values was mentioned significantly more frequently by Western participants.

However, the delineation of the three cognitive constructs: judgement/decision-making, problem-solving and smart/knowledgeable, may offer a broader and more distinctive construct which collects the inter-related meanings of the three constructs under a single unifying construct. If the responses from all three constructs are summated under a meta construct of rational capability, the differences between Chinese and Western participants disappear at the meta level. The summation of participants who referred to the three cognitive constructs (judgement/decision-making, problem-solving and smart/knowledgeable) result in mentions by 79.8 per cent of Chinese participants and 77.6 per cent of Western participants. Further references will refer to these three cognitive constructs combined as rational and analytical capability.

A priority in the SPW research approach is similar to Weberian *Verstehen*. In seeking to understand the meaning of wisdom to the Chinese participants, the Mandarin word for wisdom provides interpretive insight. Wisdom in Mandarin contains two ideas rather than one: *zhi* 智 (practical intelligence/cognition/knowledge), and *hui* 慧 (enlightened mind/intuition/insight). Chinese participants frequently referred to 'IQ' and 'EQ' as proxy interpretations of 智慧 in describing wisdom in the decision-making process and it is therefore possible that the blending of the cognitive and non-cognitive capacities of wisdom is more pronounced by the Chinese participants than the Western participants. Semantically, Mandarin provides for two constructs of wisdom that are confirmed by the understanding of most participants. The third construct of values incorporates references to ethics and a humane character and explicit mentions of honesty, integrity, trust, respect, humility, fairness, dignity, courage, empathy and care.

Whilst the three constructs of rational and analytical capability, values and intuition are the strongest groupings of wisdom attributed from a textual analysis of the participants' comments, two further categories of attributes are distinguishable in the textual corpora: self-awareness and emotional regulation. These five constructs taken together represent the main outputs from the Wisdom Project research in answering the underlying question: 'How do you, as a manager, understand and apply wisdom in making decisions?' In short form the five constructs of wise management identified from the narratives answer the question, namely, with: (1) Rational and analytical capability; (2) Intuitive insight; (3) Values / humane character; (4) Self-awareness; and (5) Emotional regulation.

To illustrate the way in which participant responses have been linked to the five constructs of wisdom in relation to managerial decision-making, example responses are reproduced below with commentary.

1 Rational and analytical capability

The majority of respondents associated a rational and analytical capability with the practice of wisdom in managerial decision-making. A typical expression of this is found in the response made by the Chief Engineer of a Chinese company:

> The ability to apply knowledge innovatively, accurately, flexibly and quickly. Have a broad span of knowledge base and know how to apply knowledge effectively.

Many respondents noted the distinction between wisdom and the intellectual, rational and cognitive processes involved in managerial decision-making. As the Russian GM of an international spices company puts it:

> There is a clear difference, as well as overlapping, between wisdom and intellect or logical mind. Being armed with wisdom you are able to get more information from the same set of facts and figures. And you will create a decision, which will be the simplest of the best, or the best of the simplest. And you will make this decision much faster, than simply a clever person could.

The role of wisdom is regarded as including the capability to use reason, logic and intellect in order to gain a greater knowledge of a situation and apply the knowledge more quickly or, in the words of other respondents: 'efficiently':

> Wisdom is the most efficient way to use knowledge and rational approach in a shorter time and pro-active to be faster than the competitors.
>
> (GM of an Austrian marketing consultancy)

> I think wisdom is the ability to comprehend, to determine accurately and correctly, to make decision efficiently, to express acceptably by others and so on.
>
> (CEO of a Chinese health management company)

The idea that wisdom adds a further but undefined dimension to the judgement process is echoed by the Romanian COO of a multinational brand consultancy. She notices a difference between a purely correct knowledge-based response and one which contains wisdom as an 'ingredient':

> Wise management implies the right use of knowledge and ensures the best future results. A decision that looks good considering the information, knowledge and rational approach can differ from the one that had wisdom as an extra ingredient, as this will also consider widely held values.

Many respondents acknowledge the limits of fact-based decision-making processes and a range of wisdom factors are mentioned as complementary to analysing the facts of a situation:

> A pure fact-based decision making process will struggle if information is incomplete or not available.
>
> (CEE Sales Director for a multinational food company)

> Wisdom is the part that cannot be measured, that cannot be assessed factually. … Wisdom greatly increases the quality of decisions, but in a way that may not always be visible to the outsider, not even at a later date.
>
> (GM of a dairy multinational, Austria)

2 Intuitive Insight

The significance of intuition and non-rational cues fits with one of the five SPW principles. In Sternberg's (1998) Balance Theory of Wisdom, intuitive insight is named as perspicacity and identified as one of six components of wisdom. In this present study, which relies on unprompted responses, over half of the Western respondents associated wisdom with intuitive insight or 'gut feel':

> Wisdom adds a non-knowledge, non-rational dimension.
>
> (GM of a machine tools manufacturer, France and Iberia)

> Sometimes the decisions are intuitive, never mind the knowledge.
>
> (Divisional Manager of an international food and drinks distributor, Bulgaria)

> In my view, intuition, gut feel and wisdom is, in many cases, the unconscious application of patterns that we connect to the present matter at hand.
>
> (Global Head of Information Services and Compliance of a governance and compliance multinational, USA)

> Wisdom is close to intuition. Insight into what might happen in the future. It combines intuition with logic and applied common sense.
>
> (Former GM of a textiles group, Austria)

> It's something instinctive; it's awareness of the bigger picture and how the pieces fit together. It comes from within.
>
> (Change Director of a dairy multinational, UK)

> Wisdom would add management intuition and decision instinct.
>
> (APAC Capital Market Managing Director for multinational consultancy)

Generally, there was an appreciation that intuition added a depth and quality of insight to complement analysis of facts and knowledge:

> The combination of analysis (knowledge) and intuition is probably more situational, but this mix has served me well for many years.
>
> (CEO of a US training company)

> Wisdom comes from the combining of analysis; intuition informed by experience; and the ability to visualise a future state beyond the data.
>
> (Managing Director of a Chinese-American management consulting group)

> The intuition is experienced by those who are working with it as exceeding by far the capacities of comprehension of our human mind and, by there, gives a capacity of decision making connected, with a much greater quality, to the globality of the factors. It is my personal experience on multiple occasions.
>
> (The Coordinator of a Belgian cultural services network)

> Wisdom is a deep and critical understanding of situations, subjects, sometime even a deep understanding of people.
>
> (Chairman and CEO of UK and Ireland of a food multinational)

> Knowledge, experience and intuition (main components of wisdom) go beyond a pure fact-based and rational approach and will complete an optimal decision-making process.
>
> (CEE Sales Director for a multinational food company)

> Wisdom comes from the combining of analysis; intuition informed by experience; and the ability to visualise a future state beyond the data.
>
> (Managing Director of an international publishing company)

3 Values/humane character

Respondents used a range of words and phrases that might be summarised under the heading of values or humane character. Wisdom is described as having an 'ethical and altruistic dimension' with 'principles and values' with values mentioned including trust, respect, goodness, integrity, grace, courage, benevolence, justice, care and love:

> A wise person is a kind one, not a saint but ethical, with high moral, his personal values are human oriented, more listening than speaking.
>
> (GM of an international spices company, Russia)

> [W]e are not talking just theoretical knowledge but also life experience and soft values/ knowledge to make decisions.
>
> (GM of an international ready meals company, Estonia and Eastern Europe)

> Wisdom requires lots of love, goodness and cleverness, and you must use all these so that not your own actions (i.e. your own biases and frailty) would be relevant, but rather listen to and understand the other, and then let love lead your words, and advices.
>
> (Partner in an international consulting firm, Hungary)

> Applying wisdom is really looking at things in another dimension, which could be said to be metaphysical and often times includes applying a moral compass.
>
> (CEO of an impact investment company, Hong Kong)

> Wisdom knits together a whole series of intangible things such as character, values, intuition, a feeling of responsibility, a preference for action, a desire for safety and order on behalf of others.
>
> (EU HR director for an international technology group)

The CEO of a real-estate company in Harbin, China referenced three well-known Chinese virtues as part of his description of wisdom: *ren, yi* and *cheng-xin. Ren* focuses on an individual's relationships within the community, defined in terms of sociability, security and status (Wang and Lin, 2009:400), whilst *yi* refers to a sense of moral rightness and discernment. *Yi* and *ren* 'often work together in unison to define morality and to guide actions' (Ip, 2009:464) and the virtue of 诚信, *cheng-xin,* meaning honesty and trustworthiness. The Harbin CEO also provided an explanation of the two parts of the Mandarin for wisdom, *Zhi Hui*:

> *Zhi* is the ability of acquiring knowledge and experience. *Hui* is the ability of using and comprehending the knowledge. Of course *Zhi Hui* also includes benevolence, justice and honesty. In another word, a person with wisdom must be one who has a very high ethics. But a person with very high ethics is not necessarily one who is with wisdom.

4 Self-awareness

Both Chinese and Western respondents acknowledged self-awareness and its synonyms as a characteristic of wisdom. Self-reflection on life's experiences and the idea of becoming more enlightened are regarded as activities of wisdom:

> We can acquire wisdom through studying cases and through self-examination.
>
> (China CMO of a multinational pharmaceuticals company)

> The intuitive thinking and judgement capability gained through self-reflection of success and failure experiences.
>
> (CEO of a Chinese investment company)

In my view, wisdom is acquired over time, when one gives conscious attention to being mindful, allowing oneself to engage in reflecting upon issues and upon life overall. Often, gaining wisdom means listening instead of speaking, observing rather than reacting, and certainly, continuing to allow the mind to remain open to endlessly increasing possibilities.

(Owner of a Canadian consulting company)

Wisdom means Enlightenment to me, a combination of Experience, Knowledge, Empathy/Emotional Intelligence, Self-Awareness/Humility, Common sense, Generosity and Inspiration.

(Asian director of an international market research agency)

For me, wisdom means operating from a heightened level of awareness and understanding. To be wise is to observe fully before acting, and to refrain from acting, when that is what is best called for.

(Owner of a Canadian events company)

5 Emotional regulation

Emotional regulation or emotional management is also linked with the ability to manage uncertainty and ambiguity in empirical studies on wisdom by a number of organisational psychologists (Ardelt, 2003; Brugman, 2006; Greene and Brown, 2009; Meeks and Jeste, 2009). The survey respondents directly relate the management and control of 'passion' and 'negative emotions' as exemplified in the selected comments below:

[Wisdom is] the ability to make fair judgements, specially in difficult situations, keeping emotions under control.

(Senior manager of a Columbian social bank)

For me the wisdom includes – life experience (professional and personal), emotional intelligence, tolerance, realism but also many other capabilities necessary to achieve personal balance. The wise people are balanced and sober.

(Divisional Manager of an international food and drinks distributor, Bulgaria)

The person must have also developed the capacity so that the negative emotions (fear, etc.) did not interfere anymore and on the contrary the emotional level must bring its full potential for the setting in action.

(The Coordinator of a Belgian cultural services network)

Dominating passion in making decision; analysing facts with objectivity; projecting in the future; integrating people emotions.

(CEO, international chemical group, Belgium)

> The capability to understand correctly, react promptly and manage flexibly and effectively.
>
> (Vice GM of a Chinese education consulting company)

> A wise person is a master of his and other[s'] emotions.
>
> (GM of an international spices company, Russia)

> Wisdom encompasses a lot of different things, but an important element is the emotional quotient of how we make decisions. Someone who possesses wisdom in a matter has the ability to look at the decision presented before them and to understand how different responses will affect/effect the parties involved and chooses 'wisely' based on that foresight.
>
> (Deputy General Manager, electronics technology company, China)

> Calmness; reflection; anchoring into something deep.
>
> (VP Leadership and Talent of an international insurance company, UK)

Wise management constructs compared with the five SPW principles

In Table 9.2, the five SPW principles are set out in the form expressed in McKenna, Rooney and Boal, 2009 (pp. 178–180). Alongside each principle are concepts and descriptions derived from the textual analysis conducted using the Leximancer tool with further elaboration from survey data in order to show the association with an SPW principle.

Table 9.2 SPW principles compared with Wisdom Project concepts

SPW principle	*Wisdom Project concepts*
1 Wise leaders use reason and careful observation 1a Wise leaders make careful observations to establish facts and logical deductive explanations 1b Wise leaders evaluate the salience and truth-value of logical propositions when applying reason to decision-making by using clear understandings of ontological categories that theoretically describe substance, process, and quality, and so demonstrate, through logical argument, correct conclusions	Rational, information processing, data, facts, decision-making, management, problem-solving, application of knowledge, objectivity, reason
2 Wise leaders allow for non-rational and subjective elements when making decisions 2a Wise leaders acknowledge the sensory and visceral as important components of decision-making and judgement 2b Wise leaders have a metaphysical, even spiritual, quality that does not bind them absolutely to the rules of reason thereby enabling vision, insight and foresight	Intuition, knowledge, experience, thinking, decision-making, insight, perceptivity, cognition, gut-feeling, voice within, higher consciousness, inspiration, foresight, spirit, heart, interconnectedness, intangible elements, reflection, spiritual values, Chinese cultural tradition

2c	Wise leaders respect and draw upon tradition as a means of apprehending who and what they are as a form of personal insight enabling them to understand the contingency of life and the constructedness of phenomena, particularly their historical and spatial contexts	
3	Wise leaders value humane and virtuous outcomes	Values, principles, respect, truth, humility, honesty, generosity, empathy, EQ
3a	Because wise leaders are humane, they produce virtuous and tolerant decisions	
4	Wise leaders and their actions are practical and oriented towards everyday life, including work	Pragmatic, problem-solving, decisions, application
5	Wise leaders are articulate, understand the aesthetic dimension of their work, and seek the intrinsic personal and social rewards of contributing to the good life	Beauty, truth, goodness, common good

While no validity can be inferred from the number of concept mentions from the survey sample and the concepts are stark insofar as they are without interpretation or definition, the unprompted responses by participants to the three questions do indicate that the five SPW principles were supported. Numerically, concepts associated with principle five were the least mentioned.

Conclusion

Following the praxeological and axiological principles of SPW, an application of the Wisdom Project survey data in business practice has been used in further management education[1] and in a preliminary model (the Wisdom Prism) with links to SPW principles (Thompson, 2013). Phronetic social science and the SPW model suggest that case studies are an appropriate element of the research structure and the praxeological dimension. This means a 'bottom-up' point of departure and an appropriate reporting of axiological aspects of practice and action.

The Wisdom Project findings, as revealed through a phronetic research approach, enables a view on how some senior managers describe the dimensions of wisdom and its practice in leadership and managerial decision-making. The contemporary application of Aristotelean *phronèsis* in the SPW model is demonstrated by the frequent allusion to virtues, values and ethics in managerial decision-making. The SPW research approach is here illustrated as an alternative to prescriptive social scientific methods and is thus open to rebuttal on grounds that no theory has been tested or developed nor have any hypotheses been proved. Indeed, on social scientific grounds the research findings are weak. However, the insights gained through an SPW approach may serve those who ask questions of vocation, motivation and practice by business leaders (Elangovan, Pinder and McLean, 2010). And these questions are being increasingly asked and measured in organisational management systems (McKinsey and Company, 2010; Larson, Latham, Appleby and Harshman, 2013; Kaipa and Radjou, 2013; Boaz and Fox, 2014; Zacher, Pearce, Rooney and McKenna, 2014; Thompson and Buytaert, 2014). Indeed the praxis of the five wisdom constructs identified in the Wisdom Project have been applied as an online self-assessment tool used by a Chinese-based recruitment and selection company.[2] The tool itself is an example of how the praxeological principle in phronetic research can be operationalised in practical output and engagement in the wise management constructs identified in the Wisdom Project. However, further work is required to suggest ways in which the five wise management constructs might be enacted and applied in management and education.

The Wisdom Project has shown how a phronetic research approach has enabled unprompted and particular narratives on wisdom and decision-making by 181 senior managers to identify agency and intentionality within five wise management constructs. The findings revealed through textual analysis show that senior managers understand wisdom to be practical, rational, ethical and intuitive and that they identify these constructs as intrinsic to decision-making. The underlying 'telos' within the narratives is clear: in the descriptions provided in answering the question regarding the source of wisdom, experience is linked to a path of continuous self-development and the pursuit of the good life.

SPW, as an example of phronetic research offers a phenomenological framework for researchers to firstly enquire and secondly to move into a praxeological mode of enquiry which respects the essentially fluid and practical nature of wisdom.

Reflective questions

1 What are the pros and cons of following a phronetic research approach versus the established social scientific research approach?
2 What further processes and applications of practical wisdom and ways of wise leading and managing might be explored and demonstrated through research, education and personal development tools?
3 The Wisdom Project survey participants were selected because of their seniority in management and to represent a broad range of countries. What might be the next stage of research required to strengthen the necessarily subjective nature of the Wisdom Project?
4 How might the five wise management constructs be practically applied to management and executive education?
5 The strength of responses which identify wise decision-making with an element of intuition or 'gut feel' is, perhaps, a surprising finding, or is it?
6 In which respects might the Wisdom Project findings help to ground and apply a (meta)-theory of wisdom learning in organisations?

Notes

1 http://www.ceibs.edu/ecclars-wise-leadership-research-and-pedagogy-event-0
2 The GLO Wise Check Up, Good Leaders Online, Shanghai: https://glo-china.com/the-glo-program/glo-wise-check-up/.

References

Alvesson, M. (1996). Leadership studies: From procedure and abstraction to reflexivity and situation. *The Leadership Quarterly*, 7(4), pp. 455–485.

Ardelt, M. (2003). Empirical assessment of a three-dimensional wisdom scale. *Research on Aging*, 25(3), pp. 275–324.

Ardelt, M. (2004). Wisdom as expert knowledge system: A critical review of a contemporary operationalization of an ancient concept. *Human Development*, 47, pp. 257–285.

Aristotle (n.d.). *Nicomachean Ethics*. Translated by H. Rackham, 1934. Cambridge, MA: Harvard University Press.

Baltes, P. B. and Staudinger, U. M. (2000a). A metaheuristic (pragmatic) to orchestrate mind and virtue towards excellence. *American Psychologist*, 55(1), pp. 122–136.

Baltes, P. B. and Staudinger, U. M. (2000b). Wisdom: a metaheuristic (pragmatic) to orchestrate mind and virtue toward excellence. *American Psychologist*, 55(1), p. 122.

Barker, R. A. (2001). The nature of leadership. *Human Relations*, 54(4), pp. 469–494.

Boaz, N. and Fox, E. A. (2014). Change leader, change thyself. *McKinsey Quarterly*, March.

Brewer, K. B. (1997). Management as a practice: A response to Alasdair MacIntyre. *Journal of Business Ethics*, 16(8), pp. 825–833.

Brugman, G. M. (2006). *Wisdom and Aging*. Amsterdam: Elsevier.

Conger, J. A. (1998). Qualitative research as the cornerstone methodology for understanding leadership. *The Leadership Quarterly*, 9(1), pp. 107–122.

Dunne, J. (1993). *Back to the Rough Ground: Practical Judgement and the Lure of Technique*. Notre Dame, IN: University of Notre Dame Press.

Eikeland, O. (2008). *The Ways of Aristotle: Aristotelian Phronesis, Aristotelian Philosophy of Dialogue, and Action Research*. Bern: Peter Lang.

Elangovan, A. R., Pinder, C. C. and McLean, M. (2010). Callings and organizational behavior. *Journal of Vocational Behavior*, 76(3), pp. 428–440.

Flyvbjerg, B. (2001). *Making Social Science Matter: Why Social Inquiry Fails and How It Can Succeeed Again*, trans. S. Sampson. Cambridge: Cambridge University Press.

Flyvbjerg, B., Landman T. and Schram, S. (2012). Important next steps in phronetic social science. In: Flyvbjerg, B., Landman, T. and Schram, S., eds., *Real Social Science: Applied Phronesis*. Cambridge: Cambridge University Press, pp. 285–297.

Gardner, W. L., Lowe, K. B., Moss, T. W., Mahoney, K. T. and Cogliser, C. C. (2010). Scholarly leadership of the study of leadership: a review of *The Leadership Quarterly's* second decade, 2000–2009. *The Leadership Quarterly*, 21, pp. 922–958.

Greene, J. and Brown, J. (2009). The Wisdom Development Scale: Further validity investigations. *International Journal of Aging and Human Development*, 68(4), pp. 289–320.

Grint, K. (2007). Learning to lead: Can Aristotle help us find the road to wisdom? *Leadership*, 3(2), p. 231.

Ip, P. K. (2009). Is Confucianism good for business ethics in China? *Journal of Business Ethics*, 88(3), pp. 463–476.

Kaipa, P. and Radjou, N. (2013). *From Smart to Wise: Acting and Leading with Wisdom*. San Francisco, CA: Jossey-Bass.

Kinsella, E. A. and Pitman, A., eds. (2012). *Phronesis as Professional Knowledge: Practical Wisdom in the Professions*. Rotterdam: Sense Publishers.

Küpers, W. (2007). Phenomenology and integral pheno-practice of wisdom in leadership and organisation. *Social Epistemology*, 21(2), pp. 169–193.

Küpers, W. and Pauleen, D. J. (2013). *A Handbook of Practical Wisdom: Leadership, Organization and Integral Business Practice*. Farnham, UK: Gower.

Küpers, W. and Statler, M. (2008). Practically wise leadership: Toward an integral understanding. *Culture and Organisation*, 14(4), pp. 379–400.

Larson, M. D., Latham, J. R., Appleby, C. A. and Harshman, C. L. (2013). CEO attitudes and motivations: Are they different for high-performing organizations? *Quality control and applied statistics*, 58(5), pp. 505–506.

MacIntyre, A. (1981). *After Virtue: A Study in Moral Theory*. Reprint 2011. London: Bloomsbury.

Macklin, R. and Whiteford, G. (2012). Phronesis, aporia and qualitative research. In: Kinsella, E. A. and Pitman, A., eds., *Phronesis as Professional Knowledge: Practical Wisdom in the Professions*. Rotterdam: Sense Publishers.

Maxwell, N. (1984). *From Knowledge to Wisdom: A Revolution in the Aims and Methods of Science*. Oxford: Blackwell.

McKenna, B. and Rooney, D. (2008). Wise leadership and the capacity for ontological acuity. *Management Communication Quarterly*, 21, pp. 537–546.

McKenna, B. and Waddell, N. (2007). Mediated political oratory following terrorist events: International political responses to the 2005 London Bombing. *Journal of Language and Politics*, 6, pp. 377–399.

McKenna, B., Rooney, D. and Boal, K. (2009). Wisdom principles as a meta-theoretical basis for evaluating leadership. *The Leadership Quarterly*, 20(2), pp. 177–190.

McKinsey & Company (2010). *The Value of Centered Leadership: McKinsey Global Survey Results* [pdf]. McKinsey & Company. Available at: www.mckinsey.com/insights/leading_in_the_21st_century/the_value_of_centered_leadership_mckinsey_global_survey_results [Accessed 5 August, 2015].

Meeks, T. W. and Jeste, D. V. (2009). Neurobiology of wisdom: A literature overview. *Archives of General Psychiatry*, 66(4), pp. 355–365.

Nonaka, I. and Takeuchi, H. (2011). The wise leader. *Harvard Business Review*, May, pp. 59–67.

Robinson, D. N. (1990). Wisdom through the ages. In: R. J. Sternberg, ed., *Wisdom: Its Nature, Origins, and Development*. New York, NY: Cambridge University Press, pp. 13–24.

Rooney, D. (2013a). Empirical wisdom research. In: Thompson, M. J. and Bevan, D., eds., *Wise Management in Organisational Complexity*. Basingstoke: Palgrave Macmillan. Ch. 3.

Rooney, D. (2013b). Being a wise organizational researcher: Ontology, epistemology and axiology: ontology, epistemology, and methodology. In: Küpers, W. and Pauleen, D. J., eds., *A Handbook of Practical Wisdom: Leadership, Organization and Integral Business Practice*. Farnham, UK: Gower. Ch. 4.

Rooney, D. (2016). *The Knowledge & Wisdom Site* [online]. Available at: https://sites.google.com/site/davidrooneyknowledge [Accessed 8 February 2016].

Rooney D., Mandeville, T. and Kastelle, T. (2013). Abstract knowledge and reified financial innovation: Building wisdom and ethics into financial innovation networks. *Journal of Business Ethics*, 118(3), pp. 447–459.

Rooney, D., McKenna, B. and Liesch, P. (2010). *Wisdom and Management in the Knowledge Economy*. London: Routledge.

Sternberg, R. J. (1998). A balance theory of wisdom. *Review of General Psychology*, 2(4), pp. 247–365.

Thompson, M. J. (2013). What does wise leadership mean? *Forbes India*. 5 April [online]. Available at: http://forbesindia.com/article/ceibs/what-does-wise-leaderhip-mean/34915/1 [Accessed 9 February 2016].

Thompson, M. J. and Bevan, D. (2013). Wise management in organisational complexity: An introduction. In: Thompson, M. J. and Bevan, D., eds., *Wise Management in Organisational Complexity*. Basingstoke: Palgrave Macmillan. Ch. 1.

Thompson, M. J. and Buytaert, P. (2014). Change management is changing. *Today's Manager*, 4, pp. 66–69.

Trowbridge, R. H. (2011). Waiting for Sophia: 30 years of conceptualizing wisdom in empirical psychology. *Research in Human Development*, 8(2), pp. 149–164.

Wang, C. L. and Lin, X. (2009). Migration of Chinese consumption values: Traditions, modernization, and cultural renaissance. *Journal of Business Ethics*, 88(3), pp. 399–499.

Yuki, G. (1989). Managerial leadership: A review of theory and research. *Journal of Management*, 15(2), pp. 251–289.

Zacher, H., Pearce, L. K., Rooney, D. and McKenna, B. (2014). Leaders' personal wisdom and leader–member exchange quality: The role of individualized consideration. *Journal of Business Ethics*, 121(2), pp. 171–187.

Zhu, Y., Rooney, D. and Phillips, N. (2015). Practice-based wisdom theory for integrating institutional logics: A new model for social entrepreneurship learning and education. *Academy of Management Learning & Education*, 27 July. doi: 10.5465/amle.2013.0263.

Chapter 10

Educating future business leaders to be practically wise

Designing an MBA curriculum to strengthen good decision-making

Dennis W. Wittmer and Cynthia V. Fukami

> We are drowning in information, while starving for wisdom.
> The world henceforth will be run by synthesizers,
> people able to put together the right information at the right time,
> think critically about it, and make important choices wisely.
> (Wilson, 1998, p. 294)

A company with which the authors are familiar (GCI, a fictitious name) is in the business of distributing organic and natural products. It has had strong growth of both sales and earnings over the last 10 years, and one of its biggest strengths is the long-standing and trusting relationships it has built with its customers. GCI is known for treating employees well, and the employees are proud of GCI's commitment to sustainability and social responsibility. Recently, GCI was approached by a "big box" retailer, potentially representing over $300m annual business. If the deal were made, GCI would become the largest supplier of organic produce and other natural foods in its stores, with great growth projections. At the "eleventh hour" in negotiations, the big box retailer asked GCI to add several non-sustainable and non-natural products into its scope of supply, including motor oil and anti-freeze. This is the last step before signing the contract. What should GCI do? Which stakeholders matter most? What about its commitment to sustainability? What wise decision can be reached?

An MBA education involves learning to sharpen various skills and competencies, introduce various analytical techniques, and engage students with problems and situations that allow them to practise decision-making under conditions of uncertainty. At the heart of an MBA education are teachers helping students learn the practice of business. More directly related to an MBA education, teachers help students learn to be effective leaders and managers in the practice of business.

As indicated by the quote that opens this chapter, business (let alone the world) needs leaders who can make important decisions wisely. That does beg the question, "What are wise decisions in business?" While perhaps not answering that question directly, we will explore the nature of decision-making in business and how practical wisdom is a key competency in business decision-making. In an MBA program, students master a variety of skills, knowledge, and tools to be successful decision-makers – e.g. skills learned about finance, accounting, and statistics. Once they graduate and move into their professional roles, the problems that they face are likely to be messy (Schön, 1983), for which cookbook approaches will not be effective (Pearson d'Estree, 2013). They also are better decision-makers when they have various competencies or qualities. These may include, for example, being innovative, being an effective communicator, being self-aware, being empathetic, being able to formulate a shared vision for the team or organization, being a good listener, tolerating ambiguity, and many others.

Students also benefit from having experience in business and life prior to their MBA education. Some students will come with "natural" capacities that make them more practically wise as MBA students. There are those students who are "old souls," wise beyond their years. Some will have technical skills and theoretical groundings that allow them to have more time to practise integrating such knowledge. Regardless of the starting point, however, our contention is that an MBA education is about acquiring the necessary "know-how" and "know-why" for becoming more practically wise in decision-making. In short, our students need to be "artful" practitioners (Lang and Taylor, 2000) who can do more than solve merely technical problems (Pearson d'Estree, 2013). Practical wisdom, we believe, should be the *sine qua non* of an MBA education.

Aristotle on practical wisdom[1]

Unpacking this notion of practical wisdom is important if teachers are to be successful in helping students strengthen practical wisdom and decision-making. It is only appropriate to include in a discussion of practical wisdom the ideas of the Greek philosopher Aristotle, who is perhaps most associated with the virtue of practical wisdom, at least from a classical perspective. For Aristotle, practical wisdom is one of many virtues or excellences required in achieving fulfillment, happiness, and success in life. Virtues, character traits, or behavioral dispositions that are important for Aristotle include courage, self-control, honesty, generosity, and friendliness. Practical wisdom is one of these virtues, but it is not just one among many others. It is a chief (cardinal) virtue, along with courage, moderation, and justice.

Practical wisdom, as defined by Aristotle, is basically the excellence or competency to know what to do in specific situations, which is just what MBA students will be tasked with in their future managerial and leadership roles. At the heart of it, practical wisdom is the capacity and skill to grasp the particular context and relevant features of situations, the capacity to deliberate, and the ability to decide and act. Practical wisdom (*phronesis*) "is a true and reasoned state of capacity to act with regard to the things that are good or bad for man" (Aristotle, 1941, p. 1026). For Aristotle, practical wisdom is not theoretical wisdom or knowledge. Theoretical wisdom and knowledge (*sophia* and *episteme* in Greek) involve understanding the nature and relationships of things. As Aristotle says, "Scientific knowledge is judgement about things that are universal and necessary" (Aristotle, 1941, p. 1027). Practical wisdom, on the other hand, "is identified especially with that form of it which is concerned with a man himself – with the individual" (Aristotle, 1941, p. 1029).

In business, understanding Porter's Five Forces model (Porter, 1979), or the pros and cons of resource dependency theory (Pfeffer & Salancik, 1978) in strategic decision-making are examples of theoretical or scientific knowledge. Alternatively, it might be useful to understand theories of human motivation in workplace settings, including expectancy theory (Vroom, 1964), Maslow's hierarchy (Maslow, 1943), or operant conditioning (Skinner, 1938). One might benefit from such theoretical understanding and knowledge, and while one might be very smart and knowledgeable theoretically, one may still be bereft of practical wisdom in regards to applying any of this knowledge in specific situations. Consider the human ironies between having theoretical understanding and being able to practise or use the knowledge. A professor who teaches leadership and teams may yet be dictatorial and dogmatic in practice, unable to think about the good of the team or common good at all. A professor who teaches negotiation and mediation may be willing to participate in organizational change only if things change in his or her desired way.

Nor is practical wisdom the same as knowing how to do things (*techne*). "Every art [*techne*] is concerned with bringing something into being, and the practice of an art is the study of how to bring into being" (Aristotle, 1941, p. 1025). Having skills and techniques are important in business and other spheres of life, of course, but they do not constitute practical wisdom. Knowing how to calculate return on investment, how to do activity-based accounting, how to do financial forecasting, or how to use statistical tests to analyze data are all useful skills to possess in business. But knowing how to do any or all of these things does not constitute having practical wisdom in business. Rather, practical wisdom (*phronesis*) involves the practitioner using all tools and skills, as well as theoretical knowledge, in making decisions in particular situations when leading and managing groups or organizations. It is wisdom in knowing and understanding what to do, when something has to be done or decided, often when there are multiple perspectives, competing interests, uncertainty of outcomes, and various responsibilities to consider. Practical wisdom is the sense of what to do in situations where there are multiple paths and no clear and obvious ways forward. It is having the good sense to "see through a situation" to a wise and thoughtful decision. It is taking into account the particulars of a situation and finding a way to balance the relevant factors and interests that deserve consideration. This is the "stuff" of managerial and executive decision-making and the role for which MBA students are presumably preparing.

The context of learning and applying practical reason

Aristotle thought all activities had a purpose or goal (*telos*), which represented the end and good for that activity. As he says at the outset of the *Nicomachean Ethics*, "Every art and every inquiry, and similarly every action and pursuit, is thought to aim at some good" (Aristotle, 1941, p. 935). The end or good could be an activity itself, or a product of the activity. So, the good of carpentry is the thing being created, whereas the good of horseback riding is the activity of riding itself.

An important aspect of practical wisdom is that it is applied in a context, in a community, or in a practice with a purpose. Better decisions emerge when there is a clear goal or overarching purpose guiding deliberation and decision. By "better" we mean decisions that more fully and adequately address the problem and situational demands, as well as decisions that are more satisfying to various stakeholders. Each profession has these overarching goals. For example, when engineers decide what designs and materials to use in their work, decisions should be made in the context of public safety as guiding choices. For legislators, decisions should be guided by the public good or public welfare. For managers of publicly traded corporations decisions should be guided by what creates most value for stakeholders. With respect to education, the overarching goal is student learning. Curriculum decisions, then, should be guided by what maximizes student learning and achieves intended learning outcomes and student mastery.

A critical question with respect to an MBA education, therefore, is to uncover the purpose or goal of business generally and also of an MBA education in particular. What is the main purpose or objective of business and a business education? What is the fundamental end (*telos*) that should govern decision-making in the practice of business and management? With respect to an MBA education, what is the basic purpose that should guide learning about managerial and leadership decisions in organizations? Answers to these questions are not obvious as they would be for activities like carpentry and horseback riding, or even practising the profession of medicine where health and wellbeing of the patient are the fundamental goals. Activities and practices as complex as business or leadership and management do not lend themselves to quick answers. Nevertheless they are equally important, since making practically wise decisions would seem to hinge on having a more clear understanding of the *telos* or purpose of the activity.

Experience and becoming practically wise

Whether wisdom is associated with age and experience is, no doubt, debatable. Given the physical and mental decline that accompanies aging, one might reject the idea. Yet, wisdom may emerge from experience, assuming that reflection and learning also accompany that experience. Indeed, Aristotle was skeptical that young people had much practical wisdom:

> Whereas young people become accomplished in geometry and mathematics, and wise within these limits, prudent young people do not seem to be found. The reason is that prudence is concerned with particulars as well as universals, and particulars become known from experience, but a young person lacks experience, since some length of time is needed to produce it.
>
> (Aristotle, 1941, pp. 1029–30)

Learning can be enhanced from having more experience in life. Many MBA programs require some experience before admitting applicants. The assumption is that one needs to gain some experience in life and business before being able to fully appreciate and benefit from an MBA education.

With experience it seems that we tend to have a better understanding of context and all those particulars that deserve consideration in a decision. With longer tenure in an organization, the more one understands how other individual members are likely to act or respond. The longer one practices a profession, the more completely aware one is of the full range of responsibilities one has to clients, stakeholders, and the public. The more experience one has about marketing and pricing new products, the more one understands the likely factors that will affect customer acceptance. Experience matters, and that is why wisdom is often associated with age.

So, does this imply that practical wisdom, however valuable, cannot be taught in academic programs? Is it the case that wisdom is only acquired from experience and that one must simply work and live longer to acquire more practical experience, and hence wisdom? Just having experience is not sufficient, of course. One must learn from what happens in life. One must reflect, evaluate, and draw lessons of life from experience. Notwithstanding the wisdom of gaining wisdom from experience, there is still reason to believe that decision-making can be practiced and hence learned, at least to some degree, in the course of an MBA program.

The American educator and philosopher John Dewey (1934) talked about the importance of "funded experience." Works of art, new innovations, or practically wise decisions do not come as insight *ex nihilo*. Rather, they come from prior experience, work, and preparation, that serves as funding of experiences. Our working assumption and contention in this chapter is that practical wisdom will continue to evolve and mature with experience, while students bring their own funded experience when they enter educational programs. Therefore students can develop and grow their practical wisdom with practice, whether through simulations, case studies, applied projects, debates, and/or discussion.

Digging deeper into practical wisdom

Before discussing more specifically how practical wisdom might be strengthened in MBA programs, it may be worth probing a bit further some features and aspects of practical wisdom and practically wise persons. Here we will draw on a recent and lucid book by Barry Schwartz and Kenneth Sharpe (2010), who capture some essential features of practical wisdom and what it takes to be practically wise. They state, "It [practical wisdom] depended on our ability to perceive the situation, to have appropriate feelings or desires about it, to deliberate about was appropriate in the circumstances, and to act" (Schwartz and Sharpe, 2010, p. 5).

Schwartz and Sharpe relate a wonderful example that captures practical wisdom in a very ordinary kind of situation. When dissected (in part from an interview afterward) the decision reveals important elements and features of practically wise choices and actions. A custodian, Luke, cleaned the hospital room of a very ill young man, whose father had been consistently at his son's bedside, but happened to be absent during this day's cleaning. Since he did not see the custodian clean the room, he proceeded to berate the custodian, demanding that Luke clean the room immediately. After some brief consideration, Luke simply cleaned the room again. An interview with Luke later revealed that Luke had an understandable initial reaction of being defensive and a bit angry. He could have repeated to the father that he cleaned the room and reported the incident to his supervisor. He could have held out for what was fair and just. He could have protected his honor. Moreover, he could have asserted his right to be treated fairly and with dignity. Or he could have brought in a supervisor immediately to handle the conflict. However, when he thought about the stress the father was experiencing and the fact that the father was convinced the room had not been cleaned, Luke decided to simply clean the room again. Luke said, "But I wasn't angry with him. I guess I could understand."

We think most would agree that Luke made a very wise, if not generous, decision. Perhaps not only was the decision wise, but he conducted himself wisely and thoughtfully. Applying the earlier quote about the features of practical wisdom, Luke perceived the situation from not only his own perspective but from the perspective of the father. Luke was able to empathize with the father. Luke also managed to regulate his own emotions of anger and defensiveness because of that empathy. Luke was also aware of options and was able to deliberate about what was appropriate for the specific circumstances and situation. Finally, he acted in a self-chosen manner consistent with how he had processed the situation.

From this and other examples Schwartz and Sharpe (2010) suggest some key aspects of practically wise people. Included in their discussion is a list of the features of practically wise people:

- They understand the goal (*telos*) of the activity and frame their decision-making in that context. For Luke, he went beyond his limited job description, and he viewed himself and his job as part of the practice of medical care.
- They are perceptive in reading social context and move beyond rules to appreciate the gray areas and decide in that context. Luke might have seen the father's demands as violating a principle of justice, but instead he saw the larger context of a father's care and concern for his son.
- They can take on the perspectives of others affected by decisions. They have empathy and can both feel and think from others' perspectives. Luke was able to understand the father's stress and emotional reaction; he was able feel and imagine what the father was experiencing. He could put himself in the shoes of the father and thereby regulate his own emotions.
- They know how to balance competing rules and goals in the context of particular situations. Luke understood multiple goals, principles, and rules that could apply in the situation, and he chose a path that reflected ordering and priority.

We will now turn our attention to how these insights on the practical wisdom of Luke help to illuminate needed change in MBA education.

The gap between knowing and doing[2]

As we argue above, if practical wisdom (*phronesis*) is the combination of theoretical knowledge (*episteme*) and experience (*techne*), then another way to conceptualize practical wisdom is through the gap between knowing and doing (Pfeffer & Sutton, 1999). In classic educational systems, excellence is often defined as intellectual performance (Martin and Martinez de Pison, 2005). Knowledge is defined as information possessed, and the primary role of a teacher is to convey information (*episteme*). Our classrooms, thus, are places where educators dispense knowledge and our students soak it up, to varying degrees of effectiveness on either side. Some have referred to this process as the "conveyor belt" model of communication. The student's performance in the class is evaluated on the basis of how much of this knowledge can be recalled in short-run, 10–16 week assignments, and the educator's teaching performance is evaluated at least in part by how effectively she or he has conveyed this knowledge. When the academic term is over, the student puts away (or forgets) this short-term information and may not access it again in other courses.

On the other hand, what to do with this knowledge (*techne*), is often left out of the picture. There is an old adage – if the only tool you have is a hammer, then every problem looks like a nail. Why is it that many excellent companies, such as Southwest Airlines, don't recruit at leading business schools, and don't show a preference for hiring MBAs

(Pfeffer and Sutton, 1999)? None other than Elon Musk and Peter Thiel, the founders of PayPal, along with other entrepreneurial ventures, have strongly argued against hiring MBAs (Tabis, 2016). Perhaps it is because our graduates possess a lot of information, but have difficulty translating knowledge into practice. In other words, perhaps they lack practical wisdom.

There have been a number of notable critiques of business education on this point. In part, they are directed at the failure to provide what is needed for developing an appropriate management style and practice. Management concepts and programs have been criticized for destroying good management practices. Ghoshal (2005) argued that business schools have been complicit in the current state of unethical behavior in organizations. "Many of the worst excesses of recent management practices have their roots in a set of ideas that have emerged from business school academics over the last 30 years" (Ghoshal, 2005, p. 75). In addition, there have been calls for a critical reappraisal of business education (e.g., Colby, Ehrlich, Sullivan, & Dolle, 2011; Mintzberg, 2004). Some have argued that these problems have arisen from the movement toward scientific rigor (*episteme*) among business schools and away from practical relevance (*techne*) (Armstrong & Fukami, 2009). Rather than thinking of business as an academic discipline, such as chemistry or physics, Bennis and O'Toole (2005) have argued that business should be viewed as a profession, like medicine and law. In professional education, knowledge and practice are integrated.

In a highly regarded and well-cited essay, Pfeffer and Fong (2002) made three remarkable conclusions. First, there has been little assessment of the impact of business schools on either their graduates or on the profession. Second, what assessments do exist suggest that business schools are not particularly effective. Third, there is little evidence that business schools have influenced management practice. Others have reported similar findings. One such study reported that 73 percent of the surveyed MBA program graduates indicated that they made little use of what they had learned in the classroom on their first assignments as managers (McCall Jr., Lombardo, & Morrison, 1988). When students successfully graduate from an MBA program, they must have performed to a standard, implying that they have gained a "passing" level of knowledge. Yet, the results listed above imply that these students were unable or unwilling to put their knowledge into practice.

Similar results were reported in a study by Baldwin and his associates (Baldwin, Pierce, Joines, & Farouk, 2011). In an extensive study of both practising managers and current students, they found modest relationships between academic performance and applied managerial knowledge. They conclude that "Acquiring applied management knowledge is a more formidable challenge than simple declarative or procedural knowledge and yet is a key to the effectiveness of practising managers" (Baldwin *et al.*, 2011, p. 587). They also comment on the wasted resources we are committing to ineffective educational systems. We couldn't agree more, and believe that the concept of practical wisdom can help us provide more value for our students' educational investments.

In short, practical wisdom implies the integration and transformation of knowledge (Eastham, 1992), such that knowledge is interpreted and applied within a context. The difference between knowledge and wisdom, then, is that wisdom requires context and perspective in applying. Thus, we must combine *techne* and *episteme* in MBA education.

How can practical wisdom be strengthened through formal education?

> The key to pursuing excellence is to embrace an organic, long-term learning process, and not to live in a shell of static, safe mediocrity. Usually growth comes at the expense of previous comfort and safety.
>
> (Waitzkin, 2007, p. 33)

So, assuming that practical wisdom can be learned and strengthened in academic programs, specifically in MBA programs, what strategies might be utilized? In an interesting book, titled *How We Decide* (2009), Jonah Lehrer explores how the airline industry came to solve what seemed an intractable problem of not being able to reduce the incidence of accidents caused by pilot error. The percentage of flight accidents due to human error remained constant (about 65 percent) over a 50-year period (1940–90). Many solutions to the problem were tried, including mandatory layovers for pilots and more classroom training, but without any significant change in the incidence of these accidents. The solution would be, in effect, getting pilots to make better and more practically wise decisions.

Then technology advanced, as did the approach to addressing the issue. Now less than 30 percent of accidents are due to bad decision-making by the pilots and crew, after a 50-year period at 65 percent. What was responsible for this reduction? Lehrer identifies three changes to explain the improvement in performance. First is the use of flight simulators. Technology improved greatly, allowing pilots to practise decision-making in sophisticated simulation devices. While not real, the situations feel real in a flight simulator. Lehrer argues that training in simulators trains the brain to respond better (more wisely) to crisis situations. The old way consisted of classroom lecture and hearing about worst-case scenarios and what to do.

The educational delivery model in higher education has historically followed a rather similar model, it would seem. "The problem with this approach," Roberts [CAE officer] says, "is that everything was abstract. The pilot has his body of knowledge, but they'd never applied it before" (Lehrer, 2009, p. 252). That is, the pilots were told what might happen, what to expect, and what to do. But they never really practiced in any systematic fashion. As we have argued earlier, isn't that more or less true of most approaches to teaching in higher education? Students learn a lot about the topic, read, and perhaps even apply theory to problems. Then they take exams to prove that they "know" the theories, tools, and perhaps a bit how to apply them. But they spend little, if no, time to systematically put them to use in business, leadership, and management situations.

Lehrer identifies another component of the new training of pilots and crews critical to its success – exhaustive debriefings following the flight simulation scenarios. Instructors scrutinize the decision-making, so pilots learn from their mistakes. Practising situations and scenarios, followed by critical assessment, became the way of learning. This is similar to a standard practice in hospitals called the "M&M" meeting, where each mistake occurring during the care of patients is reviewed by your peers. After all, whenever learning a skill, the way we master it is through practice and feedback.

In *Outliers* (2008), Malcolm Gladwell argued that one of the key factors in success and achievement is the 10,000-hour rule, or about ten years of hard and sustained practice. To really become proficient, to achieve expert status, one must practice over a significant period, as implied by Dreyfus' (2004) five-stage model of adult skill acquisition, moving from novice to expert. Again this may speak to the importance of time and experience being critical in becoming practically wise. It is doubtful that students would pay for a ten-year program, but like the pilot training, at least an MBA program can put them in sustained decision-making situations to optimize learning and strengthen their practical wisdom during their time in the program. We should remember that in the case of flight simulation training, the debriefing and critical analysis of decision-making was essential in terms of learning. Likewise, in an MBA program, the role of teacher may need to shift more to that of coach, evaluator, and mentor. That may also be true for other peer students in the program who can serve as other sources of evaluation and feedback. Mutually we can all help each other to grow and develop good decision-making skills and cultivate practical wisdom.

The third factor that led to improvements for airline crews was something referred to as "Cockpit Resource Management" (CRM). The idea came from a tragedy in which pilots did not use information from members of the crew, who had important information and perspective in a crisis situation. Rather than depending on the "God-like certainty" of pilots, CRM training requires pilots and members of the crew to practise soliciting and expressing a diversity of viewpoints in crises. They practice creating and valuing different perspectives on a problem. Weick and Putnam (2006) make a similar point in their development of the concept of mindfulness. In studying organizations where high-reliability is critical, they found that a decreased dependence on concepts and an increased focus on context will lead to wise action. Schön (1983) refers to this as the need to be reflective, both while engaged in practice, as well as after the fact.

This is precisely the method of Giving Voice to Values (GVV) suggested by Mary Gentile (2010). A key is to develop a value for soliciting and listening to other points of view, and continual practice among all members of teams to "give voice" to their views:

> The main idea behind Giving Voice to Values (GVV) is the observation that a focus on *awareness* of ethical issues and on *analysis* of what the right thing to do may be insufficient. Precious little time is spent on *action* – that is, developing the 'scripts' and implementation plans for responding to the commonly heard 'reasons and rationalizations' for questionable practices, and actually practising the delivery of those scripts.
>
> (Gentile, 2010, p. xiii, emphasis in original)

There is a likely link between this CRM system and an MBA education. From a leadership and management perspective, it makes sense to teach students about the importance of teams and team decision-making. Like the God-like pilot as decision-maker, business has a traditional myth of the strong and charismatic CEO as God-like as well. To foster a business CRM system, an MBA education needs to emphasize the responsibility of leaders for creating an environment where everyone is willing to have a voice and to express contrary points of view without reprisal. Similar to corporate environments in which management teams discuss and make decisions, an MBA education can include more scenarios for decision-making where students alternate playing roles of team leaders and team members. Then students can practice how they would actually solicit key stakeholders' perspectives, and, just as important, how they would communicate that all perspectives are valued in arriving at a practically wise decision.

The importance of seeking multiple perspectives is also noted by Peter Senge. In *The Fifth Discipline*, Senge (1990) reflects on the importance of mental models in human interaction. A mental model is one person's view of how the world, or a piece of the world, works. For example, one person's mental model of how to succeed in business may be that he should work very hard and accomplish exceptional productivity, and that his hard work will be rewarded with success. Another person's mental model of how to succeed in business may be that there is no point to working hard because you have no control over who will be rewarded. A leader in this situation, trying to solve the problem of a lack of motivation in the workforce, will need to be aware of both perspectives in order to adequately address the problem.

These ideas are hardly foreign in the MBA classroom. In fact, they are central to many analyses of effective leadership. In other words, business school educators have for many years argued that effective leaders are those, who communicate well, who are "considerate" to their employees, who empower their employees, and who can take multiple perspectives into account (Bolman & Deal, 2013). If these attributes are important in effective leadership, should we not emphasize them in our teaching?[3]

In the past, business school faculties were largely composed of experienced and reflective practitioners. These were individuals who did not have terminal degrees, but rather, had many years of experience from which they drew in the classroom. Over time, as schools started producing more PhDs in business, these "enlightened" practitioners became less common and faculty became more "scholarly" in the traditional sense of the word. The growth in the power of the AACSB as accrediting body also contributed to this shift away from practitioners to researchers, as the acceptable number of non-terminally "qualified" faculty delivering a particular program was capped and the number of refereed journal publications by each faculty member was carefully counted. It is interesting to note that, as it often does, the pendulum is swinging in the other direction as the AACSB has begun to recognize the value of practitioners as faculty members (AACSB, 2013).

Part of the trend toward research among business school faculty can also be attributed to the uneasy relationship of professional schools and traditional departments in a university setting. At least in part, our push for research may have been fueled by our quest to be taken seriously in academia. Nonetheless, if practical wisdom is the marriage of knowing and doing, experienced teachers with theoretical and practical knowledge must play an important role in the classroom.

In other words, can wisdom be taught by those who aren't wise themselves? As the old adage goes, "those who can, do ... those who can't, teach." Would our students be wiser if they were taught by life-long practitioners instead of life-long scholars? Perhaps, but the end product may merely be a shift from the wisdom of *episteme* to the wisdom of *techne*. *Phronesis*, or practical wisdom, would still be missing. So, what's to be done about this? In this vein, it would be fruitful to explore the related concept of poietic *phronesis*, which recognizes the artistry needed to creatively adapt theory and practice (Küpers, 2013). In her paper on Conflict Resolution as a profession, Pearson d'Estree (2013) argues that today's professional must be able to deal with complexity and surprise:

> Professionals today require a competence that is not merely the mastery of a substantive body of knowledge, nor the initiation into a brotherhood of experts. Professional competence would be based on the capacity to learn how to learn, the ability to create a working theory that is continually modified under real-time conditions .... What is needed most for modern professionals to be adaptive and responsive is practical knowledge.
>
> (Pearson d'Estree, 2013, p. 89)

These ideas have been mirrored in a rather remarkable program at Harvard Medical School (HMS) that uses visual arts training to improve physician performance (Katz & Khoshbin, 2014). Based on studies that showed the importance of balancing humanities education with scientific education (Seyal, 2013) and the connection between the lack of humanities education and ethical lapses among physicians (Coles, 1979), HMS created a program designed to integrate visual arts training to improve various skills of medical students. These skills include the need for multidisciplinary teamwork, meditation and reflection, improved diagnosis, empathy, and improvisation. Katz and Khoshbin (2014) argue that these skills are the more difficult to teach, and that they combine left-brain and right-brain activities. Extensive assessment of the effects of this program has not yet been reported, though feedback on the program from various stakeholders has been "overwhelmingly positive; enrollment requests for the elective ... course consistently exceed the number of positions available" (Katz & Khoshbin, 2014, p. 339).

Based on the promise of the work done in other professional disciplines, we have optimism about the development of practical wisdom in business eduction. We now turn to a discussion of some avenues with this potential.

Embedding practical wisdom in business education

We have presented a case for developing practical wisdom in graduate business education. At this point, we will turn to ideas and suggestions for the development of practical wisdom in our curricula. We will start by contrasting the different assumptions in traditional business education with the assumptions inherent in a new approach. Next, we will build on the assumptions by providing specific recommendations. In this section, we take a stakeholder approach as a foundation for our argument. We include students, faculty, and administrators as the stakeholders most critical to developing practical wisdom.

It is useful to recall that the term "education" comes from the Latin root, "*educere*," which means "to lead out." To "*educe*" means "*to bring out or develop*." Even a casual observer of our traditional educational systems would find this definition to be out of place. All too often, we view ourselves as "professors" or "instructors," rather than as educators. An instructor provides "detailed information telling how something should be done," and "provides directions or orders." A professor "affirms a faith in or allegiance to something," while an educator is "one who develops others" (Oxford Online Dictionary, 2015) As we have argued above, a cursory examination of the techniques and methods used by our colleagues suggests that most behave as "instructors" who are conveying information, rather than as "educators," and that this is one of the most important reasons for the lack of practical wisdom in our graduates.

Table 10.1 Attributes of "education" versus "instruction" by stakeholder

	Educational approach	*Instructional approach*
Students	Engaged in "problem-solving inquiry"	Satisfied with mastery of facts and theories
	Assume responsibility for their learning and the learning of fellow students	Rely on faculty to direct student learning and motivate students to learn
	Enhance their perceptual skills in terms of identifying critical particulars of situations	
	Constantly practising how to balance competing perspectives with innovative and creative solutions	Simply apply decision-making rules and procedures in solving business problems
	Comfortable with giving and taking critical evaluation of problem solving from peers and instructor	
Faculty	Create an environment where teams of students are responsible for wrestling with business problems and issues	Lecture and tell students what they need to know
	Emphasize the importance of judgment and developing practical wisdom in business	Emphasize the importance of memorizing and applying decision rules and frameworks
	Constantly challenge students to appreciate the complexity and uncertainty of problems	Measure the success of students learning almost exclusively with problems that require simple application of decision rules
	Coach students in developing critical competencies and skills	
	View their role more as facilitator, coach, mentor	View their role more as content expert, disseminator of knowledge, and disciplinarian
Administration	Create relatively autonomous teaching teams	
	Reward both team and individual performance	Create incentives that undermine team unity
	With clear focus on core learning outcomes, allow teaching teams to design student assessment and evaluation	Create rigid standards of student performance that undermine innovative teaching to achieve fundamental goals

How does the process of education differ from the process of instruction? Table 10.1 provides our assessment of the attributes of each system from the perspective on each of our three stakeholders: students, faculty, and administration.

Students

In the traditional, instructional approach, students rely on faculty to direct their learning, and to motivate them to learn. Students expect rewards (good grades) for following the rules, which usually involve mastery of facts and theories. At most, students may be placed in case-based decision scenarios, where they make decisions based on the rules of the theories they have learned. Rarely are students expected to link information from one course to another.

In contrast, in the educational approach, students are engaged in problem-solving, and are constantly practising how to balance competing solutions by reframing problems and perspective taking. Students understand the importance of context in applying theories. They assume responsibility for their own learning, and also for the learning of their peers. In short, they are learning to solve problems as much as they are learning disciplinary content.

Faculty

In the traditional approach, faculty act as professors and instructors. They hold the knowledge necessary for successful completion of the courses and the degree program. They disseminate their knowledge to students, and test the knowledge through examinations and projects where correct use of theory is assessed. Learning is likely to be short-term as memorization of theories is emphasized. Assurance of learning is provided through demonstrations of the lower levels of Bloom's Taxonomy (1956): simple application, rather than synthesis as suggested by our opening quote.

Thinking about the educational approach suggests that faculty members would create an environment where there are few universal truths, and where context and perspective lead to greater understanding. Faculty understand the importance of developing skills in their students along with understanding theory; these skills include critical thinking and decision-making under conditions of ambiguity.

Overall, the classroom is thereby converted from a theater to a laboratory or studio where students are provided with challenges to approach and to debate these approaches. Rather than disseminating knowledge, faculty are coaches and mentors, developing and facilitating the educational process.

Administrators

There is a difficult environment today facing higher education administration in general and business education in particular. Stakeholders are demanding more from educational institutions: assurance of learning, enrollment declines, and rising costs, just to name a few. The traditional, instructional, approach has created reward systems that focus on disciplinary scholarship to the detriment of the teaching role. We are encouraged to produce research and to complete our teaching assignments as individual contributors, rather than as team members. As a result, there is little sharing of best practices as faculty are rewarded competitively – why should I help a colleague to be more effective if it means that my pay increase might be adversely affected? In this way, innovative teaching is stifled.

If administrators were to use an "education" approach, we expect the situation to be markedly different. Reward systems would be adjusted to reflect collaboration and teamwork. Learning objectives would form the basis of assessment and assurance of learning. Finally, teams would guide behavior and identify best practices because the reward system would stop punishing such behavior and instead would encourage it. Most critically, teams of faculty would include multiple perspectives: those with theoretical knowledge would be paired with those with practical knowledge, thus providing the ingredients for practical wisdom.

Specific interventions in MBA education

Now that we have set the stage for the two different extreme models, we will now explore the specific interventions that are being used, or should be used, to increase practical wisdom in graduate business education. Implementing a belief in this "educational approach" will be limited only by faculty imagination and ingenuity. We will offer a few ideas, but individuals and teams of faculty members will surely discover other creative delivery methods. Indeed, it might be interesting to have a community on social media to share ideas, experiments, and results.

From the outset, we note that the pursuit of wisdom requires a close, almost apprenticeship relationship, between the learner and the expert (Talbot, 2004). But we must recognize the barriers to such a significant relationship between faculty and students, not the least of which is time. Thus, developing wisdom will be more difficult in environments that contain large classrooms, or, do not provide significant rewards for teaching excellence. It will also require the development of certain capabilities.

Lang and Taylor (2000) describe these capabilities as "artistry," and Schön (1987) argues that "In the terrain of professional practice, applied science and research-based technique occupy a critically important though limited territory, bounded on several sides by artistry" (p. 13). Artistry includes how problems are framed, how solutions are implemented, and improvisation. He concludes that professional education needs to include both experiential learning and good coaching, which are present in disciplines with a studio tradition, such as art (Pearson d'Estree, 2013).

Finally, we note that the following ideas are not merely our suggestions; rather, they are part of an overall comprehensive redesign of the MBA program at our institution, the "Daniels College of Business," where we are creating our own laboratory for the development of practical wisdom.

Challenges and competencies – not just courses

At the heart of embracing the educate-not-instruct model may be how one thinks about constructing the learning environment. Faculty have learned in a system of classes, credit hours, and the usual methods for tracking learning. Take a course in statistical methods, pass it, and move on to the next element in the curriculum. A new model might frame the goal as a set of challenges which develop competencies that are important in becoming good (practically wise) decision-makers. This requires teachers to consider a bit more systematically just what students should be able to do as a result of their time learning. The identified competencies, then, drive the challenges that might be created to develop and measure performance.

Problem-based learning and challenges

The context for developing competencies could be live problems that require identified competencies. Case studies are a typical way to teach problem-solving. However, usually cases are written with a fairly specific focus, and teaching notes are written to teach in a relatively narrow way. Live cases, of course, are not always easy to find. The payoffs of investing the time to find such cases are the relationships with potential employers and business community, as well the messy and ill-defined nature of the problems themselves.

Just-in-time content (JiTC)

Having students attack ill-defined problems should lead to the value of theoretical concepts and business tools to address the situations. Teachers, then, demonstrate expertise by being able to provide readings, materials, and lectures that will give students the knowledge and skills required to deal more effectively with the situation.

An example

A mining company is considering opening a mine in South America, and they would like another assessment of the value and viability of having a successful operation in this country. Students are provided with background information about the company, they sign confidentiality agreements, are introduced to the situation by a high-level company official, and then are given the task of taking on the project as a consulting team. With a faculty team of content experts as resources, students meet daily and are given ten weeks to develop a written and oral report to the company. The student teams figure out what they need, and faculty teams and staff are responsible for providing the tools, skills, and knowledge required. Suddenly the students must confront all the things they need in terms of quantitative tools, cross-cultural management, legal and public policy requirements, ethical and social responsibility frameworks, strategic positioning frameworks, organizational structure options, written and presentation skills, and understanding about team effectiveness and team dynamics. In effect, this forms the curriculum for the quarter and provides a vehicle for determining competency in these various areas. Moreover, with regular meetings with faculty as mentors and facilitators, faculty members are in a position to ask the kinds of questions to get students to discover useful concepts and tools that students may be missing. Presentation and writing coaches work with student teams to perfect their products. Student teams present their analyses to managers and executives in the company, and then assuming some level of success, teams celebrate and call it a day. Not so fast – something more is needed.

Debriefing and assessment

The learning should not stop with the presentation and delivery of the written report. This is where faculty play a critical role again and demonstrate their expertise. Faculty can serve as facilitators in debriefing the process and product. Team effectiveness would be one of those items. The team could review the attributes of highly effective teams, and then assess team performance, as well as providing each other with individual feedback. In addition, debriefing of the process itself, that is, how the team attacked the problem and how the process could be more effective and efficient in the next project. Moreover, a review could be done of the critical elements of knowledge and theory, as well as skills and competencies, perhaps creating the team's own checklist for future projects.

Reflection on the "*telos*" of the practice of business

As we indicated previously, practical wisdom and good decision-making should be grounded in the fundamental nature and purpose of a practice, whether law, medical care, or business. Some time can be spent debriefing the project in terms of how students have discovered (had insights) into the nature of business as a professional practice. What did they learn about stakeholders, guiding values, core principles of the practice, and balancing competing priorities and needs of those affected by their evaluation?

In general, what we are advocating is nothing less than our colleagues in the field of education have been advocating for years. For example, Newmann and Wehlage (1993) provided *five standards of authentic learning*. These include:

- higher-order thinking, such as the use of Bloom's Taxonomy and approaches to critical thinking;
- deep knowledge, such as the use of ill-defined problems;
- connection to the world, such as emphasizing the relevance of the material;
- substantive conversation, such as active engagement between students and faculty;
- social support for achievement, such as mentoring and encouragement.

Using a framework such as this will help guide the decisions of educators in providing opportunities to develop practical wisdom within business school curricula. Fortunately, schools of business have access to organizations and journals that contribute to the scholarship of searching and learning (e.g., Academy of Management Learning and Education, the Organizational Behavior Teaching Society), which provide forums for disseminating ideas for good teaching methods.

Conclusions

We offered at the outset that practical wisdom in an MBA education would simply involve helping students to become better decision-makers with respect to business problems. Then we drew on several wise scholars to help us unpack some of the attributes of practical wisdom. Following the specifics just discussed in terms of implementing an MBA curriculum, we see that the approached described included the following:

- reflection on the *telos* or fundamental purpose of business;
- simulation (real problems in this case) as a vehicle for strengthening skills and competencies;
- debriefing as a critical component in learning;
- group decision-making and team management as a mechanism for getting better decision-making;
- focus on the particulars of a situation, rather than abstract ideas and rules disconnected from real-word problems;
- development of empathy and social context by having to consider numerous stakeholders;
- practice in balancing principles and particulars, balancing the competing interests of stakeholders and balancing the various skills and talents of member of a team.

We also urge the use of the scholarship of teaching and learning to gather and disseminate tools and techniques for supporting these goals. It is critical for educators to use evidence-based teaching pedagogy (Charlier, Brown, & Rynes, 2011), to monitor and assess for student learning, not just satisfaction (Sitzmann, Ely, Brown, & Bauer, 2010), and to aim for authentic learning (Newmann & Wehlage, 1993).

This chapter has been an academic analysis and discussion of a pressing problem for MBA education, with wider application to higher education and more, no doubt. We have provided a framework and arguments for change. Yet, if we are true to our own argument and model, we should consider how this might be implemented into existing programs. One option would be to present and lecture about the model, i.e. tell faculty and administrators how they should change. However, to be true to our own principles, it would be better to try a different way. Perhaps one could first frame the issue as a challenge or problem to be solved. Most MBA programs should be open to change these days. The environment is changing, and the external pressures are increasing. After setting the context for change, faculty and administrators could attack this as a challenge. Perhaps they could probe and discuss the "*telos*" of an MBA program. If the "*telos*" is thought to be practical wisdom (by other names perhaps), the next issue will be the appropriate means to achieve that goal. That could open the door for offering some of the ideas presented here in terms of flight simulators and challenge-based education. It is perhaps important to remind ourselves that practical wisdom is context specific. Finding the "right" curricular changes will need to be sensitive to the particular faculty, institutional history, and other situational factors. Faculty and administrators will have to find their own way of being practically wise as educators.

Overall, we must create classrooms that are forums for communities to generate knowledge, together; to share, to vet, to critique, to reflect, to improvise, and to improve. We must create communities of inquiry (Pearson d'Estree, 2013). Our stakeholders, administrators, faculty, and students, as well as our ultimate customers, public and private sector organizations, will be the wiser for our efforts.

Notes

1 Perhaps the most extensive and systematic discussion of Aristotle's conception of practical wisdom is found in Chapters 5–13 of Book VI of the *Nichomachean Ethics*.
2 This section is based on an earlier chapter by the second author (Fukami, 2010).
3 This section is based on an earlier chapter by the second author (Fukami, 2010).

References

AACSB (2013). *2013 Accreditation Standards*. Retrieved from www.aacsb.edu/accreditation/standards/2013-standards.

Aristotle (1941). Nicomachean ethics. In R. McKeon (Ed.), *The basic works of Aristotle*. New York: Random House.

Armstrong, S. & Fukami, C. (2009). Past, present and future perspectives of management learning, education and development. In S. Armstrong and C. Fukami (Eds.), *The Sage handbook of management learning, education and development*. London: Sage, 1–22.

Baldwin, T., Pierce, J., Joines, R., & Farouk, S. (2011). The elusiveness of applied management knowledge: A critical challenge for management educators. *Academy of Management Learning & Education*, 10(4), 583–605.

Bennis, W. & O'Toole, J. (2005). How business schools lost their way. *Harvard Business Review*, May, 96–104.

Bloom, B. (1956). *Taxonomy of educational objectives, handbook I: The cognitive domain*. New York: David McKay and Co.

Bolman, L. & Deal, T. (2013) *Reframing organizations: Artistry, choice, and leadership*. 5th edition. San Francisco, CA: John Wiley & Sons.

Charlier, S., Brown, K., & Rynes, S. (2011). Teaching evidence-based management in MBA programs: What evidence is there? *Academy of Management Learning & Education*, 10(2), 222–236.

Colby, A., Ehrlich, T., Sullivan, W.M., & Dolle, J.R. (2011). *Rethinking undergraduate business education: Liberal learning for the profession*. New York: Jossey-Bass.

Coles, R. (1979). Occasional notes. Medical ethics and living a life. *New England Journal of Medicine*, 301(8), 444–446.

Dewey, J. (1934). *Art as experience*. New York: Capricorn Books.

Dreyfus, S.E. (2004). The five-stage model of adult skill acquisition. *Bulletin of Science Technology & Society*, 24, 177–181.

Eastham, S. (1992). How is wisdom communicated? Prologue to peace studies. *Interculture*, 25, 1–33.

Fukami, C.V. (2010). In search of enlightened leaders. In J. O'Toole & D. Mayer (Eds.), *Good business: Exercising effective and ethical leadership*. New York: Routledge, 44–57.

Gentile, M.C. (2010). *Giving voice to values*. New Haven, CT: Yale University Press.

Ghoshal, S. (2005). Bad management theories are destroying good management practice. *Academy of Management Learning and Education*, 4: 75–91.

Gladwell, M. (2008). *Outliers: The story of success*. New York: Little, Brown.

Katz, J.T. & Khoshbin, A. (2014). Can visual arts training improve physician performance? *Transactions of the American Clinical and Climatological Association*, 125, 331–342.

Küpers, W. (2013). The art of practical wisdom: Phenomenology of an embodied, wise inter-practice in organisation and leadership. In W. Küpers & D. Pauleen (Eds.), *A handbook of practical wisdom: Leadership, organization and integral business practice*. London: Ashgate Gower, 19–45.

Lang, M.E. & Taylor, A. (2000). *The making of a mediator: Developing artistry in practice*. San Francisco, CA: Jossey-Bass.

Lehrer, J. (2009). *How we decide*. New York: Mariner Books, Houghton Mifflin Harcourt.

Martin, M. & de Pison, M. (2005). From knowledge to wisdom: A new challenge to the educational milieu with implications for religious education. *Religious Education*, 100, 157–173.

Maslow, A.H. (1943). A theory of human motivation. *Psychological Review*, 50, 370–396.

McCall Jr., M., Lombardo, M., & Morrison, A. (1988). *The lessons of experience: How successful executives develop on the job*. Lexington, MA: Lexington Books.

Mintzberg, H. (2004). *Managers not MBAs: A hard look at the soft practice of managing and management development*. San Francisco, CA: Berrett-Hoehle.

Newmann, F. & Wehlage, G. (1993). Five standards of authentic instruction. *Educational Leadership*, 50(7), 8–12.

Oxford Online Dictionary (2015). URL: http://dictionary.oed.com/

Pearson d'Estree, T. (2013). Conflict resolution as a profession and the need for communities of inquiry. *International Journal of Conflict Engagement and Resolution*, 1(1), 83–95.

Pfeffer, J. & Fong, C. (2002). The end of business schools? Less success than meets the eye. *Academy of Management Learning & Education*, (1), 78–95.

Pfeffer, J. & Salancik, G. (1978). *The external control of organizations: A resource dependence perspective*. New York: Harper & Row.

Pfeffer, J. & Sutton, R. (1999). Knowing "what" to do is not enough: Turning knowledge into action. *California Management Review*, (42), 83–10.

Porter, M. (1979). How competitive forces shape strategy. *Harvard Business Review*, 57, 137–145.
Schön, D.A. (1983). *The reflective practitioner*. San Francisco, CA: Jossey-Bass.
Schön, D.A. (1987). *Educating the reflective practitioner*. San Francisco, CA: Jossey-Bass.
Schwartz, B. & Sharpe, K. (2010). *Practical wisdom: The right way to do the right thing*. New York: Riverhead Books.
Senge, P. (1990) *The fifth discipline*. New York: Doubleday Business.
Seyal, M.S. (2013). Abraham Flexner: His life and legacy. *Journal of Medical Humanities*, 5(3). Available at: www.hektoeninternational.org/index.php?option=com_content&view=article&id=162:abraham-flexner-his-life-and-legacy&catid=18&Itemid=611 [Accessed January 24, 2016].
Sitzmann, T., Ely, K., Brown, K., & Bauer, K. (2010). Self-Assessment of knowledge: A cognitive learning or affective measure? *Academy of Management Learning & Education*, 9(2), 169–191.
Skinner, B.F. (1938). *The behavior of organisms: An experimental analysis*. New York: Appleton-Century.
Tabis, J. (2016). Why you shouldn't disregard MBA hires, no matter what Peter Thiel or Elon Musk say. *Huffington Post*. January 10, 2015.
Talbot, M. (2004). Good wine may need to mature: A critique of accelerated higher specialist training: Evidence from cognitive neuroscience. *Medical Education*, 38, 399–408.
Vroom, V. (1964). *Work and motivation*. New York: Wiley.
Waitzkin, J. (2007). *The art of learning: A journey in the pursuit of excellence*. New York: Free Press.
Weick, K. & Putnam, T. (2006). Organizing for mindfulness: Eastern wisdom and western knowledge. *Journal of Management Inquiry*, 15, 275–287.
Wilson, E.O. (1998) *Consilience: The unity of knowledge*. New York: Alfred A. Knopf.

Chapter 11

Exploring practical wisdom

Teaching management in a spirit of co-creation

Ksenija Napan

Introduction: Contextualising the author and the course

Situating the author

I am a curious scholar keen to explore engaging ways of tertiary teaching and learning in order to make a positive difference in the world. I have been a teacher for most of my professional life and have always attempted to integrate practical ways of being in my academic teaching. I am a social worker by my basic qualification and in my view, practical wisdom is a prerequisite of being an effective one. The mission of social work is to create social change, but very often social workers are perceived and act as agents of social control. It is a profession which grapples with numerous paradoxes, and managers and leaders in social work need to develop creative leadership styles to be able to stand up for the 'under dog' and get funded by the 'top dog' (the 'top dog' in this context being government departments, corporations or philanthropists without whose funding social service agencies cannot exist). Bourdieu observes:

> Social workers must fight unceasingly on two fronts: on the one hand, against those they want to help and who are often too demoralised to take in hand their own interest, let alone the interest of the collective: on the other hand, against the administrations and bureaucrats divided and enclosed in separate universes.
>
> (Bourdieu, 2002, p. 190)

Social workers are stretched between radical grassroots movements and a legacy from charitable ways of practising, including the normative notions of 'deserving and undeserving poor' (Appelbaum, 2001). Because of all these tensions, exacerbated with the stress brought by working with some of the most marginalised groups, it is essential for social workers to develop practical wisdom in their practice. Furthermore, social workers are well-educated people (in some countries a completed Master degree becoming the norm) and their clients often possess a different kind of wisdom expressed through ability to survive on the streets, live and support their families with minimum funds or cope with serious mental or physical illness, often combined with various addictions. Well-educated people are not necessarily street-wise, and it requires an open mind, divergent thinking and ability to reflect in action to be an effective social worker. Similar skills and abilities are required for becoming an effective manager in social services.

I have been strongly influenced by social justice ideas and understand that an essential part of my job is to be the conscience and critic of society. In my universe, personal is professional and professional is political. I tend to blur disciplinary boundaries in my teaching practice and integrate seemingly opposing polarities. While teaching, I strive to explain complex concepts in a simple way and I tend to model what I would like my students to do in their future practice. Education has a transformative potential and I witness this at the end of each year while cheering for my graduating class. I thrive when I meet them later in social work agencies in leading positions, where they are making a difference and building on wisdom gained during their studies and practice. Unleashing students' creativity is a prerequisite on the road to becoming wisdom-seekers and enabling them to apply that wisdom in a range of situations. I teach social workers, mostly towards the end of their study, just before they get qualified. By the last year of their degree, their heads are full of theories, and they have had a chance to thoroughly examine their values and attitudes. Furthermore they have been through skills training and two fieldwork placements and have gained some practical skills and insight into how social service organisations work. However, before they can become competent practitioners they need to develop practical wisdom to cope with a range of contexts and client situations they will encounter.

Routine procedures rarely engender change, therefore social workers need to be wise, creative and able to understand the global context of their practice and translate it into specific and unique practices that are suitable for each individual situation.

If we use the Aristotelian understanding of *phronesis* being the moral will to do the right thing and the moral skill to find what the right thing is, practical wisdom is the essence of being an effective manager of a social work agency. Alongside with knowledge, skill and experience, play and improvisation are instrumental in finding out what the right thing is, while respecting the uniqueness of each particular context. What I have experienced is that playfulness unleashes students' creativity and enables practical wisdom to emerge.

Situating the course

The 'Management in the Social Services' course is offered on the second year of the Master of Applied Social Work programme. It a compulsory course and most of the multicultural group of students are not very excited to take it. It is taught in a block of two-plus-two full days while students are preparing their research reports, are undertaking another large course and have just finished their final three months of fieldwork experience. Most students are not interested in management and are more focused on jumping through the final hoops of becoming qualified social workers instead of exploring theories of management and leadership. The majority do not envisage themselves as managers and leaders, but because they graduate with a master degree in social work accompanied with their primary degree in social sciences or similar fields, many of them quickly get offered management positions.

The positioning of the course, straight after completing their fieldwork placement, means that all students have experienced being managed in their agencies and have observed some great and some not so great managers and leaders in the field. The rationale of the course is that social workers need to understand organisational and management theory and skills to support their practice and to understand the context of their future employment. It is envisaged that this will assist them to better serve their client groups, organisations and communities. Management and administration is recognised by the 'International Federation of Social Workers' as a field of practice (Lewis, Packard & Lewis, 2012) and social workers often work as team leaders and line and senior managers, and fill many roles on the professional committees and boards in the not-for-profit sector.

The aim of the course is to provide a critical examination of current management and organisational theory and its impact on management, administrative systems and professional practice in social service agencies. Critical understanding, comprehending implications of policies, identification of challenges in current social work leadership and examination of own leadership style all are closely related to the development of practical wisdom.

This chapter explores how 'Academic Co-creative Inquiry'(ACCI) (Napan, 2009) was used to enable students to develop their practical wisdom, while personalising learning outcomes through learning contracts, using self- and peer-reflection to improve their work and engender trust and collaboration while being immersed in seven qualities that ACCI proposes for inquiry-based learning.

Managing diversity or embracing difference?

In the field of social work, the focus on social justice often challenges the corporate ladder which is clearly depicted in the quote from one of the prescribed textbooks for the course:

> The real challenge for social work managers is not to emulate the more negative and perhaps distorted stereotypes of the private business world in seeing who can run the leanest and fittest organisation, the 'tightest ship', the 'biggest empire', or who can hire and fire with the greatest abandon. Rather, it is to absorb those ideas emerging from the business world which suggest that success lies in valuing fostering and listening to the workforce, hearing and responding to the 'customer', managing diversity not conformity and seeking to build in flexibility at every stage.
> (Coulshed, Mullender, Jones, & Thompson, 2006, p. 221)

In contemporary management, the notion of 'managing diversity' needs to be challenged. In a globalised world, diversity is not something that needs to be 'managed'. Rather, it needs to be embraced, cherished and utilised for development of new ideas that can happen only through collaboration and creation of a trustworthy space where individual uniqueness is appreciated. Managers in social services need to learn how to balance this appreciation of uniqueness and diversity within a collaborative and community-minded context where goals and outcomes can be achieved only through collaboration and creation of synergies.

Contemporary management theory does not need to be concerned only about outputs, financial gains, competition and exploitation. Increasingly, it is more about terms and principles traditionally connected to social sciences like human rights, social justice, community development and sustainability, as well as creating contexts where humans can meaningfully contribute to their communities by utilising their strengths, passions and special abilities. Within this framework, diversity becomes an advantage and a rich pool from which we can draw in order to enhance and enrich quality of life of communities as opposed to the more traditional view, where diversity is something that needs to be tolerated or 'managed'.

Participants

My students have a Bachelor Degree in a social work-related discipline (social sciences, education, psychology, health, sociology, law and so on) and most of them are international students, immigrants or mature domestic students, who decided to change their career for a range of reasons. The 'Master of Applied Social Work' condenses the usual four years full-time study required to become a social worker into two years of full-time study with two fieldwork placement experiences. Practical wisdom is a term my students resonate with well as they are aware that they need a lot of practical wisdom to utilise their prior knowledge while transitioning into their new profession. They need to relearn, unlearn and be proactive in changing their professional identity and become flexible and open in appreciation of different kinds of wisdom that may be culturally determined. All these factors made an inquiry approach to learning suitable for this particular group. This particular class comprised 28 students with various academic and professional backgrounds and nationalities.

The inquiry process

For the development of my students' practical wisdom, I applied qualities that permeate 'Academic Co-creative Inquiry' or ACCI (Napan, 2009). This approach is based on adult learning principles (Brookfield, 2001), whole people learning (Heron, 1996a), some principles grounded in choice theory (Glasser, 1997) and awareness of importance of critical reflection in teaching and learning social work (White, Fook, & Gardner, 2006). The ACCI model was built on John Heron's Cooperative Inquiry (1996) with awareness of the hierarchical nature of academia where it would be impossible to get away without some form of unilateral assessment which is an anathema to cooperative inquiry where two or more people research a topic through their own experience of it using a series of cycles of action and reflection. All participants are co-subjects and co-researchers and it can be seen as a most emancipatory form of action research. However, its application and epistemology is quite distinct: 'It is a vision of persons in reciprocal relation using the full range of their sensibilities to inquire together into any aspect of human condition with which the transparent body-mind can change' (Heron, 1996b, p. 1).

Heron's model needed to be modified to suit the academic reality and Learning Contracts (Knowles, Holton & Swanson, 2005) were used as means to ensure prescribed learning outcomes were covered and peer and self-reflections inform the final grade which was assigned by a teacher. Participants were engaged in the design and management of the inquiry within university parameters with clear information provided on what aspects of the inquiry were negotiable and what was non-negotiable.

ACCI embeds seven specific qualities (namely: *context, trust, relevance, choice, flow, integration* and *integrity*) that are presented in detail below. These qualities were derived from a number of courses facilitated in this manner and data from this particular study was used to illustrate how these qualities have manifested and what kind of practical wisdom emerged as a consequence.

One of the main characteristics of the Academic Co-creative Inquiry is that, each time it is applied, it is contextualised differently to honour each individual course, teaching style of the lecturer and a range of students' learning styles that participate in the co-creation of the course. Each year these qualities are manifested differently as each course is co-created to suit a particular student group. What follows is an illustrating example of how these qualities manifested in the course offered in 2015. A particular set of reflective questions related to each quality (Napan, 2011) are listed within each subheading. Additionally, critical questions that enabled the development of each quality are embedded in the text to provide clarity and focus for this non-linear process.

The following sections present the appearance of these qualities as emerging in the course for the purpose of developing practical wisdom in management in the social services field of practice.

Quality 1: Context

On the first day we got to know one another and explored various contexts we come from. The purpose of doing this was to utilise prior knowledge and create space, where students can learn from one another. I asked myself a number of questions and explored some of them with students on the first day:

- How do I convey my passion and interest for the subject I teach?
- Do I know my students' names? Can I pronounce them well?
- Am I genuinely interested in my student's thoughts, ideas and perceptions?
- What are my students' contextual strengths? (What do they bring to the course in terms of culture, prior experiences, interests and passions?)
- Do students appear to be enjoying learning?
- Which processes contribute to creating a learning community in my classroom?
- How can students contribute to make it their own?
- Is my course challenging enough? Do my students appear to be bored?

During the morning of the first lecture we connected and made links. We got to know each other, and some students knew one another from various other courses. I introduced myself in Te Reo Maori, which is a native language of Aotearoa/New Zealand. By this I acknowledged native people of the land, proceed by sharing the country of my origin, my mountain, my river and my 'tribe', situating and grounding myself and declaring that I am an immigrant as most of the students in the class. I included the photograph of a Marae (communal Maori meeting place) in the background (Figure 11.1), a specific one to which I was welcomed and where I taught in the past. I chose to present myself in that way to show my respect and commitment to native people of the land, the bicultural nature of New Zealand, to acknowledge my ancestors and share what I bring to the course. The dog in the photo symbolises the sense of home and permanence. For me as an immigrant getting a dog meant that I am committed to staying in Aoteroa/New Zealand.

Figure 11.1 Introducing and contextualising a lecturer.

This kind of personal introduction enabled students to make links between personal, professional and political, so relevant for management in social services. Then I asked students what they would like to know about me that would facilitate their learning; and what would they like me or the class to know about them that would facilitate my teaching and our learning together. A few interesting ideas were shared and I noticed that some were not comfortable to speak in front of the whole class, so I pointed to the box on the desk where they were encouraged to put a question, comment or anything that may concern them, anonymously. Exploring various contexts of where my students came from enabled them to become aware how they can utilise their prior knowledge and to create a space in which they can learn from one another.

> You are honest with me; I will be honest with you. I was late because I had a drama with my sick child at home just before I was supposed to leave. I really do not want to be here, but I have to, if I want to graduate in April. I will never be a manager, I am not interested, I just want to become a social worker and help people in need.
>
> (Course participant who approached me during the tea break, 20.8.2015)

This student was a working and studying mother. Later on she decided to write an assignment about links between managing a family and managing an agency. In her final reflection she wrote:

> Due to recent difficult personal and health circumstances, I am very disappointed that I was not able to complete my inquiry-based assignments to the standard

> that I am normally capable of. One thing I have learned throughout the duration of this course is just how determined I am to complete my work and persevere despite the chaos around me (perhaps this is good management experience for when I am out working in the future!).
>
> Through self-reflection, I have found that management is not an unfamiliar concept as I had previously thought. My experiences as a mother and a partner are not so different from that of a manager. I have found self-reflection to be a useful tool in facilitating my learning of management/leadership concepts and ideas.
>
> (Course participant, self-reflection, 2.10.2015)

This quote reflects the usefulness of utilisation of student's particular contexts and enabling them to make links with prescribed learning outcomes required to complete the course.

There were 28 students in the class and diversity was the only commonality. The Academic Co-Creative Inquiry was presented to students enabling them to have a high degree of choice in assignments they were going to produce. Coverage of prescribed learning outcomes, submission of individualised learning contracts and peer and self-assessment were not negotiable and the process of the course was co-created with students taking an active part.

Data was collected through anonymous questionnaire mid-course and at the end of the course and from student assignments and peer and self-reflections. This study is part of the larger co-operative inquiry into effectiveness of teaching conducted at Massey University.

Quality 2: Trust

The second quality, trust, slowly emerged in the group; however, without knowing how this strange course is going to be assessed, students appeared to be puzzled and slightly confused. I have presented prescribed learning outcomes and offered learning contracts (Knowles, 1986; Knowles et al., 2005) to personalise them into inquiry questions or 'I would like to' statements. Learning contracts are a useful tool for personalised learning and in this particular instance; I used them for students to translate prescribed outcomes into inquiry questions that will lead to practical actions relevant to them and their interests. Contracts are used for clarification, can change during the semester and are living documents that enable students to be focussed and yet flexible in their inquiry into management in social services. Clarity of expectations and certainty enabled trust to emerge; however, the development of trust was glaringly evident during the process of self- and peer-reflection.

Committed to the idea that only purposeful material will be taught, on the first day we discussed and explored the purpose of peer and self-reflection. In social work practice, these reflections are part of the appraisal process and clinical supervision and it was useful for students to get used to this process. Competent social workers need to be reflective, which is linked to the development of meta-reflection that enables a practitioner to see issues from various points of view and think globally but act locally. During this process students became aware that their fellow students can help them improve their learning and assignments so the usual context of competition transformed into context of collaboration with significantly increased trust in the

Table 11.1 Peer- and self-reflection feedback

Students' comments on peer-reflection	*Students' comments on self-reflection*
• It was very useful to receive views from a different angle about my work • Another chance to learn, enlightened me about my strengths and weaknesses • It gave me a chance to improve my work • It was interesting to read somebody else's work and see how there are many ways to cover same learning outcomes It inspired me to do something more creative in my second assignment • It was kind, reflective and useful • Relevant, informative, effective • It was a difficult balancing act – positive with growth opportunities and writing it with respect • I have done two and have learnt how the same thing can be done differently and effectively • I have learnt that my colleagues are bright and creative • Useful suggestions, safe confrontation, learning different perspective • It made me realise how reluctant I am to give advice • From another's understanding I can identify my strengths and weaknesses	• Self-reflection makes me think about my work and then I fill the gaps I think deeper • It was kind of confession, it made me be honest about my work • I am my worst critic! • It improved my self-awareness and become aware of my personal leadership qualities and attributes • It felt like an additional task but it allowed me to explain myself in the marking process • It was like having a silent supervision with myself • Made me assess and think beyond just completing the assignment • Good opportunity for me to rethink what I did and how it is related to my learning outcomes set at the beginning

classroom. The requirement for peer and self-reflection enabled students to go beyond the bare minimum and was evident in the quotes captured from the course evaluation shown in Table 11.1.

Peer assessors needed to answer some reflective questions and give feedback, but they did not need to mark their fellow students' assignments. The purpose of peer-reflection was to strengthen relationships and give relevant critical feedback before the assignment is submitted for assessment. The student can then choose to take feedback on board or not. Besides being a trust-building exercise, it was a useful time management exercise too. Each assignment was accompanied with student's self- reflection which served as a meta-cognitive layer enabling students to develop critical thinking and writing. These reflections were guided by a series of inquiry questions and students were able to add their own. Students were able to do assignments individually or in a group. For group assignments they needed to reach consensus through trustful dialogue about each individual contribution while evaluating their participation. During this process students became increasingly trusting and the quality of assignments 'skyrocketed'.

Questions that relate to exploration an application of the quality of trust are listed below:

- Am I trusting the process of ACCI and my students' ability to know what form of expression will enable them to expand their knowledge?
- How do I manifest this trust?
- How do students manifest it?

- How do they show care for one another?
- How do I encourage it?
- How does trust enable wisdom to emerge?
- Do I notice when respect or disrespect enters the room?
- How do I react? How do my students react?

Quality 3: Relevance

As students at the beginning of the course could not relate to it and perceive how it is relevant to their future practice, everything we did needed to be meaningful and purposeful to fully engage them. I had to answer the following questions:

- How does the content and the process of this course bring my students closer to their goals?
- Does it give them new hopes and ideas or career prospects?
- How does it arouse their curiosity?
- How will it improve the quality of their lives or lives of their families?
- Does it solve any of their problems?
- How does it satisfy their basic needs?

Relevance is a main contributing factor to student engagement. Only purposeful content was taught and linked with the overall rationale and aim of the course. On the first day, I explained the rationale of this course. I did my best to contextualise it in a current climate of social work employment. My students were on their final year of study and many of them were already seeking employment. For international students, finding employment is a condition of staying in the country. Discovering purpose and meaning for their active involvement was essential for the success of the course and student participation.

I presented the prescribed aim of the course, which is worded in a language that usually puts students off. In this case, the aim is to provide a critical examination of current management and organisational theory and its impact on management, administrative systems and professional practice in social service agencies. When students hear that, many immediately switch off. Until they perceive this aim as something that will improve the quality of their life it is not likely that they will engage. As a way to make this aim personal I asked them to write on the piece of paper what would they like to learn and share it with the person sitting next to them. I received back blank faces, so I rephrased it by asking 'How can your quality of life improve as a result of this paper?'. I followed by giving them examples including saying that:

> Similarly to social workers who are bridges between clients and social service agencies often exercising roles of social change and social control, managers are often acting as bridges between policies, social service agencies and their employees. Effective management is about relationships, effective social work is about relationships, effective education is about relationships. How can we utilise richness of our relationships to make this course relevant, effective and fun?

Blank faces suddenly started raising their eyebrows. This quote from a student demonstrates how relevance fuelled motivation:

> My original inquiry was to focus on management and leadership styles and determine how they fit with larger organisational values. Not exactly riveting stuff. If I am being honest, I can say that I had no real interest in management when starting this paper. Perhaps, similar to many social work students, I was interested in practising social work, working with like-mined individuals and engaging with service users. The idea of management never appealed to me. With that said, I can also say that I was not particularly motivated to work on this assignment and found doing the research somewhat of a chore. However, after determining to interview both of my colleagues, considering what questions to ask, reflecting on their answers and critically analysing my own observations, I can say that I have found a new appreciation for management theories. I have found the process of conducting interviews with both the social work practice supervisor and clinical coordinator of my current job/placement illuminating and providing insight into the social work sector in Aotearoa/New Zealand, the ADHB (Auckland District Health Board) and the ACOS (Assertive Community Outreach Services) team itself. The assignment afforded me an insight into how the team operates and the internal and external forces at play in determining the organisational directions, as well as leadership and management styles.
>
> (Course participant, Darren Bot, self-reflection, 27.10.2015)

At the same time the quote depicts a level of trust not common in externally assessed environments. While sharing their aims, students started making links with their fieldwork placements, life interests and career aspirations.

Quality 4: Choice

The quality of choice was manifested in clear distinction between 'negotiables' and 'non-negotiables' for this course, creative assignments and playing to students' strengths. Learning contracts enabled students to have a range of choices in completing requirements for the course.

The main inquiry questions that guided my preparation and delivery of the course were:

- Which academic requirements, proposed by my academic institution are non-negotiable and which are negotiable?
- Which academic requirements, proposed by me and my academic integrity are non-negotiable?
- How is flexibility manifested in my course?
- Which choices do I make to make the course different each year and on which basis?

Figure 11.2 shows an example of the learning contract with prescribed (non-negotiable) learning outcomes in bold and inquiry questions personalised by a student

Learning Contract for

Name: Fake Name
Paper: Management in the Social Services 179.792

Please personalise prescribed learning outcomes into inquiry questions or *I would like to ...* statements:

1. **Demonstrate a critical understanding of management and organisational theories as well as management styles.**

I would like to explore both transformational and servant leadership models and the management styles they embody with reference to a social enterprise concept of a Partnership School in Kaitaia. This will be expressed through the medium of photography and graphics presented in a slide show with background music.

2. **Demonstrate a theoretical and practical understanding of social service organisations and their management in the Aotearoa New Zealand context.**

I would like to explore the challenges involved setting up a Partnership School social enterprise in Kaitaia. I will research issues of funding, geographical location, Iwi, customer identification, barriers to success, and possible stake holders. This will be presented visually through Art on Canvas.

3. **Identify the implications of current policy and practice for the management of social service organisations and for social work practice.**

I would like to explore a business start-up including a business plan with legal structure, projected budget forecast, an ideal team, and product or service offered and the policy around that business start-up.

4. **Identify current challenges facing social work leadership and begin to examine their own leadership style.**

I would like to explore my leadership style and how I will facilitate and develop a sustainable social enterprise idea which can grow and bring lasting significant change, inspiration, education and empowerment in a low socioeconomic area. I would like to develop a pitch and a brochure for my business idea.

5. **Analyse the significance of management as a field of social work practice.**

I would like to determine my success in a five year success matrix including markers for impact, enterprise and personal targets to recognise the success of my venture.

Resources

BOOKS

Cousheld, V., & Mullender, A. (2006). *Management in social work* (3rd ed.). New York: Palgrave MacMillan.

Hughes, M., & Wearing, M. (2007). *Organisations and management in social work*. London: Sage.

Packard, T., Lewis, J., Lewis, M. (2011). *Management of human service programs* (5th International ed.). USA: Broadman & Holdman Publishers.

Senge, P., Scharmer, C., Jaworski, J., & Flowers, B. (2008). *Presence: Human purpose and the field of the future*. USA: Broadway Business.

Weinbach, R.W. and Taylor, L.M. (2011). *The social worker as manager: A practical guide to success* (6th ed). Boston: Pearson/Allyn & Bacon.

WEBSITES
Useful information
http://diytoolkit.org/ D.I.Y: Development impact & you: Practical tools to trigger & support social innovation.

http://communitylaw.org.nz/community-law-manual/introduction/about-the-community-law-manual/ Managing a community centre best practice guidelines community law 2014.

www.dia.govt.nz/cvs Legal Structures for Social Enterprise June 2013 Produced by the Department of Internal Affairs.

http://redochre.org.uk/ Extracts from Red Ochre BAME Social Enterprise Finance Toolkit.

www.stats.govt.nz/.

www.education.govt.nz/ministry-of-education/specific-initiatives/partnership-schools-kura-hourua/.

Social Service Social Enterprise Examples:

www.fiver.org/
www.oxfam.org.au/
www.zeal.nz/
www.jamieoliver.com/the-fifteen-apprentice-programme/home

Obstacles you can foresee to complete the assignment and strategies you intend to put in place?
Not enough time to study & balance my kids.
Getting carried away with research.
Strategies in place:
Regularly working on my assignments so that they don't get left to the last minute.
Focus on answering the questions.

Evidence of Accomplishment of Outcomes (list your assignments with a date you want to submit, last day being 21st September for assignment one and 23rd October 2015 for assignment two)

1. **Assignment one (the word limit is 2,500 words, if you do not use words, there is no limit)**
   Title: Part 1 'The Transformational Servant'
   Format: Photographed with graphics presented in a slideshow to music.
   Part 2 'The Gap'
   Format: Art on Canvas

Peer assessors name: Pseud Onim
Date you will submit it to your peer assessor: 14/9/2015
Date you will submit it to Ksenija: 21/9/2015

2. **Assignment two: word limit 3,500 words**
   Your title: EVOLVE Partnership School: Business plan & pitch.

Format: PowerPoint Presented and film uploaded to YouTube.

Peer assessors name: Pseud Onim
Date you will submit it to your peer assessor: 16/10/2015
Date you will submit it to Ksenija: 23/10/2015

(Continued)

Figure 11.2 (Continued)

Criteria and Means for Validating Evidence (what do you want your peers to focus on when reading your assignment, how will you know that you have been successful? Minimum of 4 criteria please, choose from the list and/or make up your own)
General criteria: (also see criteria on Stream) **Presentation and Readability (20% of total marks)** Typing – layout, errors, printing
Creativity
Structure and Content (80% of total marks) Application and knowledge of theory Logical development
Coverage of learning outcomes Objectives and key points easy to identify Relevance to Social Services in Aotearoa New Zealand and internationally Conclusion
Additional criteria:
Establish a success matrix for a 5-year plan for Alternative Education

Figure 11.2 Sample learning contract.

below it. After the initial confusion, students were genuinely surprised that they could express themselves any way they like as long as they covered the prescribed learning outcomes and fulfil criteria listed in their contract. Furthermore, it was clearly stated that assessment will be based on a comparison of what they set out to do in their contract and what they delivered. On the second day of the course we started co-creating it. Based on students' input and interests, prior knowledge and learning needs I tailored my lectures and learning activities with the course aim and outcomes in the back of my mind.

The coverage of prescribed learning outcomes was not negotiable, but students were able to personalise them in the way that made sense to them, and link them to their learning styles, career aspirations and unique experiences from practice as well as their current situation. In this co-creative process, students started making links between the choice of their career paths and leadership, their need to change the world and tools that this course can provide to do so, parenting and management, use of social media and creative ways of completing assignments and potential partnerships in facilitating their individual processes of learning.

Learning contracts modified for this specific context proved to be useful in enabling students to personalise the prescribed learning outcomes in very creative and committed ways and prescribed learning outcomes got transformed into exciting inquiry projects.

This particular student changed her contract three of four times as she was developing her own agency. Not all students were at that stage of competence. Learning contracts allowed for diversity in the classroom and contributed to each assignment being relevant to students' interests and career aspirations. Students were also invited to come for an externally organised seminar about geoleadership and a public talk by Michael Bauwens on the sharing economy and peer-to-peer design. A range of choices and options made assignments interesting and relevant for their peers and I have to say that some were so good that I could not put them down while marking them. Some touched me to tears, which is not a common occurrence within the assessment process in academia.

To demonstrate a range of creativity, assignments are grouped in a table as those where students linked practical wisdom gained from their placements and those that are linked to their personal experiences (Table 11.2).

Table 11.2 How was creativity expressed and wisdom utilised?

Assignments linking practical wisdom gained from fieldwork placements	*Assignments linking practical wisdom from life experiences and/or utilising personal strengths and creativity*
Analysis of the Rape Prevention agency	A journal reflecting on learning outcomes in the light of the personal story
A project for housing homeless	A proposal for sustainable social service agency combined with tourism and permaculture gardens
Cartoon about effective management accompanied with a critical reflection	Operating manual for a church group
PowerPoint: Wisdom in management in relation to the Vulnerable Children Act recently passed in the parliament	Design of a flyer and proposal for an alternative school for young people with autistic spectrum disorder in Kaitaia
Critical reflection on Child Youth and Family agency	Mindfulness and its relevance to management in social services
Managing the event: Gambling free day	Outline of a proposal for residential school for street kids in Nepal
Case study of a social service agency in Auckland and how it is managed	Repository and a business plan for the agency 'Unique Options'
Recruitment letter for an imaginary social services agency	Two presentations to the class about social services agencies students were planning to open when they complete their degree
Reflection on fieldwork placement focussing on management styles	A movie about transformational and servant leadership style
A proposal for a leadership course for young women in Papua New Guinea	A journal reflecting on learning outcomes in the light of the personal story
Critical reflection of management at Age Concern agency	My family as an NGO (non-government-organisation)
Critical exploration of the main functions of small business management and social services management: Based on two experiences from Boaz Ltd and Asian Family Services	How my leadership style contributes to my clients and their families
The flying cat and the bunny rabbit: A transformational management fairy-tale within Child, Youth and Their Families agency	Ongoing Resource Scheme (ORS) Funding Application: New Horizons – School to Community.
	School to Community: Carer Information & Support Group for people with disabilities finishing school

It is important to note that when students became aware of the relevance of their assignments to improve the quality of their lives, either by doing something they enjoyed (movies or art) or by creating something that is potentially useful beyond a getting mere passing mark, their motivation and engagement significantly increased and this allowed the experience of the flow to emerge.

Quality 5: Flow

The experience of the flow as studied by Csikszentmihalyi (1990; Abuhamdeh & Csikszentmihalyi, 2012) is a state of consciousness in which a person is fully involved in the activity that they enjoy doing. Intrinsic motivation and sense of purpose and meaning contributes to this experience, which is more common in arts than in science; however, inventors with a strong sense of mission report experiencing it, and it is closely linked to the experience of spontaneous joy while harnessing emotions in the service of learning and discovery. It seems that he question posed on the first day of the course – *How can your participation in this course improve the quality of your life?* – launched students into an all-encompassing engagement with the course material. This question springs from choice theory (Glasser, 1997), which explains that if clients, students, customers or employees do not perceive that engagement with the initiator (in this case a teacher) or the material the initiator wants to share with them is contributing to the improvement of their quality of life it is not likely that they will engage. The focus was on allowing the true internal motivation to emerge and allow 'the flow to flow'. While students were discussing their personal aims in pairs on the first day of the course, I wanted them to start formulating their personal learning outcomes and inspire one another to stretch their aspirations. It also got acknowledged that if their aim was just to pass the course and move on – that answer was good enough. We also explored how they can pass this course with least possible effort, and highest possible achievement. I asserted, with a dose of humour, that learning how to work smart and not hard may become a useful management and social work tool that will contribute to development of their practical wisdom on the road to becoming effective social workers, managers and leaders in social services. We explored what they can utilise from their past, who are the people they can contact to cover prescribed learning outcomes and how they can support one another on their journey. The prerequisite for the sense of flow to emerge is elimination of fear, as to be 'in the zone' one needs to love what he or she is doing. This clearly occurred when one of the students decided to do a presentation about the alternative school for children with the autistic spectrum disorder in a remote rural area of New Zealand. One of the reasons she decided to complete the Master of Social Work applied degree was for her and her partner to do this. Her creative presentation involved a video, art work and a Power Point presentation all accompanied with self-reflection linking it to prescribed learning outcomes. Her contract is displayed in Figure 11.2. Part of her creative assignment is presented in Figure 11.3.

The following reflection accompanied this part of the assessment:

> *Art Piece: THE GAP*
>
> This art piece explores the challenges with setting up and the management of a Social Enterprise Partnership School in Kaitaia. The first piece identifies the client base: A Maori child from Muriwhenua (the six tribes of the Far North)

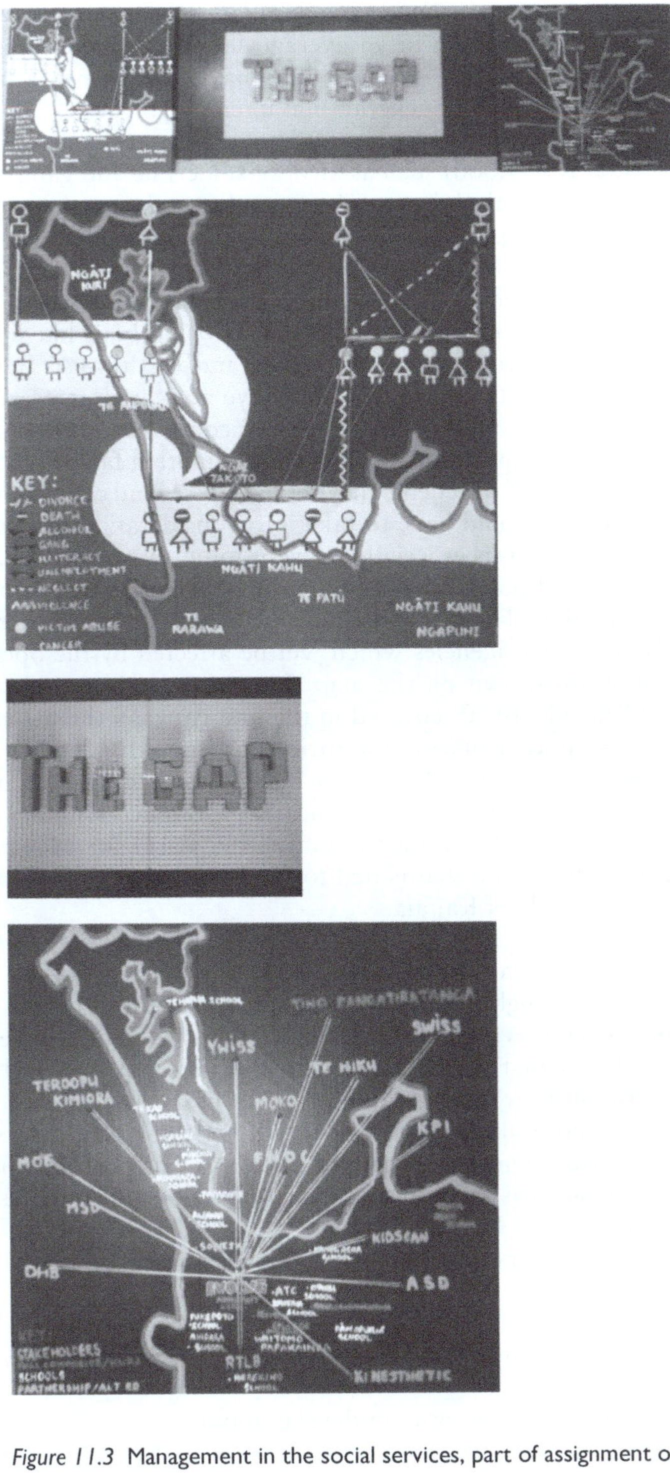

Figure 11.3 Management in the social services, part of assignment one.

> and addresses the location, environment, and social situation of the potential clients. The background – Maori flag depicts the population being largely Maori (55%). The large number of children in an average family, and the struggles of death, generational illiteracy (only 5% of adults have a degree in Kaitaia, and only 40% obtain NCEA level 1), generational unemployment (19%), geographical isolation (2 hours from nearest city, Whangarei), poverty issues (the median income in Kaitaia is $19,000) such as alcoholism, crime and gang affiliation and high sexual or physical violence. The map shows the sand, sea, and lush green land depicting the importance of land and sea and the abundance of fishing, hunting, and waka and weaving to the Maori all kinaesthetic activities! The GAP is made from red Lego bricks assembled two stacks high on a lush green backdrop which depicts the widening gap that is being built like a wall and nourished like fresh green grass by social policy and wealth distribution. The GAP could represent either the 'have' and the 'have nots' with reference to wealth of money, education, or opportunity. The GAP could also represent the gap between social services key performance indicators, limiting factors such as time or funding, and the needs of the clients they serve. The second canvas shows the strategies that a manager would have to take into consideration to make a venture economically viable. This is especially relevant for a transformational or servant leader as the nuts and bolts must hold the same weight as the vision so that the project is sustainable. The key stakeholders such as current programs and services, schools and other agencies which will be affected by the opening of a Partnership School are shown on the map. The strategic planning takes into account the problems identified (covered in the first canvas), the networking needed, the funding requirements and the various potential funders, as well as the high level of ASD diagnosed in the far north (according to the Rosemary Ayers Paediatrician) the needs of Kinaesthetic learners, the accessibility, and the ethos in the Far North of Tino Rangatiratanga (by Maori for Maori) all these pulls are shown by the cotton that is tied to the Partnership school called EVOLVE situated in the middle of Kaitaia.

This demonstrates how eliminating fear from failure and transparently stating that doing a bare minimum will be enough to pass the course paradoxically enabled students to do much more than what was required. The student reported that she invested a lot of time in this project, but that when she started she could not stop and has clearly experienced the sense of 'flow' and an outpouring of creativity. The joy this creative assignment provided, not only for the student, but for the whole class who watched her presentation with amazement, opened the doors for many other students to start experimenting with new ideas and utilising the space to do something useful that they felt passionate about.

On reflection, I spend some time pondering on following questions related to the flow:

- Have I noticed the flow in this classroom? Has anybody else noticed it? How did it manifest?
- How did I manage and encourage curiosity in the classroom?
- What brainstorm activities were used?

- How did we engender curiosity and wonder?
- How did I express my creativity?
- How did students express their creativity?

I have experienced the flow while lecturing on a topic students requested me to present while noticing full attentiveness of all 28 students. It was also experienced in some group activities when students keep requesting more time to discuss topics more. Laughter, noise and camaraderie were common and although the block course was timetabled for 9 a.m. to 5 p.m., time seemed to fly.

As flow is creative and can be very uplifting, the following quality of integration enabled students to ground their experience and make sense of their creative endeavours. It also enabled them to make links with prescribed learning outcomes.

Quality 6: Integration

Integration happened on many levels and various aspects of it permeated the process. It happened at the beginning when students started personalising prescribed learning outcomes by integrating their interests, then when they undertook projects of their choice, when they received peer-reflections, improved their assignments on reflection and finally when self-reflecting on their work. These self-reflections served as a final check that prescribed learning outcomes have been covered, which was particularly useful for artistic and alternative assignments, but also to integrate and consolidate knowledge. For traditional essays (yes, some students chose to do essays) self-reflections were like a saving grace where students were able to pinpoint what they missed and what would they cover in their assignments providing they had more time, resources and interests.

Many unexpected learning outcomes were reported and almost all students have put a lot of effort into creating assignments that were reflective of their interests, aspirations and dreams.

> There were unexpected learnings about external influences on social services in Aotearoa (neoliberalism and new public management). I suppose I had not considered or been aware of the extent of these influences, due in part of being a foreigner. I also learnt a tremendous amount about the ACOS team, where I currently work, and the DHB. I found the insights offered by my colleagues around leadership to be extremely useful; and they contribute to my ongoing education about social work in this country.
>
> (Assignment two, self-reflection, 29.10.15)

Allowance and encouragement to do assignments that build on students' experiences and resources available to them and that are relevant to their career aspirations engendered a high level of motivation and enthusiasm that contributed to a high level of engagement with the material and prescribed learning outcomes. It also motivated students to 'walk the extra mile' and gain some insights relevant for their future employment.

> I have spent a lot of time on conversation with colleagues around what they have in mind regarding leadership style and management. I feel I have not only explored

> the literature but learned from my own community. The interviews with peer has lead me to explore a unique kind of management theory but one that resonates with myself and my social work context. I can see that engaging both with literature and with my community is a beneficial practice in my field. The best part for me was gathering and analysing responses from my colleagues. I was surprised to hear some of the perceptions from my interviewees and engage with some very challenging ideas.
>
> (Assignment two, peer-reflection, 29.10.2015)

Some students integrated personal, professional and political:

> As I was reading the third section of recommended readings about social work leadership, especially the ones about challenges, I was deeply reflecting on my current work experience. I used this assignment as an opportunity to reflect on and develop my own leadership style. This helped me to work better and be happier in a stressful multidisciplinary environment.
>
> (Assignment two, self-reflection, 30.11.2015)

> In my life, I know I am a very strong leader of my family. What I now need to learn is how to be a strong leader within the confines of working for a government agency which is a challenge I hope to take on. The best part of this assignment has been applying principles that guide my family life and how we have built our own life style and applying these permaculture principles to social work practice. I enjoy this planning process through creative design.
>
> (Assignment one, self-reflection, 25.9.2015)

And insights were evident for peers while reading their colleagues' assignments:

> C. has covered this objective effectively in a variety of ways. She has not only presented the current challenges of social work leadership: the heavy caseload and the extended paperwork, but she has also set this in the context of the workings of the DHB (District Health Board). She has cleverly presented the struggle between legislation and the risk adverse policy with the social work practitioner's desire to be creative and actively find solutions that attend to client's emotional needs over the system's need to 'cover itself'...
>
> Also, the emotional impact that many medical professions can have on a client. How it is difficult for a client and a social worker to argue their opinions in the face of medical opinion. Setting this argument within a narrative is effective as it has an emotive impact that highlights the personal emotions involved in this kind of work. I have certainly learnt a lot about the impacts of policy on social work by peer reflecting on this assignment.
>
> (Assignment one, peer-reflection, 24.9.2015)

Integration of personal, professional and political dimensions was encouraged during class discussions as well as an integration of knowledge, skills, values and attitudes. Artificial dichotomies like indigenous and Western wisdom, individualistic and communal, street-wise and book-wise etc., were critically examined and allowed students to experiment with alternative views to social care and management. Transformational and servant leadership were most commonly explored, while one student focused on bureaucratic leadership and thoroughly explained its value in hierarchical institutions. However, the integration of learning into professional life and practice is going to happen when this group of students get employment, see the relevance of these projects and evaluate if practical wisdom gained will make their social work practice effective.

Quality 7: Integrity

The previous qualities are all in the service of developing practitioners who will act with integrity and coherence. Integrity manifested through role-modelling and calling for honesty in giving and responding to feedback about the process and the content of the course. Mutuality was expressed as 'compassion in action', when students supported one another and offered their feedback with ideas for improvement. In past studies on ACCI (Napan, 2012, 2013), increased academic integrity was observed by assignments being plagiarism-free (and very interesting). The quality of assignments was significantly higher than in classes where regular teaching methods were used and students were giving only their best drafts to their peers. It seemed that they would put in that extra effort to show their best work to their peers as they were aware that these people will be part of their professional network in the future. Students claimed that assigning marks to their peers' work destroys relationships, but that they were fine with me doing it as it is my job. After extended dialogue we reached a consensus that they will only provide feedback to their peers with a purpose of suggesting how their work can be improved; their peers can decide to act on it or not. Then I assign a mark, as this is my job anyway, and give them relevant feedback taking into account peer and self-reflections and their response to them. In my past experiments with ACCI and various forms of self- and peer assessment (Napan, 2009, 2012, 2013, 2014) when students would agree to assign marks, or when I mandated it, in most cases they would put a high mark as a sign of loyalty to their peers and then try to justify it instead of becoming really engaged in helping their peers to improve their assignments. Since the switch to only descriptive feedback, I started calling it peer-reflection (instead of peer assessment or peer evaluation). Since this change, student feedback has become more useful and relevant and more aligned with the qualities that permeate the process.

To illustrate how these peer-reflections were used for improvement:

> Following feedback from my peer, I attempted to edit the background information in an effort to focus more in the interviews, particularly on the reflections from interview answers, while still keeping to the word count maximum. I sourced some data on housing first initiatives and research from overseas. I also attempted to improve grammatical errors.
>
> (Assignment two, peer-reflection, 1.11.15)

> This process of reflection and peer-reflection helped to strengthen my assignment and enabled me to focus more on the learning goals I have set out. It has also made me think about what I look for in an assignment and how can I strive to make mine better.
>
> (Assignment two, peer-reflection, 28.10.2015)

Reflective questions that guided me in exploring this quality were:

- How do I act with integrity and how I teach my students to do so?
- Is integrity teachable?
- Are beliefs something people should talk about?
- How personal beliefs influence professional practice?
- How important is integrity for my student's future profession?
- How can I manage my power and not impose my beliefs on students?
- Do I 'walk the talk'?
- How do I encourage my students to 'walk the talk'?

This student insightfully summarised her understanding of acting with integrity and her development of practical wisdom in social services:

> In the same way that we advocate for our clients, we need to advocate for our profession and our staff, in general and also in specific situations. If I were in leadership, I would speak about the challenges facing my team. And I would encourage the team to stand up for social work principles and ideals, in the knowledge that I was willing to back them up. However, we also need to be smart about how we operate; as a profession we need to understand the challenges facing general management, such as securing funding and managing risk, and learn to speak in their language. We need to be marketing out profession to general management and the medical fraternity in a way that makes clear to them the value we bring to patient engagements. An improved profile would increase our ability to influence decisions and ultimately help enhance the wellbeing of our clients.
>
> As a leader, I would want to be considered supportive of change; I think it is important to encourage new ideas and be open to change, as long as there was sufficient thought put into it and justification concerning what the change aims to achieve and why it is needed, then we should welcome innovation.
>
> (Assignment two, a story, Social Work Management in the Public Sector: Balancing Rights, Risks and Obligations, 23.10.2015)

Another student expressed how he would express his integrity in practice after developing a proposal for development of alternative housing options for the homeless living in the city centre:

> I have discovered a much more nuanced understanding about how management and leadership can be instrumental in determining the viability of a potential organisation by providing necessary focus or guidance on projects that require vision. By researching and reflecting on inclusive leadership approaches, the following assignment has provided me a new-found respect for management styles and their potential to impact on not only the lives of staff, but also service users. After conduction [of] the interviews and reflecting on my own needs as an employee or how I am best led, I realised that if I were to ever become a manager or leader, I would need to work on being flexible in how I approach or work with colleagues that are different than myself. It became apparent that this is something my own manager struggles with, and I can relate to that. I need to continue to work on recognising

> when a certain approach is not appropriate and being able to confidently and sincerely change tactics. I think the qualities of a leader are varied, but being able to understand the needs of your team are paramount. This applies to other aspects of life as well; as a father, partner and friend to people who learn in different ways.
>
> (Assignment two, self-reflection, 1.11.2015)

These statements show development of practical wisdom and how students managed to integrate personal, professional and political aspects of social work and get in touch with how they want to be in this world and what acting with integrity will look like in their professional practice.

Instead of conclusion

Development of practical wisdom is becoming increasingly important in the era of rapid changes in social life and society. This study confirmed the effects of replacing the conveying and sharing of information in the classroom with working on development of inquiring minds. The findings were very much in line with Montuori's idea that:

> Creative inquirers seek to navigate and integrate the skill building, knowledge based development, scholarship and critical thinking of traditional academia with the emphasis on self-reflection, the excavation of values, the integration of the knower in the known, and the stress on transformation – personal and social – of alternating approaches, without falling into polarized excesses.
>
> (Montuori, 2006, p. 5)

Practical wisdom emerged as a result of being mindful of seven qualities that permeated the process of the outlined 'Academic Co-Creative Inquiry'. As it has been shown, the creation of an appreciative context that is conducive to transformative change reflexively engendered trust among participants and between the teacher and the students. Commitment to relevant material being taught and learned significantly increased student motivation to do much more than a bare minimum to pass a course. Clearly delineating 'negotiables' and 'non-negotiables' as well as unleashing student creativity by allowing them to choose what, how and when are they going to submit their assignments resulted in a range of creative assignments related to their own interests and career prospects. The integration and practical utilisation of theory, practice and personal experiences enabled students to think outside of the square and develop lateral thinking while daring to experiment outside of their comfort zone. This experimenting provided space to explore their values, enhance their knowledge, improve their skills, and challenge their attitudes. Practising the presented seven qualities led to the development of personal and professional integrity rarely manifested so obviously in externally assessed courses. These wisdom learning practices are intended to contribute to developing coherent, grounded and yet creative practitioners, who will be able to maintain focused on the mission and the vision of the agency they manage or lead as well as on individual needs of their diverse employees. Further exploration and contextualisation of 'Academic Co-creative Inquiry' in a range of academic settings would be a wise next step.

Reflective questions related to specific qualities are embedded it the text and following questions emerged upon writing this chapter:

- How can development of practical wisdom be further promoted at universities?
- What are the characteristics of wise educational contexts?
- How can academic co-creative inquiry be contextualised to other educational programmes?
- What are the processes that best promote wising up management education?
- Can critical thinking transform neoliberal contexts?

References

Abuhamdeh, S. & Csikszentmihalyi, M. (2012). The importance of challenge for the enjoyment of intrinsically motivated, goal-directed activities. *Personality and Social Psychology Bulletin, 38*(3), 317–330.

Appelbaum, L.D. (2001). The influence of perceived deservingness on policy decisions regarding aid to the poor. *Political Psychology, 22*(3), 419–442.

Bourdieu, P. (2002). *Weight of the World: Social Suffering in Contemporary Society*. Stanford, CA: Stanford University Press.

Brookfield, S. (2001). *Understanding and Facilitating Adult Learning: A Comprehensive Analysis of Principles and Effective Practices* (6th ed.). Buckingham, UK: Open University Press.

Coulshed, V., Mullender, A., Jones, D., & Thompson, N. (2006). *Management in Social Work* (3rd ed.). Basingstoke, UK: Palgrave Macmillan.

Csikszentmihalyi, M. (1990). *Flow: The Psychology of Optimal Experience*. New York: Harper & Row.

Glasser, W. (1997). *Choice Theory*. New York: Harper Collins.

Heron, J. (1996a). Helping whole people learn. *Working with Experience: Animating Learning*. London: Routledge.

Heron, J. (1996b). *Co-operative Inquiry Research into the Human Condition*. London: Sage Publications.

Knowles, M. (1986). *Using Learning Contracts: Practical Approaches to Individualizing and Structuring Learning*. London: Jossey-Bass.

Knowles, M., Holton, E.F., III, & Swanson, R.A. (2005). *The Adult Learner: The Definitive Classic in Adult Education and Human Resource Development* (6th ed.). Burlington, MA: Elsevier.

Lewis, J., Packard, T., & Lewis, M. (2012). *Management of Human Service Programs* (5th ed.). Belmont, CA: Brooks/Cole Cengage Learning.

Montuori, A. (2006). *The Quest for a New Education: From Oppositional Identities to Creative Inquiry*. Washington, DC: Heldref Publications.

Napan, K. (2009). Academic co-creative inquiry: Creating inclusive processes for learning. Paper presented at the refereed proceedings from Educational Integrity Conference, University of Woolongong.

Napan, K. (2011). How do I teach? *HERDSA News, Higher Education Research and Development Society of Australasia, Inc, 32*(3), 1. Retrieved from www.herdsa.org.au/wp-content/uploads/HERDSA-News-Volume-33-No-3-December-2011.pdf

Napan, K. (2012). When a question met a story: Exploration of inquiry learning on a masters level of study. *The International Journal of Learning Common Ground Publishing, 18*(1), 293–304. Retrieved from http://ijl.cgpublisher.com/product/pub.30/prod.3281

Napan, K. (2013). Walking the talk in social work education. In C. Noble, M. Henrickson, & I. Young Han (Eds.), *Social Work Education: Voices from the Asia Pacific* (2nd modified edition). Sydney, NSW: Sydney University Press.

Napan, K. (2014). Co-creating learning: A comparative analysis of two integrative and collaborative methods of teaching/learning social work. In N. Bala Raju & Z. Hatta (Eds.), *Social Work Scholarship in Education and Practice: Innovations from the Asia Pacific* (pp. 143–164). Surrey Wellers Hill, Queensland: Primrose Hall.

White, S., Fook, J., & Gardner, F. (2006). *Critical Reflection in Health and Social Care*. New York: Open University Press.

Chapter 12

Embodied "aesth-ethics" for developing practical wisdom in management education/learning

Wendelin Küpers

Introduction

What would it mean to engage bodies and minds in all learning to enliven business and management education through integrating aesthetics and ethics, transforming existing educational forms and imagining them otherwise (Greene, 1995)?

For quite some time, inquiries have been undertaken into the goals, stances, contents, didactics, and curricula of business schools and management education in a search for innovative and alternative learning models for future leaders. The ways future leaders are educated supposedly affects and influences their understanding of and dealing with organizational and leadership tasks and actions.

Increasingly there are calls for a critical reappraisal of business education (Colby et al., 2011) and rethinking management education for the twenty-first century (Wankel et al., 2012). Part of rethinking management and leadership in general (Küpers et al., 2016; Ladkin, 2010) is the daunting task of reconsidering and reviewing the principles and practices that underlie and guide education.

This is important as it seems that conventional management education does not provide forms, contents, or capabilities that correspond to challenges of increasingly complex environments and transformations in our contemporary worlds of business, economy, ecology, and society. On the contrary, concepts or programs of leadership have been criticized for destroying good management practices (Ghoshal, 2005).

Business schools have been accused of playing a major role in the financial and economic crisis by failing to emphasize ethics and responsibility (Fragueiro & Thomas, 2011). This has raised questions and challenges concerning their (paradoxical) legitimacy, respectively legitimacy-related contradictions (Alajoutsijärvi et al., 2015).

As becomes ever more evident, traditional business and management programs and education fail to provide what is needed for developing "proper" responsible leadership and organizational practices. They do not prepare students and executives sufficiently for coping with leadership trials or dealing with ethical dilemmas in contemporary corporations, economies, and societies (Wankel & Stachowicz-Stanusch, 2012).

Due to being "instrumental, dispassionate and disembodied" (Dey & Steyaert, 2007: 437), most conventional approaches lack integrating embodied and body-mediated ethical and artful learning and teaching or arts-infused and aesthetic pedagogies (Gallos, 2009; Katz-Buonincontro, 2011). What is required is not only more art and craft, and less "science" (Mintzberg, 2004), but also taking ethical and aesthetic risks in management education (Mack, 2013).

Furthermore, with its outdated contents and often anachronistic approaches, a great extent of mainstream education is complicit with a "business-as-usual" orientation that is untenable and even dangerous.

Traditional orthodox business education has possibly assisted in preserving a state of crisis in society and economy, enriching some while impoverishing others, and squandering natural and other resources in an unsustainable way (Shrivastava & Statler, 2012).

As currently constituted, obsolete forms of traditional educational contents and practices that produce unsustainable ways of thinking and acting are complicit in the "unraveling of the Earth's life support systems and the accelerating decline in life's prospects" (Brown & Erickson, 2014).

As a response to the impasses of conventional modes a shift is necessary with regard to guiding orientation and epistemologies of teaching in business school education away from information-transfer and instruction toward other forms and contents of learning, including the cultivation of practical wisdom (Nonaka & Toyama, 2007; Antonacopoulou, 2010; Statler, 2014). Business and management education calls for new, more embodied ways of learning that are part of a morally informed and integral form of education (Roca, 2008). For their incorporation, complementary proto-integral, phronetic approaches to teaching and learning (Pantzar, 2000; Küpers & Pauleen, 2015) are vital.

Bringing together embodied and mindful dimensions mediates more integral transformative forms of learning and education in general (Esbjörn-Hargens et al., 2010; Ferrer et al., 2005) and management education in particular. Such forms of integrative education make room and give time for somatic and semantic, emotional and intuitive knowing, as well as non-discursive learning, without debilitating intellectual standards of analytical rigor and reason-oriented criticism. Thus, a phronetic approach to teaching or learning combines reflexivity with realism (Grint, 2007).

Instead of sterile or formulaic views of reality captured in "sanitized" material or artificial simulations and "games" based on just a few variables or simplistic conceptualizations (Dehler et al., 2001: 494), what its required is quite the opposite. Management education and learning are called upon to bring contexts and "contextures" alive and provide students with opportunities to experience the messy complexity and poly-causal ambiguities and paradoxes or dilemmas of actual and acute management practice.

Integrating ethical and artful/aesthetic ways of learning allows interconnecting with life-world *prâxis* in organizations, the business world, and society, with all material and socio-cultural dimensions as they emerge in situated sayings, doings, and relating (Kemmis, 2012: 150). For this kind of integral *prâxis*-, practice- and process-oriented learning and education the body and embodiment play an essential mediating role.

It is the proposition of the following that the living body and embodiment need to be approached and valued, not only as a "repository of knowledge and learning" in organizations and leadership (Meyer, 2012; Gärtner, 2015; Lord & Shondrick, 2011), but as proto-integral media. They mediate between internal and external or subjective and objective as well as individual and collective experiences, dimensions, and meanings of ethical, aesthetical, and wise learning practices. In other words, body-mediated and embodied performance incorporates relations between individual inner and behavioral spheres, social relations, artifacts, and institutions, through expressive forms of inter-relations (Merleau-Ponty, 2012), also in relation to enacting of more ethical and artful ways of business and management education.

The body of the succeeding text is organized as follows. First a phenomenology of embodied learning is briefly introduced. Then the roles of embodied ethics and aesthetics for management learning and education are outlined. As an empirical illustration, insights about teaching a module on "Ethics and Aesthetics" in a master-study program are presented, including its setting, assignments, and some effects. Furthermore, the significance of relearning to wonder also in learning and education and some concluding implications and perspectives are discussed.

A phenomenology of embodied learning

Advanced forms of phenomenology, in particular Merleau-Ponty's philosophy (1995, 2012), provide an important contribution to the exploration of ignored, undervalued, marginalized, or mistreated sensual and bodily dimensions and forms of embodiment for learning.

Being a distinct style and movement of thought (Merleau-Ponty, 2012: 8), phenomenology is a flexible and vivid way of inquiry and learning, especially in relation to ethical and aesthetical dimension and its integration. A phenomenological approach takes various perspectives on phenomena and its meanings, as well as experiments with diverse ways of sensing and reasoning toward a living understanding.

From a phenomenological perspective, learning takes place primarily through experiential processes. Therefore, phenomenologically, the main intention and orientation is to go back to learning itself. That is, to the present, living act of learning as embedded in practice and process. To return to learning and to its life-worldly situatedness is to turn to that world that embodies the act of a different kind of knowing, of which knowledge always speaks, and in relation to which every scientific schematization is an abstract and derivative sign-language. Metaphorically expressed, this resembles "geography in relation to the countryside in which we have learnt beforehand what a forest, a prairie, or a river is" (Merleau-Ponty, *2012*: ix). Returning to such life-worldly learning is to relate to a meaningful world, in which embodied learners meet and co-create the likewise bodily learned. Thus, all knowledge and learning is always mediated by the living process of embodiment that allows being receptive to "sensual abstractions" that exist before a strict split takes place between subject and object.

A phenomenological understanding of embodied learning can disclose what as a consequence of traditional approaches remains intangible. Thus, it can help to reveal and revalue what heretofore has been unfelt, unseen, untouched, untasted, and even unsmelled and hence unknowable, unthinkable, or unrealisable. Such reworking and reintegrating is especially important for embodied practices of learning in relation to contexts of organization and management.[1]

A phenomenological perspective integrates the non-rational and the rational, the pre-reflective and the deliberative, and the particular and the general as part of a dynamic and decentered, emerging and inter-relational state of being and becoming and learning. As such it embraces bodily situated pre-personal, personal, and transpersonal dimensions in a continuum of professional practice and life (Kinsella & Pitman, 2012). Instead of an intellectualist, overly cognitive, or mentally biased approach, a phenomenological approach toward learning and education strives to overcome the neglect of bodily, situated, and dynamic dimensions (Küpers, 2011) and implicit knowing (Küpers, 2005b, 2011).

The incarnate status of the bodily subject and collective embodiment opens the way to a specific phenomenological description of the learner and learning. Phenomenologically, learning subjects are situated in their environment in a tactile, visual, and/or auditory way through their embodied selves. Whatever they think, feel, or do in their learning process, they are exposed to a synchronized field of inter-related senses. Thus, learners live and their learning takes place fluidly, in the midst of a world of touch, sight, smell, and sound, as well as multi-sensorial experiences and dimensions involved.

In embodied learning, students, as future professional practitioners, genuinely learn from and through their sensual, sensory, meaningful experiences, in which they are ontologically implicated. When learners and learning become mutually involved and co-entangled, perceptions, feelings, meanings, and actions can be integrated in a fluid fashion.

As bodily engagement, involving sensing, perceiving, making choices, and realizing actions, such learning generates effective, appropriate, and creative responses under changing and challenging circumstances (Kemmis, 2012).

Embodied "inter-learning" (Küpers, 2008) refers to a relational understanding of the learning process as co-constituted event. The mesh of inter-learning moves and is distributed in dynamic sets of relations within powerful historical, bodily, and emotional as well as social and structural-processual dimensions. Thus, embodied learning, learners, and their situation with others, and the learnt co-create each other within an "interworld." Importantly, the processual understanding of inter-learning tries not only to reconceive the experiential bodily base of learning, but also to open up new ways of approaching of emerging learning and unlearning (Akgün et al., 2007).

The inclusion of such an embodied and integral learning provides renewed possibilities for developing richer, more textured, understandings of how learning is part of the lived involvement, within what Merleau-Ponty (1995) calls "flesh". This "flesh" refers to a reversible carnal medium of a chiasmic processing in organizations (Küpers, 2015) and leadership (Ladkin, 2010) that is processually foundational for embodied learning of ethics, and aesthetics or art of wisdom as outlined in the following.

Embodied ethics and wisdom learning

As part of an ongoing crisis caused also by unsustainable business and management, various unethical and irresponsible practices in professional settings (Robinson, 2009) call for integrating ethics into management education, that is, cultivating responsibility and practical wisdom (Küpers, 2012, 2015a).

Conventional business ethics and its teaching have been criticized for being instrumentalized or merely reconforming and reconfirming, sustaining, and legitimizing "business as usual" (Banerjee, 2008). Accordingly, possibilities and impossibilities of rationalist business ethics (Woermann, 2013; Carter et al., 2007; Jones et al., 2005) and its ideological critique (Wray-Bliss, 2009, 2012) have ben problematized. Countering one-sided rationalist models of moral practice and normative orientation requires non-foundational critically reflective understandings and teachings of ethics as practice (Painter-Morland & ten Bos, 2011) and practical wisdom. As bodily and embodied characters of moral practices are neglected (Wray-Bliss, 2002) an integrative realization of this emerging "ethics as practice" approach (Muhr et al., 2006; Painter-Morland, 2008; Woermann, 2013: 27) considers them as media for learning. Furthermore, the dominating use of objective, functional, deliberate, and logical analysis of ethical situations in teaching does not sufficiently capture the living and complex nature of human activity (Brady, 1986; Taylor, 2012) that organizations and their management are exposed to and have to deal with.

Embodied sensing and learning requires that ethical practitioners are attuned to themselves, others, and the world. An ethics- and wisdom-orientation and its learning approach that does not take embodied relations into account loses more than its capacity for flexibility. Rather, it might be misleading and blind to (inter-)affectual processes, empathy, compassion, care, or feelings that are experienced pre-reflexively through the body (Pullen & Rhodes, 2014).

Accordingly, a disembodied approach lacks not only senses and affects, but by this also an openness to others and "othering" that are part of a common and shared reality out of which possibilities for the future can unfold (ten Bos, 2011). Instead, embodying ethics and wisdom learning involves relating to and working with situated, ongoing psycho-social experiences inquiring into what bodies can do (Thanem & Wallenberg, 2014). Such orientation toward a living embodiment allows researchers and practitioners to consider how bodies make wise and ethical sense (Diprose, 2005), individually and inter-relationally. Specifically such approach is paying attention to the spaces between bodies encountering one another within organizational life-worlds. These interrelated happenings invites inquiring into ethical issues (Linds & Trull, 2012) while giving rise to "ethically important moments" (Guillemin & Gillam, 2004) or moments of wisdom that are assisting possibilities of sensing, seeing and doing "otherwise" (Butler, 1990).

Integrating phenomenology and pragmatism can then lead to experimenting with forms of ethical and wise "pheno-pragma practice" (Küpers, 2009) in management education that incorporates embodied, inter-relational, as well as living actionable processes and responsive decision-making and behavior. Trying to overcome the traditional opposition between ethics and politics, such pheno-pragmatism is ethico-political in that it considers two dimensions: on the one hand, ethics, as what enables actors or observers to diagnose and evaluate moral and wisdom-related righteousness of organizations (or lack of it); and, on the other, politics, as the actualization of an embodied ethics that also exposes and critiques the political, institutional, and economic investments that underwrite them.

Phenomenology- and pragmatism-oriented approaches together provide the basis for a wisdom and an ethics that is sensorial and corporeal (Roberts, 2003; Pullen & Rhodes, 2014) or carnal and somatic (Bevan & Corvellec, 2007).

Accordingly, a learning and teaching about the ethos of wisdom and ethics takes the entangled bodily dimensions in organizational and practices seriously (Dale & Latham, 2014). Moreover, it cultivates corporeal ethical sensibilities of a genuine responsible and sustainable living and acting as well as the mediality of moral dispositions, feelings, decisions and actions.

As these embodied processes are sedimented in habitual modes and kinesthetic memories of the individual body or collective memories, learning opportunities for de- and rehabitualizing become important. This involves also developing new habits and forms of habitualizing different ethical practices. For this to happen and be enacted, improvisation can be used (Koppett, 2001; Küpers & Pauleen, 2015; Küpers, 2015a) for opening up possibilities of emerging formative relations between feeling, knowing, and acting or being acted-upon, between being a practitioner and becoming one s/he could be, ethically and wisely.

In the course on ethics and aesthetics, outlined in the following, students were invited to experiment improvisationally and asked to reconsider their habits in relation to actual and possible ethical situations. Interplaying with de- and rehabitualizations and exploring other ways of embodied practising and decision-making become alive, individually and in small groups. By taking one habitual and improvisational self and other selves as living cases to study and scenarios of ethical dilemmas, embodied mindfulness could be cultivated in relation to management tasks and responsibilities.

Using improvisational theater (Yanow, 2001) as means of teaching business ethics allowed learners to become "heart aroused" (Whyte, 1994). Accordingly, they became bodily and emotionally engaged in a richer way than deliberate cognitive and propositional processes alone might facilitate. (Re-)engaging sensitivities of improvising, eco-improvisatory exploration, and sensuous intimacies of interactions help overcoming dichotomies of separation and otherness (Preece, 2013).

Bringing together insights from phenomenology and pragmatism, a pheno-pragmatic teaching of ethical practice avoids both the reductionisms of a one-sided reifying constructionism and short-sighted instrumentalist "practicalism" that, due to an outcome-fixation and utilitarian biased course, collapses the "pragma" of instrumentalism with practicality. Such learning about ethics incorporates the sense-makings of the senses as embodied a(i)esthesis (Küpers, 2013b). Correspondingly, right and wrong are recognized as entwined with the beautiful and the ugly, while moral perception, imagination, and motivation are mediated. In an integral fashion, ethical and wisdom dimensions are thereby reintegrated into a(i)esthetics and vice versa (Elm, 2015; Koehn, 2010; Koehn, & Elm, 2015), realized through art-based learning.

Art-based learning

Being "in-formed" by art education helps management education to "catch the sparkling glow" thus to enhance creativity (Baker & Baker, 2012). Art-based methods (Springborg, 2015) and art-mediated learning incorporates artistic and aesthetic experiences (Kokkos, 2011), especially related to managerial development and management education (Taylor & Ladkin, 2009; Nissley, 2002), to get in touch with embodied sensing, feeling, and knowing (Lawrence, 2008). Findings of recent studies support the effectiveness of arts-based methods for leadership development as a form of a potent learning that emerges as sense-making to aesthetic knowing (Sutherland, 2013; Sutherland & Jelinek, 2015).

In particular, art-based forms of learning employ experiential, improvisational, and presentational ways of knowing (Heron, 1996; Heron & Reason, 1997). These modes relate to sensing, perceiving, feeling, thinking, and doing, while cycling through, and between, experiential, imaginal, conceptual, and practical learning and knowing as a "manifold learning" process (Heron, 1999: 3). Art-based learning via presentational knowing is engaging expressive forms of imagery and experiments by dance, sound, music, drawing, painting, photo-captioning, sculpture, poetry, drama, storytelling, play, prototyping, or improvisational theater (Huffaker & West, 2005). Although each art form has different capacities to develop moral *creativity* as well as *empathy,* all of them have specific requirements for going beyond a decorative superficiality toward a "relevant" learning or "relevating" (Paton, et al., 2014).This includes a shifting of roles of instructors and learners; the active participation in the arts by students may forge collaborations with professional artists (Katz-Buonincontro, 2015).

Embodied transformative learning is not only achieved by a cognitive, rational-analytic approach. Rather, it requires disturbing those approaches and mediates a shift in the embodied experiences and its creative processing, especially as occurring in "play-spaces" (Meyer, 2010, 2012). In these spheres, learners are embedded and co-create a "learning space/work space" (Meyer, 2009), in which it is safe to participate with their whole embodied selves. In particular, these spheres of play mediate bodily experienced, situated "felt-sense" and co-emerging "felt-shifts" as enacted through focusing (Gendlin, 1996).[2]

As a practice of understanding, interpretation, and enactment, play is not the application of general principles to practical situations, but a living dialogue, forming a practical, reasonable, and participatory way of be(com)ing (Küpers, 2013).

Creative learning may be enacted performatively through being responsively and creatively playful and in situations where aesthetic play becomes an organizing principle (de Monthoux and Statler, 2008).

In this sense, there is a close connection between embodied learning and serious play (Statler, 2005), especially for developing practically wise leadership (Holliday et al., 2007). Embodied learning is processed by non-rational tacit sensings, knowings, and doings which are integrally and relationally tied to a playful art(istry) of practice. This would involve a heightened attention to sensual experiences of sounds, sights, colors, textures, smells, and feelings as they constitute actual scenarios. Furthermore, art(istry) of practices would include perceptual and aesthetic competencies to relate to and grasp configurations of harmony or disharmony, and rhythm, proportion or fit, etc.

The art of organizing and managing reveals itself both in crucially important situations of uncertainty, instability, and uniqueness and in those dimensions of everyday practice which depend upon the spontaneous exercise of intuitive artistry. Achieving this art(istry) requires bodily sensibility, knowing, and creative imagination, as well as the ability to discern holistically and to make proper judgments about the feel and significance of a particular situation. This art(istry) allows practitioners to make highly skilled moves between and judgements on micro-, macro-, and meta-levels that are "optimal" for the given circumstances in organizational transformation (Paterson et al., 2006).

Bringing art into management education (Irgens, 2014) and learning from artists and through artistic practices and aesthetic experiences, like staying with the senses, engaged detachment and imaginative free play, offer tremendous possibilities. In particular this integration makes it possible to develop "proto-wise" moral sensitivities for more sustainable and ethical organizations and leadership (Ladkin, 2011; 2015) that can also be connected to habitualization and improvisation (Küpers & Pauleen, 2015; Koppett, 2001).

According to Eyler (2009), experiential education helps students to bridge classroom study and life in the world and transform inert knowledge into social knowledge-in-use. At the same time, it enables the learner to interact with and in the world anew and integrates new learning into old constructs, manifesting a sustainable experiential education for the twenty-first century (Higgins, 2009). Such learning is processed via the three "Hs" – Hands, Heart, and Head – as described some longer time ago by Pestalozzi (1746–1827) and in Geddes' holistic approach to education (Geddes, 1915; Higgins, 2001). Such an approach not only harnesses student curiosity (Beames et al., 2011), but realizes an aesthetic practice pedagogy while building a bridge between embodying, feeling, and knowing, for example, about sustainability (Ivanaj et al., 2014).

Creative, proto-artistic practices of learning are distinctive in that their sense-making potential is tied to the way they work with and through specific media. Existentially, these artful learnings mediate transformations that compromises also the overall (self-) understanding of others and the world as part of a life-long learning and unfolding.

An Empirical Case: Embodied "aesthethics" in teaching a master-study program on "legitimacy: ethics and aesthetics"

The following illustrates and connects the discussed issues by presenting the case of a study module called "Legitimacy: Ethics and Aesthetics." First, the module and its context, setting and goals are described, followed by outlining some specific, experimental assignments and some insights and effects.

Context, setting, and learning objectives of the module

The module is part of a master-study program at a new, private, but accredited international German business school. This culture-oriented institution is an entrepreneurial organization created with a "proto-wise" aspirational mission of education.[3] Students come from different backgrounds and countries, some having work experience. The seminar and workshops for this module were facilitated via co-teaching with a professor from an academy of arts, who is an expert in art-based learning. As facilitators, the teacher tried to create a psychologically and socially safe, trustful learning environment, where activities were offered as voluntary.

Building on previous experimental and experiential learnings during the study program, this module was part of the final phase, before a research colloquium for developing their theses. Accordingly, students had already "moved" through alternative learning processes and had experienced various other modules, including simulations, role-plays, and field-trips, particularly during specific "educational touring." This "edu-tour" incorporated embodied creative engagements in projects related to ecological, social, and/or cultural sustainabilities which emerged during self-organized field study to Lisbon or Shanghai. Also in a previous module on "strategic practice," students were invited to learn about strategies and their development by building models using Lego bricks as part of "serious play" (Statler & Oliver, 2008).

The following presentation demonstrates how students learned by experience, while being implicated in an embodied co-entanglement individually and as peers and in relation to artifactual phenomena as well as artistic, social, and culture-related realities.

The overall aim of the module was and is to create spaces and times in which students could become creative participants in experimental and experiential learning. Specifically, the design and learning objective of this course is to provide possibilities to experience and reflect moral, ethical, and art-related aesthetic dimensions, including attitudes, perceptions, imaginations, interpretations, responses, judgments, and communication (Küpers, 2004: 48). The underlying goal is to understand and tentatively enact critical, utopian, and pragmatic dimension of ethics and art/aesthetics for moving beyond a "Sense of Reality" toward a "Sense of Possibility" and "Sense of Design or Gestalt" (Küpers, 2005a).

Accordingly, as an innovative form of leadership education this module aspires to contribute to developing ethical and aesthetic capacities and competencies, as well as getting engaged in embodied applied knowledge and creative practices.

As a preparation and in the first sessions students engaged and reflected on their own experiences and implicit knowings about the topical field and then in relation to course readings, including self-researched sources and in-class activities. The latter included mind-mapping, clustering via small group work, and exercises that were sensual and helped to make sense of ethical and artistic/aesthetic processes and dimensions.

Taking inspirations from connecting ethics, art, and leadership in practices of leadership development and technique and practices from the arts (Taylor & Carboni, 2008), various experiential and creative media were integrated. Throughout the course various sensorial elements and art-related media helped to stimulate a deep and generative learning, aiming at going beyond contrived cognitive orientations and verbal learning through texts, lectures, and discussions. Correspondingly, the learning involved engaging and cultivating senses and multisensory experiences (Joy & Sherry, 2003), experimenting with various forms of embodied and collaborative inquiries, including an assigned creation of "arti-fActs" or "art-works," as outlined later.

Related to artistic or aesthetic ways of experiencing sense-mediating and sense-making media invited entering the sphere and time betwixt and between sensation and knowing. Furthermore, technology was used, particularly mobile phones, for making photos and videos, while being involved in defamiliarizing and improvising excursions into the entwined nexus of "culture-and-nature." These excursions, manifesting processually with also an exiting of conventional frames, included a blindfolded walk through the busy city into a park and a visit to and provocative tour through an exhibition of modern art. The museum was displaying abstract works of art in the style of the tradition- and rule-breaking "*Art Informel*" that was using improvisatory methodology and gestural techniques. The visit to the museum was combined with a creative play-shop in an art studio in cooperation with a local academy of design (*Hochschule für Gestaltung*) that included performative practices and interventions as well as creating "informal" art-works, hands-on, and modifying the works of others.

The distinct experiences in different environments allowed experiments with bodily (dis-)orientation and perceptual (dis-)placement, but also realizing the significance of trust, empathy and pro-social experiences. Thereby, different senses, affective subtleties, and sensory potentialities and proto-ethical qualities were addressed and processed that otherwise would be glossed over or just "labeled."

Employing these exercises was interrupted and punctuated by reflection periods, in which students were invited to think individually and critically, but also to share and discuss in small groups the experiences they had. Here, they could make connections back to other learnings and forward to their own envisioned professional practices. Conducting further exercises and experiments served then as a means of exploring the embodied, ethical, and artful moments of leadership and developing "leadership-as-practice" in real time, followed by processing, reflecting, and projective storytelling and sharing.

In this way, students learned interpreting leadership as a situated "ethical" art-form in and of itself (De Pree, 1989; Vaill, 1991) that is characterized as much by its phronetic qualities and artfulness as its skills and technical sites.

Students not only deconstructed modern notions of universal leadership and morality principles and supposed self-evident truths of modernism. Being sensually and aesthetically sensitized, they transferred themselves into taking different perspectives compared to conventional economic-analytic and managerial approaches.

As part of cultivating an ethical and aesthetic pursuit or artful craft, guided by "excellence," they learned about what it means to embody ethics and becoming a "leaders-as-aesthete" as virtuoso. The latter one will still employ conventional managerial tasks like capital budgeting and other technical methods, but will view these as just one means of making a decision (Dobson, 1998). At the same time this aesthetic-virtuoso leader is also recognizing and enacting underlying qualities, like disinterest, subjectivity, inclusivity, contemplation, internality and value judgements (Dobson, 1999; 2007), and can be extend to a "collective virtuosity" (Marotto et al., 2007) and poly-centered phronesis (Jackson, 2012).

The assignments

1 "arti-fAct"/"art-work"

The students were invited to create an artful expression, called art-work or "arti-fAct" related to the contents and experiences they have processed during the module.

Accordingly, they were invited to respond or to make connection to the ethical and the aesthetic parts as well as possible relationships or tensions between both.

Creating such an "art-work" offered an opportunity to playfully work on and express what students had experienced and learned or what had provoked or inspired them personally, interpersonally or was afforded physically respectively mediated structurally. One invited focus was on responding to the quests and questions of more responsive, responsible, and/or sustainable forms of organizing and managing.

Practically, technically, or methodologically, students could to use pictorial or sculptural forms and media as well as vignettes (hypothetical situations) and scenarios/simulations, all serving to represent more concrete and/or more abstract expressions. Optionally, for processing their ideas, they could also employ written media like stories, poems, a personal letter, picturing dreams, diary entries, fictional dialogues, or scripts for a role-play. Alternatively, they could also discuss critically self-selected quotations or texts, respectively existing works of art by others, so that they could be connected to and interpret the themes of the module.

What was actually created were, among other things: collages, fragmented pictures, photographic snap-shots, multi-layered paintings, a comic cartoon, a video-clip of a performance, a poly-material sculpture, and a multi-dimensional installation, colorful dress-models, a complex puzzle in a box, a hand-made embroidery, an interpretation and reflection of Ai Weiwei's Ghost Gu, a letter to a friend, and a poem. A selection of some of these art-works ("arti-fActs"), created by the students, is shown in the appendix. These examples of outcomes of the creative endeavors invite us to imagine the underlying creative processes that brought them to life and metaphorical and narrative richness they carry.

2 "ScholArtist"-statements

For understanding better this richness and the original intentions and background ideas, processes of creation, and possible interpretations, the students were asked to write a brief, reflective commentary statement about their work-of-art for other possible recipients. One guiding question for this so-called "ScholArtist"-statement was: "What do you want to express, and communicate, and why, in this way?" The use of non-academic literature and (academic) references or other sources was encouraged to contextualize and enrich their statements.

Offering themselves and recipients, especially the peer students, these reflective commentaries about these singular works-of-art allowed them to express their feelings and thoughts by retelling "little narratives" in a non-formulaic way. This medium was intended for helping students to reinterpret truth(-fulness) and its representation by using their genuine knowing and specific expression. Accordingly, they could ascribe meanings and value via personal "*petit récit*" as part of the cultivation of open-ended and insuppressable desire and its expression. However, students also realized the difficulties to make such statements, appearing as inept, about their often non-text-semantic work and the artist intentions and expressions.

All works of art, reflection papers, and feedback are documented in a book, published by the university, to provide access for other students and interested readers or observers.

3 Short reflection paper

Additionally, students were invited to write a short reflection paper or mini-essay on why they "sense" and make sense (or none), thus think that organizations and management/leadership should and could be ethical and aesthetical. A special focus was given to how learners could become more responsive, responsible, and sustainable. These reflective essays served as media to explore, express, and share their own personal insights, and "lessons" through the learning process as well as discussing related literature.

The following guiding questions were offered:

- Why and how are ethical and aesthetical dimensions relevant for practices of managing and organizing differently? What differences do enacted ethics and aesthetics make in organizations and management/leadership, and how?
- What roles do (formative) principles and (performative) practices of a "lived" ethics and aesthetics play within organizations and its stakeholders? What are constraints and limitations of these practices?
- What does an ethically sensitive "professional artistry" as an embodied "art of leadership" mean to you? Where do you see possibilities, problems, issues, and challengers for your own artful actual and future leading practices in and beyond organizations?
- Why are ethics and aesthetics a base or media for an extended, more integrative legitimacy of organizing and managing in the twenty-first century?

Furthermore, students were stimulated to reflect transfers and implications of what they have learned on their own envisioned career and professional practice as a imagined process of development. For showing their "mastery" they were also prompted to consider and relate their reflections to contents and insights that were processed in other modules before and connected discourses and contents. Again, they were expected to bring in and discuss some sources or references to illustrate, substantiate or to complement their lines of argument, reasoning and intuition.

Discussion: Insights, feedback, and effects

The following provides some observational, conversational, and exemplarily insights, understanding, and feedback, as well as some effects and implication and then limitations and challenges. Overall, the module confirmed the effectiveness and value of experiential learning and bringing together learning about ethical and aesthetical dimensions and practices in one course.

The following presents some understanding of why senses make sense for a transformative (wisdom) learning in relation to integrating ethics and aesthetics practically.

Why senses "make sense" for transformative (wisdom-) learning

Offering access to an embodied and social sensorium (Jones, 2006: 8), sensual experiences and vital expressive possibilities were invigorated by this learning that allowed both an intensified sensing and sense-making (Küpers, 2013a).

Staying with and coming anew to their various sensory modes (Springborg, 2010), students dwelled in moments of different states of being and connections. This included experiencing how embodied, tacit knowing corresponds to sensory-aesthetic knowing and gut feelings (Hansen et al., 2007). The learners not only noticed how their bodily states altered, but also how atmospheres and communication as well as tension-patterns had changed (Springborg & Sutherland, 2015).

The feedback by students suggests that the offered experiential approaches led to realizations and meanings that would be unavailable through rational-analytical ways with their written or spoken language. Learning experientially and the (self-) employed techniques and exercise allowed them to develop a-rational or a-logical capabilities and intensified forms of awareness and other ways of "knowing" and realizations as well as cultivating ethical and aesthetic sensibilities and competencies (Hansen et al., 2007; Waddock, 2014).

Not only was energy and motivation level higher compared to other courses and approaches, but also this learning freed up ideas, liberated a radicalized creative sensing, thinking, and action, and deepened awareness about unconscious drivers while also cultivating conscious mindfulness.

Statements like "This allowed me to awaken my inner child", "I could let the artist within me express herself, tapping into unknown potentials," and "I felt released as I did not need to fulfil any kind of expectation and the result was beautiful" confirm an activation of dormant potentials. Being involved in investments into ethical and aesthetic risk-taking (Mack, 2013), while affording opportunities to "enliven and impassion" (Dey and Steyaert, 2007), students were challenged to "find their own form" (Taylor and Hansen, 2005) and trans-&-form (Küpers, 2011a).

Transforming the actual and moving toward the possible

Doing things for their own sake, which includes not being graded, students were experiencing intrinsic values of ethical and artful events and processes, while developing, enacting, and "maintaining a reflective practice of aesthetic quality" (de Monthoux, 2000: 46) that can be linked to dimensions and components of transformational leader- and followership (Küpers, 2011a).

The module mediated via de- and rehabitualization and ethical and aesthetical learning opportunities for an integral transformation, comprising inner and outer, individual and collective dimensions. Accordingly, it provided chances for a multidimensional, cognitive, socio-emotional, and behavioral growth, as well as fostering creativity and complex skills development that are likely to be increasingly important for organizational leadership (Gallos, 2009).

The capacity for questioning the locked sense of the "real" was as much activated as the yielding of a sense of the possible and imaginative (Küpers, 2013a).

The experimental practices and reflected experiences offered a productive irritant, rendering utopian as well as pragmatic re-orientations. Through engagements with various ongoing ethic-oriented and arts-based activities, students tapped and activated potentials to find alternative and playful ways to perceive, relate, and act, and thus learned differently.

The capability of intensified awareness and enacting capacities to embrace and juxta-reposition otherness of multiple realities, heterogeneous contents, and complexifying perspectives gave them opportunities to experience and create different feelings, thoughts, social encounters, and actions, modifying their way of studying, learning, working, and living.

Ethical processing and artful/aesthetic relations and practices were transformative by experiencing, developing, and enacting sensitized bodily and emotional states, identities, and practices. The transformative qualities became alive especially as control was suspended or relinquished and receptivity allowed and encouraged. The ethical and artful co-inquiry design invited and helped students to explore how they could co-create organizations and their management realities in more empathetic and creative ways. The art-works "worked" in that the assigned tasks rendered impressive and inspiring "outcomes" and artful expressions beyond conventional formats. Creating these art-works facilitated working with overlapping meanings with a "thinking through making" (Lammer, 2012). It was an exercise in "artful making," including the interdependent and intertwined elements of release, collaboration, ensemble, and play (Austin & Devin, 2003).

Experiencing the relation between art and leadership (Küpers, 2004), they learned leading beautifully (Ladkin, 2008: 27), responding to the call to beauty (Antonacopoulou & Bento, 2016) as well as activating novel potentials also for responding differently, and thereby extending the repertoire of interpretative capabilities, and responses. For instance, perceiving organizational and leadership situations as more or less beautiful, sublime, comic, or grotesque ways and value them for its own sake (Taylor & Hansen, 2005: 1216) or as more (or less) ethically acceptable, fair, just, and wise.

In this way, the experienced and reflected transformation may contribute to realizing other and wiser forms of organizational and management/leadership practices. The experiences of explicit and implicit bodied processes, related to ethical and aesthetic dimensions facilitated discoveries of "bodied" mindful forms of knowing and dealing with not-knowing, and engaged action and non-action.

As a form of radical reflexivity this module allowed a complexifying reflexive co-agency or "re-flAction" to emerge, which unites aesthetic reflexivity and aesthetic agency (Springborg & Sutherland, 2015) and learning also how to know what is known (King, 2008) and what is not known/done or could be known or done differently.

Accordingly, this module served as medium for re-relating, reconfiguring, reclaiming, and reassessing the way students are connected to and process themselves, others, contents, issues, and problems. All of this revisiting helped them to re-form their orientation with regard to perceiving, believing, and acting that encourages critically reflective, transformational development, and learning (Gray, 2007: 497).

While some elements were more memorable than others, participants experienced that it was the complementary blend of the components properly integrated in this module that made it special and effective, which implies that isolating or removing some elements or not connecting them would be limiting.

Concerning the aforementioned holistic approach of learning by hands, hearts, and heads, participants used their entire bodies by grasping and processing materialities of various tangible media and being in embodied spaces and situations with co-present others; with regard to their hearts, they experienced flowing feelings, emotions, and moods and got engaged in an affective, empathetic "knowing" and relating, while also they used their heads for getting a reflective and critical understanding of meanings and implication of what they were doing.

Importantly, it was a practice of students' own hands, hearts, and heads, but students co-created and moved through a shared experiential field in which they were learning together, hence were gathered; a specific co-creational "we-space." This dynamic and forceful realm was enacted jointly by them as "inter-actants," in existence only for the time the interaction lasted (Krueger, 2011; Fuchs & Koch, 2014), and which embodied social "inter-learning."

Specific limitations and challenges

This final part of reporting about the module states some limitations and challenges. While the overall response was positive and most students liked being involved, some have had reservations toward or struggled with this kind of experimental approach. Despite that it was a relatively safe learning environment, some students suffered from emotional or mental hesitations and blockages. There were students who found such experiments and the tasks very unfamiliar, and felt that they lack the supposed necessary skills to engage in them. A well thought-out design, specific preparation, and continuous coaching and encouragement are vital for counteracting these tendencies.

Furthermore, the choice of possible media was selective and constrained. Students were considering also writing, composing and singing songs, acting out dramatic scenes, or choreographing dances, which would require other, more expensive forms of documentation or recording. Using again (limited) verbal and explicit language in the "scholArtist" statements and reflection paper created a tension in relation to non-verbal and more implicit forms of expression in the art-works.

Finally, questions about evaluation and the transferability of this learning to life-worldly management and organizational context arose. The use of novel, expressive forms of creation and writing that demonstrate engagement with particular concepts is challenging for any assessment and evaluation. Because arts-based, or aesthetics-integrating education, fosters different ways of learning, the corresponding evaluation needs to capture the different aspects of what has been taught and what has been learned (Eisner, 1998). As the creative expressions revealed something of students' attitudes, personalities, identities or personal relationship within the contents, and transformations, it is difficult to assess or even unethical to judge.

What are needed are sensitive designs for approaching assessment (Pavlovich et al., 2009) and specific qualitative treatments and feedback. In the given case, the reflection papers were given formative, rather than summative feedback and the art-works/artifacts were not graded at all formally. Furthermore, additional criteria for creative and reflective work were considered (Pavlovich et al., 2009), including looking for evidence that the student has imaginatively engaged with ideas and perspectives that are different than their own, as well as how being imaginative and authentic were brought together by narrative coherence and plausibility, rather than theoretical accuracy (Hibbert, 2013).

Constrained by the given institutional setting and examination system, the teacher remained the ultimate assessor and validator, reinforcing a certain degree of powerful hierarchy and inequality. However, considering various features of this innovative experiment the expressions of the embodied and reflective learners were incorporated in an emancipatory way.

Correspondingly, also for the co-teachers the educational practices not only became more flexible, creative, and artful. Rather, this experiment provided them also an opportunity for deeper learning experiences, even calling to teach what they do and do don't know (Rancière, 1991). As much as possible the role of superior or policing explicators and regimes was reduced to and a liberated inquiry facilitated, allotting students for a reflective self-assessment and serious appreciation of peer feedback.

Overall the embodied inter-learning, as it became alive in this experimental ethics-and-aesthetics-in-practice, appears to be a proto-phronetic approach for a transformative and integral education and wisdom-learning.

The feedback and interpretations for this module reveal qualities of how this embodied "Aesth-Ethics" in management education/learning made and can make a difference, allowing for other differentiations to emerge.

Relearning to wonder, or how study can become enchanted and "wonder-ful"

The course and assignments invited practice of a kind of reflective unmanaged inquiry (Gabriel, 2013). In contrast to purposeful, cumulative, formulaic, mostly joyless work, students were offered or could self-organize a space and time for inquiry that was more spontaneous and playful, even partly eccentric or purposeless. The given freedom invited students for venturing into unknown territories, expeditions of sensing and making sense, discovering journeys of feeling, thinking, and acting differently. "Playing with ideas, seeking surprises, delighting in paradoxes and enduring unresolved contradictions are all features of unmanaged inquiry" (Gabriel, 2013: 726). These practices are serving as much as a source of pleasure in its own right and as a potentially valuable media of ideas and innovation for a more managed inquiry (Gabriel, 2013: 728).

Related to the previously described module, this kind of inquiry proved for the students to be a more experimental, comprehensive, and integrated way of learning. Especially, it bolstered students' excited interest, enhanced their curious (self-) reflection, and critical analysis, and activated the capacity to wonder (Rubinstein, 2008; Curry, 2015).

All inquiries, quest(ion)s and philosophizing are stimulated and sustained by wonder. Historically, wondering has been appreciated as a pervading and guiding pathos and mood of astonishment[4] and mode of enchantment. One might wonder, why wonder has not been wondered about more and is not any more a living part of research and study in leadership/management and business education and social studies and science at all. One explanation of course is disenchantment prevailing in our times. In late-modern disenchanted, secularized times, disillusions, anomies, and alienation, as well as dominating naturalistic explanations and instrumentalizing approaches, have displaced and marginalized the capacity and enactment of wonder. The classical Aristotelian view and is tradition makes wonder a temporary irritant and prelude to objectifying taming reason, something "to ration, to rein in, to delimit, something whose entrances and exits are ultimately subject to the knowing self" (Rubinstein, 2008: 14). Accordingly, modern science has "thieved wonder" in its frenzy to pile up truths (Heidegger, 1926/1962, Ch. 5; 1937–38/1994).

Our time is in need of rediscovering wondering and the wondrous as part of exploring a critical-minded re-enchantment.[5] What would a wondrous enchantment in learning mean and how can it be realized today?

According to Curry (2015) it is all about dehabitualization – letting delight and wonder happen:

> Both individually and collectively, the way to encourage enchantment in learning is become aware of, and let go of, the habitual attitudes, practices and rules that suppress it. Leave room for it, resisting the temptation to try to meddle and control the outcome, and create the conditions it favors where profit of any kind, use-value and efficiency are not allowed to dominate.

This is not the same as making it happen. The point is to *let* it happen, and the difference is crucial. Wonder, like love, is not a method, and it cannot be applied, tested, or improved. All we can do is create the conditions it favors – usually through appropriate ritual for that purpose – and invite it to be present. As Robert Frost famously said, the movement in poetry is from delight to wisdom. "Delight is where we must start" (Curry, 2015).

As wonder is an invitation to other more creative forms of inquiries and a driver of imagination, how can we relearn to wonder again for developing social innovation and more sustainable, ethical and aesthetical research and practices?

How can we bring back wonder not only into research, but also into study and all learning? How can we make inquiries again more wonder-ful – full of wonder?

Responding to these critical, inquiring quest(ion)s: first some components and interpretation of wonder and what it serves are outlined, followed by considering why and how wonder can be brought back into inquiries in organization and management studies and educational and real-life practices.

What constitutes wonder and how does it appear?

Is wonder placed outside everyday experience as extraordinary happenings or inside humans as psychological states? Seeing wonder as an embodied practice, it unfolds in moments of stillness and dwelling in which one who wonders suspends his or her preconceptions (Merleau-Ponty, 2012, xiii) and engages with realities in a direct, immediate, and new way. Those who are in wonder are fascinated and moved by something that is beyond their understanding. In this state, they open up their vulnerability[6] and longing (Hansen, 2012) as well as belonging to what is not appropriated or in control. Being in a wondering mode motivates response patterns that do not fit with standard accounts of functions.

Phenomenologically, according to Heidegger (1937–38/1994), wonder is a kind of clearing which we cannot fully know our way into or out of. As such it is an overwhelming emerging process that has its own dynamics, while questioning what is and can be, allowing the indeterminate, unthinkable, and impossible to happen. As a singularity, wonders seem to fall outside the domain of ordinary experience, common sense, daily expectations, significations, or classifications. However, while wonder may arise often from the extraordinary, it is the extra-ordinariness of the ordinary that is the opacity of ordinary transparency which instills wonder.

Wonder conceived in this way rules out an exclusive pursuit of complete explanation, but also skepticism or relativism about our capacity to make things transparent, calling for responding with interplaying of opacity and transparency. Sometimes the sheer presence or appearance of things, together with our being there, in its strangeness, resists explanation and provokes wonder (Malpas, 2006: 291). Wonder resides in the immanence of everyday-life, yet opens to the transcendent, historical contingent,[7] while it constricts for the constringent. This implies that it is causing "interactions" to contract, and only a hospitality to wonder can open "to the possibility of the transformative" (Rubenstein, 2008: 189).

The transformative qualities or potential of wonder in relation to awareness (sense, images) and in meaning can be related fruitfully to discourses, like the ones on intuition or mindfulness in organization and management studies. Wonder is transformatively mindful also by keeping consciousness alive to the present life-worldly reality including that of research.

Furthermore, also active–passive modes seem to be another one-in-two, for example, in leading and following or "co-wondering" with rotating roles. This in turn would trigger the question how wonder can be a motivational and transformative adaptive emotion that contributes to the formation, maintenance, and restructuring of orientations and social groups also of researchers.

Differentiating between wondering *at* – in passive receptivity and appreciation of phenomena – and wondering *about* – as active search and discovery, behind phenomena – Carlsen & Sandelands (2015) discuss a typology of potentials and different phases. Following this differentiation they distinguished between moments of arousal/stimulus, expansion, immersion, and explanation (Carlsen & Sandelands, 2015) all relevant for learning.

If wonder, as embodied experience, temporarily suspends or deactivates utilitarian strivings, and seems to render people contemplative, relatively passive, and receptive, then there is the question of how this is compatible with goal-oriented practices, intentionality, agency, etc. in organizational practice and research. However, it is this very suspension of rational and purpose-driven orientation and routines or reductionistic causal principles that may help to get in touch with the relational can creative aspects of reality. Thus, wonder may serve to develop affective, moral sensitivities and moral reflections while disclosing other forms of intentionalities, meanings, and actions. What about the ambivalences or even dark side of wonder? Although wonderful often means satisfying or favorably esteemed, the experience of wonder is not always pleasant. As a sense of *pathos* (and responsiveness), *ecstasy* (*ek* – out + *histanai* – place), and *surprise* (*super* + *prehendere,* as taken over and taken up) are part of wonder(ing) it can be overwhelming. Or it can lead to paralyzing dilemmatic situations, as well as have unsettling, destabilizing, or disorienting effects. What may be experienced as wonderful is apt to be ambiguous – attractive and simultaneously repellant, calling ambivalent responses and having unforeseeable, far-reaching implications.

Limitations

Facing the mentioned potentials one has also to see limitations, ambivalences, and threats of integrating ethics and especially art and aesthetics in the context of leadership/management education.

Taking a perspective of embodied experiential learning, it is important not to give a one-sided preference to the body over the mind as a source of knowledge. Nor would it be wise to reject reflective practices as they can facilitate a learning dialogue between implicit embodied experience and conceptual aspects of consciousness (Jordi, 2010).

Furthermore, as much as ethics can fall into moralism or relativism, likewise aesthetics can lead to a surface "aesthetisation" (Welsch, 1996: 12), sensory overload (Hancock and Tyler, 2009). Furthermore, artistry can be disruptive, deconstructive, deceptive, delusional, fabricational, and just plain boring or wrong, as well as ethically problematic. Additionally, a problem with the described art and aesthetic processes is that they are idiosyncratic and evanescent and tend to be unpredictable. For all these reasons it remains important to consider ideological and control linkages between ethics regarding wisdom and aesthetics or an anaesthetizing a(i)esthetic craving in organizations (Kersten, 2008).[8]

Furthermore, integrating embodied learning of ethics and aesthetics/art can also serve conservative or elitist leader-related interests only. It can be used affirmationally for validating and reinforcing or legitimizing practiced actions, beliefs, and events. An "ethicalization" and an "aesthetication" occupied with a functional appropriation can be instrumentalized as a manipulating means or substitute for authentic genuine ethical sensitive and artful leadership practice.

Additionally, there exist difficulties of institutionalization – implementation, securing and controlling by creating adequate policies, procedures, process, etc. for embodied learning in academic curricula and activities.

Conclusion

Based on a phenomenological interpretation, this chapter has explored possibilities of embodied learning that integrates ethics and aesthetics/art into management education. The significance of ethical and aesthetical dimensions into management learning and education were illustrated by a case of a module that is part of a master study program.

Correspondingly, some observational reflective findings and insights as well problems and challenges were discussed. Furthermore, the importance and implications of wonder and wondering in learning were addressed and discussed critically.

Overall, the qualities and dimensions of mediated embodied learning can be understood as a creative, poietic practice preparing students for a different kind of a professional *prâxis*. In this sense, phronetic wisdom cannot be taught and, while being itself emergent, can be cultivated and learned indirectly, which involves a commitment in the world for living and acting in *prâxis* (Kemmis, 2012: 159).

Students learned about wisdom in the sense that

> to be wise involves submitting to and wrestling with reality in all its intended and unintended interdependencies without regret and with a sense of personal responsibility. Wise people embrace doubt, ambiguities, consequences, and

> experiences – the effects of decisions that they need to live with and not just the decisions themselves. Within this 'earthy' metaphysics, the concerns of wisdom turn from a question of adding to or expanding knowledge to one of being in close intimacy with our lived experiences.
>
> (Chia & Holt, 2007: 513)

This includes embracing ignorance, while being willing to unlearn and to relearn and to realize that this process is an interminable one – yet one that sets us on the path to wisdom (ibid., 524). The module allowed the creation of new and unforeseeable differences and in-ventions in the sense of "*in-veniens*," that is, "in-comings," that break in upon us and shatter horizons of expectations.

Embodied learning practices – through which fluid bodies and co-emergent minds interplay (Fenwick, 2006) – can integrate varied, often disconnected aspects of implicit experiencing and reflective consciousness.

As such they enact "*e-ducere*," that is, "*to lead out*," leading out of limiting boundaries and toward other ways of being. The described forms of experimenting with the unknown allowed those involved to discover or conjure up as-yet-unexplored possibilities for knowing. As an embodied knowing this comprised sensing, seeing, feeling, thinking, relating, and acting further or otherwise, as-yet-unimagined options.

Perceptual knowing of the subtlety and nuances, tacit clues, and emotional signs of meaning and contexts of the process of embodied ethical and artful learning practices provides a richer and more valid premise also for evaluation as "tasteful" judging. In its original sense – referring to the Latin "*judicium sensitivium*" – ethical and aesthetic sensible judgment is based on the "*gustus*" or the taste. Hence it is distinct from pure intellectual or cognitive knowledge and must be exercised, discussed, and negotiated case by case in an ongoing debate. As such it can also be related to moral and wise judgment.

As a bodily living and shared one (Shilling, 1993: 146–7), such creation and experience of taste can be related to a "style of practice" (Tonkinwise, 2011) in management. Engaging in styles of practices with others in continuous co-creation and appraisal, serves the rendering of presentational knowing (Seeley & Reason, 2008), meaning and actualizations of possibilities of expressions or harnessing imaginative capabilities. Moreover, as an organizing, enhancing, and directing force (Dobson, 2010), style functions as "a certain way of handling situations" (Merleau-Ponty, 2012: 342).

Importantly, embodied "aesth-ethical" learning is never finished, but an open-end dynamic process of unfoldment that leads us to go on further, developing and engaging in life-long learning, while being situated in a world of contingency and generating qualitatively different responses.

Practising this kind of learning with its focus on embodiment, intrinsic and implicit as well as indeterminate dimensions keeps a sense of "*Bildung*" as an educative process of understanding and phronetic becoming (Gadamer, 1982) and artistry of practice (Schön, 1987).[9]

A truly integral learning embraces the body (embodied incorporated dimensions), mind (cognitive, logical, rational thought), heart (feelings, emotions, moods), and "spirit" of individuals and collectives. Embodied "Aesth-Ethics" in management education as described in this chapter is not only different, but makes a difference. Bringing together sensing, feeling, knowing, and doing it effectuates a proto-integral orientation toward be(com)ing a truly embodied authentic leadership (Ladkin & Taylor, 2010) or relational authenticity and integrity in organizations. On a systemic level, incorporating "Aesth-Ethics" into business and management education mediates an autoecopoïesis for developing cultures of sustainability that manifests as an exercise in applied ethically sensitive "art-science" (Kagan, 2013). As such it contributes to accomplishing a genuinely worthwhile learning purpose and effort that meets present and future needs and well-be(com)ing of members and stakeholders of organizations (Küpers, 2005) and beyond.

Being part of an ongoing rethinking and redoing of management and business learning, teaching, and education as an "aesthethical" practice embodies the unfoldment of a more integral, sustainable, and wise process.

Notes

1 Related to management and organization studies, a phenomenological approach has been used to make explicit the implicit structures and meanings of experiences of the reflective practitioner (Schipper, 1999) and groups (Neale et al., 2002) as well as issues in organizational life-worlds (e.g. Sanders, 1982: 353) and a more integral organizational learning (Küpers, 2008).

2 Referring essentially to the perception of one's own sensory and visceral experiences, the "bodily felt sense" is a significant phenomenon in both psychotherapy and body-oriented psychotherapy. Gendlin defines *felt sense* as "a special kind of internal bodily awareness ... a body-sense of meaning" (Gendlin, 1981: 10), which the conscious mind is initially unable to articulate. By staying with a felt sense, a shift in meaning may eventually occur that brings a physically felt relief in the way the body holds that issue. Referring to a change that is actually happening, Gendlin defined *felt-shift* as "the body talking back" (Gendlin, 1996: 97) or as a kind of resonating that occurs when we check with our body about the accuracy of a felt-sense, or an initial handle for a felt-sense. This shifting is a way of recognizing the appropriateness of a felt-sense, which in and of itself is already a fulfillment, a carrying forward of the whole, a "symbolic completion" (Gendlin, 1964: 10).

3 As expressed in the following excerpt from the Mission Statement:

> We act on the assumption of the educational ideal of an educated young person with multifaceted interests, who is willing to assume responsibility, believes that leadership is an opportunity to serve others and society, is capable of changing his/her point of view and questioning his/her own construction of reality, on the basis of sound know-how and a broad academic education, is able to look 'behind the scenes' of what seems to be self-evident, is willing to cross inner and outer borders and open to new and foreign experiences and, thus, in the spirit of life-long learning, has acquired the ability of independently developing his/her personality.... We act on the assumption of the ideal of a university that – literally – considers itself a service provider for the students, the economy and society, that, through its competitive orientation, seismographically detects developments and trends and integrates them into its research and teaching – thus becoming a marketplace for the requirements of those who have a demand for education on the one hand and the requirements of those who have a demand for qualified employees on the other.... We believe that, in the performance of our tasks with regard to teaching, studying and researching, we have a special responsibility vis-à-vis our city, the region and the state of Baden-Württemberg as well as vis-à-vis the people living here and the regional businesses. We seek a trustful cooperation with all groups of society, businesses and other universities and academic institutions. We want to contribute to the University's ability to establish and maintain relationships as well as to regional, national and international networking. As a business owned by a charitable foundation, we compete with other universities for the best talents, ideas and tasks. Our services and programs are aimed at

> both, those who have a demand for education and training on the one hand and businesses and institutions on the other. In order to be able to compete and to assert ourselves as a private, state-accredited University at the interface of the education and labor market we strive for a consistently high quality in our areas of performance which we continually aim to improve. ... When developing new study programs, we focus on promising industries and sectors with a high demand for academic professionalization. With the participation of students and representatives of the business community, we assess our curricula on a regular basis with regard to changing demands in the education and labor market. In this context, we strive for a high degree of innovation in our programs and integrate the topic 'Change and Innovation' into our curricula. Our offers and target groups are geared to the concept of 'lifelong learning'. On the one hand this means that we already have offers for gifted pupils and on the other that (if possible) we continually accompany and coach our graduates and others beyond their first university degree.
>
> (http://karlshochschule.de/en/university/university/karls-values)

4 Classically, the capacity and practice *to wonder* ("*thaumazein*") has been the starting point of philosophy. Following Plato, according to Aristotle (1966: 9/ 982b):

> For it was because of wonder that man both now and originally began to philosophise. To begin with, they wondered at those puzzles that were to hand, such as about the affections of the moon and events connected with the sun and the stars and the universe.

Interestingly, both the Greek verb "*thaumazein*" that means 'to wonder' and the noun "*thauma*" ("wonder") have an association with *sensing*, and looking: "*theaomai*" means 'to look at something with wonder' and is etymologically also related to 'theatre' or "*theatron*." However, ambivalently "*thaumazein*" both opens our eyes wide and plunges us into bewildering opaqueness. *Thauma* is related to trauma; complexed by apostoria and perplexed by aporias, finding and lost, eliciting thought, not just curiosity. Thus, to wonder means that you "are in an aporia", which literally "no passage," or "no way out." Thus, wondering we are in a state of perplexity, because those in it find that there is no easy solution available (Plato, 1973: 130c).

5 Enchantment today needs to be critically reinterpreted beyond binaristic and dialectic approaches (Saler, 2006) in all its ambivalence. For example, on the one hand, the techniques of enchantment evoke the personal, the socially meaningful, and even the sublime. On the other hand, enchantment comes with the double-meaning of being "duped" or fooled (Ladkin, 2006) as an ideological cover for rationalization (Landy & Saler, 2009). Enchantment has been related to an aura of authentic presence that is resisting rationalization and promoting creative social connection (Boje & Baskin, 2011).

6 Interestingly the very term "wonder," from the Old English "*wundor*" might be cognate with the German "*Wunde*" or "wound." This makes wonder about possible links to affect and emotion in organization and management theory and practice (when being wonderstruck).

7 Confirmed by historical analysis (Saler, 2006; Landy & Saler, 2009), wonder in all its forms is always historically contingent and historicizing the emotion of wonder will prevent anachronistic accounts, and may explain socio-cultural and political usages or rejections of wonder, thus showing an undulating, nonlinear history of wonders. Instead of reverting to prior forms of wonder perhaps multiplied re-enchanted ways of wonder(ing) need to be in concord with secular reason in full awareness of pluralism and contingency.

8 Kersten (2008) sensitizes us to critically take into account that practices of ethics, wisdom, and aesthetics are shaped by their social, political, and historical context, in theory and in experience. Our ideas of what is beautiful, true, and good are bound by time and place and can serve political and ideological functions. They are closely linked to issues of identity formation and social control and they often reflect class, race, gender, and cultural positioning and biases. She specifically problematizes aesthetic craving by which people seek satisfaction in that they create a sense of beauty – form, style, and colorfulness – culminating in certainties of meaningfulness while processing an unconscious aestheticism.

9 This "*Bildung*" as a cultivating form of learning is not only different from an extrinsic-oriented training of pre-specified products, but allows integration of a flourishing learning, education, and happiness (Noddings, 2003), thus making it possible to become itself an art. As this learning is about practices of becoming good and approaching an artful excellence (*arête*), it implies habitual and reflective and actional motions and emotions in the form of "being-on-the-way." As embodied learning is processing by a non-rational tacit knowing and doing, it is integrally and relationally tied to an *artistry of practice* (Schön, 1983, 1987), operating in indeterminate zones of practice. Accordingly, the art of organizing and managing ethically, and aesthetically "reveals itself both in crucially important situations of uncertainty, instability, and uniqueness and in those dimensions of everyday practice, which depend upon the spontaneous exercise of intuitive artistry" (Schön, 1983: 240). As a practically habitualized incorporated disposition for acting, artistry strives toward what makes professional activity work at its best, and thus refers to a mastery state or condition that makes people perform tasks or functions well. The embodied artistry of learning practices and practices of artistry (Minocha & Reynolds, 2013: 173) incorporate entwined perceptions, reflections, and actions artfully. As a specific practising within a shared tradition, a professional artistry involves a blend of practitioner qualities, attunement, knowledge, practice skills, and creative imagination processes together with the ability to use them critically, intuitively, and practically (Titchen & Higgs, 2001). Being more an activity-oriented than attitude-oriented practice, professional artistry is enacted in a mature performance that is characterized by virtuosity and excellence in leadership processes (Kay, 1994).

References

Akgün, A.E., Byrne, J.C., Lynn, G.S. & Keskin, H. (2007). Organizational unlearning as changes in beliefs and routines in organizations. *Journal of Organizational Change Management*, 20 (6), 794–812.

Alajoutsijärvi, K., Jussola, K. & Siltaoja, M. (2015). The legitimacy paradox of business schools: losing by gaining? *Academy of Management Learning & Education*, June 1, 14(2), 277–291.

Antonacopoulou, E. (2010). Making the business school more "critical': reflexive critique based on phronesis as a foundation for impact. *British Journal of Management*, 21, 6–25.

Antonacopoulou, E. & Bento, R. (2016). Learning leadership: a call to beauty. In J. Storey (Ed.), *Leadership in Organizations: Current Issues and Key Trends*, 3rd edition. London: Routledge (forthcoming).

Aristotle (1966). *Metaphysics* (H.G. Apostle, Trans.). Bloomington, IN: Indiana University Press.

Austin, R. & Devin, L. (2003). *Artful Making: What Managers Need to Know About How Artists Work*. New York: Prentice Hall.

Baker, D. & Baker, S. (2012). To catch the sparkling glow: a canvas for creativity in the management classroom. *Academy of Management Learning & Education*, 11(4), 704–721.

Banerjee, S.B. (2008). Corporate social responsibility: the good, the bad and the ugly. *Critical Sociology*, 34(1), 51–79.

Beames, S., Higgins, P. & Nicol, R. (Ed.). (2011). *Harnessing Student Curiosity in Learning Outdoors: Guidelines and Principles*. London: Routledge.

Bevan, E. & Corvellec, H. (2007). The impossibility of corporate ethics: for a Levinasian approach to managerial ethics. *Business Ethics: A European Review*, 16(3), 208–219.

Boje, D.M. & Baskin, K. (2011). Our organizations were never disenchanted: enchantment by design narratives vs enchantment by emergence. *Journal of Organizational Change Management*, 24, 411–426.

Brady, F.N. *(1986)*. Aesthetic components of management ethics. *Academy of Management Review*, 11(2), 337–344.

Brown, P. & Erickson, J. (2014) Education for the Anthropocene. Paper presented at the 13th International Karl Polanyi Conference, "The Enduring Legacy of Karl Polanyi," Concordia University, November 6–8.

Butler, J. (1990). *Gender Trouble and the Subversion of Identity*. London: Routledge.

Carlsen, A. & Sandelands, L. (2015). First passion: wonder in organizational inquiry. *Management Learning*, 46(4), 373–390.

Carter, C., Clegg, S.R., Kornberger, M.M., Messner, M. & Laske, S. (2007). *Business Ethics as Practice: Representation, Discourse and Performance*. Cheltenham: Elgar.

Chia, R. & Holt, R. (2007). Wisdom as learned ignorance: integrating east-west perspectives. In E.H. Kessler & J.R. Bailry (Eds.), *Handbook of Organizational and Managerial Wisdom*, (pp. 505–526). Thousand Oaks, CA: Sage.

Colby, A., Ehrlich, T., Sullivan, W.M. & Dolle, J.R. (2011). *Rethinking Undergraduate Business Education: Liberal Learning for the Profession*. New York City: Jossey-Bass.

Curry, P. (2015). The enchantment of learning and "the fate of our times" for "re-enchanting the academy": A conference at Canterbury Christ Church University.

Dale, K. & Latham, Y. (2014). Ethics and entangled embodiment: bodies-materialities-organization. *Organization*, 22(2), 166–182.

de Monthoux, P.G. (2000). The art management of aesthetic organizing. In S. Linstead & H. Höpfl (Eds.), *The Aesthetics of Organization* (pp. 35–60). London: Sage.

de Monthoux, P.G. & Statler, M. (2008). Aesthetic play as an organizing principle. In D. Barry & H. Hansen (Eds.), *The Sage Handbook of New Approaches in Management and Organization* (pp. 423–435). London: Sage.

De Pree, M. (1989). *Leadership is an Art*. New York: Doubleday.

Dehler, G., Welsh, A. & Lewis, M. (2001). Critical pedagogy in the "new paradigm." *Management Learning*, 32(4), 493–511.

Dey, P. & Steyaert, C. (2007). The troubadours of knowledge: passion and invention in management education. *Organization*, 14(3), 437–461.

Diprose, R. (2005). A genethics that makes sense: take two. In M. Shildrick & R. Mykitiuk (Eds.), *Ethics of the Body: Postconventional Challenges* (pp. 237–258). London and Cambridge, MA: MIT Press.

Dobson, J. (1998). Three business contexts: from the technical and moral, to the aesthetic. *Journal of Business Ethics and Organization Studies*, 3(1), 1–20.

Dobson, J. (1999). *The Art of Management and the Aesthetic Manager*. Westport, CT: Quorum Books.

Dobson, J. (2007). Aesthetics as a foundation for business. *Journal of Business Ethics*, 72(1), 41–46.

Dobson, J. (2010). Aesthetic style as a post-structural business ethic. *Journal of Business Ethics*, 93, 393–400.

Eisner, E.W. (1998). Does experience in the arts boost academic achievement? *Art Education*, 51, 7–15.

Elm, D. (2015). Aesthetics and ethics. *Wiley Encyclopedia of Management*, 2, 1–2.

Esbjörn-Hargens, S., Reams, J. & Gunnlaugson, O. (2010). The emergence and characteristics of integral education: an introduction. In S. Esbjörn-Hargens, J. Reams & O. Gunnlaugson (Eds.), *Integral Education: New Directions for Higher Learning* (pp. 1–16). Albany: SUNY.

Eyler, J. (2009). The power of experiential education. *Liberal Education*, 95, 24–31.

Fenwick, T. (2006). Inside out of experiential learning: fluid bodies, co-emergent minds. In R. Edwards, J. Gallacher & S. Whittaker (Eds.), *Learning Outside the Academy: International Research Perspectives on Lifelong Learning* (pp. 42–55). New York: Routledge.

Ferrer, J., Romero, M. & Albareda, R. (2005). Integral transformative education: a participatory proposal. *The Journal of Transformative Education*, 3(4), 306–330.

Fragueiro, F. & Thomas, H. (2011). *Strategic Leadership in the Business School: Keeping One Step Ahead*. Cambridge: Cambridge University Press.

Fuchs, T. & Koch, S. (2014). Embodied affectivity: on moving and being moved. *Frontiers in Psychology*, 5, 1–12.

Gabriel, Y. (2013). Surprises: not just the spice of life but the source of knowledge. *M@n@gement*, 16(5), 719-731.

Gadamer, H.G. (1982). *Truth and Method*. New York: Crossroad.

Gallos, J. (2009). Artful teaching: using the visual, creative and performing arts in contemporary management education. In S. Armstrong & C. Fukami (Eds.), *The Sage Handbook of Management Learning, Education and Development* (187–212). London: Sage Publications.

Gärtner, C. (2015). Organization Inc.: how modern organization shape embodied understanding and cognition. *International Convention of Psychological Science* '15. Amsterdam.

Geddes, P. (1915). *Cities in Evolution*. London: Williams & Norgate.

Gendlin, E.T. (1964). A theory of personality change. In P. Worchel & D. Byrne (Eds.), *Personality Change* (pp. 100–148). New York: John Wiley & Sons.

Gendlin, E.T. (1981). *Focusing* (revised edition). New York: Bantam.

Gendlin, E.T. (1996). *Focusing-Oriented Psychotherapy*. New York: Guilford.

Ghoshal, S. (2005). Bad management theories are destroying good management practices. *Academy of Management Learning & Education*, 4(1), 75–91.

Gray, D.E. (2007). Facilitating management learning: developing critical reflection through reflective tools. *Management Learning*, 38(5), 495–517.

Greene, M. (1995). *Releasing the Imagination: Essays on Education, the Arts, and Social Change*. San Francisco, CA: Jossey-Bass.

Grint, K. (2007). Learning to lead: Can Aristotle help us find the road to wisdom? *Leadership*, 3(2), 231–246.

Guillemin, M. & Gillam, L. (2004). Ethics, reflexivity, and "ethically important moments" in research. *Qualitative Inquiry*, 10, 261–280.

Hancock, P. & Tyler, M. (2009). It's all too beautiful: emotion and organization in the aesthetic economy. In S. Fineman (Ed.), *The Emotional Organization: Passions and Power* (pp. 202–217). Hoboken, NJ: John Wiley & Sons.

Hansen, F.T. (2012). One step further: the dance between poetic dwelling and socratic wonder in phenomenological research. *Indo-Pacific Journal of Phenomenology*, 12(1), 1–20.

Hansen, H., Ropo, A. & Sauer, E. (2007). Aesthetic leadership. *The Leadership Quarterly*, 18, 544–560.

Heidegger, M. (1926/1962). *Being and Time*. Oxford: Blackwell.

Heidegger, M. (1937–38/1994). *Basic Questions of Philosophy* (R. Rojcewicz, A. Schuwer, Trans.). Bloomington: Indiana University Press.

Heron, J. (1996). *Cooperative Inquiry: Research Into the Human Condition*. London: Sage.

Heron, J. (1999). *The Complete Facilitator's Handbook*. London: Kogan Page.

Heron, J. & Reason, P. (1997). A participative inquiry paradigm. *Qualitative Inquiry* 3(3), 274–294.

Hibbert, P. (2013). Approaching reflexivity through critical reflection: issues for critical management education. *Journal of Management Education*, 37(6), 803–827.

Higgins, P. (2001). Student outcomes: heart, hand & head. *Outdoor Education: Authentic Learning in the Context of Landscapes*, 2, 10–12.

Higgins, P. (2009). Into the big wide world: sustainable experiential education for the 21st century. *Journal of Experiential Education*, 32(1), 44–60.

Holliday, G., Statler, M. & Flanders, M. (2007). Developing practically wise leaders through serious play. *Consulting Psychology Journal*, 59, 126–134.

Huffaker, J. & West, E. (2005). Enhancing learning in the business classroom: an adventure with improv theatre techniques. *Journal of Management Education*, 29 (6), 852–869.

Irgens, E.J. (2014). Art, science and the challenge of management education. *Scandinavian Journal of Management*, 30(1), 86–94.

Ivanaj, V., Poldner, K. & Shrivastava, P. (2014). HAND / HEART / HEAD. Aesthetic practice pedagogy for deep sustainability learning. *The Journal of Corporate Citizenship*, 54, 23–46.

Jackson, K. (2012). *Virtuosity in Business*. Philadelphia: University of Pennsylvania Press.

Jones, C. (2006). *Sensorium*. Cambridge, MA: MIT Press.

Jones, C., Parker, M. & ten Bos, R. (2005). *For Business Ethics: A Critical Approach*. London: Routledge.

Jordi, R. (2010). Reframing the concept of reflection: consciousness, experiential learning, and reflective learning practices. *Adult Education Quarterly*, 61, 181–197.

Joy, A. & Sherry, J. (2003). Speaking of art as embodied imagination: a multisensory approach to understanding aesthetic experience. *Journal of Consumer Research*, 30(2), 259–282.

Kagan, S. (2013). *Art and Sustainability: Connecting Patterns for a Culture of Complexity*. Bielefeld: Transcript.

Katz-Buonincontro, J. (2011). Improvisational theatre as public pedagogy: a case study of "aesthetic" pedagogy in leadership development [special edition on the arts]: how does it work? *Policy Futures in Education*, 9(6), 769-779.

Katz-Buonincontro, J. (2015). Decorative integration or relevant learning? A literature review of studio arts-based management education with recommendations for teaching and research. *Journal of Management Education*, 39(1), 81–115.

Kay, R. (1994). The artistry of leadership: an exploration of the leadership process in voluntary not-for-profit organizations. *Nonprofit Management and Leadership*, 4(3), 285–300.

Kemmis, S. (2012). Phrónêsis, experience, and the primacy of praxis. In E.A. Kinsella & A. Pitman (Eds.), *Phrónêsis as Professional Knowledge: Practical Wisdom in the Professions* (pp. 147–162). Rotterdam: Sense Publishing.

Kersten, A. (2008). When craving goodness becomes bad: a critical conception of ethics and aesthetics in organizations. *Culture and Organization*, 15(2), 187–202.

King, I.W. (2008). How we know what we know: the potentiality of art and aesthetics. In *The Sage Handbook of New Approaches to Organizational Studies, British Society of Ethics* (pp. 42–48).Thousand Oaks, CA: Sage.

Kinsella, E. & Pitman, A. (2012). Engaging phrónêsis and education. In E.A. Kinsella & A. Pitman (Eds.), *Phrónêsis as Professional Knowledge: Practical Wisdom in the Professions* (pp. 1–11). Rotterdam: Sense Publishing.

Koehn, D. *(*2010*)*. Ethics, morality, and art in the classroom: positive and negative relations. *Journal of Business Ethics Education*, 7, 213–232.

Koehn, D. & Elm, D. (2015). *Aesthetics and Business Ethics*. Berlin: Springer.

Kokkos, A. (2011.). Transformative learning through aesthetic experience: towards a comprehensive method. *Journal of Transformative Education*, 8(3), 155–177.

Koppett, K. (2001). *Training to Imagine: Practical Improvisational Theatre Techniques to Enhance Creativity, Teamwork, Leadership, and Learning*. Sterling: Stylus.

Krueger, J. (2011). Extended cognition and the space of social interaction. *Consciousness and Cognition*, 20(3), 643–657.

Küpers, W. (2004). Art and leadership. In J. Burns, R. Goethals & G. Sorenson (Eds.), *Encyclopedia of Leadership* (pp. 47–54). Thousand Oaks, CA: Sage.

Küpers, W. (2005). Phenomenology and integral pheno-practice of embodied well-be(com)ing in organizations. *Culture and Organization*, 11(3), 221–231.

Küpers, W. (2005a). Envisioning a refined existence between the sense of reality and the sense of possibility through a responsive encounter between art and commerce. In M. Brellochs & H. Schraat (Eds.), *Sophisticated Survival Techniques: Strategies in Art and Economy* (pp. 372–397). Berlin: Kadmos.

Küpers, W. (2005b). Embodied implicit and narrative knowing in organizations. *Journal of Knowledge Management*, 9(6), 113–133.
Küpers, W. (2008). Embodied "inter-learning': an integral phenomenology of learning in and by organizations. *The Learning Organisation: An International Journal*, 15 (5), 388–408.
Küpers, W. (2009). Perspectives on integral 'pheno-pragma-practice' in organisations. *International Journal of Management Practice*, 4(1), 27–50.
Küpers, W. (2011). Integral responsibility for a sustainable practice in organizations and management. *Corporate Social Responsibility and Environmental Management Journal*, 18, 137–150.
Küpers, W. (2011a). Trans-+-form: transforming transformational leadership for a creative change. *PracticeLeadership & Organization Development Journal*, 32(1), 20–40.
Küpers, W. (2012). Integral response-abilities for organizing and managing sustainability. In G. Eweje & M. Perry (Eds.), *Business and Sustainability: Concepts, Strategies and Changes, Critical Studies on Corporate Responsibility, Governance and Sustainability, Volume 3* (pp. 25–58). London: Emerald.
Küpers, W. (2013). The art of practical wisdom: phenomenology of an embodied, wise inter-practice in organization and leadership. In W. Küpers & D.J. Pauleen (Eds.), *Handbook of Practical Wisdom: Leadership, Organization and Integral Business Practice* (pp. 19–46). London: Gower.
Küpers, W. (2013a). The sense-makings of the senses: perspectives on embodied aisthesis and aesthetics in organising and organisations. In I. King & J. Vickery (Eds.), *Experiencing Organisations: New Aesthetic Perspectives, Series: Management, Policy & Education* (pp. 33–56). Oxford: Libri.
Küpers, W. (2013b). Phenomenology of embodied senses and "sense-making" and the making of sense in organisational culture. *International Journal of Work, Organization and Emotion*, Special Issue on: Sensually Exploring Culture and Affect at Work, 5(4), 325–341.
Küpers, W. (2015). *Phenomenology of the Embodied Organization: The Contribution of Merleau-Ponty for Organization Studies and Practice.* London: Palgrave Macmillan.
Küpers, W. (2015a). Embodied responsive ethical practice: the contribution of Merleau-Ponty for a corporeal ethics in organizations. *Electronic Journal of Business Ethics and Organization Studies, Business and Organization*, 20, 30–45.
Küpers, W. & Pauleen, D. (2015). Learning wisdom: embodied and artful approaches to management education. *Scandinavian Journal of Management,* 31, 493–500.
Küpers, W., Sonnenburg, S. & Zierold, M. (2016). Introduction: turns in re-thinking management. In W. Küpers, S. Sonnenburg & M. Zierold (Eds.), *Re-Thinking Management.* Berlin: Springer (forthcoming).
Ladkin, D. (2006). The enchantment of the charismatic leader: charisma reconsidered as aesthetic encounter. *Leadership*, 2(2), 165–179.
Ladkin, D. (2008). Leading beautifully: how mastery, congruence and purpose create the aesthetic of embodied leadership practice. *The Leadership Quarterly*, 19(1), 31–41.
Ladkin, D. (2010). *Rethinking Leadership: A New Look at Old Leadership Questions.* Cheltenham: Elgar.
Ladkin, D. (2011). The art of perceiving correctly: what artists can teach us about moral perception. *Tamara Journal for Critical Organization Inquiry*, 9, 91–101.
Ladkin, D. (2015). *Mastering the Ethical Dimension of Organizations a Self-Reflective Guide to Developing Ethical Astuteness.* Cheltenham: Elgar.
Ladkin, D. & Taylor, S. (2010). Enacting the "true self": towards a theory of embodied authentic leadership. *Leadership Quarterly*, 21, 64–74.
Lammer, C. (2012). Healing mirrors: body arts and ethnographic methodologies. In S. Pink (Ed.), *Advances in Visual Methodology* (pp. 173–190). London: Sage.
Landy, J. & Saler, M. (2009). *Re-Enchantment of the World: Secular Magic in a Rational Age.* Stanford, CA: Stanford University Press.

Lawrence, R.L. (2008). Powerful feelings: exploring the affective domain of informal and arts-based learning. In J. Dirkx (Ed.), *Adult Learning and the Emotional Self: New Directions for Adult and Continuing Education* (pp. 65–78). San Francisco, CA: Jossey-Bass.

Linds, W. & Trull, A. (2012). Developing ethical practice through inquiry: it's not know-what, *it's know*-how. In C. Wankel & A. Stachowicz-Stanusch (Eds.), *Handbook of Research in Teaching Ethics in Business and Management Education* (pp. 214–230). Hershey, PA: IGI-Global.

Lord, R.G. & Shondrick, S.J. (2011). Leadership and knowledge: symbolic, connectionist, and embodied perspectives. *The Leadership Quarterly*, 22, 207–222.

Mack, K. (2013). Taking an aesthetic risk in management education: reflections on an artistic-aesthetic approach. *Management Learning*, 44(3), 286–304.

Malpas, J. (2006). Beginning in wonder: placing the origin of thinking. In N. Kompridis (Ed.), *Philosophical Romanticism* (pp. 282–298). London: Routledge.

Marotto, M., Roos, J. & Victor, B. (2007). Collective virtuosity in organizations: a study of peak performance in an orchestra. *Journal of Management Studies*, 44, 388–413.

Merleau-Ponty, M. (1995). *The Visible and the Invisible.* Evanston, IL: Northwestern University Press.

Merleau-Ponty, M. (2012). *Phenomenology of Perception* (D.A. Landes, Trans.). London and New York: Routledge.

Meyer, P. (2009). Learning space/work space: can we make room for transformative learning at work? In B.K. Fisher-Yoshida, K.D. Geller & S.A. Schapiro (Eds.), *Innovations in Transformative Learning: Space, Culture, and the Arts* (pp. 43–64). New York: Peter Lang.

Meyer, P. (2010). *From Workplace to Playspace: Innovating, Learning and Changing through Dynamic Engagement.* San Francisco, CA: Jossey-Bass.

Meyer, P. (2012). Embodied learning at work: making the mind-set shift from workplace to playspace. *New Directions for Adult and Continuing Education*, 134, 25–32.

Minocha, S. & Reynolds, M. (2013). The artistry of practice or the practice of artistry context. *Journal of Management Inquiry*, 22(2), 173–192.

Mintzberg, H. (2004). *Managers not MBAs: A Hard Look at the Soft Practice of Managing and Management Development.* San Francisco, CA: Berrett-Hoehle.

Muhr, S., Meier Sørensen, B. & Vallentin, S. (2006). *Ethics and Organizational Practice: Questioning the Moral Foundations of of Management.* Cheltenham: Edward Elgar.

Neale, M.A., Mannix, E. & Sondak, H. (2002). *Toward a Phenomenology of Groups and Group Membership.* Greenwich: JAI.

Nissley, N. (2002). Arts-based learning in management education. In C. Wankel & R. DeFillippi (Eds.), *Rethinking Management Education for the 21st Century: Research in Management Education and Development* (pp. 27–61). New York: Information Age Publishing.

Noddings, N. (2003). *Happiness and Education.* New York: Cambridge University Press.

Nonaka, I. & Toyama, R. (2007). Strategic management as distributed practical wisdom (phronesis). *Industrial and Corporate Change*, 16(3), 371–394.

Painter-Morland, M. (2008). *Business Ethics as Practice: Ethics as the Everyday Business of Practice.* Cambridge: Cambridge University Press.

Painter-Morland, M. & ten Bos, R. (2011). Introduction: Critical crossings. In M. Painter-Morland & R. Ten Bos (Eds.), *Business Ethics and Continental Philosophy* (pp. 15–36). Cambridge: Cambridge University Press.

Pantzar, E. (2000). Knowledge and wisdom in the information society. *The Journal of Future Studies, Strategic Thinking and Policy*, 2, 230–236.

Paterson, M., Higgs, J. & Wilcox, S. (2006). Developing expertise in judgement artistry in OT practice. *British Journal of OT*, 69, 115–123.

Paton, S., Chia, R. & Burt, G. (2014). Relevance or 'relevate'? How university business schools can add value through reflexively learning from strategic partnerships. *Management Learning*, 45(3), 267–288.

Pavlovich, K., Collins, E. & Jones, G. (2009). Developing students skills in reflective practice: design and assessment. *Journal of Management Education*, 33, 37–58.

Plato (1973). *The Collected Dialogues of Plato* (E. Hamilton & H. Cairns, Eds.). Princeton, NJ: Princeton University Press.

Preece, B. (2013). The eco-improvisatory-theatre of Merleau-Ponty's phenomenological narrative. *Phenomenology & Practice*, 7(2): 61–77.

Pullen, A. & Rhodes, C. (2014). Corporeal ethics and the politics of resistance in organizations. *Organization*, 21(6), 782–796.

Rancière, J. (1991). *The Ignorant Schoolmaster: Five Lessons in Intellectual Emancipation* (K. Ross, Trans.). Stanford, CA: Stanford University Press.

Roberts, J. (2003). The manufacture of corporate social responsibility: constructing corporate sensibility. *Organization*, 10(2), 249–265.

Robinson, S. (2009). The nature of responsibility in a professional setting. *Journal of Business Ethics*, 88, 11–19.

Roca, E. (2008). Introducing practical wisdom in business schools. *Journal of Business Ethics*, 82, 607–620.

Rubenstein, M.-J. (2008). *Strange Wonder: The Closure of Metaphysics and the Opening of Awe*. New York: Columbia University Press.

Saler, M, (2006). Modernity and enchantment: a historiographic review. *The American Historical Review*, 111(3), 692–716.

Sanders, P. (1982). Phenomenology: a new way of viewing organizational research. *Academy of Management Review*, 7, 353–360.

Schipper, F. (1999). Phenomenology and the reflective practitioner. *Management Learning*, 30, 473–485.

Schön, D. (1983). *The Reflective Practitioner*. New York: Basic Books.

Schön, D. (1987). *Educating the Reflective Practitioner*. San Francisco, CA: Jossey-Bass.

Seeley, C. & Reason, P. (2008). Expressions of energy: an epistemology of presentational knowing. In P. Liamputtong & J. Rumbold (Eds.), *Knowing Differently: Arts-based and Collaborative Research Methods* (pp. 25–46). New York: Nova Science.

Shilling, C. (1993). *The Body and Social Theory* (2nd revised ed.). London: Sage.

Shrivastava, P. & Statler, M. (2012). *Learning from the Global Financial Crisis: Creatively, Reliably and Sustainably*. Palo Alto, CA: Stanford University Press.

Springborg, C. (2010). Leadership as art: leaders coming to their senses. *Leadership*, 6(3), 243–258.

Springborg, C. (2015). *Art-based Methods in Management Education*. Cranfield University.

Springborg, C. & Sutherland, I. (2015). Teaching MBAs aesthetic agency through dance. *Organizational Aesthetics*, 5(1), 94–113.

Statler, M. (2014). Developing wisdom in a business school? Critical reflections on pedagogical practice. *Management Learning*, 45, 397–417.

Statler, M. & Oliver, D. (2008). Facilitating serious play. In G. Hodgkinson & W. Starbuck (Eds.), *The Oxford Handbook of Organizational Decision Making* (pp. 475–494). Oxford: Oxford University Press.

Sutherland, I. (2013). Arts-based methods in leadership development: affording aesthetic workspaces, reflexivity and memories with momentum. *Management Learning*, 44(1), 25–43.

Sutherland, I. & Jelinek, J. (2015). From experiential learning to aesthetic knowing the arts in leadership development. *Advances in Developing Human Resources*. Advanced Online Publication. Retrieved May 28, 2015. doi: 10.1177/1523422315587894.

Taylor, S. (2012). The impoverished aesthetic of modern management: beauty and ethics in organizations. In D. Elm & D. Kohen (Eds.), *Aesthetics and Business Ethics* (pp. 23–36). Berlin: Springer.

Taylor, S. & Carboni, I. (2008). Technique and practices from the arts. In D. Barry & H. Hansen (Eds.), *The Sage Handbook of New Approaches in Management and Organization* (pp. 220–228). London: Sage.

Taylor, S. & Hansen, H. (2005). Finding form: looking at the field of organizational aesthetics. *Journal of Management Studies*, 42(6), 1211–1231.

Taylor, S. & Ladkin, D. (2009). Understanding arts-based methods in managerial development. *Academy of Management Learning and Education*, 8(1), 55–69.

ten Bos, R. (2011). The moral significance of gestures. *Business Ethics*, 20(3), 280–291.

Thanem, T. & Wallenberg, L. (2014). What can bodies do? Reading Spinoza for an affective ethics of organizational life organization. *Organization*, 22(2), 235–250.

Titchen, A. & Higgs, J. (2001). A dynamic framework for the enhancement of health professional practice in an uncertain world: the practice-knowledge interface. In J. Higgs & A. Titchen (Eds.), *Practice Knowledge and Expertise in the Health Professions* (pp. 215–225). Oxford: Butterworth Heinemann.

Tonkinswise, C. (2011). A taste for practices: unrepressing style in design thinking. *Design Studies*, 32(6), 533–545.

Vaill, P. (1991). *Managing as a Performance Art.* San Francisco, CA: Jossey-Bass.

Waddock, S. (2014). Wisdom and responsible leadership: aesthetic responsibility, moral imagination, and systems thinking. In D. Koehn & D. Elm (Eds.), *Aesthetics and Business Ethics* (pp. 129–147). New York and London: Springer.

Wankel, C. & Stachowicz-Stanusch, A. (2012). teaching business ethics in an epoch of catastrophes. In C. Wankel & A. Stachowicz-Stanusch (Eds.), *Handbook of Research in Teaching Ethics in Business and Management Education* (pp. 214–230). Hershey, PA: IGI-Global.

Welsch, W. (1996). Aestheticization processes: phenomena, distinctions and prospects. *Theory, Culture & Society*, 13(1), 1–24.

Whyte, D. *(1994). The Heart Aroused.* New York: Doubleday.

Woermann, M. (2013). *On the (Im)possibility of Business Ethics Critical Complexity, Deconstruction, and Implications for Understanding the Ethics of Business.* Dordrecht: Springer.

Wray-Bliss, E. (2002). Abstract ethics, embodied ethics: the strange marriage of Foucault and positivism in labour process. *Theory Organization*, 9(1), 5–39.

Wray-Bliss, E. (2009). Ethics: critique, ambivalence and infinite responsibilities (unmet). In M. Alvesson, T. Bridgman, & H. Willmott (Eds.), *The Oxford Handbook of Critical Management Studies* (pp. 267–285). Oxford: Oxford University Press.

Wray-Bliss, E. (2012). Leadership and the deified/demonic: a cultural examination of CEO sanctification. *Business Ethics: a European Review*, 21(4), 434–449.

Yanow, D. *(*2001*)*. Learning in and from improvising: lessons from theatre for organizational learning. *Reflections of Society for Organizational Learning and MIT*, 2, 58–62.

Appendix: Examples of art-works by students for module "Legitimacy: Ethics and Aesthetics"

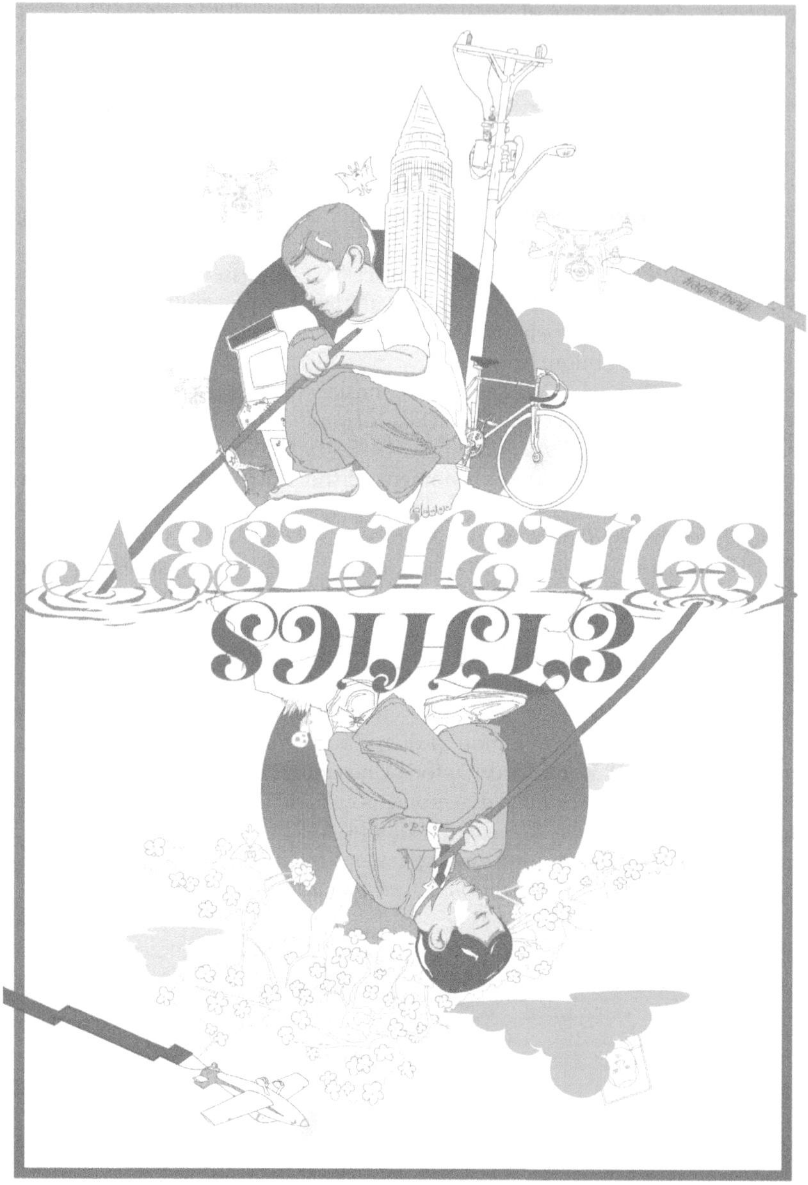

KARLSRUHE

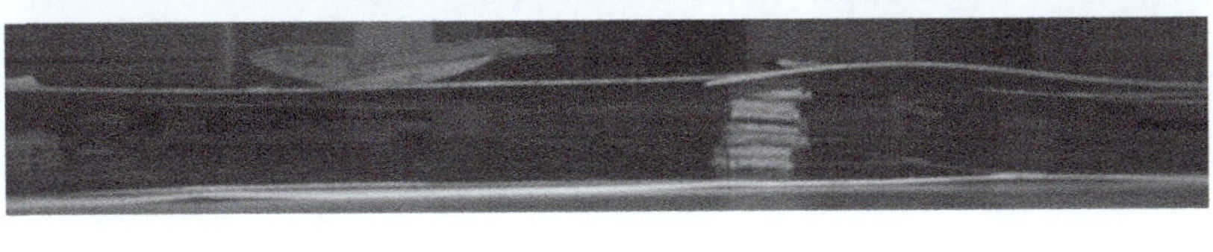

My dear friend,

Have you ever thought about ethics and aesthetics in your life? – Well - do it - because it will enrich your perception. I will explain to you why.

As you know, I am doing my Masters and in this program I took a module called 'Ethics and Aesthetics'. Dealing with the content of this module changed my perception and this is why I want to tell you about it...

YOU HAVE LIVED ABOVE YOUR STANDARDS.
EU COMMISSION
WE HAVE EATEN THEM ALL TOGETHER!
LET'S MAKE A REFERENDUM.
GREEK POLITICIANS
I DON'T TAKE BRIBES, IT IS A COMPENSATION!
GREEK DOCTOR
GREXIT IS THE BEST SOLUTION FOR GREECE.
SCHAUBLE
GOING OUT IS A BASIC NEED!
GREEK FAMILY
MEDIA
ONE STRIKE A DAY KEEPS THE CRISIS AWAY!
PUBLIC SERVANT

YOU HAVE LIVED ABOVE YOUR STANDARDS.
EU COMMISSION
WE HAVE EATEN THEM ALL TOGETHER!
LET'S MAKE A REFERENDUM.
GREEK POLITICIANS
I DON'T TAKE BRIBES, IT IS A COMPENSATION!
OXI PE ΜΑΛΑΚΑ!!!
GREXIT IS THE BEST SOLUTION FOR GREECE.
GREEK DOCTOR
SCHAUBLE
GOING OUT IS A BASIC NEED!
ONE STRIKE A DAY KEEPS THE CRISIS AWAY!
GREEK FAMILY
MEDIA
PUBLIC SERVANT

TRUST ME
100% BIO
PRO PLANET
FAIRTRADE
VEGAN
TÜV
best recruiter
ZERTIFIZIERTE NACHHALTIGE FISCHEREI
MSC
www.msc.org/de
Ohne Gentechnik
GETESTET
BIO

"Us and the Other"

War

Peace

Fear

Hope

What if these words come into life?

What if it's us that makes them shine bright?

What if they mean your daily bread?

What if you wake up each day with threat?

Anger

Calmness

Sorrow

Relief

What if it all doesn't help you to sleep?

Bombs

Tanks

Birds and the sun

What if it all doesn't help you to run?

S.N. August 2015

CREME DE DOUCHE
SHOWER CREAM

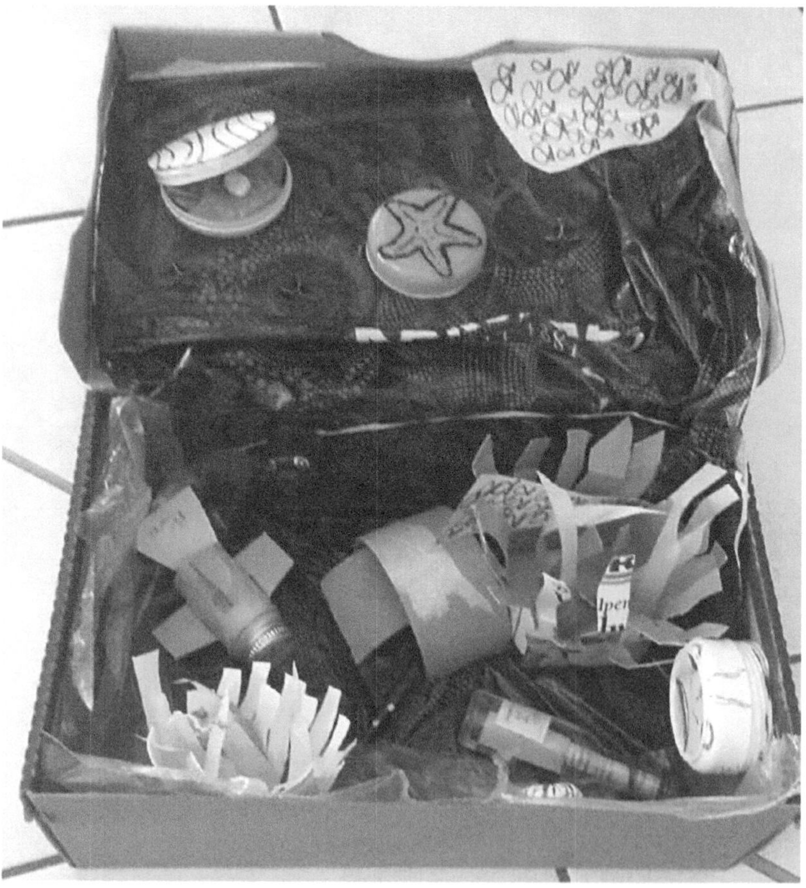

Index

Note: Page references in **bold** indicate figures and tables.

For Product Safety Concerns and Information please contact our EU representative GPSR@taylorandfrancis.com Taylor & Francis Verlag GmbH, Kaufingerstraße 24, 80331 München, Germany